HANDBOOK
OF FACULTY
BARGAINING

Asserting Administrative Leadership
for Institutional Progress
by Preparing for Bargaining,
Negotiating and Administering Contracts,
and Improving the Bargaining Process

George W. Angell

Edward P. Kelley, Jr.

and Associates

HANDBOOK
OF FACULTY
BARGAINING

Jossey-Bass Publishers

San Francisco · Washington · London · 1977

HANDBOOK OF FACULTY BARGAINING
Asserting Administrative Leadership for Institutional Progress by Preparing for Bargaining, Negotiating and Administering Contracts, and Improving the Bargaining Process
by George W. Angell, Edward P. Kelley, Jr., and Associates

Library of Congress Catalogue Card Number LC 76-50713

International Standard Book Number ISBN 0-87589-320-1

Manufactured in the United States of America

JACKET DESIGN BY WILLI BAUM

FIRST EDITION

Code 7715

The Jossey-Bass Series
in Higher Education

Preface

During the past three years we have been fortunate enough to travel throughout the country addressing groups of college and university presidents, vice-presidents, deans, trustees, faculty members, and students. It has also been our good fortune to become well acquainted with educational union officials at the national and local levels, together with labor attorneys and representatives of labor boards. In state after state our general opinion of college administrators, faculty members, union representatives, labor neutrals, and others has been strengthened by our perception of their sense of purpose, sincerity, and integrity. These people are, by and large, professionals motivated by high ideals. In addition, they are generally people of good will who harbor a spirit of generosity toward their fellow men and women. They are highly respected leaders in specialized, highly competitive fields.

There is one other characteristic which these groups share

rather widely throughout the nation: a lack of acceptance of the other's role, bordering on disrespect. Our conversations with more than a thousand college presidents and vice-presidents have yet to reveal more than three or four who have genuine admiration for the work of union leaders. In general, they appear to perceive unions as being unnecessary evils and union leaders as opportunists who are personally capitalizing on power politics during a period when the academy is already under severe economic and political strain. In turn, union leaders appear to see university executives as people who jealously guard their authority in order to make unilateral decisions in whatever way they feel best suits their own perceptions of the university's needs and with little regard for the needs of faculty members.

Open discord invites third parties (neutrals and government officials) to step in and make decisions essential to the vitality of the academy. Too often the third parties are not disinterested, especially those political office holders who have long felt that universities were too free from government controls and are not sufficiently responsive to political concerns.

In addition, although mediators, fact finders, and arbitrators have "saved" many an institution from the prolongation of insufferable, damaging internal battles, they have, through intervention, created persistent problems by their lack of understanding of, and sympathy for, the unique character, purposes, and processes that have produced academic integrity, unfettered research, and an independent source of human inspiration and renewal.

It is this continuing series of misconceptions, misunderstandings, and the ensuing weariness and pessimism everywhere present among academic administrators that pushed us to attempt a new type of book, one that looked at the brighter side of a process fully capable of eminently serving the university as a whole as well as meeting the needs of each of the parties. It would be fruitless to attempt a scholarly study of attitudes and intrigues. Such a study, rather than improving the bargaining process, would more than likely make the parties more defensive and less open to change. In addition, studies of facts and conditions are already available from the work of such authors as Carr and VanEyck, Garbarino, Duryea and Fisk, Kemerer and Baldridge, the *Chronicle of Higher*

Education staff writers, Mortimer, and Begin. These works report the facts and provide invaluable sources of knowledge about the current history of academic collective bargaining. They also quickly become out of date. It is also a fact that unions provide a plethora of union-oriented materials designed to help local faculty leaders carry out their particular union functions. But university administrators and trustees have had little in the way of positively oriented resource materials advising them in the practical matters of bargaining. The Academic Collective Bargaining Information Service (ACBIS), which we direct, provides institutions with a constant flow of information about events, procedures, and opinion, but it lacks the resources to publish a comprehensive volume capable of responding to almost any indepth bargaining problem which administrators are forced to face sooner or later. Yet more and more requests come to us for management-oriented information and recommendations.

Prior to undertaking the work of this book, we reviewed many materials designed to help managers in nonacademic, public- and private-sector bargaining. As good as they were, all lacked some characteristics essential to the volume we envisioned. Primarily, they failed to deal with the special characteristics of universities and faculty bargaining. Some were clearly biased toward union purposes; some were violently antiunion. Almost no author took a strong position as to the neutrality of the bargaining process while pointing out its capability of serving simultaneously the goals of union, management, and institution. None mentioned the feasibility of uniting union and management in opposition to outside political encroachment on internal affairs of the institution. Indeed, the affairs of academe have been discreetly omitted from most of these works.

And so we turned to a task that we knew to be formidable and time-consuming beyond our personal means. The first task was to determine purpose; the second, an appropriate approach. We decided that above all the purpose was to help institutions maintain their dedication to scholarship, objectivity, and community as they attempt to deal with forces that are potentially divisive. To do so, institutions must rid themselves of fear and mythology surrounding faculty unionization. Bargaining is a neutral process that becomes what the parties make of it. Each party must understand the opportunities which negotiation offers for shaping an agreement that encourages good will, mutual respect, and cooperation. Far too much publicity is given to the open strife that accompanies impasse on relatively rare occasions. This type of reporting covers over the fact that for every strike, approximately 160 contracts are consummated through peaceful arrangements. The intent of this book is to help college and university spokespersons (and faculty representatives) to maximize the opportunity for peaceful settlement of contractual negotiations and grievance disputes. Thus, the book opens with an introductory section suggesting the many constructive aspects of bargaining that can help the parties to approach bargaining with a positive attitude founded on careful planning and organization. To make certain that not only the more pleasant managerial opportunities are presented, we persuaded two union executives to write a hard-hitting chapter reciting reasonable expectations of unions. It must be made clear that knowledge of both management and union perspectives is essential for each party in order to develop and maintain a realistic and positive attitude essential for resolving the complex issues submitted to bargaining.

A review of the table of contents will show the reader the chronological sequence of the parts and chapters. Part One helps the reader to get in the right frame of mind by a quick overview of the general opportunities and problems generated by the bargaining processes. This part also offers a detailed explanation of the preparation essential for the major events (shaping legislation, unit determination, elections, and so forth) which always precede actual bargaining. In Part Two we bring the wisdom and experience of ten of the most talented researchers, labor attorneys, and administrators to the task of reviewing the strategies and tactics (gathering data, determining goals, designing contract language, costing demands) of negotiating viable working agreements and of avoiding violent confrontations. After the agreement is ratified comes the challenge of administering the contract cooperatively with union representatives in a manner that settles grievances fairly and quickly, while simultaneously preparing the way for a smooth approach to future contract negotiations. Part Three provides insight and suggestions about these matters.

Part Four has a special significance for institutions involved in or facing statewide or other types of coordinated bargaining. The art of accomplishing legitimate statewide objectives without destroying the identity and vitality of individual campuses is a task requiring inordinate capacity to comprehend the intrinsic relationships between unity and diversity, the interdependent elements of the American university. Nowhere has collective bargaining more seriously challenged the understanding and imagination of educational leadership. The record to date clearly identifies Pennsylvania and Montana as pace setters in approaching these problems with fresh perspectives. Part Four along with chapters Two and Fourteen reveal the insights, concerns and vision of some of the people most responsible for these achievements.

Part Five represents our effort to close the book with a series of suggestions by eminent practitioners as to how university leadership can manage the impact of unions on budgets and traditional faculty-administrative relationships, such as faculty senates, in a manner capable of producing optimism and progress.

The scope of problems and events covered by this volume requires the coordinated efforts of researchers, attorneys, and institutional executives. Thus, the approach employed by each author moves from one type of essay and notation to another. The following guide may help readers who may not be familiar with legal citations. Decisions of the U.S. Supreme Court are reported in one of three federal reporter systems. Thus, a citation to volume 395 of the U.S. Reports at page 575 would read 395 US 575. Decisions in other federal courts are reported as follows: federal district courts in Fed. Supp. and the circuit courts of appeals in Fed. State supreme court decisions are usually reported in a state reporter (for example, N.Y., Wash., Cal.) or in a regional reporter: A designating Atlantic, N.E. designating Northeastern, N.W. for Northwestern states, P for Pacific, S.E. for Southeastern, S for Southern and S.W. for Southwestern. An s added to an item usually indicates supplement, whereas 2d indicates the second series of a reporting system. Particularly for labor cases, LRRM designates Labor Relations Reference Manual while NLRB designates National Labor Relations Board decisions from 1938 to date. F.E.P. Cases designates Fair Employment Practice Cases; F.R.D. designates Federal Rules Decisions; C.C.H. E.E.O.C. designates Equal Employment Opportunity Decisions by Commerce Clearing House; and C.F.R. is the official Code of Federal Regulations. Examples of state labor board reports are, PERB for the New York Public Employment Relations Board, and MLRR for the Massachusetts Labor Relations Reporter. Statutory citations are usually made to codes, statutes, revised statutes, statutes annotated, and the like. For example, M.R.S.A. designates Maine Revised Statutes Annotated; O.R.S. designates the Oregon Revised Statutes; R.C.M. designates Revised Code Montana; and U.S.C. designates United States Code. Other general references include GERR, Government Employee Relations Report; BNA-LAR, Bureau of National Affairs Labor Arbitration Reports; and BNA-LRR, Bureau of National Affairs Labor Relations Reporter.

Finally, it is a pleasure to acknowledge the unfailing encouragement and editorial help of Grace Kelley, who suffered the usual pressures and tensions of setting aside other priorities to help us meet deadlines and numerous requests for special aid.

Our thanks also go to James Dyer of the Carnegie Corporation of New York who inspired us to undertake this book and to staff members at the American Association of University Professors (AAUP), the National Education Association (NEA), and the American Federation of Teachers (AFT), who were always cooperative in helping us to understand the issues from the faculty point of view. Finally, we express our appreciation to the staff members of the Association of American Colleges (AAC), the American Association of State Colleges and Universities, (AASCU), the National Association of State Universities and Land-Grant Colleges (NASULGC), and the American Association of Community and Junior Colleges (AACJC) for helping us to understand the needs and problems of colleges and universities.

Washington, D.C.   GEORGE W. ANGELL
March 1977   EDWARD P. KELLEY, JR.

Contents

xv

The Authors

GEORGE W. ANGELL has been the director of the Academic Collective Bargaining Information Service (ACBIS) in Washington, D.C., since his retirement in 1974 from the presidency of the State University of New York College of Arts and Science, Plattsburgh. He was president for 20 years before his retirement. Angell is the author of more than forty articles in a variety of journals, and he has authored and coauthored many of the ACBIS Special Reports. He has served as a consultant to individual institutions in the area of collective bargaining and has addressed meetings of various educational associations and institutions.

EDWARD P. KELLEY, JR. is the associate director of ACBIS. He has been an author and coauthor of a number of the staff publications of the ACBIS; he also contributed "State and Federal Legislation" in *Campus Employment Relations,* edited by T. Tice, ICLE publication, 1976. Kelley's duties as associate director of the ACBIS include preparation of the monthly fact sheet, addresses to meetings of various education associations and institutions, participation as a seminar leader in the ACBIS Cooperative Educational Service Program, consultation with individual institutions for their labor relations programs and as primary resource in the area of collective bargaining for such organizations as the National Association of College and University Attorneys, the National Association of College and University Business Officers, and the College and University Personnel Association. Kelley is admitted to the practice of law before all the courts of the state of New York and before the courts of the District of Columbia.

NEIL S. BUCKLEW, provost of Ohio University, Athens, serves as chief academic officer and executive vice-president. From 1970 to 1976 he served as vice-provost, as vice-president for administration, and as acting provost at Central Michigan University in Mount Pleasant, Michigan. In 1974 he was chairman of the writing committee for *Collective Bargaining in Postsecondary Educational Institutions (A Resource Handbook),* Report #45, (Education Commission of the States, Denver) and coedited *National Labor Relations and Collective Bargaining for Private and Public Institutions of Higher Education* (National Association of College and University Business Officers, 1974), Bucklew is a chapter contributor to *Faculty Unions and Collective Bargaining in Higher Education,* edited by E. D. Duryea and R. S. Fisk (Jossey-Bass, 1972).

RONALD W. BUSH is assistant to the president for personnel and labor relations at Middlesex County College, the largest two-year college in New Jersey. He is responsible for negotiating labor agreements, argues arbitration cases, conducts hearings, and supervises training in the areas of labor relations, affirmative action, and personnel. In addition, he is a labor relations consultant to a number of universities and colleges across the country and has written and presented numerous papers on collective bargaining, grievance handling, and union organizing techniques for various organizations and colleges.

NICHOLAS DiGIOVANNI, JR., is an associate with the law firm of Morgan, Brown, Kearns and Joy in Boston. He is admitted to practice in the Commonwealth of Massachusetts and has coauthored "NLRB Jurisdiction Over Colleges and Universities: A Plea for Rule Making," which appeared in the *William and Mary Law Review* (Spring 1975).

COLLEEN DOLAN-GREENE is director of University Personnel, Business and Finance, at the University of Detroit. Previously she held the position of labor relations manager, Employment Relations Department, at Oakland University (Michigan). She is president and secretary-treasurer for the Academy for Academic Personnel Administration and a member of the College and University Personnel Association on the Council on Faculty Collective Bargaining and Council on Staff Collective Bargaining. She was awarded a Lyndon B. Johnson School of Public Affairs Fellowship from 1971 to 1973 and has done research on such topics as "Public Employee Unions" and "The Impact of Environmental Impact Statements."

DAVID FELDMAN is dean of the School of Business Administration at the United States International University in San Diego. He is also a consultant and chief negotiator on faculty collective bargaining for the board of trustees at Southeastern Massachusetts University. Before taking on the dual role, he was professor of sociology and special services at United States International University. He has coauthored a forthcoming publication, "Collegiality Through Collective Bargaining," in the *Educational Record,* and he wrote *Human Dimensions of School Improvement,* (Research for Better Schools, 1975).

JOHN D. FORSYTH is assistant university personnel director and personnel administrator for the Medical Center of the University of Michigan, Ann Arbor. Before assuming this position in late 1976, he was manager of staff and union relations at the University of Michigan and had been contract administrator for the labor agreement between the university and 2,200 teaching and research assistants. Forsyth's responsibilities are to plan and direct personnel administration functions for the Medical Center and to direct employment, compensation, training, and staff and union activities.

WILLIAM M. FULKERSON, JR., is associate executive director of the American Association of State Colleges and Universities. He acts as the deputy for the director and handles all internal management; is responsible for programming and maintains liaison with other Washington, D.C., associations and governmental agencies; supervises all committee work for the association; and serves on national committees and projects for the association. Before coming to Washington in 1973, he was assistant to the president at California State University, Fresno, and was an American Council on Education Fellow in academic administration in 1972. Fulkerson has published several books, reports, papers, and proceedings, such as *Planning for Financial Exigency in State Colleges and Universities* (American Association of State Colleges and Universities, 1973), and *Education to Meet Present and Future Career Needs* (American Association of State Colleges and Universities, 1974).

JAMES GEMMELL served as president of Clarion State College in Pennsylvania from 1960 until his retirement at the end of 1976 when he joined the staff of the ACBIS in Washington, D.C., as associate director. He is the author of more than 30 articles in professional journals and was author of *Business Organization and Management* (McGraw-Hill, 1949). He coauthored *Principles of Economics* with H. Balsley (Heath, 1953). Gemmell was named Mellon Scholar in 1963 and was a Fulbright lecturer in 1958.

FRANK C. GERRY is education coordinator of ACBIS and directs the Cooperative Educational Service Program of the ACBIS (Ford Foundation Grant), which provides on-site skills seminars in preelection, prenegotiation, negotiation, and administration of contracts. Besides the chapters he has coauthored in this publication, he prepared "The Fair Labor Standards Act: Review and Exercises Applied to Higher Education" for the Office of Community College Affairs at Iowa.

JOHN F. GREDE is vice-chancellor for career and manpower programs at the city colleges of Chicago. In this capacity he directs career and manpower programs offered by the eight city colleges and is responsible for operation of the Chicago Urban Skills Institute. He was chief negotiator for the city colleges in 1975 and has several articles appearing in *New Directions for Community Colleges,* including "The Untried Model of the Urban Community College" (1973) and "Managing the Management Team" (1975). Grede has served on the National Task Force on Educational Credit for the American Council on Education (ACE) along with the governor's grievance panel in Illinois and has been a consultant and examiner for the North Central Association of Colleges and Secondary Schools.

JOSEPH N. HANKIN is president of Westchester Community College in Valhalla, New York. His publications have included several consultant's reports, numerous college documents, such as long-range plans, president's annual reports, and others, and contributions to a bibliographical work on community colleges, articles in the *Junior College Journal* as well as articles in magazines and local newspapers. He has served as a member of the board of directors of the American Association of Junior Colleges, and was president and vice-president of the Junior Council of the Middle Atlantic States. One of Hankin's more recent publications is *State Legislation and the Status of Collective Bargaining in Community and Junior Colleges, 1976,* Special Report #28, published by the ACBIS (August 1976).

BARRY L. HJORT recently began work as an associate in the law offices of Cannon and Gillespie in Helena, after serving as assistant commissioner for Labor Relations and Legal Affairs for the Montana University System located in Helena. He has had significant experience in labor relations and collective bargaining and has acted as chief contract negotiator in collective bargaining negotiations with faculty unions and with classified employee unions.

DAVID W. HORNBECK, recently named state superintendent of schools of Maryland, served from 1972 to 1976 as the executive deputy secretary of education of the Commonwealth of Pennsylvania. He is also the current chairman of the Chief State School Officers Study Commission and is a member of the American Bar Association Juvenile Justice Standards Project. He has had primary responsibility for the administration of the Department of Education, including the development of competency-based education programs, law-related education, training for school administrators, education in prisons and youth detention facilities, and special education programs for handicapped children. He has also had primary responsibility for labor relations, the development and implementation of a management-by-objectives system and the creation of an employee performance and development system. Hornbeck is admitted to the practice of law in the Commonwealth of Pennsylvania.

DAVID W. LESLIE is associate professor of education at the University of Virginia in Charlottesville. He has taught graduate-level courses dealing with legal aspects of college administration, and has conducted seminars in conflict management in higher education, mediation of faculty rights, and interests and legal problems in faculty employment relations. His publications are numerous and include journal articles ("Legitimizing University Governance: Theory and Practice, *Higher Education,* Spring 1975), published proceedings ("Faculty in Governance: A Rationale," in *Campus Employment Relations,* edited by T. Tice, ICLE, 1976) as well as independent publications through ACBIS, Report #2 *Impact of Collective Bargaining on Conflict Resolution Practices* (September 1975) and *Conflict and Collective Bargaining* (ERIC Clearinghouse on Higher Education, 1975).

G. GREGORY LOZIER is serving The Pennsylvania State University in University Park as university planning specialist, after holding the position of senior planning analyst, Division of Institutional Research and Planning (Office of Budget and Planning). His publications include: "A Collective Bargaining Election: Issues and Faculty Voting Behavior, in *Research in Higher Education, 4,* 1976, and "Changing Attitudes Toward the Use of Strikes in Higher Education," in *Campus Employment Relations: Readings and Resources,* edited by T. Tice, 1975, and "Collective Bargaining Rejected: Two Case Histories," which he also coauthored for *Association of Governing Board Reports, 17* (September/October, 1975). As planning specialist, Lozier worked with a faculty senate subcommittee that prepared a report on a revised university promotion and tenure policy; assessed the progress of the policy on faculty rights and responsibilities and major staff support to the president's Ad Hoc

Committee on Collective Bargaining; and had primary responsibility in the broad area of academic personnel policy.

DANIEL R. MCLAUGHLIN is president of Asnuntuck Community College in Enfield, Connecticut, having served at Cazenovia College as academic dean for a year. He was manager of education and staff assistant to the manager of industrial relations at Dow Chemical Company in Michigan for three years. In addition, he writes two weekly newspaper articles on higher education.

RAMELLE MACOY is executive officer of the Associated Pennsylvania State College and University Faculties (APSCUF). Before taking this position, he served as director of organization of Allied Industrial Workers, AFL-CIO, and as director of education, Allied Industrial Workers.

ARTHUR P. MENARD is a partner in the law firm of Morgan, Brown, Kearns and Joy in Boston and is admitted to practice in the Commonwealth of Massachusetts and before several federal courts. He is the author of several articles appearing in legal journals and law reviews, including "Exploding Representation Areas: College and Universities," *Boston College Industrial and Commercial Law Review* (vol. 17, December 1976) and "May Tenure Rights of Faculty Be Bargained Away?" *The Journal of College and University Law* (Fall 1975).

LELAND MILES is president of the University of Bridgeport in Connecticut, having previously served as president of Alfred University in New York for seven years. He is the author of numerous articles, essays, reviews, and books on literary, social, and educational subjects; and he has written extensively on the sixteenth-century humanists John Colet and Sir Thomas More. Miles has spoken on university problems at institutes and seminars sponsored by the American Council on Education and the Association of American Colleges.

MARTIN J. MORAND is director for the Center for the Study of Labor Relations at Indiana University, Pennsylvania. Before accepting his present position, he was the executive officer of Associated

Pennsylvania State College and University Faculties (APSCUF), the union representing faculties of the Pennsylvania State Colleges and University.

CAESAR J. NAPLES is chief contract negotiator for the Florida State University System. He has also served as an assistant vice-chancellor for employee relations at the State University of New York, where he participated in the first and second contract negotiations between State University of New York (SUNY) and the United University Professions, Inc., NEA/AFL-CIO. In his present position, he most recently completed negotiations with the union representing faculty at the nine institutions in the Florida State University System.

WILLIAM J. NEFF, has been serving as assistant director of personnel at the University of Michigan since 1974. His duties include contract and grievance administration, arbitration, training and development of supervisory and nonsupervisory personnel and chief negotiator. In addition, he is chairman of Michigan Employment Agency Advisory Council, State of Michigan, Department of Licensing and Regulation. Neff is an attorney admitted to practice in both New York and Michigan.

HAROLD R. NEWMAN is director of conciliation for the New York State Public Employment Relations Board. In this post he is responsible for administering the impasse procedures of New York's *Taylor Law* and directs the activities of a full-time mediation staff and a 200-man panel of mediators, arbitrators, and fact finders. He has lectured extensively in the labor relations field and has served as visiting senior lecturer at the Cornell University School of Industrial and Labor Relations.

JOSEPH J. ORZE is president of Worcester State College in Massachusetts. He has had experience in collective bargaining as chief negotiator for the board of trustees, Southeastern Massachusetts University, for the first contract with the faculty in 1969; has served as board-administrative liaison with the faculty federation for six years; and has had experience in arbitration, mediation, and fact finding. Two of his recent articles are "After It's Ratified, That

Contract Has To Work," published in *College Management* (February 1974), and *Faculty Collective Bargaining and Academic Decision Making,* Special Report #24 (ACBIS, September 1975).

LAWRENCE K. PETTIT is commissioner of higher education, Montana University system, with primary responsibilities as chief executive officer of a six-campus university system. He is also in charge of legislative liaison and has the legal responsibility for all labor negotiations, academic and nonacademic, on the six campuses. Pettit has been coeditor and contributor of three books dealing with political processes: *European Political Processes: Essays and Readings,* 2nd ed., with H. S. Albinski (Allyn and Bacon, 1974); *The Legislative Process in the U.S. Senate* with Edward Keynes (Rand McNally, 1969); and *The Social Psychology of Political Life* with Samuel A. Kirkpatrick (Duxbury, 1972). He has written several monographs, plus many articles, invited papers, and book reviews; and has participated on panels, at conferences, and in giving testimony.

WALTER H. POWELL is vice-president of personnel resources at Temple University in Philadelphia; has been a consultant for several corporations (such as Standard Oil of New Jersey, Autocar, and TRW); and has arbitrated in cases for Bethlehem Steel, U.S. Steel and Steel Workers, RCA, and others. He has written chapters in *The Personnel Man Looks at His Job* (R. F. Finley, editor) and *Dealing With a Union* (L. Marceau, editor), published by the American Management Association in 1962 and 1969 respectively, and in *Negro Opportunities in American Business* (H. R. Northrup and R. L. Rowauld, editors), Bureau of Industrial Relations, University of Michigan, 1965. His reviews of Stanley Herman's *The People Specialist* (1969) and S. Sokolik's *The Personnel Process: Line and Staff Dimensions in Managing People at Work* (1970) have appeared in Cornell's *Industrial Relations Review.* He is admitted to the practice of law in the state of New York.

RONALD P. SATRYB is assistant vice-president for business affairs and assistant to the president for employee relations at State University of New York College at Geneseo. His duties include consultation and negotiations with three local unions, reviews of grievances, application of discipline, and representative for human rights and discrimination hearing, as well as budgetary responsibilities. Recently he coauthored "Principles of Personnel Policy" in F. Kemerer's *Understanding Faculty Unions and Collective Bargaining: A Guide for Independent School Administrators* (National Association of Independent Schools, 1976). In addition to the Special Reports he has prepared for the ACBIS, he has published several articles in personnel journals.

GREGORY O. STONE is staff associate, office of the president at Southeastern Massachusetts University, in a part-time capacity, and does freelance writing, having had feature articles appear in *Popular Science, Yankee,* Sunday *New York Times,* and *Boys' Life*. He has coauthored an article with Walker and Feldman in *Educational Record* entitled: "Collegiality and Collective Bargaining: An Alternate Perspective" (Spring 1976).

DONALD E. WALKER has been president of Southeastern Massachusetts University in North Dartmouth since 1972, and previously was acting president and vice-president for academic affairs at San Diego State College. He has published several articles in both sociology and administration. His latest article is "When the Tough Get Going, the Going Gets Tough: The Myth of Muscle Administration," *Public Administration Review* (July/August 1976); and he coauthored "Collegiality and Collective Bargaining: An Alternate Perspective," *Educational Record* (Spring 1976).

WILLIAM R. WALWORTH is director of Staff Personnel Services at Mott Community College in Flint, Michigan. He has been involved in labor relations for the past seven years, both as a college negotiator and a local school board member. During the summer of 1965, he served as a consultant at the Massachusetts Institute of Technology for the U.S. Office of Education in a study of occupational, vocational and technical education in the United States. His most recent article, "The Emerging Staff Personnel Office," was published in *Michigan School Board Journal* (October 1976). He also wrote "Staff Personnel Officers: A Definition of Role" published in *Community and Junior College Journal* (November 1973).

HANDBOOK
OF FACULTY
BARGAINING

Asserting Administrative Leadership
for Institutional Progress
by Preparing for Bargaining,
Negotiating and Administering Contracts,
and Improving the Bargaining Process

Part I

To say that collective bargaining offers the opportunity for enjoyment and pleasure is almost certain to elicit denial, anger, and incredibility. Yet every executive we know seems to derive his greatest enjoyment and satisfaction from coping successfully with an especially difficult problem. Bargaining is, indeed, complex, time consuming, and unpredictable. To successfully engage in faculty bargaining, executives must proceed from a position of optimism and careful planning. Chapter One suggests a number of reasons for optimism as well as a plan for preparing one's self psychologically for meeting union demands with confidence.

From the beginning this book was conceived to be a "how to" book for administrators. Not all administrators will want to learn "how to" do everything described in each of the chapters. It is believed, however, that almost all administrators who deal with faculty unionism will want to learn more about unions and the viewpoints of union leaders. With this in mind, the editors turned to Martin Morand, the full-time executive officer of

PREPARING FOR
COLLECTIVE BARGAINING

⬭⬭⬭⬭⬭⬭⬭⬭

*Associated Pennsylvania State College and University Faculties (APSCUF),
the union representing faculties of the Pennsylvania State Colleges and
University. We chose Morand because his leadership and career clearly
indicate that he is one of the most successful liberal faculty union executives
in the nation. His forward-looking approach to union goals broadens the
bargaining perspective to include faculty development, high faculty performance standards, and institutional excellence. The pragmatic idealism
which Morand brought to the bargaining table and to the administration
of contracts is attested to in later chapters by David W. Hornbeck (who
represented the Secretary of Education) and James Gemmell (one of the
state college presidents), both of whom were on opposite sides of the bargaining table from Morand. While Morand was planning this chapter, he
decided to accept another post, a professorship at Indiana University (Pennsylvania). He was fortunate to secure the collaboration of his successor
and long-time associate, Ramelle MaCoy. Together they have prepared a*

3

short, concise analysis of actions which presidents and administrators may take to strengthen their bonds of mutual respect with unions. Morand and MaCoy see administration and union working together for the common goal of educational excellence. They make blunt, clear suggestions. Whether the reader agrees or disagrees with these union leaders, he cannot help but be impressed by their clarity, conciseness, and sincerity.

Many college and university executives remain aloof from collective bargaining activities until critical decisions require their attention, and once involved, have difficulty understanding the subtleties and technicalities that prevent them from taking quick decisive action. All authority for action is rooted in law, and administrators should understand that labor law in most states has the effect of preempting education law. Moreover, much to the unhappiness of educational administrators, labor law in the public sector is rooted in forty years of case decisions emanating from industrial experience. The antidote for this unhappiness is to help shape and reshape (amend) state labor laws. The university's first bargaining experience should be with labor unions before the legislature. The legislature (or legislative committee) is the arbitrator. It listens to arguments as to what should or should not be included in each section of labor law and then makes its decision. The resulting law is then given its first basic application to the academy when university officials go before the labor board to seek a unit determination consistent with the university's view of its own mission, authority, and organization. Failing to mount an impressively thorough argument can result in a decision by an "outside" agency (labor board) that, in fact, redistributes authority and responsibility within the university. These are only two examples of the need for college and university officials to become involved in the early stages of activity many months prior to table negotiations. Chapter Three identifies ten issues critical to the future of higher education which should be brought to the attention of legislators as they attempt to frame labor legislation. Each labor law answers these issues either directly or by omission. Union representatives bring their point of view to bear on each issue and legislators need to hear well-reasoned suggestions from institutional executives.

Chapter Four offers an exhaustive list of questions and sources of evidence which a college or university representative will find exceedingly valuable in preparing for a bargaining unit determination. Testimony and cross-examination before the labor board can be a humiliating experience for the unprepared novice. To prepare this case analysis, we turned to a dis-

tinguished Boston law firm with considerable experience in representing colleges and universities.

Three other areas of understanding are essential to preparation for bargaining: the proper role of college administration in a union election campaign, the selection and training of administrative personnel for meeting the complex demands involved in bargaining and administering contracts, and the scope of bargaining. For the first (Chapter Five) we reviewed case studies of union elections from public and private institutions in different sections of the country. For the last we reviewed laws and case decisions in the fourteen states with the most experience, and the decisions of the National Labor Relations Board regarding private colleges and universities (Chapter Seven). To offer a comprehensive picture of the why, how, and what of training administrators for bargaining, we were fortunate to prevail on Daniel R. McLaughlin to draw upon his broad experience in industrial training programs and as a college president. We encouraged Dan to look at every avenue available in order to offer the reader an exhaustive plan from which to select those ideas most appropriate to his local situation.

To prepare adequately for collective bargaining is, indeed, a time-consuming and costly endeavor. To fail to prepare adequately is to challenge fate itself, including one's own.

George W. Angell

1

⁂ ⁂ ⁂ ⁂ ⁂ ⁂ ⁂ ⁂

  The baby-boom following World War II produced a flood of high school graduates during the 1960s. Since the economy was sound, state governments responded to demands of students and parents for expanded college opportunities. Within a short time, governments expanded state universities, turned teachers' colleges into multipurpose campuses, and established new types of institutions called community colleges. Many private colleges and universities also enlarged enrollments, constructed new buildings, and, in some cases, built whole new campuses.

  The result was a shattering impact on the American educational system. The size of some colleges doubled and tripled in a matter of three to five years. High school teachers became college professors, and in many colleges graduate students with no study beyond a master's degree filled the lower ranks of the faculty as instructors and assistant professors. Not only were many of them

Understanding
Collective Bargaining
as a Constructive Process
in University Leadership

CR&CR&CR&CR&CR&CR&CR&CR

intellectually ill-prepared for research and philosophical discourse, they were psychologically unprepared for the great freedom of the university. The number of older professors on campus who could induct the young, half-prepared neophytes into college teaching was simply too small. It is no wonder that some of these young academics, fortified by the security of an overabundance of job opportunities, abused the freedom and authority to which they were unaccustomed. Many of them led the student rebellions against authority of any kind. Although, in general, the revolts of the 1960s yielded far greater positive than negative social reform, institutions of higher education paid an incredible price in loss of public opinion about how well colleges were managed and controlled. Even such prestigious private institutions as Harvard, Columbia, and Cornell shared the scars of the 1960s. But their recuperative powers are more varied and more independent of government than are those of public institutions.

The natural backlash to student and faculty abuses was civil action designed to bring campuses under more direct government control. Since expenditures for higher education skyrocketed, the first attempts at control came through budgeting. Coordinating boards with offices located in state capitals were established essentially as part of governors' executive branches. Expansion of buildings and special programs (especially costly ones such as medicine and engineering) were subjected to tight governmental supervision. Legislation designed to control faculty teaching loads and student-financed activities (such as "radical" speakers on campus) began to surface throughout the nation. This, of course, violated academic freedom and freedom of speech. However, public opinion and court review forced legislators and governors to confine their control to expenditures.

The natural response from faculty and students to the growing strictures of government control was, in turn, to develop political influence. The growth of public services and the employment of millions of people by state and local governments gave national union leaders the opportunity for expanding collective bargaining for public employees. Union leaders pushed hard for state labor legislation, and by 1967 Wisconsin, Michigan, and New York had passed such laws primarily as a political response to union pressures. Public college faculties, having less and less power and security on campus, began searching for means of redress through state government. Getting help from campus administrators and local trustees often became, in the eyes of union officials, an exercise in futility since most of the important decisions were being made in the capitol by coordinating officials who work under directives from governors, state budget officials, and legislators. The new state labor laws, never intended for college faculties, provided an ideal outside vehicle for organizing faculty political power. So faculties began to unionize, first in community colleges where they had the least influence on either internal or external decisions, and later in those particular public colleges where the administrative hierarchy, topped by the governor, made most of the decisions.

In addition, the governors and legislators of New York, Pennsylvania, and New Jersey, long irritated by their inability to control campuses (especially the prestigious state and land-grant universities), inadvertently discovered that centralized, statewide collective bargaining with faculty union representatives offered them an unparalleled opportunity for legalized, contractual control of both expenditures and personnel policy (bordering on academic policy) on campuses. Furthermore, this new found instrument of political control had the support of unions and faculty. Politicians in other states noticed the growing political control of state colleges and universities in these states. Maine passed a labor law designed specifically for the University of Maine, a statewide system of campuses. For two years Wisconsin has been formulating such a law to cover its university system. For the first time, many state legislators and governors began encouraging faculty collective bargaining in one way or another. Holding faculty at four-year campuses to salary increases at levels lower than those negotiated at unionized two-year campuses (and high schools) was one way of instigating faculty unrest and, eventually, interest in unionization. When faculty members at state universities in and near Chicago received an average of $5,000 less in salary than those who taught in the neighboring community colleges, the faculties at the five universities under the Board of Governors demanded the right to unionize. When the public school and community college teachers of Minnesota received, on the average, 11 percent increases each year for two years and college and university teachers received 3½ percent, the state college faculties unionized. The battle over unionization is still going on at the prestigious University of Minnesota. In addition, subtle but explosive political battles for campus control among coordinating boards, governors, legislators, unions, and campus administrators are currently being waged in such key states as Oregon, Michigan, Iowa, Nebraska, Colorado, Wisconsin, Massachusetts, and Connecticut. These battles, usually starting at the state college or community college level, are only the beginning of a long government campaign to bring the influential state universities and land-grant institutions under more governmental control.

At the same time, private colleges facing severe financial problems sought more and more public funding. As states expanded their support of private colleges, directly and indirectly, the institutions became more dependent on political patronage. When the financial crunch of the mid-1970s decreased state interest in private college financing, the colleges found themselves in a weak political position to compete for tax dollars. As a result, private colleges organized the Council of Independent Colleges and Universities (CICU) on the state level and in 1976 on the national level (NAICU). During this period more than sixty private college and university faculties had unionized, most of them affiliated with national unions with considerable political influence.

There are many opportunities for presidents of both public and private colleges to unite with faculty unions in a common goal of campus autonomy and a fair share of tax dollars. However, many presidents are angered by union activity and see unions in the narrowest context of adversaries fighting for control of whatever is left of autonomy on campus. Unions in turn, flushed with their initial successes in shared authority, fear subversion from local administrators and trustees. Therefore this book will help campus administrators and union leaders alike transcend the mistakes and emotions of early negotiations. The academic milieu thrives on the natural internal conflicts among the several parties (departments, deans, students, and alumni). But economic survival as well as campus freedom and integrity require a united front at the state and national political levels. Inadequate funding and internal political disunity are the enemies of higher education. When colleges and universities successfully unite the political forces of national unions with those of institutional leadership, their future will be assured. But this unity simply will not occur until both parties learn how to handle collective bargaining as a normal positive aspect of collegial life.

Responsibility of Leadership

College administrators have special talents which eventually lead to positions of academic leadership. These talents are often related to the ability to bring people together, to listen to their concerns and suggestions, and to analyze or synthesize fact and opinion that shape a resolution of the problem at hand. It is this ability to identify and use the valid elements of debate to fashion reasonable responses to problems that I shall call the constructive approach to college and university administration.

This chapter establishes the natural relationship between such a constructive approach to campus administration and the opportunities offered by collective bargaining for exercising this approach. Collective bargaining is neither good nor bad per se. The validity of any process must be established on the basis of its results. Bargaining is an administrative process, and it can be used advantageously to achieve institutional as well as union goals. This appears to be a truism, but I have met hundreds of college administrators in the last few months who have expressed fear of, or at least a deep apprehension of, collective bargaining; they think it means the end of administrative authority. This fear results from a lack of information or positive experience or both. Sometimes this fear is sustained by administrators who have unyielding attitudes about their administrative styles and who always assume that collective bargaining is incompatible with the "correct" (their own particular) style of administration. Fear, of course, produces its own tensions and makes change more difficult. It spawns a defensive reactionary response. But the constructive approach to administration leaves no room for fear to hinder one's intelligent use of the opportunities offered by the negotiation process and or to avoid its potential problems. Successful bargaining requires a spirit of freedom and openness.

Everyone with whom I talk seems to realize that collective negotiations is a powerful tool in the hands of a faculty union. Almost no one talks about bargaining as a powerful tool in the hands of a firm, intelligent administration. But it is. This chapter provides an overview of some opportunities presented to administrators in the process of creative bargaining. Ensuing chapters discuss in detail how higher education executives have used these opportunities to help achieve institutional goals.

Opportunities of Collective Bargaining

Obviously there are always more opportunities in any given situation than those perceived or acted upon by a particular individual. More and more administrators, however, are beginning to understand bargaining as a process that offers almost endless opportunities for an imaginative executive. Those listed here are neither universally perceived nor universally available. Yet all of them have been found in practice and may be available to any administrator sufficiently imaginative to help create and use them.

Efficiency

What college administrator has not waited impatiently for a faculty senate to act upon a new program, a policy change, a budget recommendation, or a grievance settlement? Faculty senates have histories of slow deliberation. For example, a grievance moves from the executive committee to the standing committee on faculty welfare to the subcommittee on faculty grievances. The senatorial process usually takes place *after* the grievant has taken his case first to the department chairperson, then to the dean, then to the vice-president, and eventually to the president. After several months of frustrating administrative review, the case comes before a committee which must review it from the beginning, since informal administrative reviews seldom produce written records of administrative decision making. The administrators present a formidable *adversary* to any faculty review committee attempting to study the case. This faculty review process may take months of frustrating emotional effort, and the case comes before the president again. The president must declare that either the administration was in error or the faculty committee was in error. By this time, the decision is further complicated by the length of time taken, and it may be too late in the year to expect the grievant to find suitable employment or accept other remedies. Then the college faces the possibility of an expensive and time-consuming court case. This procedure, of course, is not the precise one followed on every nonunionized campus. But the differences are probably not too great.

How is this example different under collective bargaining? Later chapters will show that constructive debate at the bargaining table usually leads to a more efficient due process. Here, it is enough to say that most contractual grievance procedures yield several advantages, such as (1) a limited time span for submitting a grievance, (2) a relatively short, formal procedure for resolving the grievance, usually three or four steps, (3) a skilled adjudicator, often a labor attorney, who hears the case on behalf of the institution and makes a reasoned decision based on the rules specified in the contract, (4) a provision for binding arbitration. Properly used, such procedures can reduce personality conflicts, administration-faculty confrontations, faculty-inspired student demonstrations, costly court procedures, and destructive indecision. They can lead to more timely and just decisions that faculty members are more likely to accept in general because due process was followed. Administrators are more likely to accept such decisions because a nonacademic person (a campus labor relations executive or an outside arbitrator) made the final decision, relieving the president or academic vice-president of the burden of overruling administrative colleagues or the faculty committee. In addition, the campus labor relations expert is available to advise deans and chairpersons during the early stages of review, hopefully avoiding common errors such as misinterpretation of the negotiated contract.

The bargaining table is another area of efficiency. The union table team legally represents the *entire* faculty. Where else can administration representatives meet face to face with an equal number of faculty representatives and make agreements binding on the entire faculty? Where else can the institution expect the faculty as a whole to *agree* upon personnel policies which can be reasonably administered and legally enforced? How many faculty senates have the courage to bargain retrenchment procedures and criteria? Senates normally recommend a procedure that is favorable to faculty members. When the president vetoes such action and gives reasons for the veto, the senate debates further. It will probably make another recommendation equally favorable to the faculty, one that usually places most, if not all, of the burden for "negative" decisions on the administration and requires the institution to pay heavily for relocation, reeducation, long-term leaves of absence with pay for anyone being retrenched, regardless of the institution's programs (American Association of University Professors [AAUP] *Bulletin,* 1976, p. 17). A voluntary faculty senate committee should not be expected to recommend less for a colleague. Yet few institutions have the financial means to accept such a one-sided policy. Consequently, by the time retrenchment is necessary, there is often no agreed-on procedure, and the administration has little recourse but to take emergency measures which will probably cause an emotional response among faculty and students as well as create suspicion of administration motives. At the bargaining table, however, retrenchment criteria and procedures are mandatory subjects of bargaining, and the faculty has little choice but to arrive at a reasonable accommodation with the administration. (For an example of a reasonable accommodation between the national AAUP proposal and an employer position, see the contracts which Oakland and Temple Universities negotiated with their AAUP unions.) The accommodation becomes legally enforceable.

Bargaining also increases efficiency because labor board decisions and labor laws almost universally allow the administration to act unilaterally in times of emergency. Emergencies do not relieve the executive from properly consulting with faculty as quickly as possible. But how does one achieve an emergency meeting of the senate with any assurance of general acceptance among the faculty? The executive committee of the faculty union, however, has the legal power to act on behalf of all members of the faculty, even when some faculty members refuse to join the union. Situations have proven that union representatives are willing to meet quickly with the administration in order to agree on a temporary measure that both can support for the duration of the emergency.

Legal Force of the Union's Actions

Contracts are legally enforceable, but the importance of the legal aspects as a management benefit cannot be overemphasized. Grievances properly processed in accordance with contractual procedures are seldom overruled by civil courts. In addition, formally processed grievance settlements ordinarily yield broad support among faculty and students not so much in terms of the substantive decision as in terms of due process. Perceived lack of due process, which can arise out of almost any informal or employer-determined procedure, is perhaps the most frequent cause of poor faculty-administration-student-trustee relationships. Unionization generally leads not only to more efficient procedures but to the employment of trained personnel administrators and legal counselors, who greatly increase the potential for objective personnel decisions. In addition, unionized faculty members soon realize that the actions of duly elected union officers legally bind all members of the faculty. This fact alone is considered by some college executives to be worth the entire cost of collective negotiations.

Equality of Power

Many college presidents believe that unions weaken the power of the administration because contracts require the employer to follow certain procedures of due process and consultation. Yet almost every president sincerely believes in both processes. Moreover, labor board and legislative decisions are broadening, not narrowing, the right of the employer to make unilateral decisions in such matters as the level of funding, number of employees, assignment of employees, promotions, supervision, discipline, tenure quotas, and many others. (See Chapter Seven on the scope of bargaining.) In addition, administrators are becoming more sophisticated in negotiating favorable retrenchment criteria, affirmative action procedures, merit increases, conditions for salary increases, management rights clauses, as well as other measures. Obviously, then, management has a real opportunity to require faculty to negotiate not only written standards of excellence, but more importantly, procedures by which faculty can enforce those standards through evaluations of their colleagues. By negotiating for control of criteria, procedures, and evidence, the institution can provide academic deans with ways of determining the quality of individual performance as a basis of tenure and promotion. Moreover, union support for specific criteria, evaluation procedures, and reliable evidence can help in achieving institutional standards of excellence. Unfortunately, too many administrators fail to see the opportunity to specify in bargaining contracts the *types* and *sources* of evidence that faculty committees must collect and *verify* as a basis for making recommendations. When a committee is forced to supply its evidence, sources of evidence, and means of verification, a dean can analyze whether or not the committee's recommendation is based on scholarship. Under such exposure, committees will be more thorough and demanding. Individuals facing such scrutiny will more clearly understand what is expected of them. Many unions are now negotiating into contracts the traditional AAUP requirement that administrators provide "compelling" reasons for not accepting faculty recommendations. Under normal circumstances, if a faculty recommendation appears to ignore negative evidence or fails to include an analysis of reliable evidence for all the criteria, deans are inclined to over-ride a faculty recommendation. If committees are not compelled to provide sources and verification of evidence, a dean cannot provide reasons to sustain a contrary judgment because he has no way of evaluating evidence. Bargaining the types and sources of evidence can rectify this injustice both for deans and grievants.

Unions and administrators work toward the same objectives, although not always for the same reasons. For example, in the spring of 1976 the college presidents of the Pennsylvania state colleges tried to resist orders from the governor's office to save money by retrenching eighty-two faculty positions. The presidents argued that they could save money elsewhere in the budget to better institutional advantage. But they were overruled. During spring negotiations the statewide faculty union negotiated an agreement with the state to rescind all eighty-two letters of nonreemployment. In other words, a unionized faculty can sometimes help the administration to achieve institutional goals.

Clarification and Codification of Institutional Policy

After making a nationwide study, Kemerer and Baldridge (1975) stated that "union emphasis on due process has resulted in tightening up and regularization of procedures and an elimination of informality (p. 127)." They further classify this effect as one of the major "positive aspects" of collective bargaining. Many administrators have not taken advantage of this positive aspect because they have bargained procedures defensively, reacting to union demands rather than countering with a more complete set of demands of their own. Administrative tightening up of procedures can reduce the number of careless and untimely decisions made by department chairpersons and committees. This action, in turn, can greatly reduce unnecessary grievances.

Another potential advantage of bargaining is the opportunity to have key management rights listed separately within the contract. Such a list should help faculty understand what it is that administrators have a right to do without consultation. If there is doubt about whether or not a particular subject requires mandatory bargaining, management can always refuse to bargain it. The most a union can do is turn to the appropriate labor board for a formal ruling. When this type of authoritative adjudication is not available (as on a nonunionized campus), faculty members often express the opinion that "the faculty is the university" and that administrators have no right to make any decisions without their advice and consent. This pressure may, and often does, lead to hesitant decision making by insecure administrators, constant grumbling among faculty members about administrative actions, or both.

Legally enforceable contractual clauses usually reduce procedural differences among departments. Such differences have always been a source of grievance claims. When a grievance is taken to court, the lawyer for the grievant does not hesitate to search for inconsistencies within or among departments. On nonunionized campuses such differences are not usually difficult to find. Although this situation existed on newly unionized campuses in the early stages of bargaining, it has slowly improved because unions have become vigorous in demanding that contractual procedures be strictly enforced. A loosely knit faculty senate seldom demands that trustee-established procedures be strictly and uniformly applied in each department. Senates traditionally appear to be more interested in protecting departmental autonomy than in seeking consistent application of procedures. Yet serious inequities in personnel decisions resulting from departmental autonomy often become insoluble administrative headaches because the administration is expected to remedy those inequities without weakening departmental autonomy. Such headaches can be reduced by a good contract.

Use of Professional Personnel Administrators

Academic deans traditionally administer faculty personnel policies. But deans are seldom prepared either by training or by temperament to supervise personnel standards or to override faculty recommendations. As a result, faculties have long resisted any systematic accounting of their teaching, days of service, sick leave, sabbatical leaves, office hours, research, or recommendations for promotions. Court cases have revealed the inadequacies and inequities of informal accounting. Injustices are less likely to occur when trained personnel administrators keep and administer faculty records. This does not mean that unionized faculty members will have to punch time clocks. Far from it. Nevertheless, if they are to fully enjoy the growing list of fringe benefits available to them as a result of negotiations, the union will insist that accurate records be kept. In addition, personnel administrators will require department heads and deans to make timely recommendations and decisions. This requirement alone will avoid many useless and harmful grievances.

The Use of Professional Negotiators

On nonunionized campuses, faculty members bargain individually and as groups, often haphazardly, with chairpersons, deans, and vice-presidents. The result is a great variety of decisions often made without benefit of broadly accepted guidelines. It is important to understand that academic deans and vice-presidents are often put into office as a result of faculty influence within selection committees. Teachers usually favor modest, understanding, scholarly, gentle people as deans and reject aggressive, highly organized, energetic candidates. It is no wonder that traditionally informal bargaining by such people leads to inexplicable inequities among individuals and departments. The truth is that few academic deans have the ability or desire to bargain with their colleagues. When bargaining becomes formal through unionization, however, the chief executive has an unusual opportunity to employ a well-educated, professional negotiator who knows how to plan for bargaining, how to train his table team, how to develop a unified institutional posture toward union and institutional goals, how to respond calmly to the most emotional demands of union officials, and how to lay aside differences once an agreement is reached. This same professional, if a full-time employee, could head up the employee-relations administration program, be the official campus counsel, and handle grievances and labor relations. In addition, he could be responsible for meeting regularly with union officials and reviewing grievances on behalf of the president throughout the life of the contract. These assignments relieve untrained academics of the sometimes unhappy experience of negotiating and administering contracts. It can also reduce the time of administrators spent in confrontation with faculty members. The negotiator will always be acting on behalf of the president and trustees, and his objectives must be established and reestablished in consultation with them. Finding the right professional negotiator provides an opportunity for extending the constructive approach to administration.

The Use of Impartial Mediators

College and university administrators and faculties traditionally resist outside influences in campus decision making, and usually for good reason. Too often the outsider is motivated by political, economic, religious, or other personal interests. The House Un-American Activities Committee, the Central Intelligence Agency, the Federal Bureau of Investigation, and even a "professional" committee from a national association intent upon securing a favorable personnel decision for a particular client serve as reminders of outside influence. Few such visitors were prepared to preserve institutional values or to be scholarly and neutral in their proceedings. But collective bargaining provides, usually through an established conciliation agency, a panel of neutrals trained in mediation, fact finding, and arbitration procedures. Professional conciliators have only one objective: to help the parties resolve their own differences in accordance with established rules. Chapter Eighteen explains how an administrator with an open and constructive approach to problem solving may secure invaluable help from neutrals at little or no cost.

Increased Faculty Compensation

Higher education executives have always strived for better salaries for faculty colleagues. A well-paid profession attracts people with high potential. The ability to select new additions to the faculty from a panel of highly qualified candidates assures the future quality of an institution. Administrators have long been willing to cut budgets elsewhere in order to pay better salaries. But in recent years, especially in public institutions, forces beyond administrators' control have caused faculty salaries to level off below those of other professions which require no greater preparation or potential. Bargaining generally improves both salaries and fringe benefits for the teaching profession. Administrators with a constructive approach to bargaining are finding new opportunities to join with faculty unions to improve salaries and other conditions to attract better-qualified people to college teaching.

Quality of Faculty Members

It is common knowledge that most unions will bargain for across-the-board salary raises rather than merit increases. But where administrators have insisted, bargaining has produced merit increases and promotions by which the institution may encourage and reward above-average professional services. Contractual criteria and procedures can improve institutional ability to evaluate performance and to distribute merit awards and promotions in a manner that gains more faculty, administrative, and public support. Many contracts sustain and strengthen the right of administrators to evaluate faculty. Some contracts establish internal review boards for final arbitration of grievances related to merit awards, such as tenure, promotion, and reappointment. Others use outside arbitrators. Some recent contracts include student grievance procedures for protesting arbitrary or unsatisfactory faculty performance. More contracts are helping administrators, with union support, to reallocate positions and funds to departments with the heaviest teaching loads. Many contracts recognize the need for faculty assistance in teaching and research. In these and other ways, administrators are beginning to show their ability to bargain constructively to help achieve institutional excellence. The same results may be possible through nonunion processes. But economic hard times, public scrutiny of campus affairs, antidiscrimination legislation, the intervention of courts and government in campus issues, and public demand for improved management decisions are all sorely testing the traditional collegial strategies for achieving excellence.

Faculty Security

Perhaps this outcome of collective bargaining is the least appreciated by executives. Faculty security has been bargained in many ways. Procedural safeguards against arbitrary and politically motivated decisions, reasonable retrenchment procedures, repeal of layoffs in New Jersey and Pennsylvania, consultation procedures, and other warranties have been negotiated. Of course, they may be viewed as merely union victories. But in a very real sense they have promoted institutional excellence. A secure faculty union does not have to win or even pursue weak grievances. It can turn its efforts to the improvement of programs and faculty standards with less fear of revealing the need for improvement. Younger faculty, procedurally protected by the contract, may have more difficulty finding support for tenure among their colleagues unless solid evidence of scholarship and effective teaching is forthcoming. Equally significant is the concomitant improvement in administration at all levels. As the administrative staff becomes more effective in executing the contractual procedures, more mutual respect can develop among the parties, enhancing the opportunity for cooperative action. Although *there are only a few campuses where these encouraging signs are in evidence,* their very existence signals an era of renewed faith in higher education built on mutual respect among the parties.

Tenure and Institutional Excellence

One continuing concern of faculty and administrators alike is the possible negative effects of a high proportion of tenured faculty on educational excellence. Without doubt, unions have made it difficult for management to make arbitrary or unilateral decisions about tenure awards, but this is entirely proper. In addition, some state labor boards are beginning to make clear decisions in this area. For example, New Jersey has ruled that management has the right to unilaterally determine both quotas on tenure and the procedures for granting tenure. University boards of trustees (for example, the City University of New York Board of Higher Education) have been less than successful in setting tenure quotas without the aid of labor board rulings.

Students in the Collective Bargaining Process

Many administrators and union officials believe that students have no place at the bargaining table. Yet new experiences with students at the table, especially at Montana institutions are encouraging. (The Montana story is fully explored in Chapter Fourteen.) Three states, Maine being the most recent, now require the parties to permit students to share in the bargaining process. The reports from administrators usually are more favorable than those from union reporters. To some observers, a form of tripartite bargaining will emerge as a new type of collegial governance. The presence of student interests at the table should open new opportunities for constructive approaches to resolving multiparty concerns. Such a movement is perceived by many as essential for slowing the recent initiatives toward formalized independent student unions (for example, Massachusetts Legislative House-Bill No. 4346 [1976]). If they are strong, these unions may bargain at different political levels with several different parties creating a complexity of incredible proportions in campus governances. An interesting question arises: Should students gain the right to bargain separately? Would faculty then join administration on one side of the table to bargain with students on the other?

Summary

It should be pointed out that I am fully aware of the many possible disadvantages of collective bargaining, such as increased costs, confusion about the role of the faculty senate, the union drive for egalitarianism as opposed to merit salary and promotion, more formal procedures, and so forth. These have elsewhere been discussed ad infinitum with much less emphasis on the *opportunities offered* by bargaining. Bargaining in itself does not automatically bring all of the possible institutional benefits listed above. Benefits must be earned and achieved through excellence in bargaining. Academic administrators with unionized faculties should stop grumbling about the problems of bargaining and study the means to excellence. For this reason I have attempted to demonstrate that an enterprising management may find and even create opportunities within the context of collective bargaining for achieving institutional goals. Obviously, a union must bring to the table its goals and objectives. Should management simply react to union imperatives the resulting contract will be merely an expression of those narrow union goals. Management's duty is to bring institutional goals into every table discussion and to demand that the union openly join management in its effort to achieve the broader goals of the institution. When management and union bargain with equal power, a constructive agreement will surely result.

Ramelle MaCoy
Martin J. Morand

We, the authors of this chapter, are not without our own prejudices and our own points of view. As union organizers and administrators, we believe in unions and the collective bargaining process. We believe that collective bargaining can be a positive force in an institution's drive toward excellence in higher education. We believe that collective bargaining is the best available alternative to wearying forms of bureaucratic inefficiency—an inherently democratic process that is neither better nor worse than its participants, a self-regulating mechanism operating through small social units, a substitute for excessive governmental regulation, a vehicle for participatory decision making, and the best hope for overcoming alienation and apathy on the campus.

We do approach the writing of this chapter with some reservations. We have confessed to partisanship, and if we had a formula for besting an opponent at the bargaining table, we would be loathe to share it. If we had an insider's knowledge of how to "beat" the union, certainly we would not publish it.

Establishing
Constructive Relationships
Between Administrators
and Faculty Unions

But although the bargaining process is an adversary process and both sides take, on occasion, partisan glee in outmaneuvering the other, the more profound, but less dramatic, truth is that any agreement reached at the bargaining table must be satisfactory to both parties. If it is not, the process fails and will ultimately require renegotiation and a new agreement almost always at the expense of both parties. That a satisfactory agreement must benefit both parties is frequently forgotten since, superficially at least, the union is perpetually in the position of "asking" while management "gives." We know, however, that a faculty member who feels that decisions about pay and working conditions have been fair will be a more efficient and productive member of the university team.

A Case in Point

Some years ago, we were senior executive officers of an Atlanta union employing a staff of sixty people. The staff enjoyed excellent working conditions with wages and benefits considerably above the standards of the area. We accepted, albeit with considerable personal indignation, the unionization of that staff and after one productive—or so we thought—late night bargaining session, we met at breakfast the next morning to map our negotiating strategy.

Following breakfast we drove to the office and found, to our total surprise, our employees waving picket signs with childish jubilation in full and embarrassing view of reporters and television cameras. We were angry with their traitorous ingratitude as we recalled favors bestowed, unjustified absences forgiven, unmerited pay increases granted, and personal loans made. We marveled at what we regarded as the obvious stupidity of those employees who could not understand that by damaging the reputation of their employer (a union), they would inevitably jeopardize their jobs and livelihood. We traded anecdotes about the incompetence of many of those on the picket line and deplored the fact that they lacked our own dedication and commitment to the union cause. The strikers were treating their lofty union calling as just a "job," and we ranted against their short-sighted greed. We reacted exactly as so many other employers had reacted to us.

That strike of our union staff in Atlanta was soon resolved and a contract negotiated. Perhaps the examination (with some of the objectivity that the passage of time permits) of our own attitudes and reactions at the time will show some parallels between that situation and the one which confronts increasing numbers of academic administrators.

The union, of course, was a nonprofit organization, the purpose of which was to allow workers, through collective action, to raise their standards of living and to promote, through a variety of means including education, their general welfare. The union sought to instill in its own employees an idealistic commitment to this purpose; and anyone whose primary interest in being employed by the union was his own selfish, materialistic welfare was, by definition, unfit to be a union employee. The problem of who would look after the legitimate interests of the employees, materialistic or otherwise, was seldom, if ever, addressed.

As the senior executive officers of the union, we had the responsibility (we would certainly have chosen to use the word *respon-sibility* rather than *power*) for making all decisions concerning rates of pay, promotions, working hours, working conditions, the hiring of new employees, and direction of the staff. We would have argued that with this responsibility came authority and that authority was essential for the efficient direction of the staff toward achievement of the union's goal.

Although this argument is obviously not without some validity, what we are able to see in retrospect is the extent to which our own egos were involved. The possession of power has few equals in the area of ego gratification, and we were unwilling to surrender even a portion of that power. And because of the lofty nature of the union's goal, we were able to rationalize our tenacity for power far more easily and more convincingly than we would have been able to do had we been, for instance, factory owners. We suggest an almost perfect parallel with academic management.

In the end, we discovered or, more accurately, were rather painfully taught, that most of the decisions about our own staff's pay and working conditions could be shared with the staff itself at the bargaining table without adverse effect on anything more important than our own egos. In fact, we found that employees who shared in the decisions about their working lives were able to worry less about their personal security and more about the purpose of the union.

We believe there is an irreversible trend—for which the educational community itself can claim much of the credit—away from autocratic decision making and toward shared decisions. Decision making can be truly "shared" *only* between equals; thus, it follows that for faculty to share decisions with academic management, they must achieve and exercise power equal to that of management.

Unionization and Shared Decision Making

Because of the history of labor relations in this country and because of the direction that our laws have been and are taking, we believe that unionization will be the chief means by which faculty achieve this parity of power. We think it axiomatic that management cannot confer or grant an equality of power, that it must be asserted by the faculty itself. This assertion must be a collective action representative of at least a majority and will, therefore, be a "union" regardless of any euphemisms that popular prejudices about unions may prompt.

If we can accept these arguments—that faculty will increasingly insist on shared decisions, that shared decisions can only be made by equals, and that faculty can achieve equal legal power with academic management only through collective action (unionization)—it is clear that collective bargaining is going to be a fact of life on a steadily increasing number of campuses.

Management can, without question, impede this trend toward unionization in at least two ways. Management can voluntarily grant some of the tangible benefits of collective bargaining, voluntarily share decisions (the phrase is inherently contradictory), and attempt to create the appearance of the contented, cooperative family model that managers traditionally point to when faced with an organization campaign.

Management can also launch countercampaigns and attempt to convince faculty members that unionization is not in their best interests, that they will lose some of their prized individuality and independence, that they will tarnish their professional image and, in the bargain, be forced to pay exorbitant union dues.

Academic administrators must decide how to react when the union campaign begins. Such a decision could shape the course of the faculty union-administration relationship for a whole generation. Some years ago this question was posed and answered for businessmen in *The Nation's Business* article titled, "What To Do When the Union Knocks." Unfortunately, some college and university leaders see themselves as corporate plant managers, immediately assume an adversarial posture, and, indeed, hire law firms reputed to be most tough on unions. We suggest that this reaction is inappropriate, counterproductive, and immoral.

Immoral? Yes. It has been declared public policy of the United States to "promote and encourage" the practice of collective bargaining since the passage of the National Labor Relations Act (NLRA), after which most state laws are patterned. Although the business community accepts, and even applauds, the defiance of this policy, such conduct hardly seems appropriate in academe, and it is doubly inappropriate when the college president is also an officer of the state with a duty to uphold the law.

Although management's right to oppose unionization is usually defended on the grounds of free speech, the result is usually an inappropriate and frequently counterproductive interference in what is essentially the faculty's decision. Do the administrators not have a vested interest in the outcome? Will they not have to deal with the winner? Certainly, just as the U.S. Government has an interest in who wins the Italian and Chilean elections. But intervention in the internal affairs of others not only calls into question our commitment to the free election process but also frequently produces quite unintended results.

As union organizers, there are two things we know: First, no organizer/agitator can stir up a contented group and lead them like the Pied Piper where they would not go on their own. Second, there is no greater obstacle to union organization than employee lethargy—and frequently no quicker cure for such lethargy than managerial overreaction. Administration attacks on faculty unionism may succeed only in driving out of activity and leadership in the newly forming organization those faculty members with whom the administration communicates most often and best.

Perhaps the greatest danger that the administration faces if it decides to enter the faculty organizing fray is that management may end up being captivated, as many propagandists are, by its own rhetoric. Administrators who convince themselves that collective bargaining will destroy collegial life, undermine the mission of the university, eliminate the faculty senate and end friendly interpersonal relationships, will have great difficulty in effectively dealing with the union should their campaign against unionization fail. Even if they are successful in overcoming the antiunion bias that must inevitably be nurtured during the course of an antiunion campaign, the administrators involved are not likely to convince the union leaders and activists with whom they must later deal as equals that they are capable of bargaining fairly and dispassionately.

Administration and the Unionizing Effort

At this point, regardless of your bias, you may begin to think that we protest too much, having argued that it is unethical for the administration to intervene in an organizing campaign, that administrative intervention is counterproductive and may help the union to win, and that administrative intervention tends to poison future relationships between the administration and the union. We are convinced, however, that the reasons are valid. A faculty organizing campaign is the concern of the faculty, and the interests of all parties is best served by leaving the decision to the faculty. Many administrators, perhaps all, will be tempted to at least provide information to assist the faculty in making their decision, but that temptation is best resisted since information will almost certainly be perceived as propaganda and therefore be resented.

Assuming the administration decides to adopt a neutral stance in the union organizing campaign, the first major decision that the administration will have to make will be the question of unit determination, that is, who should be included in the bargaining unit. The determination is not easily changed once made, and an inappropriate determination can cause much subsequent mischief for both parties. Statesmanship is required, and since at this point, the union must respond to the pressures and demands of those who have subscribed to its cause and pursue narrow organizational goals, it can best be provided by the administration.

Unit Composition

There is no arbitrary checklist of who should and who should not be in the unit. Circumstances vary among institutions, and department chairpersons who should clearly be included at one school may be so definitely an arm of management at another that they must be excluded. Lawyers and doctors may have a community of interests with other faculty at one school but not at another. Generally, the unit should be as large and broad as possible so long as the members have sufficient community of interest to maintain the cohesiveness necessary for orderly bargaining. Generally, labor boards will approve any reasonable unit to which both union and management agree, and the goal should be to reach agreement on the unit rather than having it determined—as it will be absent agreement—by a state or federal labor board.

Statesmanship on the question of unit determination is not

likely to be forthcoming from the union. The union will be seeking to gain legal bargaining rights to represent its supporters, and naturally it will be striving to have all its supporters included in the unit. If department chairs, for instance, are not among its supporters and if the union knows or suspects that department chairs as a group will vote against union representation, the union may seek to exclude them.

The union's stance naturally inspires—if it did not already exist—an equal determination on the part of management to include within the unit those whom it thinks will vote against the union. Under such circumstances, the important and long-enduring decisions on who should be in the unit are determined on the basis of temporary and mostly irrelevant considerations. Real statesmanship on the part of management in striving to reach agreement on an appropriate unit can avoid starting the union-management relationship off on an adverse basis and can keep both parties from being saddled, perhaps permanently, with an unworkable or cumbersome unit.

Scope of Bargaining

When the union has been certified as the bargaining agent, one of management's first questions is what the scope of bargaining should be. Management's common reaction is to seek to limit the scope as much as possible. In almost all cases, there will be certain items—wages, including fringe benefits, and certainly working conditions—that are mandatory topics for bargaining. Management must bargain about them if the union places them on the table. Other items may be permissible topics for bargaining while others may be mandatory subjects for "discussion" purposes only.

Within the legal parameters, management frequently attempts to restrict the scope of bargaining in the apparent fear that if it bargains, it must inevitably lose. That approach, we think, is ill-advised. By restricting bargaining to wages and hours, management will focus the union's energy on these topics causing it to become a narrow, expensive "business" union. A competent, confident manager can throw the bargaining table open to any subject without prejudicing the outcome as long as it understands that an agreement to bargain does not mean, or even imply, a concession. There is nothing for management to gain by refusing to bargain about class size, for instance, that cannot be gained more easily, more directly, and with less ill will by taking a firm position in bargaining about class size.

Prior restrictions and even legal restraints on bargainability are of no avail. Even while the Pennsylvania Supreme Court was ruling that class size is not a mandatory subject of bargaining, the Philadelphia School Board was negotiating class size with the teachers' union in order to settle a strike.

The Administrative Negotiators

The mystique that surrounds union negotiations and bargaining may intimidate a college president or a dean inexperienced at it, and the administration's lack of confidence is almost certain to adversely affect the success of the first negotiations. As the administration prepares to bargain, a crucial first decision must be who will serve as spokesperson for the administration's bargaining team.

There are three alternatives, none of which is completely satisfactory. The president is, perhaps, the best choice, but most presidents have too many other responsibilities to allow them to devote sufficient attention and time to negotiations. Because of personality and temperament, some presidents may be unable to accept a condition of complete equality with the union negotiators across the table.

If the president is unwilling or unable to personally undertake negotiations, a second alternative is to choose a top administration officer for the job. However, he may not be given the kind of authority required to successfully do the job. Nothing impedes negotiations more than a management spokesperson who is little more than a messenger and who must repeatedly go back to the president for consultation and permission to make decisions. In selecting a spokesperson, the president must be certain that he can not only accept and exercise the necessary authority but is also secure enough to make decisions that may turn out to be unpopular. The final agreement must inevitably contain features that the president will find less than satisfactory.

The third alternative is to hire an outside consultant with expertise in bargaining. The advantages are obvious and considerable. The disadvantages are that the consultant will lack sufficient familiarity with the structure and operation of the institution and that he may be too zealous in demonstrating his worth and expertise to the administration. Such zeal may impede negotiations and serve as a crutch so that the administration never develops its own capability for handling negotiations.

Management and Union at the Table

As the negotiations begin, there is a quite natural—and, we submit, unfortunate—tendency for both sides to strive to "win." This tendency will be exaggerated unless the administration is able to understand and fully accept the fact that the union has been legally certified as the *exclusive* bargaining agent for all the faculty and that it is in the administration's own best interest for the union to be secure. Only a strong and secure union can politically afford to make responsible decisions that are in the best interests of all the faculty and the institution but that may be unpopular with certain individuals or factions.

There is no real need for management to undermine the union's position with its members by competing for the loyalty of faculty members, but management regularly does so when it attempts to portray improvements in wages and benefits as flowing from management largess rather than from collective bargaining. Management's own position is relatively secure. Management provides the paychecks. The union, on the other hand, collects dues and, thus, is faced with the continuing necessity of demonstrating that the services it returns are worth those dues.

It is in management's own interest, both in negotiations and in the later settlement of grievances, to give the union appropriate credit for every benefit it negotiates and for every grievance it settles. The argument that some of these benefits may have been granted and some of the grievances settled without the union is, at best, speculative and there is no useful purpose served in its being advanced by management.

The task confronting the management negotiator at the bargaining table is—in our admittedly prejudiced view—far simpler than the job of the union negotiator who must strive to reach an agreement that not only provides concrete improvements for every union member but also is perceived and accepted as a satisfactory agreement by a majority of the faculty members.

If management understands this need, the union, in turn, is more likely to understand management's need for an agreement that is financially feasible and that does not disrupt the orderly functioning of the institution.

Management can avoid many future problems at the outset by furnishing the union with all of the relevant information requested even when some technicality makes it possible to conceal or refuse information. Some Pennsylvania school districts are not believed today when they plead inability to meet wage demands because they hid resources in prior years.

Since it is safe to assume that financial resources will not permit the granting of all union demands, management can make its own job easier by making the union assign priorities to its needs. If money is not available for both early retirement and dental insurance, for instance, the union should decide what to sacrifice.

Once an agreement has been reached, management should accept responsibility for it. The agreement should be regarded as a joint management-union one and not as the "union agreement." Some administrations tend to blame every problem and frustration on the union agreement, which is neither fair nor useful.

Students' Role in Bargaining

As collective bargaining occurs on more and more campuses, pressure for student participation at the bargaining table is likely to increase. Students, the argument goes, are directly affected by collective bargaining decisions and, therefore, should have a voice in making those decisions. The nature of the bargaining process, however, is inherently bipartite. Those third parties, mediators, who are placed at the bargaining table by law are also restrained by law from breaching the confidentiality that is necessary for successful collective bargaining. They may not even be subpoenaed to reveal what took place in negotiations at subsequent arbitrations. Any move, no matter how well intentioned, by academic management to foster the formal role of students in the collective bargaining process will inevitably damage the prospect of a good-faith, constructive, and creative collective bargaining relationship. Students at the bargaining table would immediately be subjected to manipulative pressures from both management and the union, and the result would be to divert attention from the negotiation of a mutually satisfactory agreement.

Administering the Contract

In addition to the administration's acceptance of the contract as a credit to the institution and as a joint agreement for which both parties are equally responsible, both parties should guarantee objectivity, sincerity, and fairness as they work together in the interests of the institution as a whole. Union representatives can hardly be expected to take the initiative since it is the role of administration to "administer" the contract. Technically unions can only object (grieve) when administrators at various levels fail to meet the requirements of the contract.

To extend the concept of shared responsibility, some administrators invite union representatives to join them in addressing meetings of administrators and faculty members to explain the new contract and how it will be interpreted in terms of daily operations. When management and union join to explain how they worked out difficult contract clauses and why it is a good agreement, the first step of good will and cooperation may be achieved. However, if either party attempts to use the forum to further personal ends or one party's goals as opposed to another, the effort will result in antagonism rather than cooperation. In the early months following ratification of the agreement, each party will carefully watch the other for possible attack. If no attack comes, cooperation has a chance to grow.

At the first sign of a grievance, the administration should take the position that a fair and quick settlement can be reached by working with the union. The administration's desire to settle grievances quickly and fairly will provide the best possible evidence of leadership within the framework of a collectively bargained contract. Some administrators are afraid that a quick settlement may be a sign of administrative weakness or fear. The result should be the opposite. Union confidence that administration will be fair and timely in handling grievances should result in real cooperation. It may also lead to union acceptance of its own most difficult job, that of screening out trivial complaints not worthy of formal processing. Only a secure union can do this with impunity.

Another aspect of grievance administration that can build or destroy union-management cooperation is the avoidance of grievance settlements based on technicalities. Often a faculty member will hesitate to bring a complaint to the union, and by the time it is initiated, the administration could refuse to process it because it came in after the time limit established in the contract. To deny the grievance is to permit the problem to fester. Sincere administrators and union representatives can often find at least a partial solution to the complaint "outside" the grievance procedure. It is in this area that real leadership on both sides makes the institution one in which excellence can flourish.

Another important area that tests the integrity of both parties is that of faculty senate-administration-union relationships. Some administrators like to pit the senate against the union. By pretending they have great confidence in the senate (by constantly consulting with it in all important matters) and no respect for the union (by avoiding contact whenever possible), administrators can weaken a union and make its representatives rely on legal rights in order to exist. This continuous and unnecessary conflict is counterproductive. A constructive move for the administration is to bring representatives of the senate and union together and to have all parties share in deciding what role each should play in making key decisions. When such a move is successful, nothing can create more good will for the administration.

Summary

It is our conviction that the collective bargaining process can be used by academic management to share the decision-making process with the faculty and that decisions reached through collective bargaining can be mutually satisfactory to both management and faculty. The process will work best, however, if management approaches it with an open mind and good faith. No administrator is likely to be able to go to the bargaining table with such an attitude fresh from "defeat" in a union organizing campaign. The decision to organize or not should, therefore, be left to the faculty. If a union is organized, management can achieve its own goals best by dealing with a secure and stable union. Management should not sabotage or impede the union's efforts to achieve status by competing with it for the allegiance of the faculty.

George W. Angell

Many trustees and campus presidents think that shaping legislation is not important because their particular state collective bargaining law already exists. This assumption is a false one because any law should be continuously evaluated and amended, and because by 1979 there will probably be a new federal law or executive regulation that will affect bargaining rights of employees in all universities, public and private.

One of the chief reasons that collective bargaining has created special difficulties for higher education is the fact that college and university officials had little or no influence in shaping the laws that govern them. Only by assiduous study of the bills and their possible effects on campus operation can higher education executives hope to understand the problems inherent in proposed laws as well as the opportunities they offer for more effective and constructive leadership. Clearly, the extent to which bargaining be-

Shaping and Amending
Collective Bargaining
Legislation

comes a constructive process depends on whether or not a law is written to meet the special needs of higher education.

The Roles of Legislators and University Administrators

Legislators' Interest in Higher Education

One serious mistake which college and university trustees and presidents make is assuming that legislators do not want their opinion. This idea simply has no foundation in fact. It may have arisen from hearsay that some legislatures acted against the wishes of some educators or acted without inviting educators to give testimony. However, when higher education representatives have made convincing arguments, legislators have listened and responded. For example, California, Washington, and Wisconsin senior colleges and universities have been exempted from omnibus labor laws because legislators required more time to study potential problems and to legislate for the special conditions of higher education. The Wisconsin Board of Regents established committees with representatives from university administration, faculty, and students before considering legislation. Thus, it is important for higher education to request hearings and sufficient time to study the implications of faculty unionization. In making such requests, educators should be well versed in labor law and its special effects on higher education and insist that legislators join with them in broad preliminary discussions. Too often educators do their committee work in isolation and then send a representative to the legislature to deliver unilateral and naive position papers. This approach does not work largely because legislators on labor committees are accustomed to industry's well-seasoned approach to labor-management relations and because many legislators feel that higher education has too long been isolated from the realities of practical economics and politics. The antidote for this is to request that several key legislators meet regularly with educators (and students where feasible) until each section of a proposed bill can be reviewed in some depth. Not only will legislators, educators, and students learn from each other, educators and students will be pleased at the understanding and responsiveness of legislators.

Understanding the Differences Between Industry and Higher Education

These differences seem obvious to educators, and it is easy for them to assume that legislators and union representatives also know and accept such differences. This assumption is a serious mistake. Labor attorneys and professors of labor relations generally seem to believe that the basic principles and processes gleaned from industrial relations apply equally well to public-sector bargaining including faculty negotiations. In general, this may be a safe assumption. Higher education, however, poses some unique conditions which should be considered fully in writing public-sector labor legislation. Such legislation is generally written to cover many types of employees including police, firefighters, sanitation workers, clerical staff, maintenance workers, public school teachers, and many others. Influential union organizations, such as the American Federation of Labor-Congress of Industrial Organizations (AFL-CIO), the American Federation of State, County, and Municipal Employees (AFSCME), and the National Education Association (NEA), help to initiate and shape bills in state legislatures and Congress because those activities allow them to extend their membership. These organizations have been largely responsible for framing existing labor legislation in New York, New Jersey, Michigan, Wisconsin, California, and in many other states. However, institutions of higher learning have made little effort to participate in shaping legislation. For example, in Maine, university officials exercised little influence in shaping a special law for university employees even though they had been invited to participate in early discussions. Unfortunately, too many university spokespersons have taken the attitude that nothing of value can be learned from experience in other states or that there is little to be gained from trying to persuade legislators that colleges and universities are significantly different from industry and elementary-secondary education. California provides another good example. University spokespersons were having little effect in shaping the Rodda Law of 1975. But after articulate university students demanded a role in bargaining, the legislature decided to exclude senior institutions at least temporarily from the bill. Some people now doubt that universities ever will be included. There are recognizable differences in the university employer-employee-consumer relationships, and they are significant. Unless college and university spokespersons convince legislators of these differences, the legislators will tend to accept bills modeled after federal law designed for business and industry.

The Structure of the University and Collective Bargaining

What are these differences? One is the triple role performed by higher education faculty members. Their roles include legislative, executive, and employee functions that are so interwoven that it is difficult to separate and consider the employee function for collective bargaining. Teaching faculty members are elected to faculty senates and councils to shape legislation (policy) that will govern the activities of students (consumers) and the students' supervisors (teachers and administrators). Indeed, faculty senates may initiate and formulate new programs, program requirements, standards for student and faculty performance, academic fiscal policy, and standards for administrators' performances. Resolutions passed by these legislative bodies must be approved by the college or university president. But so are resolutions of Congress approved by the president of the United States. This relationship does not make congressmen eligible to form a union because the very nature of their work gives them advantages which employees normally accrue through unions. Some people argue that a college president can use his own authority and take action either not permitted by or prohibited by a faculty senate. But he takes such action at the risk of public censure by the faculty senate and review by trustees. Strong U.S. presidents have also taken serious action in the absence of, or contrary to, existing law. President John F. Kennedy, by executive order, established collective bargaining for federal employees. President Lyndon B. Johnson sent troops to war without congressional approval, and President Richard M. Nixon established wage ceilings. None of these actions make congressmen employees under the Wagner Act. Although faculty senates do not raise taxes, they do share in planning budgets; allocation of funds; raising endowment and research funds; and approving expenditures for sabbatical leaves, clerical assistance, research projects, student assistance, and faculty travel.

As executives, faculty members also have additional functions. Departments enjoy a great deal of autonomy and, in effect, choose their supervisors (chairpersons and deans); assign themselves particular classes; and determine class size, class prerequisites, numbers of classes, numbers of class preparations, class time and location, numbers and types of classrooms and laboratories and equipment to purchase. They also determine types of library services, library book purchases, and library fines. In addition, they decide what new faculty positions are needed, what the qualifications of candidates shall be, where to search for candidates, when and what candidates are to be interviewed, how to conduct the interviews, which candidates shall be successful, what salaries (within limits) and ranks shall be offered, and what duties shall be assigned. They supervise and evaluate the performances of junior colleagues; assign work to clerical staff; and evaluate, reject, or accept work performance of clerical staff. This list is only a partial one and does not include the executive and legislative roles of faculty in determining standards for student admission to the institution and to special programs, as well as the selection and rejection of students who apply for admission.

As an executive, each faculty member selects texts, individual students for class, and student assignments. He also examines and evaluates student performance. Each faculty member selects his own student assistants, approves payrolls for student and clerical assistants, obtains special grants, supervises grant funds, selects research projects, decides what campus committees to serve on, chooses what community services (speeches, studies, committee functions) to perform, selects professional organizations to join and consultants to invite to classes or to campus. Yet all of these functions, executed with almost no supervision, provide the basis for tenure and promotion. Can such independent legislators and supervisors really be considered "employees" under the Wagner Act or under a state labor law? This question is a serious one, and higher education must raise it again and again until there is a clear answer. Although faculty members are bargaining on some 500 campuses, there has been no answer because federal and state laws were enacted without a thorough analysis of who should be considered an employee for purposes of collective bargaining. There is serious doubt that the Congress of 1935 meant the Wagner Act to apply to professionals who help legislate and administer institutional policy. One factor which the National Labor Relations Board (NLRB) examines when trying to determine whether or not workers are employees or supervisors is the character and size of remuneration. Are they paid wages or salaries? Is the remuneration different from that paid to supervisors? Faculty ranks and salaries are not too different from those of deans and associate deans. Top professors often enjoy higher salaries, more freedom from supervision, and more opportunity to exercise discretionary judgment than do the deans under whom professors are supposed to be serving. Many deans share the duties and privileges of teaching and tenure. They rotate back into full-time teaching and eventually into other administrative types of work. Are deans really "employers" and are professors really "employees"? Legislators need to debate these questions and find definitions on which labor boards can base their unit determinations. The NLRB admits in some of its decisions that it has not found all the answers to this vexing problem (*Adelphi University* v. *Adelphi University Chapter AAUP*).[1]

What alternatives to a definition of *supervisors* can university spokespersons suggest to legislators for purposes of exclusion from the bargaining unit? For those who are firmly opposed to faculty unionization, the first alternative is of course to classify all faculty as supervisors because of the general and specific conditions already expounded. The NLRB has denied such classification under federal law in several cases, notably at New York University[2] (*New York University and New York University Chapter, AAUP*) and at Wentworth Institute (*Wentworth Institute and Wentworth College of Technology, Inc. and Massachusetts Federation of Teachers, AFT, AFL-CIO*).[3] Wentworth refused to bargain, causing the NLRB to seek enforcement of its decision in the courts. The court decided in favor of the NLRB, but most observers feel that Wentworth was a poor test case because shared governance was not its strong characteristic (*NLRB* v. *Wentworth Institute and Wentworth Institute of Technology, Inc.*).[4] Nevertheless, as a result of these decisions, it is not feasible for a college or university to attempt further tests of the issue under the NLRA unless faculty do indeed participate in making some "effective" managerial decisions affecting conditions of faculty employment. This was the missing evidence in the Wentworth case that could have tipped the court's thinking in the other direction. Since the Wagner Act (NLRA) was written in its basic form more than forty years ago and never intended for college faculty members, nothing should prevent states from developing and testing fresh points of view about the definition of a supervisor. Some state decisions have made it clear that faculty members cannot legally be both man-

---

[1] 195 NLRB No. 107 (1972).
[2] 205 NLRB No. 16 (1973), cf. *New York University and NYU Federation of United Professionals, NYSUT, NEA, AFT, AFL-CIO*, 221 NLRB No. 176 (1975).
[3] 210 NLRB No. 53 (1974).
[4] Case No. 74-1219 U.S.C.A. 1st Cir. (March 31, 1975).

agers and employees (*Rutgers, The State University and Rutgers Council of American Association of University Professors Chapters*).[5] It may be that as additional states design new types of public-sector labor laws, they will try to resolve this knotty problem by expanding the definition of supervisor to include the types of supervisory duties performed by faculty who effectively determine their own conditions of work, criteria for evaluation and self-evaluations.

A second alternative is to exclude from the union faculty members serving in temporary or permanent supervisory positions, for example, deans, department chairpersons, and program chairpersons.

A third alternative is to exclude faculty who serve in key administrative positions: chairperson of the budget committee, chairperson of the departmental committee responsible for evaluating and supervising nontenured teachers, supervisors of grant funds, and supervisors of teaching assistants.

A fourth alternative is to simply exclude all tenured faculty on the basis that they are generally no longer supervised, evaluated, and reappointed on a regular basis and that their responsibility is to set performance standards and to supervise and evaluate the nontenured faculty. This may appear to be an extreme position at this time, but the public now has serious misgivings about the results and costs of public-employee bargaining. This may be the time to rethink the purposes and privileges of bargaining. Do tenured faculty need the protection of collective force? Is there a conflict of interest when tenured faculty set promotion standards, evaluate, and supervise union colleagues and each other within those standards? The American press and public opinion are raising questions of conflicts of interests in all areas of public service. Higher education and unions are not exempt from this review.

It is important to point out here that the employment conditions on some campuses do not support any of these alternatives. Campus administrators lose credibility when they suggest alternatives that do not conform with the duties and responsibilities currently delegated to faculty members.

Another significant difference between industry and higher education is the nature of the "consumer." Students are often con-

[5] 2 NJPER 13 (January 23, 1976).

sidered consumers of higher education. But students live on or near the campus and share in the daily efforts of production. They do not consume products of higher education. They consume services, such as lectures, discussions, counseling, library services, and health services. What is the "product" of higher education, the graduate or the learning? Did professors produce the learning or did the students produce the learning by taking notes, by studying books, and by doing experiments? Nowhere in industry or in public-sector services do consumers "live with" producers while the product is being processed. Consumers do not help produce the product. The cooperation and help of consumers are not necessary to keep production moving. Students sit on committees and help shape policy. Consumers do not help develop company policy. Students evaluate professors and administrators. Consumers do not evaluate corporate executives. Students sometimes sit on the boards of trustees. Consumers are not represented on boards of directors. In fact, the entire campus community has a shared governance system, with student government responsible for developing social programs, providing artist and lecture series, developing student governance policy, and collecting fees. Consumers do not engage in such company activity. A campus is not a bipartite community. It is one in which three constituencies (and more if alumni are counted) interface in making policy, administering policy, and in cooperatively producing the product (learning).

In shaping a law that permits two of these parties to bargain, in the absence of a third party, a legally binding contract which can seriously affect the terms and conditions of the third party's work, legislators must ask themsleves whether or not the bipartite bargaining process is valid.

Legislators throughout the country are eager to find means of solving these problems, but they find few college administrators who have taken the time to identify basic questions, project alternative responses, and predict the consequences of those responses. The National Association of State Universities and Land-Grant ﹑olleges has established a committee to study the issues involved in la﹕ ﹅r legislation. The American Council on Education (ACE) and other higher education associations are beginning to study the issues. To wait for a national policy, however, may not be feasible, especially if state or local legislation is already in process. Each state needs a concerted effort by higher education executives and trustees to produce a fair debate of the subject in each state.

University Self-Government and Labor Legislation

The Issue of University Self-Governance

The differences between industry and higher education raise questions about labor legislation for higher education. Is bipartite collective bargaining valid for the higher education enterprise? Should political office holders (legislators) thrust the university into politics? Will bipartite bargaining destroy the self-governing nature of higher education by subjecting university policy and internal relationships to a bargaining process often governed by political office holders rather than by university officials?

There is considerable evidence (Mortimer, 1976, p. 12) that governors and legislators are using collective bargaining to gain control not only of university budgets but of university personnel policy and faculty supervision as well. There apparently has never been any question about the right of legislators and governors to determine the level of funding for public education. But the American people have historically expressed serious doubts about political control of faculty appointments, promotions, work assignments, and other conditions that affect the character and purpose of higher education. For example, many states have established state universities as a fourth branch of government with constitutional powers. Despotic governments are known for thought control through carefully regulated public education. But thought control is inimical to a free and democratic society. Yet a labor board decision in Kansas declared that academic freedom is a policy decision, and therefore faculty cannot negotiate it unless the employer (the state) is willing (*NEA of Shawnee Mission* v. *Board of Education*).[6] The ruling itself may be innocuous. However, it could inaugurate a series of actions whereby states during a period of economic crisis attempt to abridge traditional freedoms through

[6]512 P.2d 426 (1973).

the traditional limitations on the scope of industrial bargaining.

In New York the faculty of the State University no longer officially discusses with trustees and administrators broad policies regarding such matters as salary increases, hours, teaching loads, appointment procedures, tenure policies, leaves of absence, holidays, promotion procedures, and teacher evaluation, except as a matter of interpreting a contract negotiated between faculty representatives and the governor's office. In addition, the governor's office reviews grievances between the faculty and administration. What happened to university self-governance? What happened to the fundamental concept of academic freedom from political interference? The same type of intervention is occurring in New Jersey, Pennsylvania, Minnesota, and other states where the state insists that it is the employer; it negotiates directly with faculty, leaving trustees and administrators a minor role, if any, in the determination of the conditions of faculty employment. What kinds of professional leaders are willing to be middle management deans and presidents, acting as branch managers for state politicians? Why should faculty members respect deans and campus presidents when they can "go over their heads" in both negotiations and grievances? Why should trustees and presidents abdicate the authority delegated to them by education law simply because no one realized that a collective bargaining law could jeopardize their authority?

There is an alternative to state controlled bargaining with faculty that will better protect the integrity of the university: bargaining under a trustee resolution rather than under state law. University faculties are bargaining in Nevada, Ohio, and Illinois under trustee sanction and without benefit of enabling legislation. Faculties bargain with trustee representatives, and the entire governance-negotiation process is within the jurisdiction of the university. The university rather than a labor board decides the subjects of bargaining and the methods of grievance. These actions have been supported by national unions.

Legislators, motivated by normal desires to control university expenditures and to extend bargaining rights to public employees, should not overlook the fundamental safeguards essential for achieving the purposes of higher education. Whether higher education should be politicized through collective bargaining and whether there are adequate alternatives should be analyzed before labor laws governing colleges and universities are passed.

Analyzing the Issues of Collective Bargaining Legislation

Some legislatures are convinced that faculty members should be given the right to unionize and either have passed or are considering new legislation. What determines whether or not a bill or an existing law is sound for education?

Who Should Be Named as Employer for the University?

This question deals with fundamental authority, capacity, and integrity of the university to achieve its public purpose. Yet only eight of the twenty-four state laws identify someone within the university as the employer, usually the board of trustees. This means that in two-thirds of the states, the governor is free to designate the state's representative to negotiate with faculty, and governors generally designate political appointees outside the university. One cannot blame a union for wanting to negotiate with that political office most capable of guaranteeing funds to support a negotiated contract. There is an interesting exception: the University of Iowa faculty litigated its demand to negotiate with trustees rather than with the governor's office.[7] University spokespersons generally insist that faculty bargaining with the governor's office produces such debilitating effects as (1) the faculty union bypasses the trustees and administration thereby disrupting normal campus processes of cooperative self-government; (2) political officials bargain teaching loads, hours, calendars, promotion procedures, disciplinary procedures, and grievance procedures, which affect the character and quality of education; (3) faculty can disregard the needs of students, alumni, and administrators when they bargain outside the university; (4) grievances regarding internal campus decisions are adjudicated outside the control of the university; (5) the authority of trustees as stated in the state constitution or in education law is eroded without a corresponding change in responsibility; and (6) neither the state officials nor the faculty

[7]GERR, March 8, 1976, B-17.

unions who bargain the contracts can be held responsible for the successful operation of the university.

What Should Be Included or Excluded from the Scope of Bargaining?

Unions tend to prefer a simple statement of "wages, hours, and other terms and conditions of employment." University spokespersons generally prefer a clear specification of what is bargainable and what is not. Unions generally believe that bargaining (supported by the prohibition of unfair labor practices) is the best means of determining what the parties are willing to put into an agreement. Trustees want their duties and responsibilities as specified in education law to be accompanied by equivalent authority in the labor law. Some trustees feel that collective bargaining laws are often written without regard for education law, and that their authority has, in some cases, been emasculated by labor laws and negotiated contracts. For these reasons trustees and administrators want a specific list of bargainable issues which define the meaning of "terms and conditions of employment." In addition, they want the collective bargaining law to list management duties (for example, the right to appoint, promote, assign work, discipline, and allocate funds) as nonmandatory subjects of bargaining. Presidents and deans point out that bargaining determines the conditions under which they administer policy and supervise employees, and that they, not union or government officials, are fired for ineffective policies and working relationships on a given campus. Presidents, therefore, are in favor of a clearly specified list of bargainable and nonbargainable subjects. (See Chapter Seven for a list of bargainable and nonbargainable issues.) This issue created so much concern among school boards and administrators in Nevada that after several years of bargaining, the state law was rewritten to include long lists of bargainable and nonbargainable subjects.[8]

Who Should Be Included in the Bargaining Unit?

Generally a union wants to strengthen its resources by including as many members as possible. Similarly university trustees

[8]51 GERR 3713 (1975).

want to keep their administrative team intact and therefore want the law to exclude from the union department chairpersons, directors, assistant and associate deans, deans, librarians, and anyone else who supervises other employees. When the law does not specifically exclude these administrators from union membership, the decision is left to a labor board on a case-by-case basis. A labor board frequently assigns chairpersons, librarians, and lower-echelon administrators to the bargaining unit, making it difficult for these administrative staff members to make managerial decisions that may be challenged by their own union colleagues. When the staff members are made part of the unit, deans become directly responsible for final departmental personnel decisions, for collecting personnel data, for keeping personnel records, and generally performing lower-level management duties. The result is that the administrative organization is affected by shifting responsibilities and authority. Trustees claim the legislature never intended such upheaval when it enacted the law. Legislators should be apprised of such viewpoints. One possible solution is to write into the law a statement that makes the trustees the sole determinants of membership in the bargaining unit.

Should Faculty Strikes Be Permitted Without Limitation,
Permitted with Specified Limitations, or Prohibited?

Union representatives generally feel that collective bargaining without the right to strike is meaningless, since they believe a union has no other adequate means to sustain its rights during an impasse or to enforce a negotiated contract. Others argue that by striking, unions are denying taxpayers services for which they have already paid. Older arguments involve the concept of government sovereignty. Other arguments are based on the importance of public health, public safety, and the denial of essential services. Many states have tried to resolve the problem of striking teachers through legislation, but few people believe they have found a method to prevent strikes. Most forms of penalties have been ineffective in deterring militant teachers from striking. When teachers lose pay for days on strike, schools often make up "extra days" for which teachers are paid. New York State withholds two days' pay for every day of strike,[9] yet New York is a leader in the number of education strikes (PERB *News,* 1976, p. 1). In assessing penalties, labor boards and courts have generally modified stipulated fines in accordance with types and causes of strikes. Some people believe that strict enforcement of serious penalties would decrease the number of strikes, but others feel that courts must have the power to adjust penalties to fit the character and causes of strikes in order to assure justice. Nebraska attempted to prevent strikes by creating a Court of Industrial Relations with authority to settle impasses.[10] To date there have been no strikes in Nebraska, but it is too early to determine whether the presence of such a court has prevented strikes. Some observers feel that the court has had a deleterious effect on good-faith bargaining since either party or the attorney general may call upon the court to intervene and make final decisions binding on both parties. Such intervention is tantamount to substituting court review for party negotiations.

Since the 1975 fiscal crisis in New York City, labor boards and courts have generally become more strict in assessing individual as well as union fines and penalties for participating in a strike. The result has been fewer strikes in 1976. With public attitudes hardening toward strikes, some public employers have welcomed a strike in order to test the strength of the union on a particular issue or to save funds gained through fines. The 1976 strike of craft workers in San Francisco is an example. The taxpayers supported the city administration by "taking" a strike for several weeks until the union yielded in its demands for larger public expenditures. Thus, the strike is not always a win for the union. One helpful factor, perhaps, is to specify strict enforcement of penalties in the law in order to bring the issues to an early decision.

Who Should Approve a Negotiated Agreement Before It Is Signed into Contract?

Ordinarily an agreement is ratified by union membership. Should it also be ratified by others whose work is directly affected?

[9]51 GERR 4119 (1975).
[10]51 GERR 3613 (1974).

For example, should contracts with colleges and universities be ratified by boards of trustees (especially when the governor's office negotiates the contract), by the administrators, by the student body (especially in Montana where a student representative is elected to represent students' interest at the table), and/or by the legislature responsible for providing funds to support negotiated increases in salaries and benefits? Universities and unions in Michigan and Rhode Island (Semus, 1975, p. 6) have had serious contractual problems because the legislature failed to provide necessary funding. Lack of the right to approve or veto a contract can create conditions conducive to strikes, trustee resignation, administrative resistance, and student demonstrations. To prevent such conditions, the law should stipulate that an agreement must be ratified by the board of trustees. In addition, the salary and fringe benefits clauses should not become effective until the legislature appropriates the necessary funds. Some provision for student participation in the processes of bargaining and ratification should also be considered.

Who Should Administer the Collective Bargaining Law for Universities?

In some states the legislation creates a special public employment relations board. The question most often raised is whether or not such a board established to deal with employment conditions governing state, city, and municipal workers can be expected to have the knowledge and understanding essential to adjudicate professional relationships within a self-governing academic community. In some states the existing labor agency for private industry is given jurisdiction over public-sector bargaining. Is knowledge of industrial labor relations processes and problems valid for administering a law governing the academic enterprise? The 1975 California law created a third model, an education employment relations board.[11] This model raises a new set of questions. Will it become a superboard with jurisdiction over existing university coordinating boards, the board of regents, boards of education,

[11]51 GERR 1415 (1975).

and campus trustees? Can university trustees successfully fulfill the administrative role usually reserved for labor boards? No bargaining law covering higher education exists in Ohio; however, at least four state university boards of trustees have determined bargaining units, conducted elections, and authorized presidents to negotiate contracts. This method affirms the integrity of the campus community by precluding campus intervention by labor boards. These experiments will no doubt have problems, but are worth observing and evaluating. The faculty union at one state university (Youngstown) took pride in publicizing its contract in the national union's newspaper (NEA *Advocate,* 1975, p. 3). Similar experiments under the authority of the university boards of governors are in process in Illinois and Nevada. One worthy alternative, then, is to exempt universities from the jurisdiction of labor boards and give each board of trustees the power to authorize and administer collective bargaining policies within its own jurisdiction. Another alternative would be to limit the labor board's jurisdiction over university negotiations to procedural matters such as conducting elections, providing neutral services for mediation and arbitration, and conducting hearings for unfair labor practice charges dealing with matters other than scope of bargaining.

*Should a Faculty Referendum on Unionization Be Held
Before a Union Election?*

Analyses of faculty elections (Lozier and Mortimer, 1975, p. 11) indicate that when several unions are on the ballot, many voters who prefer no union tend to vote for one of the unions because they do not want to "waste" their votes. Many people argue that faculty voters should have the opportunity to vote first on whether or not they want a union at all. If the referendum is in favor of unionization, then an election among the competing unions can properly determine which union has majority support. Oregon law has made provision for such a two-stage election.[12] Unions argue that the referendum is a delaying action that may prevent unions from campaigning under proper election conditions. To many observers, however, there is no convincing argument against a two-stage election.

[12]51 GERR 4614 (1975).

*Should Binding Arbitration of Grievances (and Impasses) Be
a Permissible, Mandatory, or Prohibited Subject of Bargaining?*

It is argued that binding arbitration is the only way to settle difficult disputes without the use of strikes, thereby preserving orderly and uninterrupted government service. Some groups (for example, right-to-work advocates) believe that since an arbitrator is neither elected nor appointed to public office, he should not have the authority (by negotiated contract) to substitute his judgment for that of a government official because the people's government has sovereign powers. Unions generally want both arbitration and the right to strike, saying that without these bargaining tools the worker and union are deprived of their primary sources of power to bargain effectively. University spokespersons feel that internal "professional judgment" on such matters as tenure and promotion is the only valid basis of decision and that outsiders, regardless of training, have no way of making proper decisions about substantive academic matters. Therefore, they want the law to limit arbitration to procedural grievances and to require an arbitrator to remand cases involving substantive judgment to the campus for a proper procedural determination.

*Should Students Be Permitted (Required)
at the Bargaining Table?*

Montana was the first state to require its universities to include student representatives as members of the management team.[13] Oregon assures students the role of observers at the bargaining table and the right to confer with each party.[14] Individual institutions in Michigan and Massachusetts have permitted students to observe and comment at the table (Shark, 1975). Unions have varied in their attitudes about student participation but recently appear to be taking a strong stand against tripartite bargaining and student participation in general. University spokespersons have taken various stands in different parts of the country. (See Chapter Fourteen for a discussion of the most comprehensive student experience to date in academic collective bargaining.) However, they are more favorable toward student participation than are

[13]51 GERR 3511 (1975).
[14]51 GERR 4618 (1975).

union spokespersons. Legislators should also seek opinions of students on the matter since students are organizing strong lobbies to extend their role as bona fide constituents in campus governance. By spring 1976 at least six state legislatures considered amendments to existing laws that provide limited student participation. Maine's new law permits students to meet with each party separately in order to know the issues and to offer comment without actually being at the table.[15] This is an accommodation less demanding than that in Montana or Oregon.

Should the Law's Effectiveness Be Researched and Evaluated?

The New York, California, and Maine legislatures answered this question in the affirmative by establishing and funding a research service to evaluate the effectiveness of, and to make recommendations for improving, the existing law. These services were established within the agency of the administrative board. Most state laws lack this element; as a result, reliable information is difficult to obtain in some states. A research component is important because both parties can benefit from research data developed by a neutral agency, and when reasonable, the legislature will have reliable information on which to amend the law.

Integrity in Legislation

For each issue there are several points of view and facts to be carefully considered. As a matter of honesty in legislation, a legislature should require that each issue be openly discussed and recorded, that union representatives and university spokespersons be given equal time to review each issue, that each issue be *resolved* by the legislative committee prior to writing new legislation, and that a clear statement of conclusion and reasons be made. In addition, conflicts with existing civil service, education, and municipal law should be clearly delineated and resolved by preemptive clauses in the new legislation. When collective bargaining legislation or its resulting negotiated contracts may override the intent of existing law, amendments to existing law should be introduced with the new labor legislation, so that everyone may understand the im-

[15]26 M.R.S.A. 1022 (1976).

pact of the new labor legislation before it is debated by the full legislature. Complete records of committee debates and actions should be made available so that labor boards, courts, and arbitrators may have them as a basis for reviewing unfair labor practice charges and grievances.

Arthur P. Menard
Nicholas DiGiovanni, Jr.

Colleges and universities should understand that collective bargaining begins long before the first contract is negotiated. The first major encounter with union negotiators for public institutions is probably before state legislative committees in shaping legislation requiring public employers to bargain with a certified union of employees. Unions have generally been far more successful in legislative bargaining than university employers who, by and large, have failed to adequately prepare and present their case to the various state legislatures. This matter is fully discussed in Chapter Three.

The second major encounter with union negotiators is in the matter of unit determination. Any university employer may, if it wishes, bargain directly with the union about who is to be included or excluded in the employee unit. Labor boards will usually accept any reasonable agreement between employer and employees' union.

Preparing for
Unit Representation
Hearings Before
Labor Boards

Disagreement, however, leads to full-fledged hearings and bargaining before a labor board which will then make a final determination in order to expedite elections and contractual negotiations.

A university's success or failure in these two preliminary encounters will greatly affect the character and success of its ability to negotiate and administer future contracts with a union. Although this chapter is specifically prepared for private institutions under the jurisdiction of the NLRB, the procedures, issues, and documentation outlined herein are directly applicable to proceedings before a state labor board which generally follows the arguments and principles set forth by the NLRB.

The preparation of representation cases before a state labor board or the NLRB is often a frantic undertaking for an employer, frequently done in too short a time period with too little guidance.

Once the board's processes are set in motion by a union petition for representation, the time in which to adequately prepare is necessarily circumscribed by the board's obligations under the law to expedite the procedures.

This chapter provides the college or university employer with some guidance as to what questions to ask and what areas to explore in determining its unit position in preparation for such proceedings.

Background

It has been seven years since the NLRB first asserted jurisdiction over private colleges and universities. While the three major educational unions and numerous independents have scrambled for faculty representation rights, their organizational efforts have led to some of the most perplexing unit problems which the board has had to face in its forty years of operation.

In trying to establish appropriate faculty bargaining units, the board has had to struggle with the status of department chairpersons, assessed and then reassessed the community of interest between full- and part-time teachers, discussed faculty governance, considered units where faculty are popped into and out of the unit based on the funding source of their salaries, and made the collegial concept a major factor in its deliberations. From a maze of new terms and amorphous organizational structures, the board has now begun to develop an identifiable body of case law on the major unit issues.

The college employer, faced with a faculty representation petition, must deal with many pressing decisions. However, its most immediate problem will be to determine what position to take before the board regarding the bargaining unit. Whom should the college seek to exclude as its supervisory and managerial personnel? Should the part-time faculty be included in the bargaining unit? Are there nonteaching professionals who should or should not be in the unit? These and other questions must be considered and answered in a relatively short period of time once a petition is filed.

Several factors enter into deliberation of these questions. The college employer should carefully consider what unit will provide maximum ease in administration in the event the union should win the election. If the institution's department chairpersons truly function as first-line supervisors, having them included in a unit of faculty members may be intolerable. If a union seeks to exclude from its petitioned unit one or more professional schools of the university, the administration must decide whether such fragmentation is acceptable.

Politics, of course, enter into all unit proposals. The petitioning union will invariably frame its proposed unit upon pragmatic considerations, not the least of which is the need for favorable votes in the forthcoming election. It may, for example, have very few votes among the law faculty and thus specifically exclude them from its petitioned unit. The college administration may take this into consideration in deciding upon its response before the board on this issue. On some issues, either or both of the parties may decide not to take any firm position. In such cases, the board, on the basis of evidence presented, will decide the unit issue on its own.

No matter what the college employer's unit position will be, extensive evidential preparation will be required to successfully support that position during the formal hearings before the board.

Department Chairpersons

If an institution wants to exclude department chairpersons or similar personnel, the preparation of its unit position should be given top priority and should be extremely detailed, for the board has taken into account a considerable array of factors in framing its decisions on whether such personnel are supervisors within the meaning of Section 2(11) of the NLRA. Whether the college seeks to include or exclude them from the unit, there will be two broad areas to examine in preparing its case on department chairpersons: (1) their status, (2) their function.

Status

The first area, status, is a study in perspective. The different ways in which the administration and the faculty view the department chairperson has been a significant factor in several board cases. Thus, for example, in arguing for their exclusion as supervisors or managerial personnel, institutions have tried to prove that chairpersons are accorded very special status at the college which reflects their basic position as front-line management. The main argument is that, although reflecting elements of both, the department chairperson's interests are more closely aligned with the administration than with the faculty. This position is often difficult to prove, even at institutions with strong chairpersons. However, the question "Who is the chairperson?" will pervade the entire unit hearing, and thus the development of this line is important.

Every institution will differ on the facts it can present on the chairperson's status. However, certain potential evidence can and should be examined carefully. Such evidence should include, but not be limited to, these areas:

1. Do chairpersons receive a special increment in salary for those positions, and are they the highest paid faculty?
2. Do they have reduced work loads because of administrative duties? Is their course work reduced? Are the number of students they advise reduced?
3. Do they have more or different fringe benefits than other faculty?
4. Do they have special offices and equipment?
5. Do they have private secretaries or priority on the use of departmental secretaries?
6. Do they have other support staff to assist them in their duties, including nonprofessional and student help?
7. Do they progress into higher administrative positions from their present position?
8. Do they participate in regular deans' councils or other management meetings in which faculty do not participate?
9. Do their contracts differ in length, or do they have contracts?
10. Are chairpersons the highest ranked faculty in their departments, and are they tenured?
11. Is the evaluation process different for chairpersons than for faculty?
12. Are chairpersons appointed by the administration or elected by the faculty? (The greater the extent of faculty participation in the selection process, the less chance

there is to show that chairpersons are really management appointees rather than faculty agents.)
13. Do chairpersons promulgate policy and report back to their faculty on behalf of the administration?

Function

Function may include a variety of duties, such as assigning courses, recommending new faculty for hire, and making major evaluations and recommendations on faculty personnel actions. Two questions evolve in trying to establish the chairperson as a supervisor:

1. Do chairpersons' recommendations meet the statutory requirement of being "effective"?
2. Are supervisory chairpersons' functions diluted because they exercise such functions in consultation or in conjunction with the department faculty?

The first, and most significant, line to develop at the hearing is the role of the chairperson in faculty hiring. The two general questions here are:

1. To what extent do chairpersons have a role in determining the need for new faculty?
2. Once it is determined that new faculty will be hired, what role do chairpersons play in the hiring process?

Other questions related to the first center on whether chairpersons determine the needs for new faculty and how significant their opinions are. Very often, chairpersons have great autonomy in determining whether to hire part-time faculty or not. Close attention should be given to this point. Once it is determined that new faculty will be hired, chairpersons' roles are crucial:

1. Do they draft job descriptions?
2. Do they participate in advertising?
3. How much do they independently recruit at conventions or from other colleges?

4. Do applicants contact chairpersons directly?
5. Do they screen and veto candidates without higher approval?
6. Do they select applicants for interviews?
7. To what extent do they have authority to set up committees to assist them in these functions? To what extent *must* they set up such committees?
8. Do they recommend, and if so, how effective are such recommendations?
9. If faculty or committees also make recommendations, do chairpersons' recommendations carry more weight?
10. Do they contact the new hires?
11. Do they arrange or recommend initial salary?
12. How much more autonomy and power do they have over part-time hiring?

Most department chairpersons have a role in faculty evaluations, and their authority to recommend personnel changes on the basis of such evaluations can be a central factor in weighing supervisory status. Methods of evaluation should be explored:

1. Do chairpersons engage in direct classroom observation?
2. Do they review formal student evaluations of faculty?
3. Do students come to see chairpersons with complaints or praise for their professors?
4. Do chairpersons review research and publications of faculty?
5. Do chairpersons take into consideration the faculty members' participation in departmental affairs?
6. Do chairpersons check with graduate assistants, teaching assistants, and fellows for their opinions about faculty with whom they work?
7. Do chairpersons evaluate for reappointment?
8. Do they evaluate for promotions in rank, granting tenure, dismissal, salary increases? Do they evaluate for improvement of instruction?
9. Who else or what committees evaluate faculty performance? Which recommendations carry more weight

with the dean? Whose recommendation does the dean usually accept when recommendations are in conflict?

Under the NLRA an individual is a supervisor if he can discipline or effectively recommend discipline for employees under him. In the college setting faculty discipline by a chairperson may seem completely inapplicable. However, there are numerous questions which can be explored. Discipline can be exercised through:

1. verbal reprimands
2. written warnings
3. withholding favorable committee assignments
4. withholding travel money or other benefits
5. removal of a faculty member from classroom or other contacts with students
6. suspending with or without pay or recommending such action
7. recommending dismissal of nontenured faculty during his contract years
8. recommending dismissal of a tenured faculty member

Although it may seem difficult to think of examples for which discipline could be meted out, some items immediately suggest themselves:

1. failure to meet classes
2. consistently late for classes
3. verbal abuse of students
4. failure to turn in requested data
5. drunkenness or other addiction
6. failure to meet committee assignments
7. violation of institution rules
8. discussion of irrelevant material in class
9. personal improprieties with students
10. violation of institution regulations, such as parking, speeding, or smoking in restricted areas

The ability to grant time off can be a key supervisory duty. Some questions to raise in this area are:

1. How much time off can chairpersons grant without dean approval?
2. How final are their recommendations for leaves of absence?
3. If a faculty member is ill and unable to meet his duties, does he have to contact his chairperson?
4. If so, will the chairperson reschedule or reassign the class?
5. To what extent do chairpersons screen and recommend candidates for sabbatical leaves? In making such recommendations, will chairpersons take into account worthiness of each candidate's project, departmental staffing needs, and other departmental sabbatical applications?

Work assignments exist even for relatively independent faculty members, and department chairpersons will usually play a role. For example, chairpersons may assign courses, particularly nonspecialized, introductory-level courses. A faculty member hired to teach a course on Romantic poets may not have to be assigned to such a course, but the chairperson may decide whether or not the course needs to be offered each term. In addition, the chairperson may decide who teaches how many sections of required and elective English courses in order to offer the program that will best meet the needs of students majoring in English and that will attract the largest number of nonmajor students. A loss in student enrollment may lead to a loss in faculty positions the following year.

Work assignments may also include assignments to committees, assigning faculty as student advisors, assigning faculty to work at registration and preregistration and joint assignments by chairpersons for interdepartmental courses.

Other areas of exploration on the chair issue include general departmental responsibilities (course scheduling, student affairs, presiding over department meetings, and budget preparation and administration) and supervisory responsibilities over support staff (technicians, secretaries, students, administrative assistants). On the latter point, the board has adopted a so-called 50 percent rule, whereby an individual supervising only nonunit employees is only considered a supervisor if he spends more than 50 percent of the time supervising.

Managerial and Confidential Employees

The board has developed through its case decisions certain exclusions for managerial and confidential employees. If these exclusion arguments are an issue, several other areas of inquiry may be necessary.

For managerial exclusion, most of the questions on the chairperson's status reviewed earlier can be used, particularly in regard to participation in management meetings with deans and higher administrators. In addition, special attention should be given to the role of the chairpersons in determining the direction in which their departments may move. For example, a chairperson may gear his department toward a particular academic emphasis or school of thought through the development of certain courses and by hiring faculty with a certain philosophical perspective. A chairperson who participates with other units in collective bargaining activity for the college also demonstrates an important management function.

Confidential status involves the maintenance of personnel files, knowledge of confidential wage and personnel data to which other faculty do not have access, and relationships to the dean and others who are involved in framing labor relations policy, in handling grievances, or in shaping responses to union demands.

Exhibits

Many types of exhibits and data can be used in presenting the college's case. A complete list of faculty and support staff reporting to each chairperson is a helpful exhibit early in the hearing. Sample evaluation forms with the completed recommendations of each chairperson can be introduced. Confidentiality can be preserved by blanking out the name of the individual faculty member. Completed sabbatical forms can be introduced showing the chairperson's evaluation and recommendation. Effectiveness of a chairperson's recommendations in personnel matters can be shown by specially prepared exhibits which indicate the number of positive and negative recommendations made by each chairperson in reappointment, promotion, and tenure decisions and the number of such recommendations finally accepted by the administration. Correlation is essential in preparing such exhibits.

Minutes or agenda of dean's meetings with chairpersons can be helpful in showing the chairperson's unique status. In situations in which chairpersons receive no identifiable salary increment, wage comparisons between them and other faculty can be shown by taking the average chairperson's salary in a college and comparing it to similarly ranked faculty.

If there is no fixed reduction in work load for chairpersons, but reductions do exist, exhibits can be prepared showing the average work load of faculty in a department and the actual work load of the chairperson. In the area of work assignments, any course schedules or similar documents signed by chairpersons can be integrated into evidence with testimony on how chairpersons assign and schedule courses.

Letters to new faculty signed by chairpersons are useful in showing chairpersons' roles in hiring. Letters of discipline signed by chairpersons are also helpful in showing actual supervisory duties.

Part-time Faculty

Whether part-time faculty should or should not be included in units of full-time faculty has been another significant issue in college unit cases. The board, after originally including regular part-time faculty in units with full-time faculty, has now been excluding the part-timers.

At the focal point of the issue is the 1973 New York University decision in which the board first excluded part-time faculty from a unit of full-time faculty on the basis of four general factors: (1) compensation, (2) governance, (3) tenure eligibility, and (4) working conditions.[1] In preparing its case for inclusion or exclusion of part-time faculty, the college employer should examine these four areas closely.

Compensation

1. Are part-time employees paid a percentage portion of a full-time salary, or are they hired on a per-course arrange-

[1]205 NLRB No. 16 (1973).

ment? If extrapolated, what would a part-timer's full-year salary be compared to a full-timer's?

2. Are part-timers hired by the year, by the semester, or by the course? Are there multiple-year contracts for part-timers? How are the contracts different from or similar to full-timers?
3. Do part-timers receive their primary income from the college, or do they have other jobs?
4. Do they enjoy the same fringe benefits as full-time faculty?

Governance

1. Are part-time faculty eligible for election to the faculty senate or other comparable bodies? If so, can they vote?
2. Are they eligible for, and do they participate in, standing college or departmental committees?
3. Do they otherwise participate in departmental decisions with regard to personnel, curriculum matters, and student affairs?

Tenure and Appointment Considerations

1. Are part-timers eligible for tenure?
2. Is there a presumption of renewal of contract for them?
3. Does a part-timer accumulate seniority for tenure (if he later becomes a full-timer)?
4. What is the turnover rate for part-time as opposed to full-time faculty?

Working Conditions

1. How do part-timers' responsibilities differ from full-timers', if at all? Do part-timers engage only in teaching, or are they expected to perform research and service as full-time faculty members are?
2. Do they have to keep office hours?
3. Are they evaluated in the same way and upon the same criteria as full-timers?

4. Can they grieve dismissals or other actions through normal academic channels and grievance procedures?
5. Are they assigned counseling services for students, either formally or informally?
6. Are part-timers located in particular departments of the college? Do they teach only general or overloaded courses, or are they spread out throughout the curriculum?
7. Does the part-time faculty member have an obligation to publish?
8. Do part-timers generally teach during normal school hours or at night or weekends?
9. Do they moderate any clubs or organizations?
10. Are they hired through the same procedures and with the same forms as full-timers?
11. Are they eligible for promotions in rank and general faculty salary increases?

Graduate and Professional Schools

For universities with professional schools, such as law, medicine, or dentistry, a potential issue for unit determination is whether such schools are appropriately included or excluded from an overall university unit. This problem often arises because a petitioning union may believe that it has little, if any, support in these schools and, consequently, wants them excluded from the petition. The university administration must decide whether it wants such schools segregated or whether it should argue that a universitywide unit, including the professional schools, is the only appropriate unit. Various factors should be explored in light of several NLRB cases in this area.

Personnel Policies

1. Does the professional school in question set its own personnel policy, such as compensation, tenure, standards, hiring criteria, leaves, promotion procedures, or are such areas governed by general university policy?

Governance

1. Do the faculty members in the professional school serve on any university committees or on the university senate? (An exhibit showing senate and committee representation can be helpful here.)
2. Do faculty from other schools serve on any governance bodies within the professional school?
3. Does the school in question have its own independent governance body, such as its own senate?

Geographic Proximity

1. Is the professional school on the main campus of the university?
2. Does it share a building or other facilities with other schools?

Interchange

1. Do faculty in the professional school teach in any other schools of the university and vice versa? (A detailed breakdown of the numbers involved would make a useful exhibit.)
2. How much daily contact is there between the professional school's faculty members and other faculty in the university?

Influences of the Profession

1. Is the professional school in question subject to special accreditation standards by any professional associations?
2. Are other schools in the university? What are the consequences of a denial of accreditation by the reviewing body?
3. Are minimum standards imposed on the school by extra-university sources, such as minimum days of school, mini-

mum credit hours, required courses, student-faculty ratios? (Many law schools, for example, are subject to exacting standards by either the state courts or the bar associations in terms of which courses must be taught or how many days of class students must take.)

4. Are the professors more aligned with academia or the profession? For example, do law professors maintain private practices?
5. Do medical professors attend American Medical Association conventions?
6. How does this differ from the faculty elsewhere in the university, if at all?
7. What types of consulting arrangements are made for the "professional" faculty as opposed to others in the university? Are there any "group practice" plans set up, for example?

Autonomy

1. What autonomy does the professional school have compared to the rest of the university?
2. Does it have a separate budget?
3. Are graduation exercises separate?
4. Does it have independent control over hiring and firing of faculty and staff?
5. Is the academic calendar different?
6. Are there separate lines of supervision?
7. Are there separate admissions and placement offices?

Funding

1. Is the professional school significantly funded from outside sources, such as federal or state grants?
2. How much of its operating budget is from the general university budget? (An exhibit showing source of funds for *each* school in the university should be used.)
3. Is there a smaller student-faculty ratio for the professional

school compared to the others, or is it comparable?

4. Is there a greater percentage of full professors in the school, a significantly greater or smaller percentage of tenured professors?

5. Are the professional school faculty members on different contracts from the rest of the university faculty, such as twelve-month contracts as opposed to academic-year contracts?

6. How do the salaries for the professional school faculty compare to the rest of the university faculty? (This area should be covered by an exhibit showing average salaries throughout the university compared to the professional school faculty. High and low salaries can be included to indicate comparable or differing ranges. Care should be taken to convert twelve-month salaries to nine-month salaries where necessary to reflect accurate comparisons.)

Other Considerations

1. If the faculties of the special schools are in the general union, will bargaining be easier or more complicated?

2. Will faculties of professional schools actually bargain if they receive separate units? (Experience indicates that many do not; they merely do not want to be governed by a campuswide union and opt for a separate unit.)

3. Will professional school faculty members vote for no-union in an election which includes them in a campuswide union?

As a general matter, traditional graduate school faculties are included within the greater faculty unit. Arguments for exclusion should be limited to those arguments which would exclude any faculty member, such as community of interest or geographic dislocation. For an example of this kind of exclusion, see University of *Miami-Coral Gables*, wherein faculty at the Graduate School of Marine and Atmospheric Science were excluded as a result of geographic dislocation and a lack of interdisciplinary activity.[2]

[2]213 NLRB No. 152 (1974).

Other Professionals

Whether or not other professionals such as librarians (the librarian issue may be settled in light of the New York University case), coaches, or counselors should be included in a faculty unit will rest on two key factors: (1) professional status and (2) community of interest with faculty.

Professional Status

1. What type of work does the position entail? Is it predominantly intellectual in nature? Does it require the constant exercise of discretion?
2. Is an advanced degree or training required for the position?
3. What are the backgrounds of the individuals currently serving in the position?
4. What salary and fringe benefits are given? Are the employees exempt or nonexempt? Are they salaried or paid by the hour?
5. Do they have their own offices?
6. Do they set their own hours or are the hours fixed?
7. Are they in a contractual relationship with the university?

Community of Interest

1. Do the professionals receive the same fringe benefits as faculty? Are their salaries comparable?
2. Are they eligible for tenure?
3. Are they eligible for sabbaticals?
4. Can they participate on faculty governance bodies? Do they have their own governance bodies instead?
5. Do they hold faculty rank?
6. Do the professionals participate and vote in academic departmental meetings? Can they serve on departmental personnel committees?
7. Do they hold the same type of contract as faculty? Is the renewal sequence comparable? Are the notice requirements the same for nonrenewals?

8. Do the professionals engage in any teaching functions? Do they counsel students?
9. How much contact do they have with faculty?
10. How much contact do they have with students?
11. Are professionals evaluated through normal academic channels? Are the same criteria used? Are the same evaluation forms used?
12. Can professionals grieve through normal academic appeal procedures?
13. Are the professionals' work location geographically close to the faculty's?
14. On what basis are professionals promoted? Does promotion for a professional usually involve a change in job duties as distinct from faculty promotions?
15. Is the hiring procedure for professionals the same as or different from that of faculty?
16. What are the administrative lines of supervision for professionals?

Organization and Strategy

Organization is essential for preparation of cases involving any of these issues. An administration faced with a petition for representation should carefully plan assignments and preparation. Initial meetings should be held between the top administrators and labor relations counsel to discuss the ramifications of taking certain unit positions. All employee categories should be discussed for potential litigation. Unions may amend their petitions at any time during the proceedings, and an administration should not be caught unaware and without a position on an issue.

Once the college's unit position is ascertained, preparation should begin immediately. Selection of witnesses should be reviewed and decided on first. Typically, the deans, provost, or vice-president for academic affairs can cover such issues as department chairpersons and part-time faculty. The union may, however, use a chairperson as a star witness. In such a case, the administration may wish to counter with another chairperson who will provide the desired evidence from his daily experience. A personnel officer may be the best person to review other professionals and any questions of fringe benefits. Each witness should be thoroughly familiar with the various questions that may be asked on these issues. Labor relations counsel should prepare the witnesses for the hearing and develop testimony for the witnesses' review prior to the hearing. Documentary exhibits should likewise be discussed, and one person or one office assigned to develop such exhibits for review by counsel.

Although representation cases are not formal court proceedings, certain rules of evidence still prevail and, consequently, consideration should be given as to who the best witness would be to introduce specially prepared exhibits. The witness should be able to explain how the exhibit was prepared, what it means, its source data, as well as how accurate it is.

A great deal of time can be squandered through poor organization, overlapping assignments, and faulty communications. Consequently, a plan of action should be carefully developed with counsel as soon as possible. If, for example, a petition is imminent, work can begin ahead of time in anticipation of a formal filing.

Informing the Faculty

During the preparation of the representation case, faculty members are bound to have many questions. In the early unit determination cases, administrations took unrealistic positions either because they misunderstood the constraints which the law placed on them or because they did not want to interfere in intrinsic faculty matters. They raised no issues for faculty consideration and answered no questions concerning representation matters.

Administration awareness of the importance of a fully informed faculty electorate has now been heightened by numerous faculty elections since *Cornell University* (a nonfaculty case).[3] There appears to be general agreement that a proper role for the administration is to inform and advise faculty on representation issues during the course of union organizing efforts. This role is both legally proper and administratively appropriate. In addition, it habituates faculty to reading the administrative memos or weekly newsletter for accurate and complete information.

[3] 183 NLRB No. 41 (1970).

The following questions might be raised and answered in this context:

1. Can the administration continue to interact with the faculty senate and various faculty committees in a pre-election situation?
2. Will this interaction depend upon whether the senate or committee deals with wages, hours, and conditions of employment?
3. As a practical matter should an administration take a highly legal and technical position on this question?
4. Does the propriety of interaction and cooperation between the administration and the senate and committees depend upon whether a union is certified and the faculty's exclusive bargaining representative? (The potential for unfair labor practice is high when dealing in this area.)
5. Must the administration limit itself to dealing with matters that are clearly outside wages, hours, and conditions of employment with faculty bodies other than the union?
6. Does the faculty senate then become a totally ineffectual organ for governance on the campus?
7. Does the faculty, individually or collectively, realize that it may no longer deal with "supervision" over "wages, hours, and conditions of employment" if a union is certified?
8. What are the bargainable issues if a union is certified?
9. Does the phrase "wages, hours, and conditions of employment" include:
   a. tenure (if so, may it be bargained away or modified?)
   b. selection of courses
   c. work load and work hours
   d. class size
   e. existence of governance forms which do not deal with bargainable subject matters
   f. selection of administrative hierarchy, including deans and department chairpersons
   g. issues of academic freedom

h. financial records and budget preparation?

10. What recourse does the faculty have if the administration refuses to bargain subjects which are nonmandatory?

11. Will the faculty be required to join a union and pay dues as a result of certification and bargaining?

12. Does the faculty understand the distinction between a union shop and an agency shop?

13. Do faculty members understand that they may be discharged by refusing to pay dues, or an equivalent amount, under one of two forms of union security clauses?

14. Can the faculty strike?

15. Does striking depend upon extant state law?

16. If a strike is called, may all faculty participate in the strike vote or only those who are members of the union?

17. If a strike vote is taken, what constitutes a *quorum* under the union's constitution and bylaws?

18. If there is a strike, do faculty members understand that the administration has no obligation to pay wages and fringe benefits?

19. If there is a strike, may faculty members collect unemployment benefits or welfare benefits under existing state or federal law?

20. Does the faculty understand that the union has a legal right to impose fines upon its membership if any of its members cross a union picket line or refuse to participate in such a strike?

21. Does the faculty understand the nature of the impasse concept of collective bargaining?

22. Do members realize that if a declared impasse is reached upon any single issue, the administration is free to put into effect its own offer or demand pertaining to that issue?

23. Does the faculty realize that the administration is free to put forth its own demands relating to mandatory bargaining subjects and negotiate to an impasse on them?

24. Has the administration made the faculty aware of the nature of the bargaining process and the type of con-

tingent that has historically represented faculty when a collective bargaining representative is chosen?

25. Has the administration recently apprised faculty of their salaries and fringe benefits and related them to comparable colleges or universities? When is such action most likely to have a favorable effect?

26. Is the faculty aware of the service costs of union representation?

27. Is the faculty aware of the national union's position on such issues as merit, evaluation and confidentiality?

28. Does the faculty understand the prospects for decertifying a union, should it no longer choose to be represented?

29. Is the faculty familiar with other collective bargaining agreements which the organizing union has actually negotiated?

30. Does the faculty know how long it typically takes to negotiate such contracts?

31. Has the faculty been apprised of which institutions' faculty have supported collective bargaining and which have not?

There is abundant reference material from which to answer some of these questions. Other questions require new argument. However, the proper and legal use of these materials can involve difficult questions of law and timing. Certainly, however, any administration that does not raise them and provide its faculty with the resource material or the means of finding such material is doing a grave injustice to those who will be called upon to decide an issue of such far-reaching impact as whether or not the faculty will have union representation.

Edward P. Kelley, Jr.

Once a union organizing effort begins on campus, there is little time for the trustees or administration to consider the whys and wherefores of this so-called attack upon the institution. Rather, they must plan and implement a program to educate the entire institutional community of the possible effects of bargaining on the operations of the college, on the relationships among parties, on the impact on trustees, on the possible political implications of governmental agencies, and on the perceived advantages and disadvantages.

Many presidents find themselves torn between marshaling a strong campaign against unionization and a "do-nothing" attitude, which grows out of the misconception that the law requires they do nothing. Both approaches have failed. At one major university

Taking the Initiative During Organizing and Election Campaigns

the faculty responded to a study of voting behavior by indicating that a high-powered media campaign launched by the president against unionization pushed the undecided vote into the prounion camp. At another institution a study indicated that the president's inactivity was interpreted by the faculty as support for the unionization effort.

Planning Administrative Activity

Although the election is a faculty election and although the administrator has no vote in the issue, the administration does have an appropriate role. The role is one of leadership which expresses confidence in the faculty's participation in all university affairs and not just those within the scope of bargaining. The administration should provide all faculty with whatever facts, periodicals, research, and consultants it may want or need in order to make an informed decision.

The first course of action should be the collection, review, and dissemination of facts and information about the present state of the institution. Details of the existing structures or patterns of faculty input should be provided to the entire education community as a matter of self-study:

1. personnel decisions (administrative decisions and faculty committee recommendations concerning hiring, promotion, merit salary, tenure and termination, the planning of staffing needs and control of the professional life of the institution),
2. budgetary planning (overall budget advisory committees, salary committee, library and other educational resource committees, building committees, and periodic fund-seeking committees),
3. appropriations and allocations (the general allocation of available funds, determination of fiscal priorities, how they relate to budget planning),
4. salaries and salary decisions (the institution's salaries at various ranks, salary determination, department flexibility in salary decisions),
5. curriculum control (course offerings, instructional staff needs; program, laboratory, media equipment needs; service courses and degree granting programs),
6. student affairs (admissions committees, academic progress committees, grading standards and graduation requirements), and
7. grievance decisions (reviewing and adjudicating grievances).

Without basic up-to-date information in these areas, the faculty cannot be expected to make an intelligent comparison between the present state of the institution and the likely state under collective bargaining.

Just as it is the obligation of the administration to provide information to the faculty on the present state of the institution, so, too, must the administration provide information about collective bargaining. Such administrative communication should complement and clarify information disseminated by union representatives. The administration's obligations extend to gathering and disseminating information on unionizing and collective bargaining in general and on faculty organizing and bargaining in particular. Rather than avoiding the issues or giving the impression of indifference toward collective bargaining, administrators should make their positions known, basing arguments for or against unionizing on such factors as the special purpose of the institution, the collegial responsibility for decision making, the importance of having all faculty and staff equally represented regardless of their willingness to join and pay dues to a particular organization, the progress made in recent years in salary, working conditions, quality of programs and students.

One of the most important things an administration faced with an organizing effort can do is to encourage the broadest possible discussion of the topic rather than debates. One way in which this can be done is by establishing and maintaining one or more collective bargaining minilibraries. A team composed of an administrator, an "undecided" faculty member, a union supporter, and a member of the student body could be assigned the task of identifying the most valuable informational materials on collective bargaining in higher education. Such information, available from the campus library, the National Center of the Study of Collective Bargaining in Higher Education, the Academic Collective Bargaining Information Service (ACBIS), university schools of labor relations, and state or federal labor departments and boards, should be located in a central place convenient to all campus constituencies but not in an area open to administrative surveillance.

Another way is by assisting in, or agreeing to, the organizing of faculty forums where members of each of the campus constituencies can make their positions and questions known through speeches, open panel discussions, or questioning of invited collective bargaining specialists. The administration must be careful in this activity not to exclude, directly or indirectly, one or more unions from full participation. The administration should avoid adversarial debate formats, and should suggest programs which permit the inclusion of the broadest spectrum of ideas on faculty unionization by bringing to the campus outside specialists as well as having inside advocates of differing positions take part in programs.

A third way of allowing full discourse of views is the presentation of well-considered and carefully analyzed position papers by respected academic leaders such as deans and department chairpersons, if the latter are excluded from the bargaining unit. These papers should state the position of each author based on his firsthand experience with collective bargaining or in-depth study of faculty unionizing. Under no circumstances should such papers be used to describe rumors and anecdotes associated with collective bargaining or to pass on misinformation. Rather, they should be thought-provoking, factually based papers that live up to the faculty's expectation of respectable, scholarly, objective presentation of facts supporting a particular view.

Still another method is an expression, in the form of a position paper or memorandum to the faculty, of the trustees' willingness to deal with the faculty in whatever mode it chooses. Although the trustees may express an opinion about the institutional governance they consider most appropriate, the paper or memo should note that the selection of an exclusive bargaining representative will not change their opinion of the faculty, that the parties will maintain professional working relationships, but that a certain amount of role playing will be necessary and that following the rules set down by legislators, labor boards, and others outside the educational community will be required.

In the very last stages of the election campaign, but not sooner than three to four days before the election, the chief executive officer of the institution, after consultation with the labor relations staff, should convey to the entire educational community in a personal letter, his opinions on the state of the institution and on the merits and limitations of collective bargaining. The following paragraphs come from one chief executive's letter:

I have listened carefully to all the arguments, including those advanced at the very important University Senate meeting last Friday, I have deliberately not taken an active part in the debate, although I think it has been generally known that I believe a union is not needed here. Now that the debate is closed, my first concern is that all of you vote so that whatever option is chosen is a reflection of the will of the whole faculty.

At this stage, I think I should comment specifically on the issues that have been raised. It is my own conclusion that faculty unionization would not be in the best overall interests of this University and I do hope that our faculty will decide for "no representative." I favor and support the goals and the benefits of the American labor movement, but I do not feel that industrial labor practices are appropriate in this academic community. . . .

Much has been said about collegiality, professionalism, and excellence in recent days, and I know that many union advocates agree upon the primacy of these values and feel that they could be preserved in an environment of collective bargaining. However, while there has been little experience with collective bargaining in a comprehensive university such as ours, studies of campuses that have been unionized show some alarming tendencies:

—Collegiality soon gives way to an adversary relationship between faculty and academic administrators, characterized as they are, under law, as "labor" and "management" (with students on the sidelines), with acrimony and suspicion becoming a serious part of the bargaining game.

—In the long term economic factors inexorably come to weigh more than professional academic concerns—for example, tenure may come to be justified as simple job security, rather than as a safeguard for academic freedom and a means for maintaining a distinguished faculty.

—The influence of faculties of departments, schools, and campuses declines in favor of the monolithic faculty union.

—There is a growing sense that excellence cannot flourish, in its essentially diverse and selective form, once the practices of standardization of pay scales and work loads take hold. Within a university faculty the true value of our

*work is unmeasureable, and the recognition of merit should
be individual. . . .*

*The economic aspects of collective bargaining are
often of deepest interest in a union election. Here I say simply
that at this University we have worked diligently to give substantial and equitable compensation increases, although resources here, and in all of higher education, have been eroded
by inflation. We pursue our state appropriations vigorously,
and we have fought successfully for their augmentation with
strong faculty support and involvement. Around the country,
there is no proof that collective bargaining contracts influence legislators to appropriate more money for higher educational institutions; in fact, there are indications to the reverse.
Some union contracts have led to retrenchments; and under
the rule of seniority junior faculty members, including women
and minorities, can suffer. In our own state, [one] university,
which does have a union, is not marked for any more fund
increases this year than are [this university] and [the] State
[university]. In respect to private financial contributions,
on which this University is unusually dependent, there is
strong reason to believe that unionization would be harmful.*

*In our debate much attention has been given to the
topic of governance. Here I affirm that the most important
kind of authority of the faculty is academic, pertaining to
matters of curriculum standards, appointment, and promotion. Academic authority in our present system is autonomous,
strong, and pervasive within the faculties of the schools, departments, and campuses. Although under law all authority
at the University stems from the Trustees, academic authority
at our University is largely devolved to schools and departments on the basis of the independent, professional competence of their faculty members. We must ask ourselves whether
the presence of a union at [this University] would diminish the
pluralism and autonomy of our faculties' academic authority.*

*At the more general level of the University Senate,
there is widespread discussion of a need for greater strength.
We hear on the one hand that a union could strengthen the
Senate and on the other that a union would likely supplant
it. I would argue that there is as much faculty influence pos-*

*sible in the Senate, Senate Council, and Senate Committees
as the faculty chooses to use. The real question is whether the
faculty will exercise this influence itself or through a union
structure. We do have a system of governance by consensus.
It is my consistent practice to refer important decisions for
review and comment by organs of the Senate. Their advice
is nearly always followed; and, should it not be, I am obliged
fully to explain the reasons why. In vital matters of the budget,
the faculty has been brought into the closest counsel of the
administration. Our chief budget officer meets regularly with
the Senate Budget Policies Committee, and the chairman of
that Committee and Senate officers sit with me throughout
my budget meetings with all the schools and other important
units of the University and at our appropriate hearings in
[the Capital]. . . .*

*My concerns notwithstanding, the decision on union-
ization is, of course, entirely yours. Again, I urge you to vote.
Whatever the outcome, I trust we will find a way to work together with a shared resolve to preserve and advance our
University, and to serve our common goals of excellence in
teaching and research (Personal letter to colleagues from
Chancellor Posvar, University of Pittsburgh, March 4,
1976).*

These suggestions for administrative action are not without
support and encouragement in both state and federal law and in decisions rendered. For the sake of brevity, I will deal here only with
the NLRA, since most state laws are modeled on the federal law and
since most of the decisions of state labor boards follow those of the
NLRB, at least in this narrow area of elections. Although most of the
case discussion which follows is based upon the industrial experience, it is my opinion that these issues confronted by the NLRB, state
boards, and the courts in cases involving higher education would be
disposed of in a similar manner, with decisions often referring to
the very cases I shall later cite. Therefore, you may substitute at any
point in the following discussion, *administrator* for *employer, faculty
member* for *employee,* or *state labor law* for *NLRA.*

Although the basic purposes of the NLRA are to protect the
rights of employees to (1) organize for the purposes of bargaining,

(2) bargain collectively through representatives of their choice, and (3) engage in concerted activity in support of collective bargaining, all the protections of the Act do not inure to employees alone. Although section 8(a) of the NLRA deals with employer unfair labor practices as for example at subsection (a)(1), which states it is an unfair labor practice for an employer "to interfere with, restrain or coerce employees in the exercise of the rights guaranteed" by the Act, section 8(c) of the Act permits the employer to freely express his views in oral or written form as long as the expression contains "no threat of reprisal or force or promise of benefit." Additionally, one may expect some protections from the First Amendment of the Constitution guaranteeing freedom of expression. However, as with most freedom guarantees, the right of employer free speech is not absolute, especially in view of the economic power and influence an employer has over an employee. The specific limitations on employer free speech should be clearly understood in order to avoid certain penalties.

Employer Speech

If an administrator as employer predicts adverse consequences if employees vote in favor of a union, he may be subject to a charge of unfair labor practice. However, in most cases, the employer will only be found guilty of an unfair labor practice if the prediction of adverse consequences is based on factors over which the employer can or does exercise control. If the employer controls the factors decisive to the negative prediction, the statements will ordinarily be deemed coercive by a labor board. On the other hand, if the employer prediction is based on factual data and on factors over which the employer has no demonstrable control, then the speech will be protected under the standards of NLRB v. Gissel Packing Co.[1] Thus, a factually accurate account of a union's past activity would be protected even if the account revealed information detrimental to the union, or suggested that adverse consequences would result should the employees elect that union.

It is, however, important to know that even when the employer's speech appears to contain neither threats nor promises of

[1]395 U.S. 575 (1969), cf. Town of Clay and Service Employees International Union Local 200, AFL-CIO, 6 PERB 3117 (November 7, 1973).

benefit, the context in which the speech is uttered may be sufficient to result in unfair labor practice. In one case the United States Supreme Court found that a company poster urging individual bargaining, posted at a company meeting urging a company union, could be taken into consideration with an apparently noncoercive speech to determine if section 8(a)(1) had been violated. In essence, the Court found that although the employer speech alone was not sufficient to establish a violation, the fact that the speech was given at a company meeting at which company posters were displayed could be sufficient to result in a violation of the NLRA (*NLRB* v. *Virginia Electric and Power Co.*).[2]

Another facet of the combination of context and content was revealed in *International Association of Machinists* v. NLRB[3] wherein suggestions, expressions of preference, and the like were viewed as coercive; employees could cite from past experience the consequences of angering the employer.

An additional factor to be taken into consideration along with an employer's statement is the time and place in which the statement is made. For example, an employer may give an antiunion talk to employees on company time, on company grounds, and even deny the union(s) an equal opportunity to reply as long as the talk is not coercive (*Livingston Shirt Corp.*).[4] However, these so-called "captive audience" speeches are prohibited during the twenty-four-hour period immediately preceding the election. Violation of the twenty-four-hour rule has been found to be sufficient grounds for setting aside the election and directing the employer to bargain (*Peerless Plywood Co.*).[5] This does not mean that all activity within twenty-four hours of the election is prohibited. On the contrary, employers and unions alike are not prohibited from making speeches, distributing literature, and engaging in other electioneering conduct as long as attendance is voluntary, is on the employees' own time, and the conduct is noncoercive.

---

[2]314 U.S. 469 (1941), cf. *Wisconsin Employment Relations Commission* v. *City of Evansville*, Wisc. Cir. Ct., Rock County, 80 LRRM 3201 (1972).

[3]311 U.S. 72 (1940), cf. Wisconsin, footnote 2 above.

[4]107 NLRB 400 (1953), cf. Conemaugh Valley Memorial Hospital, 2 PPER 115 (1972).

[5]107 NLRB 427 (1953), cf. McKeesport Hospital, 3 PPER 21 (1973) and discussion therein.

Employer statements which are factually inaccurate, exaggerated, or false, especially when made late in the campaign, will be judged more critically since the union has had little or no opportunity to reply. In addition, the statements commonly called *propaganda* will be treated in a special way. The test announced in *Sewell Manufacturing Co.*[6] is that when the propaganda has significantly violated or destroyed the laboratory conditions under which elections are to be conducted, there is sufficient ground to set the election aside. The test is further defined in *Hollywood Ceramics Co.*[7]; it was held that where a gross misrepresentation may "reasonably" be expected to have made a substantial impact on the election, the election will be set aside. The NLRB assumes that employees are capable of evaluating employer propaganda and, in effect, overlooks minor factual misstatements; however, it should be noted that the more limited the opportunity for rebuttal, the greater the chance that the NLRB will set an election aside (*Dal Tex Optical Co.*).[8] In one instance where the employer intentionally used an outdated and, therefore, misleading NLRB publication which dealt with the reemployment rights of strikers, the Board held that there was sufficient ground for setting aside the election (*Thiokol Chemical Co.*).[9]

In summary, it can be said that employer speech will be protected when the content, context, place, and time of the statement do not violate the conditions necessary to a free and unobstructed election.

Early Employer Conduct

An employer may limit union solicitation on company premises to the employees' free time (*North American Rockwell Corp.*),[10] and this limitation may also be imposed upon distribution of authorization cards (*Rose Co.*).[11] The actual distribution of union literature,

[6]138 NLRB 66 (1962), cf. Kent County Road Commission, 1969 MERC Lab. Op. 134.

[7]140 NLRB 221 (1962), cf. Lebanon County, 5 PPER 55 (1974).

[8]137 NLRB 1782 (1962), cf. Monongahela Valley Hospital, Inc. (Monongahela Div.) 3 PPER 374 (1973).

[9]202 NLRB 434 (1973).

[10]195 NLRB 189 (1972).

[11]154 NLRB 228 (1965).

or propaganda, may legally be limited to nonworking areas and nonworking time as declared in NLRB v. *Walton Co.*[12] These limitations may not be established in such a manner as to create a preferential position for one or more unions (*Mason and Hanger-Silus Mason Co.*).[13]

Solicitation and propaganda distribution by nonemployee organizers may be prohibited on company premises at any time when the union has other available means of communication with the employees (NLRB v. *Babcock and Wilcox Co.*).[14] However, denial of access which discriminates against one or more unions may be declared an unfair labor practice (see *Mason and Hanger-Silus Mason Co.*).

Section 8(a)(2) of the NLRA prohibits employer interference or dominance of a labor organization or financial or other support of these organizations. These prohibitions have been defined in the following areas: (1) In *Watkins Furniture,*[15] the Board held that favoring one union over another by granting it the use of employer facilities and services while denying the same to other unions is unlawful support prohibited by Section 8(a)(2); and (2) the Board held in *Stainless Steel Products Inc.*[16] that an employer may not actively solicit members on behalf of one union or allow one union to solicit members while prohibiting solicitation by rival unions.

Other Employer Conduct

An employer faced with organizing or an election campaign should not be dissuaded from granting general wage and other benefit increases out of fear of commiting an unfair labor practice. When the customary time for yearly increases is at hand, the employer should not withhold those increases based on the employees' union activities (*Pacific Southwest Airlines*).[17] However, the conferring

[12]126 NLRB 697 (1960).
[13]167 NLRB 894 (1967).
[14]351 U.S. 105 (1956), cf. Salem Hospital and District 1199, Massachusetts National Union of Hospital and Health Care Employees, RWDSU, UP-2249 (8/24/74), 1 MLRR 1008.
[15]160 NLRB 188 (1966), cf. discussion, City of Worcester and IBPO, MUP-2016 (2/6/75), 1 MLRR 1037.
[16]157 NLRB 232 (1965).
[17]201 NLRB 647 (1973).

of irregular wage increases or other economic benefits upon employees immediately prior to an election may be found to be an unfair labor practice (*NLRB* v. *Exchange Parts Co.*).[18] Thus, the employer should conduct "business as usual" as if there were no representative election taking place (*Singer Co.*).[19]

Employer questioning of employees about the union is not unlawful per se, but it will be the subject of close scrutiny (*NLRB* v. *Dale Industries*).[20] Although questioning when the employer is unaware of union activity may not constitute an unfair labor practice (*NLRB* v. *Ralph Printing*),[21] continued questioning in an intimidating manner will surely result in an adverse finding. Polling the employees about their union sentiments may be permissible if the following safeguards are maintained: (1) The employer's questioning must be for the purpose of determining the validity of the union's claim of majority status. (2) The employees must be made aware of the purpose of the questioning by the employer. (3) The employer assures the employees that no reprisals will be taken against them for answering truthfully. (4) The employer must not have engaged in any previous unfair labor practice or otherwise engaged in creation of a coercive atmosphere (*Strucksnes Construction Co.*).[22]

Although it may be unwise for an employer to question his employees about the union or to discuss the union with individual employees especially in supervisory areas or offices, nothing bars an employer from listening to whatever his employees may wish to volunteer.

Surveillance of employees by the employer carried out under circumstances tending "to instill in the minds of employees fear of discrimination" may provide sufficient grounds for setting aside an election (see generally *NLRB* v. *West Coast Casket Co.*).[23] More re-

---

[18]375 U.S. 405 (1964).

[19]199 NLRB 1195 (1972).

[20]355 F.2d 851 (1966), cf. Baraga County Memorial Hospital, 1969 MERC Lab. Op. 6.

[21]379 F.2d 687 (1967).

[22]165 NLRB 1062 (1967), cf. Town of Clay and Service Employees International Union, Local 200, AFL-CIO, 7 PERB 3059 (November 27, 1974).

[23]205 F.2d 902 (1953), cf. Green Lake County, WERC Decision No. 6061 (1962).

cently the NLRB held that any use of informers by employers, whether concealed or not, is prohibited in any phase of organization (*Excelsior Laundry Co.*).[24] A recent decision in *Montgomery Ward Co.* v. NLRB[25] states that the fact that the employer caused or authorized the use of informers must be proven.

It has long been settled that employer discrimination against an employee by hiring or firing, promoting or demoting, transferring, or in any way modifying or changing the terms and conditions of employment based on the employee's union activities is unlawful (*Phelps Dodge Corp.* v. NLRB).[26] So, too, has the decision standard been long settled; "taking union activities or affiliation into consideration" will be sufficient for a finding of discrimination (*Edward Budd Manufacturing Co.* v. NLRB).[27]

In most of these activities, it has been held that when a reasonable person might interpret the acts of a subordinate as representing the attitude of the employer, those acts will be imputed to the employer (NLRB v. *Pacific Gas and Electric*).[28] To relieve the employer of the burden of any unfair labor practice charge arising from such activity, the courts have required the employer's affirmative disavowal of the subordinate's prohibited activity (*H.J. Heinz Co.* v. NLRB).[29]

It is suggested that the best way for the administration to avoid the possibility of union objection to the conduct of an election or an unfair labor practice is to organize and educate the entire administrative team about objectionable conduct and unfair labor practices and to coordinate all official and unofficial statements. All administrators should be made aware of their responsibilities as representatives of the employer and of the various ways that objections to elections and unfair labor practices may arise. This plan is best accomplished by appointing an officer to coordinate communications. One very important suggestion in this regard is to remind all administrators to record, in a uniform manner, the date,

[24] 186 NLRB 914 (1970).
[25] 385 F.2d 760 (1967).
[26] 313 U.S 177 (1941), cf. *Muskego-Norway Consolidated Schools v. WERC*, 35 Wisc.2d 540, 151 N.W.2d 617 (1967).
[27] 138 F.2d 86 (1943).
[28] 118 F.2d 780 (1941), cf. Muskego-Norway, footnote 26 above.
[29] 311 U.S. 514 (1940).

time, place, and substance of all oral conversations with faculty which concern unionization.

Conclusion

Administrators should speak out and act in a reasonable and "business as usual" manner. They should consider all their statements and actions carefully. The following tests will govern the disposition of a union objection to the conduct of an election or the disposition of an unfair labor practice charge.

1. Substantiality: Was misrepresentation sufficient enough to influence a voter's choice?
2. Materiality: Was the subject matter of a misrepresentation sufficiently related to election issues to influence voters?
3. Timing: Was there adequate opportunity for an opposing party to reply to any misrepresentation?
4. Source: Was the source a party in a position to have special knowledge on which voters would rely?
5. Voter independent knowledge: Was the misrepresentation related to subject matter about which voters lacked independent knowledge (McGuinnes, 1976, p. 164)?

It has been said by experts in the field that enlightened employers agree that full and open discussion of the benefits and drawbacks of unionizing and bargaining will permit an untrammeled election. I suggest more: the obligation on the part of the employer to speak out can be inferred from important decisions of the NLRB. One decision which immediately comes to mind is *Excelsior Underwear, Inc.*,[30] in which the NLRB in reasoning the requirement that employers provide name and address lists of employees, suggests that an opportunity for both employer and competing unions to reach all employees "is basic to a fair and informed election." The Supreme Court supported the Board's position in this regard in a 1969 case, *NLRB* v. *Wyman-Gordon Co.*,[31] when it held that "the requirement that companies furnish worker lists to unions furthers

[30]156 NLRB 1236 (1966).
[31]394 U.S. 759 (1969).

the free-choice objective of encouraging an informed employee electorate. . . ." Thus, it is not only important, but may be obligatory, that employers make their opinions known and disseminate information available to them in order to balance the flow of information to the faculty so that each faculty member casts an informed, as well as free, ballot.

Daniel R. McLaughlin

There is no quick way to train existing administrative and classified personnel to handle collective bargaining. If collective bargaining is to be a success, it is important to understand that (1) it is the existing administrative and secretarial staff who will have to be trained, (2) the level of training will be both general and specific, the latter depending on position and function in collective bargaining, and (3) the training must begin with the chief executive and the board of trustees. If there are two or three years before collective bargaining is to arrive on campus, the following can be an outline of a successful training program; if time is critical, all the sections must run concurrently.

Developing a Training Program

Training staff to operate successfully under collective bar-

Training Administrative
Personnel for
Collective Bargaining

gaining requires attention, time, energy, creativity, and a small budget. The major obstacles to training are resistance to changes in procedures and relationships and the scarcity of good collective bargaining training material, meetings, and courses. In the last few years meetings and courses have improved, but training material for campus bargaining is almost nonexistent. For this reason, some of the material referred to here is designed for industry, business, or government; some is old. These items will have to be translated into the language of higher education by the campus staff.

Every college should consider assigning the function of training to one of the middle-level administrators. This person should be held accountable for finding, evaluating, and assigning all administrators to proper collective bargaining training programs for their positions, and for staff development both on and off campus.

ACBIS can assist this person through its knowledge of training materials and programs.

Training Top-Level Administrators

Collective bargaining forces new, and in my judgment, better systematic management on campus. But most administrators and members of boards of trustees fear it because it is an unknown, and the very concept implies conflict. It need not be so. Therefore, the training for the chief executive and the board of trustees should begin by reading *Unions on Campus* (Kemerer and Baldridge, 1975), *Management of Change and Conflict* (Thomas and Bennis, 1972), *The Functions of Social Conflict* (Coser, 1956), and *Collective Bargaining Comes to Campus* (Carr and Van Eyck, 1973). (See also Recommended Training Aids at the end of this chapter.)

There is no single model of collective bargaining in industry, and there will not be one in higher education. Yet, all collective bargaining has similarities. Even though most educators dislike the thought of comparing themselves to industry, industrial firms have been involved in collective bargaining for many years and have much to offer. They are no longer novices; they can be a great help to educators who know how to sift out the basic principles that have validity for their particular situations. Therefore, the next step in the training program is to engage a number of people such as the chief labor relations person from a nearby company, the bargaining agent or superintendent from the local school system, or the management bargaining agent from a nearby city in a series of discussions on collective bargaining. A former union person who has no connection or interest in the campus union activities would be particularly helpful. I strongly suggest that these discussions be held on some day other than a regular board meeting day. One note of warning is needed here: companies and governmental units, like colleges, treat people in different ways. Therefore, exercise care in selecting discussion visitors. Well-managed companies usually pride themselves in good human relations and effective collective bargaining. The best-managed companies are mentioned periodically in such places as the *Sunday New York Times* business section, *Fortune* magazine, and *Dunn's Review*. Some of the top chemical companies such as DuPont, Monsanto, or Dow are known for their excellence in and attention to, human relations. These companies may also have inhouse labor relations training seminars which might be useful. The purpose of this series of discussions with industrial, government, and, hopefully, union people is to cover, at the barest minimum, the following topics: what can and cannot be done during union organizing efforts (see Gardner, 1976), management rights, the process of collective bargaining and typical labor relations problems, contracts and problems to avoid, normal conflicts in collective bargaining, collective bargaining training programs which the company uses for its management, the union point of view, and possible exchange internships. This last suggestion could bring to campus a seasoned labor relations person for a short period of time and also give the college an opportunity to develop one of its younger, more promising administrators who later might become the campus's collective bargaining expert. These same agenda items should next be discussed with a consultant from a university labor studies center such as the one at Cornell University. Care should be exercised in selecting this consultant because some of these centers and their people represent management views, whereas others hold the labor point of view. Although it is important to understand labor's view of collective bargaining, especially since many education unions are merging with industrial or public employees' unions, the chief executive and his board must first understand collective bargaining from the viewpoint of experienced management. The last step in this sequence is to have a discussion with a labor lawyer familiar with the pertinent labor laws and the rulings of the national and state labor relations boards. It would be ideal if this person also had an intimate knowledge of laws that pertain to higher education as well as acquaintance with local and state barristers, judges, and courts. The purpose of these discussions will be to develop an overall understanding of the laws and legal processes governing collective bargaining and how they might be used to benefit the college. This last point is all too often overlooked! It is important to realize that courts and laws, the collective bargaining process, conflict and change are fearful items to many trustees and administrators. Encouragement from the chief executive and the board as well as a training program will help overcome this fear and make collective bargaining, laws, courts, and labor boards work for the institution.

The next step is to provide general training for all administrators, for clerical staff, and, perhaps, for some members of the
board of trustees. In the early stages of discussion, the participants
will probably state and restate that collective bargaining problems
result from poor communications, lack of ability to interpret and
abide by the contract, administrative weakness or authoritarianism,
and reaction under stress or in conflict situations which results in
poor human relations. The better-managed companies have training programs for their managers in these areas, much of which is
directly applicable to colleges and universities. The first general
training then should be in written and spoken communications.
Academic people often write to impress rather than express. Communications of all forms including job descriptions, policies, letters,
memos, and discussions under collective bargaining require clarity
and simplicity. The writer must understand the reader who is now
a union member. Three books can be used to begin this training:
The Elements of Style (Strunk and White, 1959), *How to Take the Fog
Out of Writing* (Gunning, 1964) and *Writing for Results* (Ewing, 1974).
An administrator with a writing background can conduct training
sessions which emphasize the importance and process of clarity and
simplicity in all communications from administrators. Although secretaries and clerks may not write memos or other communications,
they do read, correct, and type them. Their participation in communications training may prove to be an invaluable asset to the administration. Some industrial firms have found transactional analysis
to be extremely helpful in communications training. Furthermore,
for those administrators and secretaries who must meet union members face to face, *Body Language* (Fast, 1970) and, perhaps, *The Silent
Language* (Hall, 1973) would be excellent reading. These people
should then see and hear themselves through video- and audio tape
recordings of routine verbal communications, including telephone
conversations, with faculty. Since the revelations at the Watergate
hearings, many people are afraid of having their conversations
taped. Therefore, the college may need to simulate rather than
record or videotape these actual communication situations. Administrators playing the roles of faculty members in these conversations will show other administrators the need to exercise care in

communicating with union members. The Bell Telephone System has a business phone trainer unit that might be available to teach people how to handle different kinds of callers. In addition, a person from one of the telephone companies might demonstrate different techniques used by telephone operators to handle different types of callers. Sometimes the campus has a secretary or two capable of demonstrating successful telephone techniques. The purpose of this training is to learn not only how to handle different types of people, but also how and when to end a telephone conversation. One 16mm film which might be helpful is *Correct Telephone Courtesy* (Business Education Films). The more day-to-day situations and procedures used in each of the areas in this general training section, the more effective the training will be. For example, copies of nonconfidential memos and letters can be circulated in some patterned way, such as deans to deans and chairpersons to chairpersons, with a request they be read and criticized for clarity and simplicity. Staff meetings can be videotaped and then analyzed for communications, including unintentional messages through body language, inattentiveness, choice of words, boring presentations, monotones, and discussions without meaning. The more people practice these training items in their daily work, the better they will become at them and the better prepared the campus will be for collective bargaining. One warning for chief executives is that they must not only set the best example, but they must also reinitiate this daily practice from time to time to ensure that the habits acquired are maintained. Studying videotapes of an occasional cabinet or board meeting will set a good example.

Understanding Contracts

The second general training area involves sensitizing all administrators to what a collective bargaining contract means and how important it is to understand, interpret accurately, and follow its wording. The college attorney should be able to do this using existing contracts from other institutions or the institution's own personnel policies. The purpose is to show problems caused by differing interpretations of ambiguous language through default of process or record. A labor relations person from a nearby industry can also contribute to these sessions by pointing out problems that have resulted from administrators not paying careful attention to the contractual agreements. Administrators must clearly understand after these sessions that, regardless of past practice, the contract way is now the only way. As soon as a contract is ratified, these sessions can be repeated to analyze and interpret each significant clause in the contract. These sessions should be continued every few months as needed to point out how interpretations of various sections in the contract may have changed procedures or may have led to grievances. An analysis of past grievances and the conditions that led to each grievance can be enlightening. The purpose is to show administrators what causes grievances. In this reporting of grievances, care must be exercised so that the discussion centers on the problems rather than on the people. Discussions often bring out the fact that grievances can be, and are, used by the union to harass the administration. This is more likely to occur when the union needs visibility to help retain membership.

Overcoming Fears of Bargaining

The third general area of training concerns the fear that collective bargaining engenders in many administrators. This fear is sometimes translated into various forms of docility or hostility in dealing with unions; neither works in collective bargaining. Two things can be done to begin to overcome this situation: (1) provide assertiveness training (Jakubowski-Spector, 1973; Albano, 1975) and (2) provide management training. The assertiveness trainer can be found by contacting the women's center on campus or at a neighboring campus. If this training is not needed by all administrators and secretaries, the administration of Rotter's Internal-External (I-E) Scale (Rotter, 1966) will help to make a rough determination of who needs it most. The higher a person scores on this scale, the more assertiveness training appears to be needed. Management training should be considered a long-term training project, but a beginning can be made by providing administrators with the following material: books: *Management* (Drucker, 1973), *How to*

Manage by Objectives (Mali, 1975); tape recordings: "Drucker on Management" (Drucker, 1974), "Management by Objectives" (EFM Series, American Management Association Bookstore [AMACOM], 1975), "Executive Skills (Odiorne, 1972); films: *Effective Executive Series* (Drucker, 1968). Collective bargaining management: books: *Unions on Campus* (Kemerer and Baldridge, 1975), *Grievance Handling* (Baer, 1970); tape recordings: "Handling Complaints and Grievances" (Stanley, 1966), "Collective Bargaining" (Emmett and Howe, 1975), "Faculty and the Law" (Nolte, 1975), "Labor Relations and the Supervisor" (American Management Association, 1975b), "Constructive Discipline on the Job" (American Management Association, 1975a), "Union or Not: The Supervisor's Role" (American Management Association, 1975c); films: labor arbitration films and pamphlet (American Arbitration Association).

The third general area of training involves conflict and stress. The book, *Managing Intergroup Conflict in Industry* (Blake, Shepard, and Mouton, 1964) along with those mentioned earlier should be read. In addition, industrial firms and the American Management Association (AMA) indicate that some form of meditation is helpful to people in stressful situations (Goleman, 1976; Jensen, 1976; Schwartz, 1974). Among others, the AMA's tape, "Transcendental Meditation" (1976c) can prove useful in this area. Additional material in all of the above general training areas is available; what has been suggested is only a beginning.

The third phase of specialized training will require different experiences for different functions and people. The negotiating team alone cannot make collective bargaining a success. Administrators must perform duties to the best of their abilities, and collective bargaining requires new skills. This means different training for different positions. People on the negotiating team and top-level supervisors will normally require the most training, predominantly in the areas of handling people, enforcing the contract, conflict resolution, and communications. The negotiating team is ordinarily composed of the chief negotiator spokesperson, a high-level business officer, a high-level academic officer, a high-level administrator who is a manager (not the president), and a lawyer. (Because of different organizational charts and campus sizes, each campus should insert its own appropriate titles.)

Training the Spokesperson

The chief spokesperson for a college has often been a lawyer who has a private practice; industry has not necessarily followed this pattern. The size of the institution and the character of its personnel will determine whether or not the spokesperson is inhouse or employed from an outside consulting firm. The smaller the college, the more likely it will need outside help. If the spokesperson is to be selected from an outside firm, that firm and the individual should have had previous collective bargaining experience in higher education. Inexperienced people can lose management rights before hard bargaining even begins; the first contract is the most important one (see Chapter Nine). This chief negotiator acts as a team captain. He controls the management's team during bargaining sessions as well as the regulations governing the process. Therefore, he needs direct communication with the chief executive and the board of trustees to learn about current policies, administrative organization, grievance resolution, and fiscal resources. If this person is a member of the staff, he will require outside training. At the barest minimum, this person should attend a one- to four-week training seminar on collective bargaining offered by a university with a labor studies center or by a professional organization, such as the Public Personnel Association or the Professional Institute of the American Management Association, before bargaining begins. In addition, this person would do well to attend one or two conferences on collective bargaining offered by groups, such as McGinnis Associates or the College and University Personnel Association, to understand practices and trends in collective bargaining. The chief negotiator should also visit at least two campuses that have negotiated contracts to learn from their negotiator what mistakes should be avoided. Preferably, campuses selected for these visits should be bargaining with the same union. In addition, this person should read everything he can obtain on collective bargaining and subscribe to publications such as the *School Law Newsletter,* the *Chronicle of Higher Education,* the American Arbitration Association's *Labor Arbitration in Government,* the *Journal of College and University Law,* and reports from the ACBIS.

Knowledge of collective bargaining alone is not enough to

make a chief spokesperson successful. Some industries have found that by using T-grouping, their negotiating performance improves as does their management grievances. Therefore, the chief negotiator and perhaps other members of the table team might well go off campus for this experience. Make sure this is offered by some reputable group such as the National Training Laboratory in Bethel, Maine. If all table team members go away for T-group training, it is usually best that they do so first as individuals rather than as a group. Once they have all had the experience, a trainer can be brought to campus for a team group experience. This is excellent preparation for bargaining if done one or two months before the team is seated at the table.

Team members other than the spokesperson need most of their training in the areas of special responsibility. The business team member, with the aid of his back-up team members, must be able to analyze proposals for their immediate and long-range fiscal implications. Familiarity with cost accounting and availability of computerized cost modeling programs such as the National Center for Higher Education Management Systems (NCHEMS) "Costing and Data Management System" and "Resource Requirements Prediction Model" are essential. The academic table team member analyzes union proposals for their implications for governance, existing and future academic programs and policies, course scheduling, availability of faculty for students, faculty load, tenure, promotion, and assignments. A creative person in this role can be invaluable (see *The Chronicle of Higher Education,* July 19, 1976, p. 4). This person, like the spokesperson, should read everything available about collective bargaining and its impact on the academic community. Some sources are listed in the references, but the academic team member must watch for new publication lists as the most recent information becomes available. In addition, this person should read the *Chronicle of Higher Education,* the *School Law Newsletter,* and ACBIS publications to observe trends. The management member of the table team is responsible for analyzing union proposals in terms of existing polices covering personnel, administration and student rights (that is, students' right of access to faculty, counselors, library, and so on). Management rights are seldom discussed on campus. Therefore, the management person should be sent to two or three unionized companies of at least medium size (1,000 employees) for discussions with one of their top managers and one of their negotiators to determine what they perceive to be essential management rights. One essential question is, "What authority to make which decisions does management need in order to manage the organization?" Another question is, "What rights would improve the operation of the organization?" On these visits, it is wise to have one or two people from the college's back-up team accompany the table team representative because once back on campus the language used by industry or business will have to be translated into collegiate areas and terms. This same group should visit other campuses that have collective bargaining and analyze existing higher education union contracts. In addition, other idiosyncrasies of higher education management, such as tenure determinations, peer evaluations for promotion, will have to be examined for management rights. Visiting companies sensitizes the management people to the whole thought process surrounding management rights. Before making the visits, management people should listen to the series of tape recordings, "Drucker on Management" (Drucker, 1974) and "Executive Skills" (Odiorne, 1972).

If the chief negotiator is not a lawyer, a fifth member of the table team is needed. This person must be a lawyer whose responsibility will be to analyze union proposals for their legal implications, not only in terms of court cases, but also in terms of labor laws under which the campus must operate. This person should know the leanings of state labor relations board members as well as situations such as those caused by a closed shop (Tomlinson, 1975). Information from notorious cases can be used at appropriate times to weaken union positions. Since collective bargaining in education has been conducted primarily by lawyers, most of these people have sufficient training. However, great care should be taken to train this lawyer to understand higher education if he has not been on the campus for at least one year. This person should keep abreast of changes and trends through both legal publications and associations, such as the National Association of College and University Attorneys.

There is a sixth person, but he should not be considered a member of either table team. In fact, he must be acceptable to both teams; he is the recorder who is held accountable for accurately recording and transcribing in detail the minutes of any bargaining session. These minutes must be confidential. A court recorder or someone who can synthesize what is being said by each side is the kind of person needed. If agreeable to both sides, tape recordings should be kept of the sessions, but they usually prove too cumbersome for transcribing minutes. Their purpose is to check the accuracy of statements as they are transcribed.

Once the team has been selected and the members have had their individual and group T-group sessions as well as developed their own areas of expertise, training through simulation can become meaningful. Other campuses are suffering similar problems with collective bargaining and should also be training their teams for negotiations. Bringing these campus teams together to simulate table sessions with each team taking turns on either side of the table can be a stimulating experience. Another helpful device is to videotape these sessions with a consultant from either or both higher education and industry periodically stopping the sessions to review the tapes. The consultants should comment on both the conduct of the process and a team member's strengths and weaknesses. This is a serious business which requires practice! Contract proposals used in these sessions can be either originally written by back-up teams or obtained from other campuses. Team members should develop their sensitivity to communications, including body language, and team rules for operation. Techniques such as stalling for time to think by filling a pipe and asking for recess should also be practiced in these simulated sessions. Like preparation for any team, this practice should continue until the members are ready for their appearance at the table. Although simulation can be used throughout the year, it is most effective during the last two months before negotiations begin.

Training the Back-Up Team

The back-up teams work behind the scenes. These people do the research and analytic work for the table team. They are essential as negotiations advance toward a contract. They can participate in the simulation exercises. The usual back-up teams cover business, academic, and management areas. A large institution may also want a legal back-up team. The business back-up team should consist of: (1) a top business person who has a total view of the institution, (2) a budget manager and, (3) a detail person such as an accountant or bursar. On a small campus one person may handle all three areas. The business back-up team's function is to actually analyze union demands, check their impact on fiscal policies and operation, cost them out, and write counter proposals for the table team. At least one of these people should attend a NCHEMS general training seminar some time before bargaining begins. Ideally, a person from both the academic back-up team and the management back-up team should also be sent to this seminar to develop a team approach to using different NCHEMS software. A catalog of NCHEMS products is available from NCHEMS, Western Interstate Commission for Higher Education. This training seminar should be attended as soon as possible to allow the necessary programming and information collection to be completed long before union proposals are accepted.

The academic back-up team will analyze union proposals for their impact on tenure, promotions, and governance. They should carefully review trends on such things as peer evaluation, both academic and student counseling, and governance structures. Faculty loads, committee and other assignments as well as class schedules, class sizes, and other academic administrative rights are also their responsibilities. Like the people in the Pennsylvania State College system, these people must be prepared to make counterproposals that will not only keep flexibility for academic programming but also provide creative ways to change programs to insure excellence. In addition to attending a NCHEMS seminar, these people should read such publications as *Faculty Participation in Academic Governance* (American Association for Higher Education, 1967), *Collective Negotiations in Higher Education* (Hughes, Underbrink, and Gordon, 1973) and *The Tenure Debate* (Smith, Bardwell, and others, 1973) to name a few. Members of the academic back-up team should also review publications of the higher education associations and the faculty organizations such as the *AAUP Journal* and the *Chronicle of Higher Education*. The back-up team must have a firm understanding of academic management rights. The members should have several discussions with the spokesperson and the table academic representative. About once each year, one member of this academic back-up team should be sent to a general collective bargaining conference, especially if the conference concerns governance, tenure, or trends in academic assignment under collective bargaining. Since faculty load is often a bargaining item, information on this matter from surrounding states should be collected and reported to the table team. State coordinating agencies or departments of higher education usually have this information. People assigned long-range bargaining should learn a personnel point system from either a manager on a military base responsible for civilian employees or an industry. It is my belief that as collective bargaining in higher education seeks more equity, faculty loads will have to be calculated in different ways. The personnel point system adapted to faculty loads might provide one answer.

The third back-up team is the management back-up team. Depending on the size of the institution and the complexity of the bargaining situation, an attorney and the dean of students may be included in this group. This team analyzes union proposals in terms of existing administrative and personnel policies, state and federal laws, including affirmative action and Title IX laws, management rights in business and personnel procedures, and, if students are involved in collective bargaining, student rights. If students are involved, the dean of students should either be on this team or form a fourth team to analyze proposals affecting students. This management team should be prepared to make counterproposals in the area of campus management. Because of the nature of the counterproposals, the team should be composed of an administrative officer, a personnel officer, the affirmative action and Title IX officer(s), and the registrar. The administrative and personnel officers should read *American School and University* for collective bargaining articles and develop several industrial labor relations and personnel advisors who can be consulted when they are needed. In addition, depending upon the availability of an attorney or legal assistance, these people should participate in seminars offered by the Public Personnel Association, the National Association of Employer Negotiators and Administrators (NAPENA) and a legal seminar such as the one offered by the University of San Francisco School of Law entitled, "Practical Labor Law." NAPENA also has a negotiations aid kit and case study kit which may prove beneficial to this team. Finally, this team should discuss with the chief negotiator and the management table representative how to preserve particular managements' rights. In all management rights discussions priorities should be assigned to the items so that mistakes in giving up items will not be made. Furthermore, there should be a careful discussion as to which rights can be sacrificed for certain items wanted in return from the union. The people on all of these back-up teams should be considered as future table team members. Therefore, if time and money allow, they should be sent to the same conferences and experiences as the table team.

Training Contract Administrators

Once the contract has been negotiated and signed by both sides, it must be administered. There are many ways to handle this aspect of the contract and the problems that interpretations will bring. Two such ways are: (1) assign all labor relations to one individual or office usually located within the personnel department and (2) invest the negotiating table team, or part of it, with continuing responsibilities. The second way has some advantages because these people were at the table when the agreements were made. A disadvantage of administration by the table team will be the probable physical and psychological fatigue of the individuals after long hours at the table. In addition, someone will still be needed in the personnel office to maintain and supervise a records system. Regardless of the choice, this individual or table team should meet with the union representatives on a regular basis; the larger the organization the more likely these meetings should occur at least weekly. The purposes of these meetings are to resolve conflicts between union and management, discuss fiscal problems, new problem areas, interpretation of contract and process, including unresolved grievances. The recorder should keep accurate notes of these meetings and have both sides sign them to indicate that they do represent what transpired. Communications play an important part in these meetings. Therefore, repeating earlier training in transactional analysis, on campus T-grouping, communication practice, including body language analysis, with videotape equipment is beneficial. A nonparticipant observer in communications or a social science consultant can be extremely helpful in these meetings. However, the observer's critique should be given only to the management team.

Some form of automated personnel records should be established. This system is to ensure that the individuals in the personnel office responsible for supervising these records can provide the required information to administrators. It allows for the proper administration of the contract provisions, including policies and procedures on appointments, evaluations, promotions, tenure, dismissal, and retirement. In organizing or reorganizing personnel files, care must be exercised that national and state laws are observed as well as any contract agreements. The personnel officer or office should be charged with training top supervisors so that they and their secretaries know and practice proper personnel procedures and accurately maintain the necessary records. One record often overlooked is an hour-by-hour diary of the top supervisor's conferences and the subject discussed; a guest sign-in book is helpful. Other records that must be kept and other activities required of top supervisors should also be part of the personnel department's training program. Other supervisors (deans, associate deans, and directors) should also participate in these training sessions. A calendar of events with their deadlines should be established, communicated in these training sessions, and adhered to by first- and second-line supervisors. Such deadlines include evaluations of faculty, promotion consideration as well as submission of grades. If students play any role in the contract, the dean of students and other appropriate student personnel officers should also be included in this training.

Some industries have found that the addition of a special administrator is beneficial in the administration of the contract. This person is called a labor relations coordinator and works for and between the personnel (labor relations) department and the individual academic department. The purpose of this position is to assist the first- and second-line supervisors as they administer the contract on a day-to-day basis. The coordinator spends considerable time acting as an ombudsman to resolve minor conflicts or to obtain interpretations before grievances occur. This person should participate in the weekly meetings between the union and management and will need special competence in human relations, investigative, and conflict resolution skills. Training in these areas is primarily achieved through experience with some help from university short courses in labor relations.

The first- and second-line supervisors, hopefully department chairpersons and division directors or deans, need the second greatest amount of training. I say hopefully because not all campuses have been able to keep department chairpersons out of the bargaining unit. There is a direct relationship between the success of collective bargaining on campus and the management skills of first- and second-line administrators. Besides the general training, these people should participate in a detailed examination of the contract and its clauses as soon as it is available. It is best if this training is done by members of the table team who know the innuendoes behind clauses. A new contract often requires changes in record keeping, filing of dates, evaluation procedures, and grievance review. This training should take place simultaneously with examination of the new contract. For the management training, Peter Drucker's series of films on effective executives (Bureau of National Affairs) and the American Arbitration Association's labor arbitration films and pamphlets will be helpful. (See the references for additional management articles.) These people should read the American Arbitration Association's monthly summary, *Labor Arbitration in Government; Management* (Drucker, 1973); and *Harvard Business Review on Management* (Harvard Business Review, 1975). Three films on grievances in industry will also be of help: *Grievance* (McGraw-Hill Text Films) and *The Grievance* (National Film Board of Canada), and *Knowing Your Employees—Individual Differences* (American Management Association). Each film presentation should be preceded by a discussion outlining the grievance procedure. It must be made clear that a grievance is not always "won" by the administration. First- and second-line administrators must be prepared for a higher grievance level which may reverse decisions they have made. The labor relations coordinator can help the first-line supervisor in making grievance decisions that will be in keeping with the contract and top management's decisions. But in this training, first- and second-line administrators must learn that to "lose" a grievance (have their decision reversed) is not to lose face. Good administration always attempts to seek justice for every grievant and for every supervisor whose action is being grieved. Justice often depends on a technicality, and a good training program brings out the nature of those technicalities.

After each showing of grievance films, there should be a discussion of the technical situations, or processes, on which the final resolution of the grievance was based. The state of the collective bargaining art in higher education has not developed to the point where faculty grievances are available on film or videotape. This means that the campus trainer will have to translate into campus jargon the films and other excellent materials developed for industry. Basic concepts in grievance resolution can be easily taught using these materials. The next step in this training, following the showing of the grievance films, is to simulate grievances with first- and second-line administrators in role-playing sequences. Depending upon the contract, typical grievances often arise from decisions relating to promotion, schedule, tenure, offices, and other assignments. A short scenario could be written (possibly by teams) on the most prevalent areas of grievances depicting the union member's problem, the first-line supervisor's early response, and the basic arguments used at each step of the grievance procedure ending in arbitration if that is part of the contract. A consultant from industry or a school of labor studies is helpful in constructing the scenarios and in analyzing the progress of the grievance. Periodically throughout the process the role playing should be stopped, giving first- and second-line administrators an opportunity to say verbally or in writing what they would do, to which the consultants can respond. This process should continue through each step. A few situations should be staged so that higher levels of management reverse first- or second-line administrative decisions.

Training first- and second-line administrators should also include procedural details: what is not grievable, note taking during informal and formal stages, who should and should not be present when the grievance is discussed, what equipment and supplies should be available for union members' use. Another part of the training program should include specific methods of communicating to top management the problems created by poorly worded contract clauses, omissions and commissions. This is the most fundamental of all ways to improve the next contract and to resolve potential grievance situations before they occur.

Training Other Officials

Other campus officials will have other duties to perform which require little or no training but require caution and care. The business or administrative office should ensure that a copy of the contract be in the hands of all professional and clerical staff as quickly as possible. It is best if the contract is printed as a part of the administrative and personnel policy handbook. Pages in old administrative and personnel policy handbooks should be corrected and reissued at the same time. Changes in procedures should be issued to union personnel by first-line management using printed matter prepared by the administrative office. The union will also notify its members of these changes, but it is best if the members' immediate supervisor does this as a representative of management. The first-line supervisor's position must be part of management. The affirmative action and Title IX officers should review the contract to ensure that it complies with the law. In the event of fiscal or student enrollment decline, business-office people and students should be involved in the contract review to ensure that discrimination does not occur as a result of staff reductions.

Finally, the public relations office should work with the union to develop news releases that eliminate unnecessary fighting through the newspapers. In addition, this office, along with the office of administration, should develop emergency communications procedures and techniques in the event of a crisis. Part of this preparation should be emergency assignment plans for all administrators who will speak to the union, press, or public on behalf of the institution in the event there is a strike.

The only remaining function not mentioned is that of the chief grievance officer. The person filling this position needs the same training as the table team. If he can intern in an industrial labor relations department while the campus is preparing for the contract, it will be time well spent. Before hearing grievances, this person must ensure that all people, board members, top administration, first- and second-line supervisors and even groups of students and alumni accept the need for fairness in the grievance process. This means that college management will sometimes make errors and lose grievances. To win all grievances is to assure future battles at the negotiation table. The grievance procedure could be called a test of the whole collective bargaining process. Although the position of the chief grievance review person is the last one covered in this discussion, it in no way indicates a lack of importance. On the contrary, effective grievance resolution may be the key to good labor relations. Grievance officers should develop a circle of professional associates who fulfill similar functions at other colleges, in business, and in industry. Contact with these people, and reading available materials on trends, laws, and arbitration decisions should be a continuing source of training. One danger to avoid is overwork and tension. A beleaguered person can easily forget fairness. It is important that top administration give full support to grievance review officers in order to reduce tension. The mental and physical health of people in administration is basic to success.

Collective bargaining can work successfully on any campus where all parties are well trained. In many ways administrators were bargaining with faculty members long before unions came into existence. The change is that now there will be only one way and that is the contract way. If top administration thinks of its training program as a day-to-day exercise in improving the systematic and uniform management of campus resources, it will see training as a normal part of the daily operation. Training is a continuing investment essential for helping academics learn the art of managing. No institution of higher learning can long exist without an abundance of this art. Collective bargaining has focused attention on the need for better management and has created a positive force on campus.

Recommended Training Aids

Books

ALBANO, C. *Transactional Analysis on the Job and Communicating With Subordinates.* New York: AMACOM, 1975.

AMERICAN ASSOCIATION FOR HIGHER EDUCATION. *Faculty Participation in Academic Governance.* Washington, D. C.: 1967.

AMERICAN ARBITRATION ASSOCIATION. *You Be the Arbitrator,* 10th ed. New York, 1974.

ANDREE, R. G. *The Art of Negotiation.* Lexington, Mass.: Heath Lexington Books, 1971.

BAER, W. *Grievance Handling.* New York: AMACOM, 1970.

BAER, W. *Strikes.* New York: American Arbitration Association, 1975.

BALDRIDGE, J. *Power and Conflict in the University: Research in the Sociology of Complex Organizations.* New York: Wiley, 1971.

BELCHER, A. L.; AVERY, H. P.; AND SMITH, O. S. *Labor Relations in Higher Education.* Urbana, Ill.: College and University Personnel Association, 1971.

BLAKE, R.; SHEPARD, H.; AND MOUTON, J. *Managing Intergroup Conflict in Industry.* Houston, Texas: Gulf Publishing, 1964.

BLUMER, D. (Ed.) *Legal Issues for Postsecondary Education, Briefing Papers I.* Washington, D.C.: American Association of Community and Junior Colleges, 1975a.

BLUMER, D. (Ed.). *Legal Issues for Postsecondary Education, Briefing Papers II.* Washington, D.C.: American Association of Community and Junior Colleges, 1975b.

BRANFORD, L.; GIBB, J.; AND BENNE, K. (Eds.). *T-Group Theory and Laboratory Method.* New York: Wiley, 1964.

BRUBACHER, J. S. *The Courts and Higher Education.* San Francisco: Jossey-Bass, 1971.

CARR, R., AND VANEYCK, D. K. *Collective Bargaining Comes to Campus.* Washington, D.C.: American Council on Education, 1973.

COFFIN, R. *The Negotiator, A Manual for Winners.* New York: AMACOM, 1973.

COSER, L. *The Functions of Social Conflict.* Glencoe, Ill.: Free Press, 1956.

COULSON, R. *Labor Arbitration—What You Need to Know.* New York: American Arbitration Association, 1976.

DRUCKER, P. *Management.* New York: Harper & Row, 1973.

DURYEA, E. D., FISK, R. S., AND ASSOCIATES. *Faculty Unions and Collective Bargaining.* San Francisco: Jossey-Bass, 1973.

EWING, D. *Writing for Results.* New York: Wiley, 1974.

FAST, J. *Body Language.* New York: M. Evans, 1970.

FRENCH, W., AND BELL, C., JR. *Organizational Development*. Englewood Cliffs, N. J.: Prentice-Hall, 1973.

GUNNING, R. *How to Take the Fog Out of Writing*. Chicago: Dartnell, 1964.

HALL, E. *The Silent Language*. New York: Doubleday, 1973.

HARVARD BUSINESS REVIEW. *Harvard Business Review on Management*. New York: Harper & Row, 1975.

HUGHES, C.; UNDERBRINK, R.; AND GORDON, C. *Collective Negotiations in Higher Education*. Carlinville, Ill.: Blackburn College Press, 1973.

KALIN, R., AND OTHERS. *Organizational Stress*. New York: Wiley, 1964.

KEMERER, F. R., AND BALDRIDGE, J. V. *Unions on Campus: A National Study of the Consequences of Faculty Bargaining*. San Francisco: Jossey-Bass, 1975.

MC CLELLAND, D. *Power, The Inner Experience*. New York: Irvington, 1975.

MC CLELLAND, D. *The Achieving Society*. New York: Free Press, 1967.

MC CLELLAND, D. "The Two Faces of Power." In D. Klob, I. Ruben, and J. McIntyre (Eds.), *Organizational Psychology*, second edition. Englewood Cliffs, N. J.: Prentice-Hall, 1974a.

MC CLELLAND, D. "The Urge to Achieve." In D. Klob, I. Ruben, and J. McIntyre (Eds.), *Organizational Psychology*, second edition. Englewood Cliffs, N. J.: Prentice-Hall, 1974b.

MC CLELLAND, D. "Toward a Theory of Motive Acquisition." In H. Tosi and W. Hamner (Eds.), *Organizational Behavior and Management, A Contingency Approach*. Chicago: St. Clair Press, 1974c.

MALI, P. *How to Manage by Objectives*. New York: Wiley, 1972.

MARCEAN, L. (Ed.). *Dealing With A Union*. New York: American Management Association, 1969.

MARX, H. *Collective Bargaining for Public Employees*. New York: Wilson, 1969.

MOSES, S. *Collective Bargaining Agreements in Higher Education*. Columbia: Department of Higher and Adult Education, University of Missouri, 1973.

NATIONAL ASSOCIATION OF PUBLIC EMPLOYER NEGOTIATORS AND ADMINISTRATORS. Skokie, Ill.: Various Publications.

NIERENBERG, G. *The Art of Negotiating: Psychological Strategies for Gain-*

ing Advantageous Bargains. New York: Hawthorn Books, 1968.

SCOTT, W. *The Management of Conflict.* Homewood, Ill.: Irwin and Dorsey Press, 1965.

SHULMAN, C. *Collective Bargaining on Campus.* Washington, D.C.: American Association for Higher Education, 1972.

SMITH, B. L., AND ASSOCIATES. *The Tenure Debate.* San Francisco: Jossey-Bass, 1973.

STEVENS, C. *Strategy and Collective Bargaining Negotiation.* New York: McGraw-Hill, 1963.

STRUNK, W., JR., AND WHITE, E. *The Elements of Style.* New York: Macmillan, 1959.

TAYLOR, B., AND WITNEY, F. *Labor Relations Law.* Englewood Cliffs, N. J.: Prentice-Hall, 1971.

THOMAS, J., AND BENNIS, W. (Eds.). *Management of Change and Conflict.* Baltimore: Penguin Books, 1972.

TICE, T. (Ed.). *Faculty Power: Collective Bargaining on Campus.* Ann Arbor: University of Michigan, Continuing Legal Education, 1972.

TROTTA, M. *Arbitration of Labor-Management Disputes.* New York: AMACOM, 1974.

WARNER, K., AND HENNESSY, M. *Public Management at the Bargaining Table.* Chicago: Public Personnel Association, 1967.

Journal and Magazine Articles

CHRONICLE OF HIGHER EDUCATION. "State Trust Helps Retrain Pennsylvania Teachers," July 19, 1976.

GARDNER, J. "Faced With A Union Organizing Drive?" *American School and University,* June 1976, *48,* 8–18.

GOLEMAN, D. "Meditation Helps Break the Stress Spiral." *Psychology Today,* February 1976, *9,* 82–93.

HALL, J. "What Makes a Manager Good, Bad or Average?" *Psychology Today,* August 1976, *10,* 3.

JAKOWBAUSKI-SPECTOR. "Facilitating the Growth of Women Through Assertive Training." *Counseling Psychologist,* 1973, *4,* 75–86.

JENSEN, M. "Management Using Meditation to Unwind." *New York Sunday Times,* June 11, 1976.

JOE, V. "Review of the Internal-External Control Construct As A Personality Variable." *Psychology Reports*, 1971, *28*, 219–640.

MC CLELLAND, D., AND BURNHAM, D. "Power-Driven Managers: Good Guys Make Bum Bosses." *Psychology Today*, December 1975 (9), 69–70.

ROTTER, J. "Generalized Expectancies for Internal Versus External Control of Reinforcement." *Psychology Monographs*, 1966, *80* (Whole No. 609).

ROTTER, J. "Some Problems and Misconceptions Related to the Construct of Internal Versus External Control of Reinforcement." *Journal of Consulting and Clinical Psychology*, 1975, *43*, 56–57.

SCHWARTZ, G. "Part II. TM Relaxes Some People and Makes Them Feel Better!" *Psychology Today*, April 1974, 7, 39–44.

SHAPERO, A. "The Displaced, Uncomfortable Entrepreneur." *Psychology Today*, November 1975, *9*, 83–88.

TOMLINSON, K. "A Tale of Two Teachers." *Reader's Digest*, November 1975, *107*, 29–35.

Films and Cassettes

AMERICAN ARBITRATION ASSOCIATION. New York: Labor arbitration films with pamphlet.

AMERICAN MANAGEMENT ASSOCIATION. *Constructive Discipline on the Job*. Prime Audio I. Workbook, programmed notebook, tests, guide, and two cassettes, 1200–9. New York: AMA, 1975.

AMERICAN MANAGEMENT ASSOCIATION. *Labor Relations and the Supervisor*. Prime Audio II. Workbook, programmed notebook, guide, and two cassettes, 1202–5. New York: AMA, 1975b.

AMERICAN MANAGEMENT ASSOCIATION. *Union or Not: The Supervisor's Role*. Supplement to Prime Audio II, 1303–x. New York: AMA, 1975c.

AMERICAN MANAGEMENT ASSOCIATION. *How To Be a Successful Negotiator*. Workbook and twelve cassettes. New York: AMA, 1976a.

AMERICAN MANAGEMENT ASSOCIATION. *Know Your Employees—Individual Differences*. Film. New York: AMA, 1976b.

AMERICAN MANAGEMENT ASSOCIATION. *Transcendental Meditation*. Film, 2189–x. New York: AMA, 1976c.

AMERICAN MANAGEMENT ASSOCIATIONS EXTENSION INSTITUTE. New York: Various publications and management courses, AMACOM cassettes.

DRUCKER, P. "Drucker on Management." Sound recording, eight cassettes with guide, 9060–3. New York: AMACOM, 1974.

DRUCKER, P. *Effective Executive.* Film series, five films. Washington, D.C.: Bureau of National Affairs, 1968.

EMMETT, T., AND HOWE, R. "Collective Bargaining." Sound recording, three cassettes. Chicago: Teach' Em, Inc., 625 North Michigan Avenue, 1975.

Grievance. Film. New York: McGraw-Hill, 1954.

Grievance, The. Film. New York: National Film Board of Canada, 1953.

Grievance Hearing. Film. New York: McGraw-Hill, 1953.

Management by Objectives, EFM Series. Sound recordings, six cassettes with workbook, 80019. New York: AMACOM, 1975.

MASSEY, L. *Computer Fundamentals for Managers.* Sound recordings, six cassettes with workbook, 80010. New York: AMACOM, 1974.

RAYMOND, F. "The Goal Setting Sessions." Sound recording, one cassette, 9041–7. New York: AMACOM, 1967.

Educational Resources Information Center (ERIC) Publications

BLACKBURN, R., AND BYLSMA, D. *Changes in Organizational Structure and in Focus of Decision Making: A Test Theory in Community Colleges Before and After Collective Negotiations.* Washington, D.C.: ERIC, 1970.

BYLSMA, D., AND BLACKBURN, R. *Changes in Faculty Governance and Faculty Welfare: Some Empirical Consequences of Collective Negotiations.* Washington, D.C.: ERIC, 1971.

Interim Report. Committee to Study Faculty Collective Bargaining, Kalamazoo, Mich.: Western Michigan University, 1970.

Faculty Collective Bargaining in Postsecondary Institutions: The Impact on the Campus and on the State. Background and Recommendations. Denver: Education Commission of the States, 1972.

FLANGO, E., AND BRUMBAUGH, R. *Preference for Bargaining Representative: Some Empirical Findings.* Kutztown, Pa.: Kutztown State College Educational Development Center, 1972.

GILROY, T. (Ed.). *Dispute Settlement in the Public Sector-Research Series I.* Iowa City: Center for Labor and Management, Iowa University, 1972.

GORMAN, R. *Statutory Responses to Collective Bargaining in Institutions of Higher Learning.* Washington, D.C.: American Association of University Professors (AAUP), 1968.

HAEHN, J. *Collective Bargaining in Higher Education: An Empirical Analysis in the California State Colleges.* Chico, Calif.: Chico State College, 1971.

HANKIN, J., AND ANGELL, G. "Collective Bargaining in Junior Colleges." Papers presented at a conference sponsored by the Junior College Council of the Middle Atlantic States on Collective Bargaining in the Community Colleges, New York City, October 27, 1972.

HIXSON, R. *A Position Paper.* Washington, D.C.: American Federation of Teachers, Department of Colleges and Universities, 1968.

An Impartial Review of Collective Bargaining by University Faculties. East Lansing: Michigan State University, Faculty Affairs Committee, 1971.

MC DEAKE, J., AND STANTON, C. *Collective Negotiations and the Community College System in Massachusetts: A Case Study.* Boston: Boston College, 1970.

MARKS, K. (Comp.). *Collective Bargaining in U.S. Higher Education: 1960–1971. A Selective Bibliography.* Ames: Iowa State University Library, 1972.

METZLER, J. *A Journal of Collective Negotiations.* Trenton: New Jersey State Federation District Boards of Education, 1967.

MOORE, J. *Pennsylvania Community College Faculty: Attitudes Toward Collective Negotiations.* University Park: Center for the Study of Higher Education, Pennsylvania State University, 1971.

MORTIMER, K., AND LOZIER, G. *Collective Bargaining: Implications for Governance.* University Park: Center for the Study of Higher Education, Pennsylvania State University, June 1972.

NOLCE, M. (Ed.). *Labor Law and Education.* Report of the Work Conference on Collective Bargaining. Denver: University of Denver, July 1968.

NORTH, J. (Comp.). *Collective Bargaining in Higher Education. Bibliography Number 2.* Montgomery: Alabama State University, 1972.

REISS, L. *Faculty Governance in Turmoil—Who Speaks for the Junior College Professor.* Long Beach: California Junior College Faculty Association, 1967.

SHANNON, T. *Significant Legislation Trends in Negotiations: Federal Law-State Law-No Law Situations.* Phoenix: Annual Conference of the Association of School Business Officials, October 22, 1969.

SHOEMAKER, E. *Act 195 and Collective Negotiations in the Commonwealth of Pennsylvania.* Harrisburg: Pennsylvania State Department of Education, 1971.

SHULMAN, C. *Collective Bargaining on the Campus.* Washington, D.C.: American Association for Higher Education, 1972.

SPITZER, A. (Comp.). *Public Sector Labor Relations, 1972. Bibliography Number 1.* Montgomery: Alabama State University, 1972.

STEVENS, C. *The Professors and Collective Action: Which Kind?* Portland, Ore.: Reed College, 1971.

WARNER, K. *Collective Bargaining in the Public Service—The Road Ahead.* Chicago: Public Personnel Association, 1967.

WATTENBARGER, J., AND MARTORANA, S. *The Laws Relating to Higher Education in the Fifty States: January 1965–December 1967.* ERIC Clearinghouse for Junior College Information, Topical Paper 14. Los Angeles: California University ERIC Clearinghouse.

WEBER, A. *Academic Negotiations—Alternatives to Collective Bargaining.* Chicago: University of Chicago, 1967.

WING, D. *Legislation, Achievements and Problems in Education: A Survey of the States, 1971.* Denver: Education Commission of the States, January 1971.

Seminars

American Management Association

1. Effective Handling of Discipline and Grievances by Supervisors.
2. Handling Grievances and Arbitration.
3. The Nonunion Employer: Personnel Practices and Legal Obligations.

For other seminars, review associations' and fraternities' calendars.

Supplemental Journals and Magazines

American Association of Community and Junior Colleges. Various publications; see especially October 1972.

AAUP Bulletin; American Association of University Professors

Change

Chronicle of Higher Education

College and University Business

College and University Personnel Association Journal

College Management

Current Issues in Higher Education

Daily Report for Executives, Bureau of National Affairs

Education Record

Industrial Relations

Journal of College and University Law; National Association of College and University Attorneys.

Journal of Higher Education

Journal of Law and Education

Labor Arbitration in Government

Labor Law Journal

Liberal Education

News and Notes; Association of Governing Boards

School Law Newsletter; Box 722, Dallas, North Carolina, 28034

School and Society

Names and Addresses of Organizations Dispensing Collective Bargaining and Management Training Information

Academic Collective Bargaining Information Service (ACBIS)
1818 R Street, N.W.
Washington, D.C. 20009

American Arbitration Association
140 West 51st Street
New York, New York 10020

American Management Association Extension Institute
135 West 50th Street
New York, New York 10020

Business Education Films
5113 Sixteenth Avenue
Brooklyn, New York 11204

College and University Personnel Association (CUPA)
1 DuPont Circle, N.W.
Washington, D.C. 20036

Committee for Economic Development
477 Madison Avenue
New York, New York 10022

McGinnis Associates
526 Crafton Avenue
Pitman, New Jersey 08071
(609) 589-7842

McGraw-Hill Text Films
1221 Avenue of the Americas
New York, New York 10020

National Association of College and University Attorneys
1 DuPont Circle, N.W.
Washington, D.C. 20036

National Association of Public Employer Negotiators and
    Administrators (NAPENA)
Westmoreland Building
9933 Lawler Avenue
Skokie, Illinois 60076

National Center for Higher Education Management Systems
    (NCHEMS)
Western Interstate Commission for Higher Education
P. O. Drawer P
Boulder, Colorado 80302

National Center of the Study of Collective Bargaining in Higher
    Education
Baruch College
City University of New York (CUNY)
New York, New York 10010

Teach 'Em, Inc.
625 North Michigan Avenue
Chicago, Illinois 60611

George W. Angell

Administrators are beginning to feel optimistic about collective bargaining because of the growing number of labor-board decisions which are upholding management's right to refrain from bargaining those subjects it considers uniquely managerial in character. Administrators, of course, are responsible for making the higher education enterprise successful, for seeing that educational programs needed for the public interest are, indeed, offered at a reasonable cost and in a manner which attracts students, and for seeing that students and society can expect to benefit from the instruction offered. The need to assure administration's ability to make unfettered decisions regarding the amount of money to be invested in each part of the enterprise, the programs to be offered, the students to be instructed, and the assignments of employees is the underlying reason for reserving management's right *not* to bar-

Knowing the Scope
of Bargaining

gain such subjects with employee representatives. Faculty members obviously have a personal interest in these matters, and for them to make or share in such decisions could be viewed as a conflict of interest. Any subject held legally to be a management right is called a *permissible* subject for bargaining since it can only be bargained when management "permits" it.

On the other hand, the interest and support of faculty members is obviously essential to the success of a college or university, and they should have the opportunity to bargain about those conditions of employment which will directly affect their ability to effectively perform the particular duties assigned to them.

It is clear that the college president has responsibility for the overall operations and will lose his job if the campus becomes ineffective. A teacher is responsible for those particular teaching and related functions assigned to him by management and will lose that teaching position if those functions are not performed well. Each person, manager and teacher, must work under conditions that make success a reasonable possibility. To achieve this end, those institutional decisions which clearly do not seriously affect the conditions under which a particular faculty member works are generally reserved for management.

Similarly, there are some decisions concerning a teacher's work load, work schedules, grievances, and those procedures by which one is evaluated, that are generally recognized as being inseparable from the quality of individual teaching performance. Such decisions are subject to a reasonable accommodation between the desire of management to operate efficiently and the desire of the worker to perform in a professionally acceptable manner. These conditions of employment are clearly *mandatory* subjects for collective bargaining, that is, they must be bargained in good faith by both parties should either party place that subject on the table.

Landmark Decisions

There are, however, a great many subjects which do not appear to fit either category. As a result, the early years of academic collective bargaining (1968–1976) were marked by uncertainty and argument over such issues. When employers refused to bargain a controversial subject, negotiations would come to a stop while labor boards reviewed union charges that management was refusing to bargain "in good faith." The early decisions of labor boards tended to support union claims that a particular topic was, indeed, sufficiently a condition of employment to be designated a mandatory subject of bargaining. Just as important was that college and university administrators, not fully aware of the requirements and limitations of bargaining under law, negotiated many subjects the bargaining necessity of which they later doubted. As a result of these doubts, management began to refuse to bargain many issues in order to obtain an official determination of what had to be bargained. Subsequent case decisions by the NLRB and by various state labor boards began to shape a body of case law which provides more direction to both parties at the table and may hopefully reduce needless arguments.

One of the early landmark decisions was made by the New York Public Employment Relations Board (PERB) *(Board of Higher Education* v. *Professional Staff Congress).*[1] In this case the faculty union at City University of New York insisted on including in the contract a clause that would prohibit students from being appointed to committees assigned to evaluate faculty members for purposes of tenure and promotions. The university refused to bargain the issue and the PERB upheld the university's position. "Collective negotiations is a valuable technique to resolve questions between an employer and its employees concerning terms and conditions of employment. It is not designed to resolve policy questions regarding the structure of governance of a public employer or the nature of that public employer's responsibility to its constituency. Questions in the latter category involve issues of social concern to many groups within the community. . . . It would be a perversion of collective negotiations to impose it as a technique for . . . disenfranchising other interested groups."

One can see that labor boards must face difficult judgments about subjects which have an impact on *both* managerial responsibilities and on conditions of teaching. The issue was clarified by a decision of the Supreme Court of Pennsylvania *(Pennsylvania Labor Relations Board* v. *State College Area School District).*[2] The Pennsylvania Labor Relations Board had established a long list of nonmandatory subjects. The teacher's union appealed, and the case eventually came before the state supreme court which refused to judge individual items in the list. Rather, it remanded the case back to the labor board, ordering it to make an item by item review: "Where an item of dispute is a matter of fundamental concern to the employees' interest . . . it is not removed . . . [from] good faith bargaining . . . because it may touch upon basic policy . . . the board [must] determine whether the impact of the issue on the interest of the employee in wages, hours, and terms and conditions of employment outweighs its probable effect on the basic policy of the system as a whole. . . ." In making its decision, the court referred to a similar decision in Kansas *(NEA of Shawnee Mission* v. *Board of Education).*[3]

[1] 7 PERB 3028 (1974).
[2] 337 A.2d 262 (1975).
[3] 512 P.2d 426 (1973).

Thus, the courts began to refine the issues and provide labor boards with a criterion on which their judgments were to be founded.

In the meantime, the NLRB began to face equally perplexing issues arising from labor disputes at private universities. In another landmark decision, the Director of Region 29, NLRB, reviewed a charge of an unfair labor practice in which the faculty union was attempting to bargain such matters as: "Incorporation into the new . . . agreement . . . (1) the [AAUP] 1966 statement on Government of Colleges and Universities; . . . (2) faculty representation on the Board of Trustees; (3) a statement of administrative responsibilities, which includes a general declaration that the administration of the University . . . should function in an atmosphere of collegiality, a list of academic qualifications for academic deans and vice-presidents, and a general statement of the responsibility of administrators; . . . and (4) selection of presidents and deans. . . ." The Director declared that, "the disputed proposals do not constitute mandatory subjects of bargaining and . . . insistence to impasse upon the proposals would be viewed as violative of the bargaining obligation. . . ." *(St. John's Chapter of the AAUP v. St. John's University).* [4] Thus, both state and federal government agencies have begun to clarify the scope of bargainable subjects for educational institutions. Moreover, these decisions sufficiently broadened the scope of management rights to encourage colleges and universities to pursue the matter further.

One of the most critical matters of concern to colleges was the impact of bargaining on faculty senates and the right of a college president to consult with faculty committees other than union representatives. Every labor law, state and federal, requires that a certified union be given the right of *exclusive representation.* In essence, this means that the employer must negotiate exclusively with union representatives and with no one else. As a result, a number of faculty senates, for example, in the state colleges of Pennsylvania and Minnesota as well as in community colleges of New York, either went out of existence or became, in effect, social clubs. Most college presidents, however, refuse to stop normal communications with their faculty senates, leading to constant conflict between union

[4]NLRB Case No. 29–CB–1858 (1975).

officers and senate officers as to who has the right to consult with the campus president about a variety of matters including salaries, budgets, promotion, and appointments. It must be said here that some faculty unions took leadership in strengthening faculty senates by negotiating senatorial responsibilities into the contract. This action had the distinct advantage of giving those senates legal status when originally they were voluntarily established and could be dissolved at the will of the trustees.

Regardless of senatorial recognition or nonrecognition in the contracts, the proper status of a faculty senate on many campuses continued to be a matter of contention between the administration and the union, and it was only a matter of time before the issues would be faced formally by labor boards and courts. The New Jersey Public Employment Relations Commission (NJPERC) made a decision directly affecting the relationships among unions, senates, and management. It came to the conclusion that, "there is no reason why the systems of collegiality and collective negotiations may not function harmoniously."[5] In essence the decision was that except for grievances and terms and conditions of employment, the university could continue normal consultation with the senate about "management functions" which will be described in this chapter. Generalized, this decision indicates that the university can meet and discuss with anyone it chooses about those topics which are not mandatory subjects of bargaining. It is a tremendous boost for administrators who attempt to consult with a variety of people before making significant decisions. For example, a dean may call together a dozen of the most influential professors and consult with them about any management decision he wishes. Since formal negotiations are limited generally to the impact of management decisions on conditions of employment, it leaves the administrator wide latitude in consultation.

The Michigan Employment Relations Commission reached an almost simultaneous decision; the trustees of a university have the right to determine and announce, without consulting a faculty union, a new policy concerning the evaluation of faculty members

---

[5]*Rutgers, The State University v. Rutgers Council of the AAUP*, 2 NJPERC 13 at 15 (1976).

(Central Michigan University v. *the Faculty Association).* [6] Management's right to determine work standards for evaluation of employees was thus upheld. The *impact* of those decisions on working conditions still remains negotiable.

The distinction between a *managerial decision* (nonmandatory or permissible subject of bargaining) and the determination of *procedures* (mandatory subject) will no doubt be a subject of continuing debate, especially when a union attempts to negotiate a share of the final decision. The employer, of course, may refuse to negotiate any demand to diminish its right to make the final decision.

Two Iowa rulings concern this issue *(Bettendorf Community School District and Bettendorf Education Association,* and the *Dubuque Community School District and Dubuque Education Association).* [7] The Iowa PERB ruled that "management has sole discretion to evaluate its employees and determine the substance or essence of that evaluation. In other words, management has the right to establish the criteria or standards upon which its employees shall be evaluated. Employees . . . have the right to negotiate the procedure or manner by which management's evaluation of them is accomplished." The decision went on to say that although the employer had the right to determine unilaterally such matters as an evaluation instrument, a probationary contract, and a job classification, to the extent that these decisions ". . . relate to mandatory items such as evaluation procedures, wages, or hours, bargaining . . . would be mandatory."

Another approach to delineating mandatory and permissible subjects of bargaining is found in Nevada. In an effort to clarify the general provisions of the state's law regarding the scope of bargaining, the labor board made a series of decisions, many of them favorable to labor. The ensuing outcry from public employers became of such political significance that the legislature had to rewrite its law with specific provisions for the scope of bargaining. Section 288.150 of the new law listed twenty mandatory subjects starting with salary, sick leave, and holidays and ending with safety, teacher preparation time, and procedures for reduction in work force. [8] Included among subjects "not within the scope of mandatory

---

[6]MERC Case No. C 74 A–19 (1976).
[7]IPERB Case Nos. 598 and 602 (1976).
[8]51 GERR 3713 (1975).

bargaining and which are reserved to . . . employer . . ." are the rights to hire, fire, direct, assign, transfer, lay off, and to establish such matters as staffing levels, work standards, work loads, and the "means and methods of offering . . . services." Thus, employers are using not only boards and courts but also legislatures to sustain and broaden the parameters of executive decisions.

It is obvious from these judicial and legislative decisions that not only are faculty unions and university management becoming more sophisticated about the parameters of bargaining, but so is the public in general. The widely publicized fiscal crisis of New York City during 1975–1976 focused nationwide attention on public employee unions, including their tactics, political influence, efficiency of public service, and costs. Public attention also centered on public employee strikes. In the fall of 1975, over two million children were out of school as a result of teacher strikes. Firefighters, police, and sanitation workers mounted serious threats to public safety and property in cities such as Kansas City, Cleveland and New York. Transportation unions tied up traffic and slowed vital services in many parts of the country. One of the most publicized employee strikes to date was in San Francisco during the spring of 1976. The citizens there exemplified two important public attitudes by "taking the strike" over a period of several weeks. Public refusal to even attempt to disenfranchise the union reaffirmed the people's general acceptance of the right of public employees to bargain and to strike. At the same time, public support for the city administration's attempt to hold salaries and other costs within reasonable limits clearly indicated the people's desire to meet the powerful influence of unions with equal determination and power. The strike was eventually defeated when the union agreed to go back to work in return for the city administration's promise to withdraw a bill from the Board of Supervisors which would make employee wages subject to ratification by public referendum. A few months later the voters passed a referendum that changed the city's charter, prohibiting strikes and tying salaries of public employees to those in certain other cities in California.

These events chronicle a new era of public-sector bargaining. Public officials, including college and university presidents, are beginning to understand that the public wants them to manage and to manage well and that they should forego few initiatives in collective bargaining unless they intentionally bargain for additional services and benefits from faculty employees and unions. Therefore, academic employers should be optimistic about the bargaining process as a constructive means for achieving institutional goals.

In the early years higher education employers tended to negotiate only those subjects that unions placed on the bargaining table. Thus, they permitted unions to preempt the scope of bargaining. Yet the employer has legitimate means not only to bargain the usual mandatory subjects of bargaining such as hours, wage increases, increased work loads, and greater efficiency of performance, but the employer also has the right to place a "permissible" subject of bargaining (management right) on the table in return for union support of management programs. How this has been done successfully in such institutions as Southeastern Massachusetts University and Temple University is described in later chapters.

Classified Subjects of Bargaining

Permissible Subjects

The word *permissible* in the bargaining context generally refers to management rights, and it means that a permissible subject of bargaining is one that either party can refuse to bargain without being gulity of an unfair labor practice. Unions, of course, may refuse to bargain a management right even when the employer permits it. However, a union spokesperson usually demands that certain management rights be bargained, and it is the employer who either refuses to bargain or bargains at a "price." An analysis of board and court decisions in fourteen states (Academic Collective Bargaining Information Service, 1976b) indicates that the following subjects are broadly accepted as management rights and become subjects of bargaining only when permitted by management:

mission and purpose of the institution
hiring and discharging employees
assignment and transfer of employees
supervision and direction of employees' work performance
employment of substitutes

size of work force, number of employees
retrenchment of funds, programs, number of employees
distribution of resources (funds and employees) to departments
type of organization, reorganization of departments and divisions
emergency executive powers in all matters
overall budget, level of funding, allocation of funds within units
selection and composition of programs
evaluation of programs
changes in programs
evaluation of employee performance
establishment of performance standards
promotion of employees
wages, hours, and work conditions for employees not in the bargaining unit
nonjob-related prerequisites for employees
discipline of employees
employer's business procedures

This is a formidable, but by no means total, list. Some states reserve to the public employer such rights as:

class size
college calendar
teacher evaluation procedures
code of ethics
academic freedom
preparation time for teachers
selection of texts
procedures for granting tenure
right to bargain in public

Massachusetts was the first state to amend its labor law to force the union to bargain the traditional management prerogative of "standards of productivity and performance." Although a management right, colleges and universities have traditionally refused to define faculty standards of productivity or of performance, probably because faculty members perform some broad, indefinable, and immeasurable tasks. To measure a professor's performance only in terms of measurable services is considered by many to be an injustice both to the employee and to the employer. Yet the public demand for economy and better management led to the Massachusetts amendment which, in effect, means that should the employer (the state) place a request on the table to negotiate performance standards, the union must negotiate it in good faith (or vice versa). This does not mean that the union must agree to standards demanded by the state, but it does mean that an accommodation must be reached within the context of the contract. This is a peculiar situation because ordinarily the employer establishes work standards and evaluates employees against those standards. In higher education, however, it is traditional for faculty and administration to agree upon generalized critieria, such as teaching effectiveness, research, and university service; and it usually becomes the duty of *faculty colleagues* to evaluate performance and recommend subsequent appropriate action to the administration. This difference in the higher educational milieu is just one of the many perplexing problems that arise when legislators attempt to intervene directly in the working relationships between college professors and their university employers. To date, public colleges and universities in Massachusetts have all but ignored the amendment with support of faculty unions.

Mandatory Subjects

The generally agreed-upon mandatory subjects include:

grievance procedures, including arbitration
work hours
work loads
hours and work schedules
pensions, unless established by state law
insurance benefits
sick leave and other types of leaves of absence
holidays and vacations

parking space and other perquisites related to employment

procedures for evaluation, retention, promotion of unit employees

procedures for discipline and discharge

union security, except where specifically prohibited by law

wages and salaries, merit increases

safety rules and policies

savings clause

management rights clause

impact of management decisions on work conditions

This last item deserves special discussion. An employer may decide to cut its institutional budget by two million dollars or may decide to cut 10 percent across the board, department by department. These kinds of decisions may be made unilaterally without negotiation or consultation with the union. But the *impact* of the decision on "wages, hours, and terms and conditions of employment" must be bargained on the request of the union. For example, if the administration cuts the budget by two million dollars, and takes one million dollars of the reduction from the instructional budget, the faculty union may try to negotiate an agreement that most of the two million dollars be taken from noninstructional funds. Management does not have to negotiate the one million dollars cut from instruction. However, management does have to negotiate the procedures by which it will arrive at the necessary savings whenever those cuts affect wages, hours, or conditions of faculty employment. The union cannot ordinarily demand a share in determining which programs are to be affected since "programs" and "distribution of resources" are generally held in most states to be a management right. But the union can demand that retrenchment of employees be made on seniority. Before agreeing to such a policy, the administration can demand that it have the right to make exceptions whenever its affirmative action program is jeopardized or whenever it deems the last person hired in a particular department is too important to the instructional program to be fired first. Some institutions try to bargain a retrenchment policy solely on the basis of quality of performance and importance of each employee to the instructional or research program. Unions seldom agree to this plan. Similarly, until they make some accommodation to employers' wishes about quality of program, affirmative action, and wages unions seldom get their wishes about layoffs; they usually prefer layoffs based on seniority, part-time faculty before full-time, and probationary before tenured appointees. Thus, collective bargaining protects fully neither the desires of management nor those of the union, and wisely so. There must always be room for flexibility to resolve the most difficult problems without completely subjecting one party to the wishes of another. To fully understand the options available to an imaginative executive is to increase the scope of institutional leadership and influence. Knowledge, supported by skill and imagination, is truly power at the bargaining table.

Prohibited Subjects

Only a few subjects are completely prohibited from negotiations. Federal law prohibits a *closed shop* in which only members of a union may be candidates for an unfilled position in the university. Many states also prohibit an *agency shop* in which all employees in the bargaining unit must either join the union or pay it a service fee roughly equivalent to union dues. A few states prohibit the bargaining of pension and retirement benefits because they are already stipulated by law. States vary as to whether or not a negotiated contract takes precedence over local ordinances or state law. New Jersey, New York, and Hawaii permit the contract to take precedence over most state laws and regulations, whereas Minnesota takes the opposite view, namely, that contracts must not be inconsistent with existing state laws or regulations.

Such limitations are usually stipulated in the labor law and are well known by both parties. Any limitation, however, is seen by the union as a loss of bargaining power; management generally views limitations as a retention of management authority.

College administrators and negotiators must understand precisely which subjects are mandatory, permissible, or prohibited at the bargaining table; which subjects are likely to be laid on the table by union representatives; what impact the negotiation of each subject may reasonably be expected to have on the quality of programs and of faculty morale; and what compromises will best serve the purposes of the institution. The fact that the administration has the authority to limit the subjects of negotiation can be of immense importance, and this advantage should neither be lightly regarded nor naively handled since union negotiators are generally knowledgeable and skillful in taking advantage of such lapses. Knowledge is power, and power wisely used commands respect and cooperation.

Part II

*F*ew human events can match the ever-changing patterns and pageantry of drama, art, science and craft set in motion simultaneously by table negotiations. To predict even the sequence of pageantry is impossible since every move, word, phrase, or facial expression on one side of the table may trigger meaningful or meaningless responses, happiness or anger, interest or diffidence on the other side. When the number and types of thrusts and parries are unlimited and when the stakes can shift in seconds from the trivial to the crucial, there is only one way to prepare, and that is in great detail for every possible turn of events.

President Hankin, a researcher and practitioner of the bargaining arts, suggests the kinds of data to collect and for what purposes (Chapter Eight). Vice-Chancellor Grede shares with us his 10-years experience as he reviews the pitfalls and continuing impact of clauses bargained in the all-important first contract (Chapter Nine). President Walker and his colleagues describe the art and science of securing union cooperation in pursuing institutional goals as well as union objectives (Chapter Ten). Researcher Leslie and administrator Satryb draw on fact and experience to fashion basic principles for guiding those who seek sound contractual grievance procedures (Chapter Eleven). More than twenty contract administrators helped Kelley

NEGOTIATING THE CONTRACT

⊂⊃⊂⊃⊂⊃⊂⊃⊂⊃⊂⊃⊂⊃⊂⊃

find contract language that may help reduce future grievances (Chapter Twelve), while Lozier researched more than a hundred negotiated contracts for common elements among retrenchment clauses (Chapter Thirteen).

Only Montana law requires the management team to include a student member. Labor attorney Hjort had the unique experience of negotiating three institutional contracts with the help of students (Chapter Fourteen). Neff, another labor attorney, and his associate, Forsyth, take the reader through the difficulty of computing the potential costs of a variety of union demands (Chapter Fifteen). The master philosopher of American dispute settlement, Newman, exposes to the unsuspecting reader his delightful style as well as the viscera of mediation, fact-finding, and arbitration (Chapter Eighteen), whereas negotiator-administrator Dolan-Greene quickly suggests a plan for withstanding a strike in case Newman's philosophy and skill fail to stem the emotional tides of impasse (Chapter Nineteen). Avoiding common errors in discrimination practices and in management rights clauses requires incredible patience and much thought. Chapters Sixteen and Seventeen address these problems.

All of the above suggests, we hope, that style and a sense of humor has almost as much to do with success in bargaining as knowledge and skill.

Joseph N. Hankin

Just as in other phases of collective bargaining, a constructive approach and relationship must be struck in preparing for table negotiations. Mutual respect must pertain, and both sides should be as well prepared as possible in order to earn this mutual respect. Collective bargaining can help the administrator to achieve institutional goals, protect institutional purposes and programs, involve personnel constructively, and keep good relationships with employees during the important contract implementation stages. However, to accomplish these goals, the groundwork must be laid in the earliest stages of preparation for table negotiations. This is especially important when there has been no contract before or when the institution is attempting to regain a constructive relationship with a bargaining agent with which it has already bargained one or more contracts.

Preparing for Table
Negotiations

Solid preparation by the college breeds a begrudging respect and a feeling that the institution means to negotiate in a business-like fashion. Similarly, when the bargaining representative prepares well, the college knows that the union is serious and expects to be taken seriously in discussing proposals which will obtain significant benefits for its members.

This chapter will concentrate on two major areas: selection of team personnel and the type of information needed prior to bargaining.

Selecting Team Personnel

Daniel R. McLaughlin discusses the selection and education of key administrative personnel for collective bargaining (Chapter

Six) and lists many of the characteristics team personnel should possess. However, there are times when one would choose particular personnel for the table team, and other times when these same personnel would be assigned to the back-up team. For example, one eastern institution included both the academic dean and a division chairperson in the bargaining for its third contract, but left both off for the fourth because negative feelings remained after the third round of negotiations that carried over into the ongoing academic relationship during the year and made curriculum development and instructional evaluation more difficult. It was felt that the value of having these two key persons at the table was outweighed by their inability to recoup the positive relationship they had with the faculty prior to that round of negotiations. Their qualifications and talents, however, could be well-used (and were) as members of the back-up team in analyzing proposals of both sides.

Flexibility is important. Using what works and changing things around in order to effect better combinations of talent for different occasions is also essential. The team should reflect the administrative style and structure of the institution. If management is participative, then there are some real advantages in involving a larger number of people in one capacity or another (not necessarily at the table). On the other hand, some institutions feel more comfortable in involving as few individuals as possible in the key decisions. Most institutions have found that smaller teams provide better confidentiality and flexibility, and some try to give the impression that the administrative team is outnumbered. Probably not more than three to five people should serve on the team. A back-up team, comprised of subcommittees to study particularly knotty issues, is never, or rarely, present. Whatever works best for the institution on a year-round basis should be used. The size of the team should reflect the circumstances of the bargaining "this time," the success the institution may have had in the past, and the comfort and ease with which the chief characters in the case can work with large or small numbers of individuals.

Who should be included on the bargaining team? Conventional wisdom suggests board members, commissioners, legislators, presidents, and deans should not be included. For example, deans and presidents have to deal on a daily basis not only with the union team members but also with the whole faculty. It is very easy for the faculty to associate the dean and the president with the adversary at the bargaining table. A natural faculty antipathy toward administrators may be seriously augmented and reinforced during battle at the bargaining table. Board members who must approve a contract and legislators who must fund it in order to make it effective should help plan the prebargaining strategy and be briefed about what has happened at table sessions, but rarely should they be involved directly in the negotiations. Everyone else is often ignored when they are at the table. The result can be the removal of a healthy buffer between negotiators and these governing bodies. In addition, board members at the table can create a direct line of communication with union officials that later may disrupt normal governance channels.

The team should include a top-level administrator, not necessarily the dean of the college or the president of the institution. It might be the business manager, or the personnel or labor-relations person, if the institution is large enough to have one. Academic personnel could be represented by a division chairperson or associate dean, depending on how the institution is organized. Use of a division chairperson can also firmly establish this level of administrator as a contributing part of the administrative team. Perhaps the director of institutional research could also serve on the table team. In future years there will be increased pressure to have students present at the table, although not necessarily on the team, and to have negotiations open to the public. This team could be joined by legal counsel and other specialized personnel; this is usually the case if the institution is a public one and the local or state governing unit wants to protect its investment. In fact, governmental agencies frequently do the actual bargaining for public institutions, and the institution may not be able to control who is present at the table. Finally, the increasing complexity of table negotiations would suggest a professional negotiator for both sides. However, the disadvantage of a professional negotiator is that management and union have to live with a contract which they did not negotiate. Perhaps the answer to this dilemma is to create a high-level opening in the administration and employ a trained negotiator who can also serve as chief contract and personnel administrator. This type of position is becoming commonplace.

The characteristics of individuals selected for the table team are very important. They should be able to remain objective under stress. They must keep some aspect of dialogue going and avoid saying "no" too directly and creating an impasse. Negotiating is a tremendously time-consuming task—not only the sessions themselves, but also the preparation. Individuals must be able to devote a great deal of time to both aspects. They must control their temper. They should be persuasive, patient, logical, analytical, and skilled in clear, direct prose. They must be familiar with negotiations procedures and with the entire organization and community. A sense of humor is particularly helpful. Each team member must be detached, refrain from personalizing the issues, and have a good sense of timing. A close relationship must exist between the team and the administration. Team members should be able to listen and read cues. They should be outgoing and tactful but firm. These individuals have to make each side think it is the winner; they must be respected. They will need physical stamina. They also must have the authority from the board and the president to bargain with firmness and finality. Finding all these qualities in one individual may seem impossible, but these are the primary characteristics to be sought. "The Compleat Negotiator," according to 17th and 18th century manuals on diplomacy, "should have a quick mind but unlimited patience, know how to dissemble without being a liar, inspire trust without trusting others, be modest but assertive, charm others without succumbing to their charm, and possess plenty of money and a beautiful wife while remaining indifferent to all temptation of riches and women" (Ikle, 1976).

Members of the back-up team should have many of these same characteristics for several reasons. They may be called upon to take the place of a negotiator who is absent. This year's back-up team member may sit at the table next year. Back-up team members often become part of subcommittees to analyze issues and save valuable table time. The back-up team will frequently discuss all of the proposals from both sides and provide additional insights than would otherwise be available.

There should be several preliminary meetings of the entire team (table and back-up) for determining both strategy and tactics. One spokesperson should be designated for the team and should be given authority to control comments from the team members and to make contractual offers. Unplanned statements by someone other than the individual so selected should be considered as commentary only and not as authoritative commitments.

The importance of controlled internal communications to the board, the president, the faculty, and other employees who must be kept informed during negotiations should be stressed at these meetings. This should not be left entirely to the bargaining representative. Of course, the institution has to be careful not to commit any unfair labor practices in doing so, but information given to the faculty should not be all one-sided or in response to what has already been made public.

Employer proposals should be thoroughly discussed at an early meeting. They should be cogent, important, easily defended, well thought out, and discussions should ensue about the strategy of presentation. Above all, no proposal should be so ill-conceived or ill-presented as to draw the ridicule of the union representatives. All work emanating from the administration's team should be work behind which the institution can unite.

Information Needed in Preparation and at the Table

Administration and union teams should keep bargaining books including three classes of information: background documents, external data (comparisons with similar institutions), and internal data.

Background Documents

1. laws, charters, and constitutions
2. existing regulations, by-laws, and policy manuals
3. interpretations of laws and regulations
4. other contracts from nearby institutions
5. grievance records and arbitration reports
6. fact-finding reports and interpretations and analyses
7. current contract

Because bargaining representatives will be in touch with one another and attempt to whipsaw benefits already won at other institutions, it is important for employers to be thoroughly familiar with developments elsewhere. Nothing is so effective as being able to counter a demand for a reduced teaching load by comparing teaching loads and other faculty responsibilities at the college with comparable institutions.

External Data

1. proportion of faculty with advanced degrees by type of institution
2. average base salaries and relationships of instructional staff (see, for example Tables 1 and 2 at the end of the chapter).
3. instructor, assistant professor, associate professor salaries and as percent of professorship salary (see Table 3).
4. benefits as percent of salary and dollar value
5. compensation beyond base salary
6. minimum, maximum, and average class sizes and exceptions (see Table 4).
7. course load and overload compensation (see Table 5).
8. summer and evening compensation (see Tables 6 and 7).
9. adjunct faculty compensation versus overload compensation
10. contract increases versus Consumer Price Index increase
11. length of academic year
12. other salary information (see Table 8).
13. comparative financial status information, such as tables, charts, and graphs to show:
    a. the amount and rate at which revenues and expenditures have been increasing or decreasing
    b. cost per student data
    c. percentages spent on instruction, salaries, benefits, and administration
    d. faculty-student ratios
14. faculty retention and turnover rate
15. data on assessable base

Presenting a great deal of little-known information about faculty benefits is effective. Thorough grounding and preparation pays dividends in respect and makes the bargaining representatives feel that, in turn, they must be thoroughly prepared.

Internal Data

1. average salary by rank
2. benefit cost per individual in each rank for
   a. retirement
   b. health insurance
   c. dental insurance
   d. Social Security
   e. liability insurance
   f. workmen's compensation
3. average adjunct load by rank
4. advanced degrees by rank
5. quantity and usage of leave benefits
6. analysis of increments, such as dates due, number at each step, and cost
7. class size and number above norm
8. enrollment by department and curriculum faculty member

Lists like these are meaningless without seeing the data; see sample copies in the tables at the end of the chapter.

A number of other questions and details must be considered before bargaining begins. Should bargaining take place at the college? Faculty bargaining representatives often want negotiations to take place away from the college. They may feel at a disadvantage having the bargaining on the home grounds of the institution. Others prefer negotiations at the campus because of the ease of transportation and finding faculty members available. What should the seating arrangement be? The seating of collective bargaining representatives has often been fraught with tension and argument. Should there be privacy? Many feel that public negotiations tend to be performances and that there should be privacy. How shall the agenda and the timetable be established? There probably should be a firm timetable to avoid stalling and frustrations on either side. Recordkeeping is essential. Notes are better than minutes or tape recordings. Notes help to pinpoint the moment of agreement or other specifics in case there is later controversy. It is not wise to announce the demands and the progress because the final agreement may be compared with the starting position. However, publicity is often used to some advantage, especially in forcing settlement.

Postnegotiation implementation should be decided early. It should be decided, for example, who is going to duplicate the contract and how many copies should be made. Finally, the institution should attempt to estimate the goals—what it is trying to reach in the final agreement. The team should be working toward some specific package.

There are three levels of bargaining: what management would like, what the union would like that management could live with (the retreat or fall-back position), and what is unacceptable, a no retreat issue. The administration should set realistic goals. Each negotiator should place himself in the other negotiator's shoes to understand his problems. There is an old school debater's motto that he who knows only his own side, knows little. It is important for individuals on both teams to know or make educated guesses about what the other side is going to say. The team should know at the outset the total package and price the institution can offer in the end. Items cannot be negotiated in isolation from the total financial picture, but too frequently they are. Bargaining from the budget favors the administration, especially in these days of tight dollars. The better the institution prepares now, the better the negotiations will go, the easier it will be to live with the contract, and the better the next negotiations will go.

TABLE 1
Average of Estimated[1] Percentages of Full-Time Teaching Faculty
with Advanced Degrees, 1976

	Masters as Highest Degree	Doctorates	Total of Both
Our Community College[1]	78.2	10.6	88.8
(19) State Community Colleges	79.3	9.8	89.1
(8) Urban Community Colleges	Data Not Available		
(5) Public (4-yr.) Colleges in Nearby States	41.5+	55.7	97.2+
(13) Private (4-yr.) Colleges Nearby	29.7	67.4	97.1
(5) Private—Ivy League	4.9	95.7+	99.6+

[1]SOURCE: Telephone conversations with respondents January through April 1976.

TABLE 2

Base Annual Salaries (Weighted Averages), 1975–1976[2]

	Source/Time Effective	Instructor	Assistant Professor	Associate Professor	Full Professor
Our Community College	1975–1976 Survey	$14,595	$20,613	$26,605	$31,002
(25) State Community Colleges	1975–1976 Survey	$12,451	$16,293	$19,497	$26,008
(8) Urban Community Colleges	Data for current academic year not available				
(4) Public Colleges in Nearby States	1975–1976 AAUP Survey Responses	$13,114	$15,847	$20,361	$27,033
(14) Private Colleges Nearby	Same as Above	$13,021	$20,613	$26,605	$31,022
(8) Private—Ivy League	Same as Above	$13,154	$16,064	$26,605	$31,022

[2]Adjusted to ten-month basis as necessary for comparison with our community college.

TABLE 3

Base Annual Salaries (Weighted Averages), 1975–1976
Lower Ranks' Salaries as Percentages of Professors' Salaries

	Source/Time Effective	Instructor	Assistant Professor	Associate Professor
Our Community College	1975–1976 SUNY Survey	47.1	66.5	85.8
(25) State Community Colleges	1975–1976 SUNY Survey	47.9	62.6	75.0
(8) Urban Community Colleges	1975–1976 data not available			
(4) Public Colleges in Nearby States	1975–1976 AAUP Survey Responses	48.5	58.6	75.3
(14) Private Colleges Nearby	Same as Above	42.0	66.4	85.8
(6) Private—Ivy League	Same as Above	47.0	66.4	85.8

TABLE 4
Work Load Provisions Affecting Full-Time Faculty
at Nearby Colleges: Class Size, Preparations[3]

College	Class Size	Preparations per Semester
College 1	Set by Dean, grievable, maximum of 25 in Freshman English	2
College 2	30 normal, 25 in English Composition	3 maximum
College 3		3 maximum per quarter
College 4	Adhere to 1973–1974 maximums, may increase any class by up to 3 students	3 maximum
College 5	Variable: 16–35	2–4
College 6	25	3
College 7	Recommended by Dean	3
College 8	Norm of 30, maximum overload by ⅓ of norm	3

[3]SOURCE: State Agency Annual Report

TABLE 5
Work Load Provisions Affecting Full-Time Faculty
Credit and Contact Hours[4]

College	Standard Semester Credit Hours or	Work Load Contact Hours	Maximum per Year
College 1	26 per year	33 per year	720 student credit hours
College 2		14, 15, or 16 English, 12	30 contact
College 3	15	18	47 teaching credit hours or 56 contact hours (trimester schedule)
College 4	18 teaching hours maximum		Maximum 60 teaching hours over 2-year period, maximum 32 in 1 year
	English, 15 teaching hours maximum		24 teaching hours
College 5	Lecture only Combined lecture and laboratory Physical education		12–26 hours 15–30 hours 18–36 hours
College 6			30 credit or 40 contact
College 7			30 credit (all except English)
College 8	15		Teachers with 6 or more composition classes: 25 credit maximum

[4]SOURCE: State Agency Annual Report

TABLE 6
Evening Compensation[5]

College	Compensation Basis	Rate of Payment for Evenings and Overloads			
		Instructor	Assistant Professor	Associate Professor	Full Professor
College 1					
(Part time)	Credit hour	$263	$301	$339	$376
(Full time)		$202	$232	$261	$290
College 2	Net Contact Hour	—	—	—	—
College 3	Credit hour	$300	$338	$383	$432
College 4	Teaching hour	$275			
	1/60 th of current annual salary				
College 5	Contact hour	$210	$230	$260	$300
College 6	Contact hour	$290	$310	$330	$350
College 7					
(Part time)	Credit hour	$230	$260	$290	$320
(Full time)	Based on qualifications				
College 8	Credit hour	$260	$275	$290	$305

[5]SOURCE: State Agency Annual Report

TABLE 7
Overload and Summer Session Provisions[6]

College	Other Provisions	Summer Session
College 1	Maximum overload is 3 credit hours per semester. Full-time faculty has preference.	
College 2	Maximum of 3 additional contact hours per semester except by permission of the president.	Same as evening
College 3	Full-time faculty has preference. Some faculty may have evening assignments as part of regular load.	Same as evening
College 4	1 evening course per semester may be required.	Same as evening
College 5	Full-time faculty has preference. Maximum of 2 paid overload courses per semester.	Same as evening
College 6	Maximum of 1 course per semester, 2 per year.	$350 per contact hour section of 10 or more students; $100 per in sections of 5 to 9 students.
College 7		
College 8	Full-time faculty have preference.	Same as evening

[6]SOURCE: State Agency Annual Report

TABLE 8
Salary Schedule — 1975–1976

Instruction	College 1					College 2				
	No. of Pos.	Salary	Min.	Max.	No. of Empl.	No. of Pos.	Salary	Min.	Max.	No. of Empl.
Professors	28	$22,226	$16,782	$23,617	9	29	$19,622	$16,196	$21,410	10
Assoc. Professors	40	19,003	14,360	20,206	9	68	16,841	14,548	19,190	10
Asst. Professors	83	15,013	12,370	17,407	9	69	14,623	12,492	17,003	10
Instructors	11	12,446	10,627	14,953	9	53	12,079	10,620	14,455	10
Asst. Inst./Lect.	6	9,797	8,015	11,278	9	Varies	17.25 hr.			
Tech. and Other Assts.	7	9,549	8,675	10,529	12	13	9,488	8,356	10,809	12
Div. and Dept. Chairmen	22	3,935	1,212	8,132	PT	9	21,511	18,355	24,526	10
Clerical	20	7,157	6,118	8,315	12	22	7,719	7,108	9,110	12
PT Fac. Even. and Sum.	111	1,063 275 cr hr			PT	400	17.25 hr.	16.25 hr.	18.50 hr.	PT
Library										
Chief Librarian	1	17,407	12,371	17,407	9					
Asst. Librarian	6	15,720	13,563	17,454	9	2	14,574	12,492	16,309	10
Library Assts.	1	9,161	8,531	10,651	12	4	12,316	10,620	13,865	10
Clerical	7	7,110	6,253	7,624	12	3	7,459	7,108	9,110	12
Student Services										
Counselor for Dean of Students	7	16,985	12,303	20,206	9/12					

TABLE 9

Overview of Salient Factors in the Compensation of Teaching Faculty
(Differences Between College and Survey Data Shown in Parentheses
as Percentages of Survey Data to the Nearest Tenth)

Institutional Category	(A) (Modal) Course Load	(B) Average Base Salary Four Ranks	(C) B Plus Average Costable Benefits	(D) Average Overload Midrange
Community College	30 co. hrs. Norm (approx. same as 30 cr. hrs. max.)	$23,076	$28,107	$296/co. hr. (333/cr. hr.)[7]
State Community College	(8) 30 cr. hrs. max.	(25) 18,237 (+26.5)	(6) 21,866 (+28.5)	(9) 277/co. hr. (+6.9) (9) 312/cr. hr.
Public (4-yr.) in Nearby States	(1) 24 cr. hrs. max.	(4) 20,208 (+12.4)	benefit data varies widely	(4) no overload
Private (4-yr.) in Nearby Estates	(8) 24 cr. hrs. max.	(14) 24,705 (−6.6)	(13) 28,386 (−0.1)	(9) 319/cr. hr. (+4.4)
Private—Ivy League	no institutional standards	(5) 25,200	(6) 29,560	(6) no overloads

SOURCE: *Previous Tables in this Report*

[7] For purposes of comparison with survey credit-hour data, contact-hour data is converted to credit hours on the basis of the relationship between New York State community colleges credit-hour and contact-hour averages in the same column.

John F. Grede

The growth of faculty unionism in higher education, particularly in the community colleges which represent two-thirds of all the higher education institutions under collective bargaining agreements, has not been a peaceful one. Our own experience in Chicago has included six strikes in five contract periods. Much of this extremism is characteristic of industrial-type unions in urban community colleges, institutions which evolved rapidly under strong administrative direction and control and without the traditions of a career faculty. One may say such institutions are exceptions in higher education. Nevertheless, the successful patterns of union organization in which material benefits have been improved have

Negotiating the
First Contract

been, in large measure, the result of the adoption of the industrial model, a union external to the institution but dependent on it. These success patterns may very well expand to all of higher education despite the desire for what some call a collegial model of collective bargaining.

What then do we seek? One goal was identified, although for private business and industry, in 1946 at the height of discussions on the emerging Taft-Hartley legislation which sought to respond to a rash of violence and unsettled relations between management and labor in the early post-World War II years. Yale labor economist E. Wight Bakke saw then the goal of mutual survival when he pointed out that unfortunately both labor and management are concerned primarily with individual survival (Bakke, 1946, p. 82). The process of negotiations and all relationships between the two parties seeks to preserve for each its own "structure of living." This goal takes precedence over institutional peace. Some accommodation for these drives for individual survival is essential to continued existence of labor and management as free institutions. Alternatively, public control through legislative or governmental agency action will impose peace. Accommodation of survival needs of both parties as an alternative to imposed institutional peace is probably as realistic and timely a need today for the public sector, including higher education, as Bakke saw it for the private sector in 1946.

Institutional peace and effective working arrangements between labor and management do not necessarily preclude conflict which, in itself, is not always destructive. Basic differences in objectives, traditions, and perceptions usually exist between faculty and administration. If the differences were not obvious, they have been made so by the survival needs of the external faculty union patterned after the industrial model. But differences and conflicts must be contained without bringing either party to its knees. "Peace in industrial relations is best defined in Sumner's phrase, as a state of antagonistic cooperation. Although pursuing each his own interest, the parties recognize their mutual dependence upon each other, agree to respect the survival needs of the other, and to adjust their differences by methods which will not destroy but rather improve the opportunities of the other." (Bakke, 1946, p. 81).

Defining the goal was simple. What needs to be done to establish and maintain the mutually beneficial relationship, the equilibrium of antagonistic cooperation, is more complex. Bakke's formula was to determine as objectively as possible the reasons for the behavior of the other party without necessarily approving that behavior and from this basis to determine one's own pattern of action. Implicit in this approach was an emphasis on knowing why the other behaves as he does rather than making judgments about how he ought to behave.

With this thesis in mind, it would probably be useful to treat the negotiation of the first contract in terms of how it can aid in mutual acceptance of the process and in tandem movement toward the goal of cooperation, be it antagonistic or otherwise. One caution should be advanced. There are no simple answers, no certainties, no pat formulas. What works in one constituency may not be effective in another. What seems to produce results in a first contract may not necessarily be appropriate for a second, third, or fourth contract. The time, place, and climate of negotiations vary as do the personalities of the individuals involved.

Contract Rationale

Negotiating Mutual Contract Obligations

Before discussing the kinds of details that make a contract agreeable to both sides with a minimum of adversarial relations, it is important to understand some basic perceptions of the nature of the contract, perceptions gleaned from experience over a ten-year period and five contracts. The first contract is important because it becomes the foundation for other contracts, and because the union regards it, not as an agreement between the board and the union, but as the union's own, something that it has expended much time and effort to get, and perhaps even has gone through a strike and lost wages to secure. It is a kind of Magna Charta, a document surrounded by great emotion and defended almost as an article of faith. Such reverence is not misplaced, since the contract typically binds the board much more than it does the union. The board started with everything and the union started with nothing; anything the union gets is what the board has given it. Thus, it is the board, not the union, which agrees to perform certain functions, to provide guarantees. Boards provide credibility for the union's assertion that the contract is its own, since in very few areas do they obligate the union and, through the union, the faculty. For example, the board commonly agrees not to institute reprisals after a strike. The Chicago experience indicates that to maintain discipline in its ranks, the union is much more likely to punish its own faculty members for crossing picket lines or for engaging in other noncooperative actions than the board is likely to discriminate against faculty for prounion activities. Should not both parties be bound to forego reprisals? The answer is, of course, that the institution must negotiate an agreement that forbids either party to engage in reprisals. The union should be obligated to the contract in the interests of making it a more balanced document in return for improvements in salary and fringe benefits and for expanding faculty involvement in governance and decision making. A few important faculty obligations that could be specified are:

1. student advisement
2. regular evaluation of teaching effectiveness
3. productivity as measured by credit hours generated or course completions
4. nonabuse of academic freedom in the classroom
5. effective limitations on outside employment
6. reasonable availability on campus
7. provision for faculty substitute service as a professional obligation and without compensation
8. participation in regular inservice education
9. acceptance of limitations on seniority when student welfare is affected

One potentially useful contract provision, as evidenced in the Chicago contract (Agreement, 1977, p. 52), is a reciprocal grievance arrangement by which the board may file a grievance against the union. To date, this provision has been used very sparingly, in large part because the union is scarcely obligated under the contract. An effective mutual grievance procedure would make a better balance in the obligations of both parties and a more positive attitude toward the contract by the board as well as the union.

Although this concept of mutual obligation sounds reasonable, there is a caution. It is standard operating procedure in negotiations *not* to propose something that administration has an inherent managerial right to require anyhow. If such is proposed and not won, it is commonly assumed in arbitration that the administration believed it did not initially have that right or else it would not have sought it through negotiations. The goal is probably worth the risk, however. Furthermore, some recent court decisions are defining managerial rights, including employment and tenure, as virtually absolute and incapable of being given away (*Board of Trustees of Junior College District No. 508, County of Cook* v. *Cook County College Teachers Union Local 1600, et al.*).[1]

Negotiating a Living, Adaptable Agreement

Not only is the contract regarded as the union's, but the union commonly represents it as a rock, a shield, an unchanging guardian of faculty rights and privileges. In the last round of negotiations in Chicago, the union never failed to charge the board with attempts to erode the contract. The union saw nothing inconsistent in accretions, adding limitless proposals, some 105 in the last series of table talks. However, the board, particularly after several contracts, tends to see the agreement as a more flexible instrument to be amended or adjusted as circumstances, particularly economic circumstances, change. The view is comforting if one is trying to get back some things already given away; after four or five contracts the union should have negotiated some arrangements that it can afford to give back in order to work under more peaceful, cooperative arrangements. After all, the union can benefit from cooperative efforts as much as the institution.

Because of this very protective union attitude toward the contract, it may be extremely difficult to remove an item or change language once it is part of the agreement. In addition to the protective approach of the union, language tends to become fixed because it is the basis for grievances, particularly for arbitration cases. Arbitration decisions, in effect, constitute interpretations of the language in the contract. Some fifty arbitration cases as well as a dozen court decisions in the Chicago experience related directly to specific written language in the contract. Consequently, there is a reluctance on both sides to change contract language because of its effect upon interpretations established by arbitration decisions.

Ideally, the contract language should be rather general, permitting flexibility in operational interpretations as conditions change.

[1] 343 N.E. 2d 473 (1976).

Such general language, however, is indicative of an atmosphere of mutual trust. In adversarial situations in which emotions run high, there is a strong tendency to be as specific as possible and include minute details in the language. Thus, the size of the contract directly reflects the specificity of language and tends to be inversely proportional to the amount of mutual trust.

The importance of contract language, particularly in the negotiation of the first contract, means that much of the discussion at the table as well as in caucuses deals with interpretations and implications of the wording in a proposed contract provision, and there are some advantages in this situation. Our own experience indicates that sections of the contract which were readily agreed on and about which there was little controversy during negotiations, often proved to be the most troublesome in application. On the other hand, where there were many discussions, proposals, and counterproposals, the wording was subject to much closer scrutiny, and there has been less postcontractual dispute. For example, the Chicago contract provides that every effort will be made to avoid programming of faculty members for more than two classes in a row. In grievance hearings the union has argued that this provision was meant to apply at the option of the faculty member in order to prevent his being imposed upon by the administration. The board, however, believed that the intent was to provide, at the administration's option, a schedule of classes that permitted time for teacher preparation between classes and that would keep teachers on campus available for office hours and faculty meetings. A few words added to the provision could have clarified the issue, but since there was minimum discussion during negotiations, the opposing perceptions of this particular clause were never aired.

The importance of contract language calls for some kind of a specialist in the area, perhaps a labor attorney. Such a specialist needs to be on hand during the first contract development so that the langauge incorporates the flavor of negotiations. If the relationship between the two teams is a compatible one and if the pace of negotiations permits, then perhaps a non-negotiating editing team organized to work simultaneously with negotiators would be of great help in preventing future misinterpretations.

Organization

Administration commonly enters the collective bargaining process at an unnecessary disadvantage because of a casual attitude toward organizing. Administrative representatives are often hostile to the very thought of collective bargaining. Its approach is to wait and see what the union comes up with before making preparations. It is amazing how much the union prepares for negotiations and how much expertise it brings to the process. The large training network currently in operation by the national public employee organizations, particularly teacher organizations, to prepare local negotiators virtually ensures a well-prepared, disciplined, aggressive union team at the negotiating table.

The administration's preparation for the first contract negotiations should be in the hands of professional personnel administrators who are capable of handling the table talks as well as the routines of the personnel office. For future contracts, inhouse personnel who have had legal training and experience are more promising than outside negotiators hired on a temporary basis. Such an inhouse professional staff provides the negotiations team with enough status to override special interests of academic deans and department chairpersons and to work out with the principals, probably board members, a clear and understandable set of parameters for the negotiations process. Such a team must enjoy an easy working relationship with board members since parameters established at the beginning must be reviewed periodically because of changing conditions at the table and the economic and political climate of the public arena. Away from the table the table team is negotiating with its own board about as much as it is with the union team at the table. There is a kind of vertical negotiations process going on between the management table team and its superiors simultaneously with a horizontal process of negotiations with the union representatives across the bargaining table.

A personnel unit specifically organized to handle negotiations and employee relations is essential to provide continuity, to tie negotiations and contract administration into an inseparable process, and to handle the technical details of grievances and arbitration in a routine and nonpolitical fashion. The assignment of grievances to a nonacademic office should reduce conflict between deans and their faculties and, at the same time, assure more objectivity in the adjudication of their differences.

Mental Preparation for the First Negotiation

The attitude with which the team approaches negotiations is important. Negotiators must be mentally and emotionally prepared for a time-consuming, expensive, and initially frustrating experience with endless communications, correspondence, and records, for a process that will be continuous and probably expanding even after the contract is signed. They also must be prepared for sessions where charges, threats, table pounding, and name calling punctuate the discussion. They should expect sensitivity about status, even on what appear to be small items. These kinds of activities are not new to administrators, and many can see the process as a game of wits not unlike a debate.

Management teams which include administrators who were former teachers may be unwittingly sympathetic. More commonly, however, administrators and board members tend to see the union as curtailing management rights and making the job of running a college much more difficult. As a result, their attitudes tend to be continuously antagonistic.

The obviously ideal approach is a balance between the extremes. A consistently antagonistic attitude creates a tremendous barrier to effective communication and destroys any leverage a team may have by varying the tone of approaches and responses to the opposite side. We have seen this kind of leverage, sometimes called the "roller coaster method," used very effectively by the union team which before lunch may be a roaring lion but which may come back after lunch all sweetness and light. Furthermore, a consistent opposition couched in noncooperative language may be self-defeating. In our last round of negotiations, the union sought to include within the bargaining unit a new category of employees called "Project Personnel–Training Specialists" who are funded on "soft money." These employees follow a different time schedule and require qualifications different from those of the traditional college faculty. The board team was unwilling to identify the total membership of this new group for the union. In its anxiety to do something, even with inadequate information, the union bargained for a wage increase for only part of the new group, not realizing that fully half of the members would be excluded from the wage increase. By its attitude to the union proposal, the board put itself in an untenable position since in giving an increase to only a part of a group which worked together it created a severe morale problem. The board had outsmarted itself in holding back information and had to grant raises to a larger component than the union had bargained for simply in the interests of maintaining some degree of morale and managerial efficiency. The union would accept no blame for inadequate negotiations but claimed all the credit for the final settlement.

Attitudes are singularly significant in setting the pace for the first contract and establishing a precedent for subsequent contracts and for the entire relationship with the union over the years. The Chicago experience shows that by correcting inequities suffered by community college faculties over many years, the board and the administration overextended themselves in the first contract by granting rights and privileges, salary increases, and fringe benefits beyond the expectation of the faculty union negotiators. The union got not only money but important governance concessions which the board has subsequently regretted. These extensive concessions, partly wrested from the board by a very effective strike and partly by a sympathetic, if naive, posture on the part of the board negotiators, set a destructively fast pace for the succeeding four contract negotiations. In essence, too much was given too fast, and the level of union expectations appeared to be totally out of keeping with the board's subsequent ability to give, particularly with the advent of less affluent times. The board has been defensive, if not hostile, in subsequent negotiations because it thinks the first contract was overly generous. The union, on the other hand, has felt obliged to press for more and more, to the irritation of the board, in order to meet increasing expectations of its members and to maintain its credibility as an effective bargaining agent.

In the interest of a continuing, harmonious, and balanced relationship, both sides should consider the first contract and subsequent contracts not as ideal but as an acceptable beginning. Management must keep what it needs to operate effectively and must retain the flexibility to adapt to changing conditions in managing the college. The union must maintain credibility with its constituency without reliance on a continuous series of strikes and work stoppages which move the board to extremes.

In summary, the kinds of actions and attitudes that seem to contribute to mutual acceptance of the bargaining process and the agreement resulting from that process include:

1. mutual board and union contract obligations and responsibilities,
2. a somewhat general, but mutually understood, expression in contract language of those obligations and responsibilities,
3. an accepting attitude on the part of the board's negotiators and the board itself toward the process, as well as a realistic approach on the part of the union negotiators, and
4. a pace of union gains in the first contract that does not create an impossible expectation for future rounds and does not encourage an increasingly defensive "roll-back" attitude on the part of the board.

Contract Content

Scope of Agreement

Some boards, to their regret, have included in the first contract a provision which reads as follows: "During the life of this agreement, the board will continue its existing policies and uniform practices with reference to salaries, fringe benefits, and working conditions of faculty members which are not specifically covered by this agreement." This provision, more commonly used in contracts in the private sector, may expand the contract items to an infinite number of written and unwritten policies, procedures, and practices that have been in effect earlier, even prior to collective bargaining. The board and administration may thus be obliged to continue past practices whether they are specifically covered in the formal agreement or not. A better alternative would be to negotiate a provision, commonly called a "zipper clause," along the following lines: "All matters and items related to salaries, working conditions, and fringe benefits of faculty members in the bargaining unit have been included in the written agreement, and matters or items relating to working conditions, salaries, or fringe benefits not expressly contained in the agreement are not subject to the grievance procedure."

Duration of the Contract

Many faculty contracts include a specific termination date for the contract with a provision for the reopening of negotiations well in advance of that termination date. A union commonly seeks to have the contract continue as long as negotiations are continuing so they do not have to work without a contract. This approach presumes a kind of continuity of contractual relationship which is advantageous if the relationship between the administration and the union is a harmonious one. The alternative, a specific termination date, permits the contract to expire and makes it possible for the board to take unilateral action in emergencies. This alternative results in a highly explosive situation, but it may be the only alternative if the relationship between the two parties is not harmonious.

Most contracts run for two years. In the affluent 1960s, administrations tended to seek longer contracts. With the decline in funding, particularly for community colleges, managements now seek shorter contracts so that salaries can more closely follow funding variations. The union thrust, of course, is often the opposite. One common alternative is to agree upon a two- or three-year contract with a salary reopener at the end of each year. This means that future negotiations are limited to salary only during the life of the master contract.

Automatic Increments and Cost-of-Living Increases

A common practice, particularly in community colleges, is to develop a salary schedule with built-in annual increments granted automatically without any necessary proof of improved faculty proficiency or productivity. Similarly, the cost-of-living increase is automatic. The board gets little or no credit for agreeing to automatic increments and cost-of-living increases in the first contract. It can seldom use them as leverage for negotiating other items in the first contract or in subsequent contracts because the union regards them as already gained and as a basis from which additional wage increases can be negotiated. Much of the union's argument for a cost-of-living increase may be blunted by adjusting the Bureau of Labor Statistics' figures, based on median salaries of all workers, to typically higher faculty salary levels and by making allowance for fringe benefits such as medical and hospital insurance which may already be provided in the contract for the faculty. A firm stand on built-in salary increases is especially important in the first contract to establish a sound base of expectation in future negotiations.

Working Hours

One of the most difficult and sensitive items for administrations to deal with in contract negotiations is that of making sure faculty members are available on campus beyond the bare teaching load requirements. Even though the faculty union argues that professional integrity is impugned by such efforts, after an institution has been under a negotiated contract for a few years, a kind of cultural change takes place, and faculty members tend to abide only by hours specified in the contract. If obligations or hours and days of required physical presence on campus are not specified, it is difficult to take action against the few who set a bad example, and, as a result, the average availability of faculty on campus tends to decline.

The alternative to specific requirements of physical presence on campus is to limit outside employment of faculty. This alternative is less direct, is fraught with complex enforcement problems, and is generally less palatable to faculty. Unions may more readily accept the physical presence requirement in the first contract since it represents little change from traditional professional expectations. If introduced in later contracts, however, it can be viewed by faculty as a distinct loss of privilege and freedom, or even as a severe penalty.

Faculty Qualifications

The assignment of faculty to teach particular courses is normally an administrative function to ensure the best match of faculty qualifications with the requirements of a particular course. It is based on the management right to assign resources in a manner that best serves institutional programs. However, unions try to establish a minimum qualification level and then allocate available extra work, particularly overtime, on a seniority basis. In practice there is a difference between qualified and best qualified, particularly for new courses for which recent practical field experience is essential. Unless this management prerogative is firmly established in the first negotiation, the union will insist that seniority is more realistic than excellence.

Registration

A number of small but potentially significant first contract items may revolve around the nonteaching processes, particularly registration. In the interest of efficient management and maximum service to students, it is important for administration to retain unqualified control of the assignment of faculty members to this function. In its first contract proposals, the union may try to include a restriction on the number of days of registration, a restriction on faculty obligations to participate in the registration process, including what faculty will or will not do. The union may also try to make the cutoff date for final class changes as early as possible. Such union proposals restrict administrative flexibility in organizing and assigning human resources. If this issue is omitted from the first contract, it can appear in future negotiations and become a strong union issue to be used as a negotiating weapon, if not an objective.

Determination of Class Size and Teaching Load

Although the union prefers to have specific limits on teaching load and class size, it is to the advantage of effective administration to have them defined in the first contract in broad terms such as "reasonable" and "proper." There are several reasons for this approach. In practice many classes never reach maximum enrollment if a limit is set in the contract; yet one student over becomes a grievable violation, and the administration never gets the full measure to which it believes it is entitled. Commitment to a specific teacher load creates inflexibilities across semesters when unbalanced loads are needed, and it makes adjustments difficult where laboratory and shop courses have more contact hours than credit hours. Furthermore, limits on class size and teaching load make it difficult to equalize productivity among faculty members. What is most desirable in the first round is to keep such determinations flexible and in the hands of administration with the agreement to be "reasonable." This establishes clear responsibility, a tone of cooperation, and a general goal of excellence for everyone's benefit.

Union Security Measures

A faculty union contract commonly contains a cluster of provisions loosely identified as union security measures. These are particularly prevalent when the union is an external one based on the industrial model. Such a union is an entity which has its own life, its own political drives, and consequently its own maintenance and security needs. Security measures include the dues checkoff, with or without an administrative charge for the service; an agency shop; restrictions on other organizations in the institution; and released time for union functions. The extent to which the administration agrees to these security measures must be measured against the presumed value of a strong union. In general, the administration is advised to be cautious about these items, especially the agency shop, until the union proves over time its concern for, and cooperation in, achieving institutional objectives. Faculty, as a whole, seldom want an agency shop which forces everyone to pay for union services whether he wants to join the union or not. So in the initial stages of bargaining, few faculty would strike to secure agency shop. After several years, a union may have only 30 percent to 40 percent of the eligible people as dues-paying members. Agency shop, therefore, becomes very desirable to the union officers who then, in later negotiations, may be willing to give up substantial gains in salary or governance policies in order to secure more union dues and membership.

These considerations might have been helpful in the early Chicago negotiations in promoting a more effective long-range, cooperative relationship between unionized faculty and administration. They will be valuable in first contract negotiations with any union that is highly organized, brings in sophisticated outside negotiators, or has elected aggressive officers to conduct negotiations. This chapter suggests a calm, calculated response designed to retain administrative flexibility and control and to establish reasonable union expectations in the future. Conceding too much in the early stages does not bring cooperation and a spirit of a common need for excellence; rather, it brings unreasonable expectations for the future and a drive for more power, backed by an organized campaign for outside political support.

Donald E. Walker
David Feldman
Gregory O. Stone

The question of how to achieve institutional goals and academic excellence in spite of collective bargaining is frequently asked, in one form or another, by visitors to the campus of Southeastern Massachusetts University because it was one of the first four-year institutions in the nation to have a collective bargaining contract with its faculty. The question is interesting, for it reveals some built-in assumptions which are difficult to accept. For example, excellence in an institution is usually viewed as faculty, not administration, territory. Obviously, it should be the concern of both. But, the way the question is usually asked implies something different. It implies that lofty improvement goals will not come from the faculty. The goals of the faculty are presumed by the questioner to be self-serving and narrow. The broader goals of excellence must come from the administration. How can the administration, greatly outnumbered, hope to save an institution from mediocrity when

Achieving Institutional
Goals Through
Collective Bargaining

obviously everyone else will be aggressively dedicated to it and the contract will be a structure which guarantees it?

Excellence in an institution is hard to define. John Gardner (1961) points out that what may be excellence for one institution may not be excellence for another. Excellence is relative. However, many institutions in the United States are commonly accepted as excellent, whereas others are not. What separates them? Several factors do, some very special. But certainly the following items are nearly always present: (1) a high percentage of publishing research scholars, (2) heavy faculty involvement in the decisions of the institution, but most notably curricula decisions, (3) high salaries, (4) a relatively longer list of Nobel prize winners or other distinguished scholars than other institutions, (5) a rather rigorous set of standards of what constitutes scholarly achievement and an understanding as to how those standards will be applied in retaining or rewarding faculty members serving the institution, (6) students of exceptional quality who probably excelled in secondary school to qualify and who will continue to excel after they graduate, and (7) perhaps a general feeling that makes people inside and outside it perceive the institution as excellent.

There is no evidence that any of these characteristics of institutional excellence is inhibited by collective bargaining. Circular reasoning similar to that of some early California judges is often heard about item (7). These distinguished gentlemen wrote decisions arguing that Orientals were intellectually inferior because, during their time of residence in California, they had given no evidence of being able to sustain a complicated, Western-type civilization. After all, no Chinese at that time were recognized in the West as scholars, doctors, judges, or industrial tycoons. Similar faculty reasoning regarding collective bargaining appears to be extant in the literature and at many institutions. Harvard and Berkeley are not visibly unionized; therefore, it is argued in reverse, if they were unionized, they would not be Harvard and Berkeley.

If this sounds a little too didactic and sure-footed, it is only because an attempt must be made to create a balance to that persistent point of view that somehow collective bargaining means the end of academic excellence. Contracts can stifle creativity, but they do not have to. One must be sensitive but not overwhelmed by the possibility that the union contract is cramping individuality and hurting the school.

We have heard such complaints. They come from a minority, but certainly a minority which must be taken seriously. However, when the complaints are examined closely, case by case, another cause is usually found. What really stifles creativity and initiative are budgets so tight that faculty members cannot be spared to do anything except teach the courses they have always taught, personal squabbles and jealousy within departments, territorial struggles between departments, and individual goals that have little relation to institutional goals. These problems are found in any academic institution. They do not arise from the presence or absence of collective bargaining. In fact, a properly designed contract can attack some of these problems, reduce debilitating personal conflict, and provide an atmosphere in which individual institutional politicking is decreased and intellectual pursuits increased. If some aspect of a contract is really stifling intellectual growth, that aspect is cause of genuine concern. Administrators should take it up informally in one of the regularly scheduled meetings with faculty union leadership.

Positive Force Toward Goal Attainment

Collective bargaining can be a positive process for achieving institutional goals. We agree with Cohen and March (1974) when they speak of a university as being an "organized anarchy" meaning that a university's goals grow out of a loose collection of ideas. The university tends to discover its preferences through action rather than on the basis of predetermined preferences. Academics are not quite as cerebral as we would like to pretend.

It would be nice to say, for example, that the grievance procedure at Southeastern Massachusetts University was the result of applying a brilliantly conceived plan (the administration's, of course) to a pressing problem. It was not. When we started out, neither the administration nor the faculty really knew precisely what it wanted in a grievance procedure. There was, however, a guiding philosophy of letting people solve their own problems. Neither side had a preference. So, we developed a procedure we thought we could live with; then, through the experience of living with it, we began to discover what each side preferred. The procedure was modified accordingly. Now, we have a process based on a jury of peers that avoids the obvious pitfall of having the grievance committee, in part, consisting of administrators. This latest incarnation works, but it is viewed as just that—the latest incarnation. More experience may dictate more changes. This principle can be applied broadly to the entire contract. *The first contract should be viewed as a trial and kept flexible.*

McGill and Wooton (1975) of Southern Methodist University speak of "third-sector" organizations having three distinct characteristics: They institutionalize activism, defer their own problems in preference to solving problems of others, and have goal ambiguity. We feel these three traits apply to the typical academic institution. Certainly, the antiwar movement of the 1960s grew into institutionalized activism. How often have universities with many problems of their own reached out in an attempt to solve a problem of the larger community? More than one college or university, beset with its own problems, got involved in the Civil Rights Movement and ignored internal matters. Academics seem to thrive on developing lists of goals. It is impossible to get several hundred highly intelligent, well-educated individuals from a wide variety of disciplines and interests to agree to goals and issues.

It is this organized anarchy and goal ambiguity that makes flexibility crucial in developing institutional goals. *As a general rule, a contract should not be too specific. Forcing specific time-related goals into a collective bargaining contract or letting groups, such as faculty, trustees, or students, abuse the contract through special demands, makes the contract inflexible.* Specific goals show a disregard for the nature of a collective bargaining contract within the university. The contract should not be regarded as a document to be constantly adjusted, although it should remain open—especially during the first few years. Although a contract can contain items subject to change as experience dictates, it should include items that are fixed. A contract more closely parallels a constitution. In fact, it is a good idea to get into the habit of referring to it in these terms. Perhaps if we did, we would stop denying that academic institutions are like industry, while we draw up contracts patterned after industrial models.

Goal Generation

Before getting into detail about goals, it is best to take a look at how they are generated. The first step is to recognize that goals come from a variety of sources. Administrators are not the only ones concerned with institution-wide goals. Many others have legitimate concerns. If the institution's goals are not clear, the faculty, the students, the nonacademic staff, and even the trustees should be consulted. It is one of the major tasks of a university president to be able to recognize the legitimate concerns of the variety of special interest groups on campus and to get these groups to understand one another.

A faculty member has one perspective of the university which is based largely on his field of expertise; a student's perspective is based on his career and life needs; a trustee is concerned with keeping peace and promoting progress in a diverse community; and the community which supports the university or college wants to get the most out of its investment. The university cannot be turned over to any single group, and many presidents see their main task as constantly trying to balance these groups and help them recognize the legitimate interests and relationships of each to the others. Collective negotiations can be a powerful instrument in encouraging these diverse groups to work together, to develop goals for the university that reflect its diverse concerns and constituencies.

A university, in many respects, is a pluralistic, democratic community. Authority and power is divided, although the legal structure does not reflect these divisions. The legal structure locates authority and power in the hands of trustees. But, in a society based increasingly on expertise and in institutions heavily dependent upon expertise, authority and power often fall to those who possess expert knowledge. Students also have a relevant interest. They are both a product and a part of the process and, as such, should be consulted. However, conflict occurs between where power and authority are dispersed and where they are legally assigned. A collective bargaining agreement can rectify this disparity by recognizing this division of authority and power.

Goal Attainment Through Bargaining

In an effort to find the smoothest way for the university to function, we, at Southeastern Massachusetts University, have used the collective bargaining process. Our contract recognizes faculty expertise by giving faculty the authority to make meaningful recommendations regarding the future of their colleagues in terms of promotion and tenure. The contract was not drawn up merely out of a sense of symmetry or because administrators were trying to be diplomatic. It was drawn up because it works best for us.

Two provisions of the Southeastern Massachusetts University contract reflect this philosophy. First, each department elects its own chairperson for a term of three years. All department members are eligible to vote and the voting is by secret ballot. If the department members are dissatisfied with the performance of the chairperson, they can have that person removed by 30 percent of the department members signing a recall petition to hold a recall election. If two-thirds of those voting vote for recall, the chairperson is removed and a new election is held to elect another. Second, the contract requires each department to establish an evaluation committee composed of its entire tenured faculty. Each year, this committee is required to evaluate department members for retention, tenure, and promotion by contractually prescribed criteria. The committee's recommendations are forwarded to the department chairperson, who is also contractually required to evaluate the individuals by the same criteria. Upon completion of this process, each individual is called in by the department chairperson and given a copy of these two sets of recommendations. The individual has the opportunity to add materials, or the individual can file a grievance against either the recommendations of the department chairperson or the department evaluation committee. Such a grievance is heard by a college-wide academic council composed of one faculty member elected from each of the departments in the college. A copy of their findings and recommendations must be forwarded to the department, the alleged grievant, and the president of the university for his action. The grievance and findings become a part of the individual's record.

Every effort is made to keep clear lines of distinction. Students, for example, evaluate a faculty member's *teaching* performance in the classroom. They are not involved in assessing his value as a scholar or researcher or his contribution to the university or community. Faculty evaluate the scholarship of a department chairperson, but the dean formally evaluates him as an administrator.

We feel that this system works because people closest to the problem can usually make the best assessments, not only because of their proximity to the problem, but also because if they have significant input into the decision-making process, they will be more enthusiastic about implementing whatever decision is made. In short, they own both the problem and the solution. *Thus, the bargaining process is used to assign responsibility where legitimate (albeit de facto) authority exists and where it can be exercised more effectively for the good of the entire academic community.*

This example illustrates the kinds of goals that can be part of a collective bargaining contract. Everyone is interested in excellence. However, it is difficult for individuals to perform at their best when they are frustrated by their environment and when they believe their performances will be arbitrarily and unfairly judged. *One of our basic goals has been to create an atmosphere in which individuals can function best by assuring themselves of due process through grievance procedures.* The contract is extremely helpful in this process as well. Too many academic institutions run on the "Old Boys Club" model. It is often difficult for a young faculty member, whose philosophical and political views differ from the department chairperson's, the dean's, or a trustee's, to get promoted. Without clearly defined procedures and regulations, administrators can overlook good research and publication and excellent teaching. The significant fact is that personal, arbitrary action hurts both the individual and the quality of the academic community. The university suffers not only from the loss of a valuable individual, but also because it will be clear to others that their professional performance is not the only criterion of promotion.

The fruitfulness of the collective bargaining process is that faculty and administrators are given the opportunity to cooperatively reaffirm the institution's mission each time they agree upon procedures for promotion, tenure, and salary increases. For example, if teaching excellence and research and publication are truly goals of the institution, then they should be included in the contract. Regular ways of evaluating research, publication, and teaching and of determining how much each activity counts in a faculty member's record for promotion, pay increases and tenure, should be established.

However, these three activities should not be the only bases for evaluation. If the contract says that research and publication or teaching excellence counts for 50 percent of the total evaluation, the other 50 percent should not be left blank. Some administrators prefer to work out an entire system for judging such things as teaching, research, publications record, service to the university, and service to the community. *Thus, faculty criteria and evaluation procedures may be negotiated into the contract in conformance with the basic goals of the institution.* Such a contract demonstrates to trustees, faculty, and others concerned that the goals they have developed for the institution are being taken seriously.

Other administrators and faculty prefer a more flexible system to better serve the changing needs of their institution. For example, individual contracts can be made a part of the larger contract by establishing ground rules in the main document for drawing these individual contracts. This system gives the administration the opportunity to apportion individual contracts in relation to the institutional goals. That is, if the goal is research and publication, then the majority of individual contracts should emphasize research and publication as the major criterion for advancement.

In an individual contract, the individual is allowed to state his personal goals for the year in terms of research, teaching, and university service. In personal negotiations with administrators, he can agree on the emphasis placed on these various areas as he is judged for advancement. However, this procedure can revert to the "Old Boys Club" atmosphere if adequate safeguards are not provided in the main contract. That is, the main contract should clearly outline who is to negotiate the individual contracts, the type of items that may be included, and the constraints on them. This protects both the individual and the university.

It cannot be emphasized enough that contractually delineated procedures be established that are applied equitably to all and followed by all. Regular procedures are frequently considered a detriment to advancement. They sound terribly bureaucratic. Good procedures should liberate, not confine. Realistic and contractually delineated procedures facilitate due process and justice. They reduce, if not eliminate, debilitating personal conflict and possible court cases. A faculty member who is accorded the same process as others is more likely to perceive the process as fair. People free from undue concern about the personal predilections of their managers are more creative.

One frequently raised point is that the faculty is just interested in a few selfish goals. We do not believe it is. Since both faculty and administration are presumably dedicated to preserving the excellence of the institution, it is essential that each group trust the other's interest in attaining that goal.

Communication and the Trust Relationship

In establishing trust, the most important single tool is open communication. This means no secrets, no surprises. That is not as hard as it may sound. As one colleague is fond of pointing out, "A secret in a university is something you tell to one person at a time." We would add, it is not what people know that hurts an institution. What they don't know—what they suspect—is always far worse than the truth.

Discussing open communication in detail is far beyond the scope of this chapter, but there are a few concrete ways to improve communications between an administration and a faculty union. One effective method is to have regular, informal meetings of the two groups. Such meetings are actually required under our contract to be held on a monthly basis. The faculty union leadership must meet not only with the president, but also with the deans. These meetings serve several purposes. They are not, however, negotiating sessions. They stay informal. Each group learns what is on the other's minds at any particular time. The meetings also build a base for future negotiations. Both sides become aware of what will be the major issue at the next formal bargaining session. That way, no one walks into a major surprise that would otherwise stall negotiations. Both sides also begin to appreciate each other's limitations before formal bargaining begins. *Establishing a system of open communications which prevents surprise is a basic step.*

Such sessions mesh with another principle we try to apply in developing institutional goals and in relating them to the contract. *Contract negotiations are a problem-solving process. We do not want to approach negotiations in an "us against them" frame of mind.* We see problems. We see collective bargaining as a tool that can be used to solve problems. It is not a bludgeon to keep faculty in line, and we hope that the faculty does not see it as merely a shield against the administration. Such a view is one reason why the informal meetings are so necessary. It is only through constant communication that we begin to realize the legitimacy of varying viewpoints and can get down to workable compromises.

Another device that maintains this problem-solving orientation is open communication at the outset of negotiations. There should be no hidden agendas. There should be no extravagant demands. The goal is to come up with a workable contract. This is, of course, contrary to the way bargaining is usually carried out in industry and many educational institutions, and it is contrary to the way some persons on both sides would prefer to negotiate in the university. But we feel that the academic community should avoid tough, adversary-type negotiations as an unrealistic way of dealing with the problems of the university.

The Negotiator and Institutional Goals

We chose to bring in an outside negotiator. This course is not necessarily the best one for everyone, but there are some solid arguments favoring it. Although this person is the negotiator for trustees, he should be knowledgeable in collective bargaining and should have an academic background. Ideally, to understand and relate to the faculty perspective, he should have had experience on a faculty. He should be viewed as a resource person who understands the process. He should have a good relationship with the faculty leadership as well as with the trustees. It is no accident, for example, that when our outside negotiator comes in for a bargaining session, the union leadership picks him up at the airport. In this way, they get the first face-to-face meeting with him. This reinforces communications and the problem-solving mode we are constantly trying to promote.

The choice of an outside negotiator also serves to insulate the academic deans from the actual negotiations. No matter how good these deans may be in their day-to-day relationship with the faculty, they are bound to be a little less objective at the bargaining table. However, such exclusion does not mean isolation. The deans are kept informed about the negotiations and are consulted regularly. They will have to live with the results, and living with the results may be a little easier if their input is real but indirect.

Both the outside negotiator and the president have the role of constantly reminding the participants of the basic philosophy. This means they must remain emotionally aloof. Since neither one has to deal with the day-to-day minor problems involving the contract, they are in a unique position to maintain some emotional detachment. They are the ones responsible for keeping everyone in the problem-solving mode and for seeing that basic goals everyone has agreed to are honestly reflected in the contract. Again, this does not mean writing the goals, per se, into the contract. It means making sure that the contract is constructed in such a way that it sets up procedures which will facilitate the reaching of university goals of excellence.

However, care must be taken *during the negotiations to eliminate from the contract anything that inhibits initiative*. For example, a stringent faculty publication requirement could be written into the contract. But, if the primary mission of the institution is to teach and if research is a secondary mission, an unreal publications requirement in the contract could stifle an excellent classroom teacher and work against institutional integrity and excellence.

Contract Ambiguity—Goal Ambiguity

Finally, both parties should beware of ambiguity. It is impossible to ferret out every ambiguous statement beforehand, but the attempt should be made. *Leaving new or doubtful sections open for further study and negotiation is one way of avoiding this problem.* A three-year contract does not necessarily remain entirely untouched for three years. Regular, informal sessions with administrators and faculty union leadership can show whether or not the questionable sections are really working. If they are not, they should be renegotiated. The contract should not restrict the institution from achieving excellence, nor should the institution restrict the contract. Both should be growing and changing together.

Summary

These are the major points we see in relating academic collective bargaining to goals of institutional excellence:

1. Look on the first contract as a trial. Keep it open and flexible.
2. Do not try to force specific, time-related goals into a document which should be a constitution rather than a con-

tract, and do not allow other campus groups to abuse the contract in this way.

3. Let the bargaining process reflect the legitimate, de facto division of power in the university, and use the contract to assign power and responsibility where it most logically belongs for the good of the entire academic community.

4. Make it clear that in your collective bargaining you are assuring individuals of due process. Include fair grievance procedures. Create an atmosphere in which individuals can function best because they feel they are being judged honestly.

5. Negotiate faculty criteria and evaluation procedures which mesh with the institution's basic mission. If yours is primarily a teaching institution, for example, make sure the contract evaluation procedure puts proper emphasis on teaching performance.

6. Establish procedures through the contract and then make sure they are applied equitably to all.

7. Build trust through open communications.

8. Negotiations must be seen as a problem-solving, rather than an adversary, process.

9. Bring in an outside negotiator who can come to the negotiating table free of the emotional encumbrances of day-to-day problems within the university.

10. The outside negotiator and the president should remain emotionally insulated so they can keep others on the problem-solving track.

11. Don't let petty problems of the moment work themselves into the contract, inhibiting initiative.

12. Leave new or doubtful sections of the contract open and meet often with faculty union leadership to discuss these.

There is no reason why contributions to university excellence cannot be included in a contract and strengthened by the collective bargaining procedure. This includes faculty involvement in institutional decision making, standards of performance for promotion and retention, a differential reward system for achievement, and a general performance standard for faculty. A contract is not going to turn every institution into a Harvard or Berkeley, nor would that be desirable. But collective bargaining can be an effective tool for helping an institution grow and reach its own goals.

David W. Leslie
Ronald P. Satryb

A collective bargaining agreement does not automatically resolve the issues and conflicts between management and labor. Once the contract is signed, the two parties must have methods established for dealing with misunderstandings, errors in contract administration, and questions about their relationship which the agreement never resolved.

The history of regulated labor relations under the NLRA and state public employment relations laws clearly and explicitly favors the development of grievance procedures in contracts to deal with unforeseen problems of interpretation and administration. A grievance procedure is a mandatory topic for negotiation under the NLRA (*Hughes Tool Co.* v. *NLRB*).[1] Many state laws covering public employees are similarly supportive, normally making grievance

[1]147 F.2d 69 (1945).

Writing Grievance
Procedures on the
Basis of Principle

procedures a mandatory item for negotiation. Some state legislation directly prescribes grievance procedures, leaving little to negotiate.

In the increasingly formal, procedurally elaborate arena of faculty employment relations, the grievance procedure is rapidly becoming an important tool of conflict management. Indeed, it is becoming a central part of the procedural common law surrounding faculty rights. Collective bargaining has introduced and tends to encourage the spread of formal grievance processing, but a recent study of campus personnel policies shows that the nonbargaining sector is rapidly adopting the idea also (Leslie, 1975). Yet little has been written about the principles that might guide the formulation of effective grievance procedures. With the goal of improving campus employment relations through imaginative grievance administration, this chapter will: (1) describe the common elements of grievance procedures currently in force, and (2) discuss some principles which should underlie the design of grievance procedures.

Four separate approaches have been employed to derive the basis for our major points. One is an intensive analysis of the grievance appeals process under the first contract between the State University of New York and the Senate Professional Association (Satryb, 1974). The second is a study of informal conflict resolution patterns on unionized campuses (Satryb, 1976b). The third is a survey of grievance procedures in higher education contracts and in a sample of institutions not covered by negotiated contracts, but which had been matched to the "bargaining" population on a variety of measures (Leslie, 1975). The fourth is a review of judicial decisions, arbitration awards, and labor relations practice affecting grievance procedures.

A special word of caution should be offered. Studies of grievance processing have yet to examine informal stages of the conflict adjustment process. Data are generally unavailable on this level, and controlled observation is obviously impractical. Thus, we remain uninformed about some of the essentials of grievance management (Leslie, 1976; Peach and Livernash, 1974).

Formalizing Conflict Management

The goal of grievance and similar mechanisms is essentially to manage conflict. The history of labor relations in the United States can be traced by reviewing the emergence of agreements among parties to deal with conflicts in systematic ways and by reviewing the emergence of federal and state machinery designed to provide for the peaceful adjustment of labor-management disputes. Experience with destructive strife between industry and the unions has led to an elaborate structure of rules through which the parties accommodate their necessarily divergent interests.

Collective bargaining and formalized employment relations have been viewed by some as ultimately destructive of the sensitive, traditionally based normative agreements which have been inculcated in generations of academics through careful apprenticeship and socialization experiences (Ladd and Lipset, 1973). But two assumptions compel a hearing for the merits of formalized relations on campus. The most obvious is that modern colleges and universities are hotbeds of conflict. In an era of expanding demands and shrinking resources, conservative supporters and new clienteles, traditional goals and a changing society, colleges and universities are necessarily faced with hard choices and unpleasant decisions. Dislocation, conflict, and crisis seem inevitable in such an environment, and the virtues of being able to deal with these forces through a widely acceptable formalized procedure should be intuitively clear. Constitutions and laws which impose regularity, predictability, and dependability on the way disputes are resolved can help the organization avoid the rending, coercive strife that threatens when no structural framework exists in which disagreements, large and small, can be handled (Fisk, 1970).

The second assumption favoring formalized employment relations on campus centers on the hypothesized failure of traditional norms to reach new faculty and students. In past decades, the academic labor market moved slowly. Faculty positions were carefully rationed to properly socialized graduates. The elite graduate schools, the "old boy network," and the more tightly knit disciplines could maintain a careful watch for violations of the gentlemanly traditions of academe. Such a model seems no longer to exist. The revolution of the 1960s seems to have broken the hold of traditional agents of socialization. New faculty and new students proclaim the irrelevance of the traditional patterns of behavior. Aided by an expanding body of law which grants procedural rights to campus constituents and which protects their substantive freedoms to dissent, to argue, to express their views, faculty and students have adopted new values and behaviors which must be respected with procedural protection rather than punished with moral retribution (*Board of Regents of State Colleges* v. *Roth*).[2]

It may be too late to defend the old models of campus relations. Adoption of procedural mechanisms for the resolution of disputes may be essential if the rapid and substantial changes currently churning through the academic system are to be accommodated peacefully. Certainly, a variety of models for the management of conflict can be posed. Experience in crisis intervention,

[2]408 u.s. 564 (1972).

labor relations, and politics can provide the outlines of effective structures (Leslie, 1972). It is not our goal, however, to explore all the avenues which might ultimately prove fruitful. What is clear at present is that the formalized grievance procedure will become a part of campus relations at most institutions in the very near future. Consequently, the following outline recommends specific qualities to be sought in the grievance procedure and general behavioral patterns which should accompany its implementation.

Basic Elements of a Grievance Procedure

Three fairly typical grievance procedures are presented in the last section of this chapter. It is clear from existent surveys, however, that no standardized model is available (*Collective Bargaining Negotiations and Contracts,* 1976; Leslie, 1975; Mannix, 1974). The purpose of this section is to identify key elements of a procedure and the range of possibilities in the design of each element.

The *scope* of a grievance procedure is the most basic element: it refers to the range of grievable matters. A substantial portion of all contracts (between 20 percent and 30 percent) place no restrictions on the kind of complaint that might be pursued through the grievance procedure. These procedures often characterize a grievance as "any dispute," "a disagreement," "a complaint," or "any conflict." Between 50 percent and 60 percent of all grievance procedures define a grievance as an alleged misinterpretation or misapplication of the contract or policies governing the employment relationship.

The remaining 20 percent to 30 percent of all grievance procedures handle definition of grievable matters more explicitly by inclusion or exclusion. A number of contracts in higher education, for example, explicitly exclude the nonrenewal of a term or probationary appointment from the range of grievable matters. Salary matters, decisions to retrench, appointments of deans or chairpersons, and similar "management rights" are also frequently excluded. On the other hand, some contracts include a limited range of matters beyond the actual terms of the contract. An allegation of "arbitrary or capricious" administrative action is a common inclusion. Where a contract leaves board policies intact on certain issues, the contract sometimes includes application and interpretation of those policies as a grievable matter.

Structure is another basic element of a grievance procedure. Existent procedures range from the simple to the complex. One step may describe the entire grievance process, but procedures with as many as eight steps have been found. The modal number of steps in higher education contracts appears to be four, but three- and five-step variants are common. The final step in roughly three-quarters of all higher education contracts is binding arbitration, with the remainder calling for mediation or nonreviewable administrative disposition as the final step. More detailed attention to the stages of a grievance procedure will be pursued below.

Access to the grievance procedure is also an important item. Four issues arise: (1) who is covered, (2) does the individual have the right to pursue all steps in the grievance procedure, (3) are "class" grievances permitted, and (4) how much discretion does the union have in filing and appealing grievances?

The simple answer to the first question is that members of the bargaining unit are covered by the grievance procedure. This normally means that a campus must consider establishing several grievance procedures to cover the various classes of employees. Separate bodies of policy and distinctive authority relationships cover faculty, part-time professional employees, nonteaching professionals, technicians, clerical employees, and service workers. Each might constitute a separate bargaining unit with its own contract, and hence its own grievance procedure. Some very complex institutions may grant considerable autonomy in personnel policy matters to individual faculty units, resulting in widely varying standards and practices. Law schools, for example, have occasionally won the right to form separate bargaining units based on the unique set of factors surrounding employment of highly specialized professionals. Where these conditions exist, and where diverse campuses are covered by a master agreement (for example, State University of New York), substantial "localizing" of grievance management takes place.

Individuals cannot lawfully be prevented from filing to remedy their perceived or actual grievances, and the union will normally represent individual members of the unit who file grievances. However, since the contract is an agreement between union and management, most unions insist upon the right to use the grievance procedure as a means of enforcing their interpretation of contractual terms. At a minimum, this means that they will wish to monitor the filing and resolution of grievances. More likely, the union will want the right to file grievances whenever it feels a misinterpretation or misapplication of the contract has occurred.

Few grievance procedures leave the individual entirely free to pursue his case through the whole process. Successively more restrictive conditions which protect union interests are normally imposed as higher appeal steps are involved. Thus, at the lowest (usually informal) step, individuals may have complete autonomy; the only union rights might be to have a representative present at the session or to receive a written copy of the decision rendered. Individuals may have the option of representation, but cannot be required to use it. At intermediate steps (appeal steps), where the facts have been previously determined, and policy interpretation becomes more central, union rights to pursue the grievance become paramount. At the arbitration stage, the individual grievant may have little or no say in the decision to invoke this final expensive and binding step. Some contracts preserve the individual's rights at each step, phrasing union rights in permissive language and leaving the option of representation to the grievant.

Class grievances are permitted in about two-thirds of all higher education contracts. Groups of individuals alleging a particular condition may initiate a complaint either with or without union representation. And finally, a few higher education contracts contain an interesting aberration: management may present allegations of contract violation by the union through the grievance procedure. (It is not clear how this variation actually works, or why it is necessary.)

Powers of remedy are inherent in any judicial, quasi-judicial, or administrative proceeding. Unless a hearing officer or other official has the power to restore to the grievant his property or liberties, the procedure may be rendered impotent. However, it should be noted that grievance procedures cannot require administrative authorities to provide remedies which are beyond their statutory powers. Most grievance procedures are silent on this matter, although limits on arbitrators' powers are usually made explicit.

Procedural elements may be described in several ways. First, time limits are normally placed on all phases of the procedure. Initiation of a grievance must normally be undertaken within a specified period after occurrence of the alleged offense. Thirty days is a common period, but variants from as few as five days to as many as 120 days exist. Some contracts do not establish explicit time limits, requiring only that the grievance be pursued within a "reasonable period." Others simply fail to place any limits on initiation of a grievance. Most procedures specify brief periods (five to ten days) for adjudication of grievances or for filing of appeals. When either party fails to meet its burdens of "timely" action, the procedure normally invests such failure with explicit meaning. A grievance undecided in a specified period is normally understood to have been denied. An appeal unpursued is assumed foreclosed.

Second, formality increases when complaints and decisions are written (rather than oral), when evidentiary standards are imposed on hearing panels, when rules govern the prescribed proceedings, and when records of testimony are kept. Most contracts suggest informal resolution of disputes as the prime avenue of grievance management, but impose increasingly formal requirements on appeal steps. Arbitration, for example, may be highly formal. Even so, the strict formality of a criminal proceeding is virtually never reached, and grievance procedures remain essentially oriented to compromise and informal methods of dispute settlement. Baird and McArthur (1976) show how grievance and arbitration procedures frequently fail to meet even the permissive standards of formality for due process hearings as defined by the federal courts.

Third, procedures may incorporate standards prescribed elsewhere. State statutes may directly prescribe a grievance procedure, or they may extend coverage of administrative procedural acts to personnel matters. Similarly, standards of the AAUP or other organizations for procedural protection have sometimes been incorporated to cover academic freedom and tenure grievances. In addition, rules for the conduct of arbitration proceedings are frequently incorporated; reliance is generally placed on the rules of the American Arbitration Association, the Federal Mediation and Conciliation Service, or a state agency.

Delegation of power to resolve grievances is a complex topic. Much litigation has been pursued by both sides to contest or defend management's reluctance to permit shared authority for resolution or to permit the involvement of external agents (arbitrators) in dispute resolution. The normal outline of delegation in existent grievance procedures is to encourage informal resolution at the lowest organizational level. Thus, department chairpersons or deans usually have the primary power to hear and resolve most grievances. Appeals taken from this first step are pursued through administrative channels in about two-thirds of all higher education contracts. (Department to dean to vice-president or personnel officer to president or board is the obvious appeal hierarchy.) Adjudicatory authority is shared by faculty and administration at one or more steps in nearly 30 percent of all higher education contracts. This means that either a joint faculty-administration committee adjudicates the grievance or that a pure faculty committee reviews and decides or recommends a solution.

An important delegation issue stems from provisions to submit unresolved grievances to arbitration. Three-quarters of all higher education contracts delegate binding authority to an arbitrator, but substantive limits may be, and often are, placed on arbitrators' powers. For example, he may be restricted to resolution of "grievances concerning the interpretation and application of this contract." More commonly, arbitrators may not "add to, subtract from, or modify the agreement or make any decision which requires an act inconsistent with the law." Some restrictions limit arbitral decisions to questions of procedure or exclude the substance of institutional policy from review. Others place more explicit restraints on arbitral review, omitting "disputes relating to termination or suspension of a tenured faculty member or of a nontenured faculty member during the period of a contract." In addition, a contract may restrain the arbitrator from reviewing "appointment, reappointment, promotion, (or) academic freedom and tenure" decisions.

Just as exclusions may be explicit, the arbitrator may be specifically empowered to review certain issues, with the understanding that powers not explicitly granted do not exist. Thus, he may have power to review disputes over "wages, hours, and terms and conditions of employment," or to "resolve questions of interpretation of the agreement." Also, available remedies in the arbitrator's arsenal may be specifically enumerated: "The arbitrator is empowered to include in his award such financial reimbursements as he judges proper." In one grievance procedure, the arbitrator's powers of remedy were so implicitly broad that the drawing of limits required a court decision: "In the event that the grievant prevails," read the clause in question, "he shall be made whole" (Weisberger, 1976, p. 13).

Issues of Principle

At each step within and among grievance procedures, there are many options and there is little standardization. No precise advice can be given to an institution negotiating a grievance procedure, but certain principles of law and experience suggest directions.

The first premise is that the grievance procedure is usually a mandatory subject for negotiations and the first suggestion, as a matter of principle, is to design the grievance procedure so that it reflects the institution's structure, experience, and values. Accepting a packaged or standardized procedure may prove more disruptive in contract management than seems likely at first glance. An example from the industrial sector will emphasize the point. The grievance procedure in question provided for the presence of a union official at any disciplinary or grievance hearing. This is a standard clause (and one that is an anathema to the traditions of professionalism and confidentiality in certain academic personnel actions). The company repeatedly refused a union officer access to discipline proceedings, as one might expect a department head or dean to do for good reason. Yet such a refusal in clear violation of the contractual terms led an arbitrator to award back pay, to order the employee's record expunged, and to direct the company to circulate announcements clearly outlining grievants' rights to have union officers present (In *Re Eaton Corp.* v. *International Union of Allied Industrial Workers, Local 967*).[3] Since the grievance procedure remains in force throughout the life of the contract and since it will be the basic path used to resolve disputes, a proposal offered at the table should be thoroughly examined for its probable effects on desirable ways of handling disputes in personnel matters.

[3]F.M.C.S. Case No. 76K/03235, 66 L.A. 581 (1976).

Since the scope of a grievance procedure is affected most directly by the range of the contract itself, it may be assumed that mandatory subjects for bargaining (once included in the contract) are, ipso facto, grievable (*Red Bank Board of Education* v. *Warrington*).[4] Beyond this, whatever the contract defines as "grievable" must be allowed. Conversely, whatever the contract excludes need not be allowed.

The clearest illustration of these points has arisen in judicial review of arbitration, but the term "grievance procedure" could usually be substituted directly for "arbitration" in the decisions. One example is drawn from a civil service employees' case: "A collective bargaining agreement containing an arbitration clause presumptively makes arbitrable all disputes arising thereunder in the absence of clear language in the contract to the contrary" (*County of Westchester* v. *Westchester County Civil Service Employees Association*).[5] Where a doubt exists as to grievability or arbitrability of an issue, the courts will place a heavy burden on the parties arguing for exclusion. "Doubts should be resolved in favor of coverage. . . . In the absence of any express provision excluding a particular grievance from arbitration, we think only the most forceful evidence of a purpose to exclude the claim from arbitration can prevail, particularly where . . . the exclusion clause is vague and the arbitration clause quite broad" (*United Steelworkers of America* v. *Warrior and Gulf Navigation Co.*)[6]

An employer may voluntarily broaden the range of the contract and the scope of grievable issues beyond mandatory subjects of bargaining. Once it has done so, it must allow grievances to proceed, although it may have negotiated away prerogatives it could originally have refused to bargain. For example, a school board faced with budget cuts decided to trim the number of special education teachers in its system. The teachers' union grieved, alleging that the contract allowed such retrenchment only in the event of a decline in enrollment. Because the board had originally negotiated this nonmandatory procedural item, it was required to submit the decision to arbitration as provided in the contractual grievance

[4]351 A.2d 778 (1976).
[5]378 N.Y.S. 2d 952 (1976), at 959.
[6]363 U.S. 574 (1960), at 584–585.

procedure (*Brookhaven-Comsewogue School District* v. *Port Jefferson Station Teachers Association*).[7]

The duty to bargain does not include all conceivable subjects: "[B]oards should not be required to enter negotiations on matters . . . of educational policy, management prerogatives, or statutory duties of the board. . . ." (*Seward Education Association* v. *School District of Seward*).[8] So the second suggestion, as a matter of principle, is that grievance procedures should be negotiated in a manner to exclude clearly these issues either explicitly or by reference to statutes excepting such matters from mandatory collective bargaining. In such negotiations it is important to recognize that the broader the terms used to reserve management rights, the less control exists over subjects open to grievance. Courts recognize the difficulty of separating "educational policy" from "terms and conditions of employment" and will adjudicate union claims for grievance or arbitration of these issues on a case-by-case basis. Even the statutory duties of the board are open to such interpretation (*Board of Education of the City of Englewood* v. *Englewood Teachers Association*).[9] Consequently, specific items that are to be excluded should be enumerated. Specific exclusions should seldom, if ever, form the limits of nongrievable matters. Another suggestion, therefore, is to qualify any list of exclusions with the standard disclaimer, "Including . . . but not limited to. . . ."

Grievance procedures which allow complaints on issues not covered in the contract should probably be avoided, especially if grievances are subject to arbitration. If the policies covering grievable matters are clear and are included in the contract, the only issues before a hearing officer, arbitrator, or court trying to determine whether or not a complaint is grievable are (1) whether the parties had the power to negotiate that item, and (2) whether it has been correctly applied. If an open-ended complaint about unfair or inequitable treatment can be filed, then the parties before the adjudicator have essentially entered new negotiations over terms and conditions of employment with no clear limit on the outcome. The fourth suggestion, as a matter of principle, then, is that a griev-

[7]91 LRRM 2824 (1975).
[8]199 N.W. 2d 752 (1972), at 759.
[9]311 A.2d 729 (1973).

ance procedure be limited to established written policies by having
the contract state something like, "Items not covered by this contract are explicitly reserved to the board and are excluded from
the grievance procedure."

This suggestion raises a question about using collective
bargaining grievance procedures to handle sex discrimination
complaints. Title IX of the Education Amendments of 1972, as
administered by the Department of Health, Education and Welfare,
requires adoption of ". . . grievance procedures providing for
prompt and equitable resolution of student and employee complaints alleging . . . [sex discrimination]."[10] There are several reasons why grievance procedures that are part of negotiated contracts
cannot satisfy the requirements of Title IX.

First, the grievance procedure is normally designed to provide a forum for continued examination of the meaning of contract terms. Although women may win certain changes in past (discriminatory) policies at the bargaining table (Smith, Bardwell, and
others, 1973), the definition and prohibition of sex discrimination
is normally beyond the scope of negotiations. Unless an agreement
on nondiscrimination is part of the contract, neither union nor
management would be obliged to deal with this kind of grievance.
Also, grievances that are outside the scope of the original contract
merely open a new agenda for negotiation. Sex discrimination
would have to acquire a negotiated meaning agreeable to both sides
before a grievance resolution could proceed very far. Further, a
substantial risk exists that the labor-management agreement on this
item would not coincide with the HEW definition, making the whole
arrangement a shaky one subject to veto by external authority.

Second, access to a negotiated grievance procedure is restricted to members of the bargaining unit. Title IX grievance procedures should cover students, nonprofessional employees, and
administrators, none of whom would be covered by the contract
with a faculty union. Pragmatically speaking, unions would be most
reluctant to take on "fair representation" of sex discrimination
complaints brought by those outside the bargaining unit. To do so
would tax union resources and legitimacy.

[10]45 C.F.R. 86.8(b).

Finally, union contracts provide for avenues of appeal that seem inappropriately situated for handling sex discrimination complaints under Title IX. For example, if a contract procedure ends in final and binding arbitration, a strong legal argument might be made that women could exercise no further appeals to HEW or other courts. And there is no adequate provision in existent grievance procedures for appropriate appeal routes for students' or others' complaints, appeals which should logically flow to deans of students, personnel departments, or other nonacademic units. For these and other reasons, it seems important that unionized colleges and universities establish Title IX grievance procedures independently of collective bargaining agreements and the procedures contained therein.

A fifth suggestion is to include in the contract a statement indicating that the grievance procedure is limited to members of the bargaining unit. Individuals not covered by the agreement or policies contained in the contract do not have access to the grievance procedure. If, for example, department chairpersons are excluded from the bargaining unit, neither they nor the union in their behalf can grieve changes in their status (*Board of Education of Greenburgh School District #7* v. *Greenburgh Teachers Federation, Local 1788*).[11]

Powers of remedy inherent in a grievance procedure present some of the most difficult issues of principle. On the one hand, redress is essential, yet the board cannot be compelled to grant what it does not have, nor to act contrary to its powers and duties. Punitive damages are probably unenforceable if they result from grievance and arbitration proceedings, but compensatory damages which are fair and realistic assessments of the grievant's actual loss normally fall within the power of the arbitrator: the grievances which were submitted to arbitration are provided for in the agreement, which states that "any dispute concerning the interpretation or application of the agreement may be raised as a 'grievance' by either party." Such language absent, a separable provision that damages may not be awarded "does not limit the authority of arbitrators to an adjudication of the breach. It is authority to assess damages against the party in default" (*Belmore-Merrick United*

---

[11]91 LRRM 3002 (1976).

Secondary School Teachers v. *Board of Education*).[12] By implication, separability of damages is impossible under this holding. Logically, limits on powers of remedy might be imposed also.

A relevant example is provided in a case in which a probationary faculty member was denied tenure despite favorable peer recommendations. She alleged that sex discrimination was at the root of the denial, and such discrimination was grievable under the contract. Failing to reach a satisfactory settlement with the university, she took her case to arbitration, asking for a tenured position as the only acceptable remedy. The grievance procedure specifically restrained the arbitrator from overturning "academic judgments," yet provided that, "in the event that the grievant finally prevails, he shall be made whole." Under the latter provision, the arbitrator held that reappointment (which automatically conferred tenure) was the only meaningful remedy. Thus, the effect of the decision was to overstep the arbitrator's powers and intrude on the right of the board to prevail in matters of academic judgment. A state court overturned the decision (*Legislative Conference of the City University of New York* v. *Board of Higher Education*),[13] but the lesson is clear; the institution, by signing a contract which gave the arbitrator very broad powers (". . . shall be made whole") very nearly lost its legal right to make final determination in nonreappointment cases.

Had the court's decision in *Legislative Conference* gone the other way—which it probably would have in the absence of the "academic judgment" reservation—nontenured faculty would arguably have attained procedural rights well in excess of those provided under the Constitution. Two United States Supreme Court cases (*Board of Regents* v. *Roth*,[14] *Perry* v. *Sinderman*[15]) clarified Fourteenth Amendment rights to procedural due process for nontenured faculty. The Court could find no property right to continued employment in nonrenewal situations, and consequently refused to impose any procedural protection on decisions to nonrenew. Had the university lost the *Legislative Conference* case, it would have had to con-

---

[12]379 N.Y.s.2d 513, (1976), at 514, citing *Matter of Marchant* v. *Mead-Morrison Mfg. Co*, 252 N.Y. 284, at 298–299; cf., *Publishers Association of New York City* v. *Newspaper and Mail Deliverer's Union of New York and Vicinity*, 114 N.Y.s.2d 401, (1952).

[13]330 N.Y.s.2d 688 (1972).

[14]408 U.S. 564 (1972).

[15]408 U.S. 593 (1972).

cede that nontenured faculty were entitled to grieve their non-renewals despite the *Roth* and *Sinderman* holdings.

A sixth suggestion, then, is that powers of remedy of the arbitrators and other adjudicators in the grievance process should be restricted or explicitly enumerated. Weisberger (1976) points out that even this approach cannot solve all of the various unforeseeable problems which emerge from sensitive employment situations. But it may have the effect of preserving important lines of authority and valuable standards of judgment which underlie academic decisions.

Grievance procedures are structured with one essential purpose: to reach a fair settlement of legitimate complaints promptly and informally. Experience indicates that the large majority of all grievances are, indeed, resolved by informal means. This indicates that costly tests of will and principle can usually be avoided. Because informal resolution has a compelling record of success, the seventh suggestion is that it be accorded a prime spot in any procedure. It should normally be the first step, and it should clearly be required in the language of the contract.

Once informal resolution has been tried, the procedure requires appeal rights. At this point, questions about the structure of the procedure can only be answered by a description of delegated authority to act on grievances, for unless a hearing panel or officer has the power to correct a condition, the appeal step(s) will be meaningless.

Because the power to resolve is unevenly delegated, many grievance procedures allow varying treatment of different subject matter (See *Collective Bargaining*, 1976, sec. 51:68–70). Common structural variants may be invoked, for example, in dismissal cases. If the action takes place at the hands of a campus-wide judicial body or a college officer (dean or vice-president), the grievance process should not require "an informal discussion with the immediate supervisor." Obviously, authority to act has been removed to a much higher level. Another variant from normal procedure may arise when employees from several departments allege an institution-wide error of inequity. Since the grievants' interests have been joined in a "class grievance," it is only logical to agree that individual department chairpersons should not remain free to work out potentially inconsistent resolutions. Rather, the "case" should be removed to the administrative level with the power to ensure consistency. In other cases, such as salary administration, responsibility for implementing a policy is handled centrally, indicating that a salary grievance should be initiated at the level of central administration. The eighth suggestion, then, is that provisions for initiating grievances at the appropriate authority level be included in the procedure. This provision will prevent the frustrating, meaningless steps from undermining the legitimacy and effectiveness of the grievance procedure.

Different sorts of concern argue for internal delegation of as much authority to resolve grievances as possible. One is the customary decentralization of authority in academic institutions. It is assumed that personnel judgments and many other kinds of decisions require departmental expertise. Another argument is purely pragmatic: no institution can withstand constant high-level tests of principle. The political resources of presidents and boards are too fragile and often too thinly spread to sustain the grind of continued conflict resolution, especially where personality conflicts and tests of individual will are involved. Only bona fide policy questions should reach the highest level of the grievance procedure.

A prime risk of delegation lies in inconsistency among departmental units. To avoid inconsistency completely, however, requires removal of authority and responsibility with a consequent loss of autonomy and initiative at the department level. Choosing experienced grievance review officers who are normally careful to avoid couching their decisions in precedent-setting terms can ameliorate most concerns relating to inconsistency among departments. By restricting settlements to the facts and circumstances of isolated disputes, they can preserve a departmental common law or even avoid issues of principle entirely. A recent sex discrimination case illustrates this kind of decision making. The judge, evidently concerned about the effects of finding a pattern of sex discrimination, narrowed the grounds for his decision, finding only a clear case of arbitrary treatment in the plaintiff's situation (*Pace College* v. *Commission of Human Rights of the City of New York*).[16] A ninth suggestion is to preserve as much department level autonomy as possible in the structure of the grievance procedure, but to foster in practice

---

[16]377 N.Y.S.2d 471 (1975).

carefully circumscribed decisions that will avoid testing campus-wide principles.

Another serious delegation problem lies in the question of whether grievance-hearing officers or panels should have the authority to override the substantive decisions of other individuals or bodies to which authority was originally delegated. Many grievance procedures under collective bargaining agreements, for example, limit the authority of arbitrators to procedural questions. Arbitrators are left without the ability to review substantive decisions of internal bodies. In other words, termination of a tenured faculty member would be reviewable only as to procedural correctness and not as to the actual merits of the decision. The dilemma here is that the grievant usually feels the wrong substantive decision has been made and may have a strong point even when the procedure has been followed to the letter. Whether or not the grievance procedure should be the proper vehicle for appealing certain substantive decisions that have been correctly processed becomes a central issue. A sex discrimination grievance procedure seems necessarily to deal with substance. Job security grievance procedures in recently negotiated contracts are also moving from the procedural to the substantive.

Clear guidelines do not yet exist to ensure the security of delegated authority over substantive decisions. One obvious approach is to reduce decision making to a mechanical process, thus making the process and standards of deciding so explicit that error is unlikely. Or if an error is committed, it would be grievable as a procedural mistake. Seldom, though, can personnel decisions be so reduced in academic life. In the end, it is ultimately those charged with substantive decisions who must account for and justify their behavior. Decisions that can be characterized as "unfair" are reflections of institutional pathologies. They are basic flaws or mirror basic flaws in the expression and interpretation of institutional values. When a substantive wrong is alleged, the only meaningful recourse is through the person or body responsible for the decision itself.

Many labor-relations experts will argue that grievance decisions should adhere strictly to contract language and procedural issues. To act otherwise would expand the contract or contradict institutional policies. However, this does not address the problem of "unfair" substantive matters that are common to faculty personnel decisions in the areas of promotion, renewal, and tenure. This problem does not have to be an "either-or" one. Grievance decisions should adhere strictly to the procedural issues, but other avenues are available to make the grievant "whole" outside of the procedure. One campus president has established an ad hoc committee to make recommendations on a substantive issue outside the grievance procedure after a formal denial of a nonrenewal grievance has been issued. Another president issues a one-year renewal of term to a faculty member based on a substantive flaw in departmental evaluation after the grievance has been denied on procedural grounds. These types of informal processes which preserve traditional substantive authority can aid conflict management and gain the respect and trust of union and faculty leadership.

An analogy lies in the legislative-judicial process. A grievance procedure functions much as the court system does with an eye to consistent application of the rules. The issue of substantive wrongs that require changes in laws are handled finally through the legislative process. New laws and congressional oversight serve as corrective mechanisms for an administrative agency which oversteps, misinterprets, or otherwise violates the authority it was granted. Accordingly, the tenth suggestion is to keep the original lines of delegation intact. Senates, committees, or administrative officers charged with making substantive decisions (on promotion, for example) should remain in a position to answer for the substance of their actions. Appeals for "unfair" substantive decisions should be reviewable only within the lines of such delegated authority as exists to make the decisions in the first place. Grievance procedures are essentially mechanisms to ensure procedural integrity. They should not supplant existing legislative or administrative functions in a self-governing academic community. This could upset the delicate balance of authority and diminish the ability of the community to make legitimate substantive commitments and decisions consistent with its purpose and character. Academic institutions must retain sufficient authority to sustain their commitment to essential goals.

A balancing of these concerns leads to the eleventh suggestion. Although a grievance review officer may be restricted to pro-

cedural matters, he should have open access to the chief administrator if it is sufficiently clear that a substantive question is at the
root of the grievance. The goal is to ensure restraint of the grievance
mechanism to procedural matters while requiring a report of substantive issues of discriminatory, arbitrary, or capricious nature
to appropriate executive and legislative bodies within the institution. Fairness and justice cannot always be reached by simple adherence to appropriate procedures.

The most important delegation issue involves binding arbitration. Having traditionally enjoyed considerable autonomy in the
management of their own personnel affairs and having generally
relied upon balanced or shared authority with faculty for resolution of the more difficult issues, college officials experience a rude
awakening when the first grievance is removed entirely from their
hands at union initiative and is left to the discretion of an "extramural neutral," the arbitrator. The record is now replete with management after-thoughts, expressed by litigation of arbitral powers.
The record also contains numerous union victories in this kind of
litigation.

The NLRA, which many states follow, makes binding arbitration a permissible way to resolve grievances concerning construction and application of the contract. In many states, it is also
considered a "mandatory subject of negotiation between the parties" (*West Hartford Education Association* v. *DeCourcy*).[17] Once a public employee bargaining law is in place, the courts will probably hold
that binding arbitration, if allowed and if limited to the meaning and
application of the contract, does not represent an unlawful delegation of management's statutory rights (cf. *Board of Education, City
of Englewood* v. *Englewood Teachers Association*).[18] The item is negotiable and lawful with the confines of the various state and federal laws.

At the bargaining table, binding arbitration is usually the
union's exchange for a no-strike agreement. So widely accepted is
this practice that the Supreme Court seems to have elevated it to a
matter of principle: "the agreement to arbitrate and the duty not

[17]295 A.2d 526 (1972), at 538.
[18]311 A.2d 729 (1973).

to strike should be construed as having coterminous application"
(*Gateway Coal Co.* v. *United Mineworkers of America*).[19]

The key to arbitration clauses lies in limits on arbitrators'
authority. Court decisions, guided by the "Steelworkers' Trilogy"
precedent now favor a presumption of arbitrability unless a matter
is explicitly excluded from arbitration. Similarly, courts will decline to review an arbitrator's award unless it is clear that he has
exceeded his authority. Consequently, negotiations over what authority will be delegated to an arbitrator should include a list of
explicit limits. The placing of limits on arbitrators' authority has
another legal advantage because it tends to foreclose claims of unlawful delegation of authority when either party sues to overturn
arbitral decisions. The twelfth suggestion, then, is to consider thoroughly and enumerate clear limits to arbitral authority.

The topic will not be discussed here, but a number of higher
education contracts have included advisory rather than binding
arbitration. Cohen (1975) has suggested that this form of arbitration is essentially consistent with the traditional role of the AAUP
in faculty employment disputes. An extramural party emerges in
fact-finding, negotiations, and other efforts to mediate particular
disputes. Although without powers to command any given result,
the arbitrator fashions the most acceptable (or least unacceptable)
solution and leaves the parties to their own judgment.

Access to the grievance procedure (and its several steps)
is controlled by the nature of the collective bargaining agreement.
The agreement is between a union, which acts as the exclusive representative of faculty, and management. A grievance, although
originating often with an individual, is a question for the parties to
the agreement to settle. Consequently, most grievance procedures
provide an important role for the union in the process of reaching
grievance settlements. In higher education, with its strong traditions of individual negotiations, the issue of exclusivity comes to a
head in grievance processing, for it may be the union's right to
decide when to settle on what terms and when to push appeals
upward.

There is virtually no room for negotiating the union's central role. Under the NLRA, the union has a right to "be present" at

[19]94 s. ct. 629 (1974), at 639.

any grievance adjustment. Individual employees or groups have a right to present grievances and have them adjusted "without intervention" of the union. If management refuses to consult the union in settlement of a grievance, it may be an unfair labor practice (Cox, 1956, p. 623). But it is not an unfair labor practice for management to refuse to process an individual's grievance despite court opinions guaranteeing individual access to all steps of the procedure (Cox, 1956, p. 624). Individual unit members may seek remedies in the *courts* if they are unsatisfied with disposition of their grievances on the merits. Two conditions attach: Employees must have exhausted internal appeals, or they must be able to show that the union is acting arbitrarily, discriminatorily, or in bad faith when it refuses to represent their claims. An alternative route for employees is to complain to the relevant labor board of a breach in the union's duty of "fair representation" (Friedman, 1972, p. 258). The effect of these somewhat confusing points of law is to establish a presumption that grievance settlements should be handled bilaterally between union and management. Individuals' rights are presumed to be protected unless they can prove a breach by either union or management. This, Friedman (1972) points out, is "an enormous burden on an employee who is legitimately motivated and entitled to relief" (p. 259).

The goals of negotiating access to a grievance procedure are: (1) to ensure a balance between union and individual interests and, in the words of Cox (1956): "In my judgment the interests of the individual will be better protected on the whole by first according legal recognition to the group interest in contract administration and then strengthening the representative's awareness of its moral and legal obligation to represent all employees fairly than by excluding the union in favor of an individual cause of action" (p. 657). The authorities and general experience suggest that indiscriminate individual access to the grievance procedure and all its stages destroys the very notion of collective negotiations. Yet the employee's right to fair treatment by both union and management is essential to the integrity of the relationship.

The thirteenth suggestion aims to ensure these conditions; grievance procedures should require provisions for "phased" negotiations. First, the principals to the dispute need to negotiate an informal settlement if possible. Then the individual and the union need to negotiate and agree on their respective interests. Finally, union and management need to negotiate a settlement that respects the contract and standards of equitable treatment for the individual.

The fourteenth, and last, suggestion is to provide time limits on *all* phases of grievance processing. Unlike a due process situation in which the substantively correct result is sought by elaborate procedure, the grievance procedure handles ongoing issues in interpretation of the contract. A major goal is to force agreement or compromise on the meaning of the contract. Time limits require the parties to pursue agreement promptly. One obvious advantage of time limits to management is that they prevent excessive processing of dead issues. A recent arbitration decision handed down by the Federal Mediation and Conciliation Service overturned a management attempt to have a grievance, filed eight months after the incident, declared "untimely." Management evidently claimed a thirty-day common law limit on filing grievances. But since the contract contained no explicit limit, the arbitrator ruled that the grievance had to be allowed (*in re Walgreen and International Brotherhood of Teamsters, Local 705*).[20] Without time limits, then, indiscriminate filing of grievances is possible, even where the issues appear to be dead ones.

Conclusion

This chapter has established a central place of the formal grievance procedure in a collective bargaining contract. It is suggested that campuses not engaged in collective bargaining feel pressures to provide increasingly formal avenues for the resolution of conflict, and that many of the principles outlined here will apply to nonbargaining situations in which the grievance procedure is adopted. Existing dispute resolution practices and current labor law have been surveyed with special attention to the problems of dispute resolution in the academic environment. Six major elements of grievance procedures have been identified and common practice in the design of each has been outlined. Issues of principle in the design of each element have been discussed, and fourteen suggestions have been offered for consideration in designing and applying the grievance procedure.

[20]F.M.C.S. Case No. 76K03535, 66 L.A. 443 (1976).

Sample
Grievance Procedures

Sample One. Informal Procedure

An employee may orally present and discuss a grievance with his immediate supervisor on an informal basis. At the employee's option, he may request the presence of a union representative. If the employee exercises this option, the supervisor may determine that such grievance be moved to the first formal step.

Should an informal discussion not produce a satisfactory settlement, the grievant may, within three work days, move the grievance to the first formal step.

Formal Steps

Step One. A grievant shall initiate his grievance in writing and present it formally to his dean, or the appropriate vice-president who shall meet with the grievant and a representative of the union for the purpose of discussing the grievance within five (5) calendar days. The decision shall be rendered in writing to the employee and union representative within five (5) calendar days of the conclusion of the discussion of the grievance, then,

Step Two. If the grievant is not satisfied with the decision rendered at step one, he may submit the grievance to the college president. The president or a designee shall hear the grievance. Witnesses may be heard and pertinent records received. The hearing shall be held within seven (7) calendar days of receipt of the grievance, and the decision shall be rendered in writing to the employee and the union representative within seven (7) calendar days of the conclusion of the hearing, then,

Step Three. If the grievant is not satisfied with the disposition of the grievance at step two, he may appeal to the chancellor on the record. The appeal shall be accompanied by the decisions at the prior steps and any written record that has been made part of the preceding hearings. The chancellor may sustain, modify, or reverse the decision made at step two on the record or may in his own person or through his designee conduct a hearing concerning the grievance. If the chancellor acts upon the written record, the decision shall be rendered in writing to the aggrieved employee and the union representative within ten (10) calendar days of receipt of the grievance. If a hearing is directed, such hearing shall commence within ten (10) calendar days of receipt of the grievance. Witnesses may be heard and pertinent records received. The decision shall be rendered in writing to the aggrieved employee and the union representative within ten (10) calendar days of the conclusion of the hearing.

If the chancellor acts on the record, the grievant, within seven (7) calendar days of such decision, may request a hearing by the chancellor, who may in person or through his designee, conduct a hearing. Witnesses may be heard and pertinent records received. If the chancellor directs a hearing, it shall commence within ten (10) calendar days of the receipt of the request.

Should a decision of the chancellor or his designee, after a hearing, be unsatisfactory to the grievant or should the chancellor refuse a request for a hearing as provided above, the union may appeal the grievance to arbitration as provided below.

Hearings shall be completed within ten (10) calendar days of the date of commencement, absent extenuating circumstances.

Step Four.   If the aggrieved employee is not satisfied with the disposition of the grievance at step three within ten (10) calendar days from the determination at said step, the union as representative of the employee may, upon written notification of intent to arbitrate to the chancellor and the director of the office of employee relations, appeal the chancellor's decision to arbitration. The arbitrator shall conduct a hearing and investigation to determine the facts and render a decision for the resolution of the grievance. An arbitrator's decision shall be binding as to grievances alleging a breach, misrepresentation, or improper application of the terms of this contract. The decision shall be advisory and nonbinding as to grievances alleging arbitrary or discriminatory application of, or failure to act pursuant to, the policies of the board related to terms and conditions of employment. In any case, an arbitrator's decision relating to nonreappointment or promotion shall be advisory and nonbinding. In no event shall an arbitrator's decision have the effect of adding to, subtracting from, modifying, or amending the provisions of this agreement, or any policy of the state, the board of higher education or any board of trustees. The arbitrator shall not substitute his judgment for academic judgments rendered by the persons charged with making such judgments.

Any costs resulting from this procedure shall be shared equally by the parties.

The arbitrator making a binding determination of the grievance has the authority to prescribe a compensatory award to implement the decision.

Within thirty (30) days of the execution of this agreement the parties shall mutually agree upon a panel of three arbitrators. Each member of the panel shall serve in turn as the sole arbitrator for a given case. Where a member of the panel is unable to serve, the next member in sequence shall then serve. In the event the parties are unable to agree upon a panel of arbitrators within thirty (30) days, arbitrators shall be selected, on a case-by-case basis, under the selection procedure of the Public Employment Relations Commission, until such time as the parties agree upon a panel.

[This sample grievance procedure is a modified version based on the 1974–1976 New Jersey State Colleges contract. Agreement, the State of New Jersey/Council of New Jersey State College Locals, NJSFT-SFT, AFL-CIO, February 22, 1974 to June 30, 1976.]

Sample Two. Case Study

It is the declared objective of the Employer and the Association to encourage the prompt disposition of grievances as they may arise and to require for their resolution recourse to the procedures set forth in this Article.

A grievance is an allegation by an employee, a group of employees, or, if ten or more employees are aggrieved, by the Association that the Employer has misinterpreted or misapplied the terms of this Contract or of an existing college rule, policy, or practice.

In the event of a grievance, the aggrieved employee, employees, or the Association shall be required to submit the grievance in writing, on a mutually negotiated form, as set forth below within fifteen (15) calendar days of the date when the aggrieved knew, or with reasonable diligence should have known, of its occurrence.

Step 1. The aggrieved employee, employees, or the Association shall submit the written grievance to the Department Chairman involved, or in the case of counselors and librarians, to their respective Directors, who shall note on the grievance the date of receipt, and shall reply in writing within seven (7) days from the receipt of the grievance.

Step 2. If the Department Chairman (or Director) fails to reply within the time specified, or if his reply is unsatisfactory to the aggrieved, the grievant may submit his written grievance to the Dean of his school, who shall hold a hearing thereon and shall have ten (10) days from the date of its receipt to reply in writing.

Step 3. If the Employer's representative fails to reply within the time specified in Step 2, or if his reply is unsatisfactory to the aggrieved, the grievant may submit his written grievance to the President of the College who shall hold a hearing thereon and shall have twenty (20) days from the date of its receipt to reply in writing.

Step 4. If the President fails to reply within the time specified in Step 3, or if his reply is unsatisfactory to the aggrieved, the Association shall determine whether it wishes to submit the matter to arbitration. In the event it wishes to do so and the grievant concurs, it shall within ten (10) days of the President's reply (or within ten days of the end of the twenty day period in Step 3), notify the Employer in writing of its desire to submit the grievance to arbitration.

A. Within one week following the receipt of such notification, a representative of the Association shall meet with a representative of the Employer and attempt to agree on the identity of the arbitrator for the grievance in dispute. If the parties are unable to agree, they shall promptly request the American Arbitration Association to submit the names of seven qualified arbitrators.

B. Within five (5) days following receipt of said list, a representative of each of the parties shall meet and, by alternately striking names on the list, determine the identity of the arbitrator. The parties shall immediately notify the American Arbitration Association of their choice.

C. The Arbitrator shall conduct the arbitration hearing as soon as practically possible and shall issue his award within thirty (30) days following the close of the hearing.

D. The arbitration shall be conducted in accordance with the then-current rules of the American Arbitration Association.

E. All of the Arbitrator's charges shall be shared equally by the Association and the Employer.

F. The award of the Arbitrator shall be final and binding upon all parties to the proceeding and on all employees; provided, however, that the Arbitrator's jurisdiction shall be limited solely to the application and interpretation of this contract. He shall have no power to add to, modify, or amend in any respect the provisions of this Contract.

[This sample grievance procedure was taken from "Community Colleges Collective Bargaining Contract—Administration Case Study," prepared by Dr. D. Anderson and Dr. F. Gerry, Office of Community College Affairs, University of Iowa; consultant: Dr. Anthony V. Sinicropi.]

Sample Three. Grievance and Arbitration (Article VIII)

A. *Definition of Grievance*:

A grievance is a dispute concerning the interpretation, application, or alleged violation of this Agreement.

B. *Settlement of Disputes*:

The Administration and the AAUP shall make an earnest effort to resolve potential grievances informally at the departmental level.

C. *Formal Grievance Procedures*:

1. Step I

The grievant (or the AAUP) shall file a written grievance with the appropriate Dean within one (1) month after the occurrence of the event which gave rise to the dispute. However, if the occurrence of the event is not immediately known to the grievant (or to the AAUP in the case of a broader dispute), the time within which to file a grievance shall commence when the occurrence of the event is discovered by the exercise of due diligence.

The Dean shall hold separate or joint conferences within two (2) weeks after receipt of the grievance to discuss the dispute with all relevant parties, including appropriate department heads, in an attempt to reach a satisfactory settlement.

If the dispute is not settled, the Dean shall, within

one (1) week after the conference, deliver to the grievant and the AAUP a signed statement of his position regarding the matter.

2. *Step II*

The grievant (or the AAUP) shall be entitled to obtain review of the Dean's Step 1 position by filing a written notice of appeal with the Dean of Faculty within one (1) week after actual receipt of the Dean's written statement of position.

The Dean of Faculty shall hold separate or joint conferences within one (1) week after receipt of the notice of appeal to discuss the dispute with all relevant parties, in an attempt to reach a satisfactory settlement.

If the dispute remains unsettled, the Dean of Faculty shall, within one (1) week after the conference, deliver to the grievant and the AAUP a signed statement of the Administration's position regarding the matter.

3. *Step III*

If the grievance is not satisfactorily resolved at Step II, either the AAUP or the Administration may submit it to final and binding arbitration provided, however, that the right to arbitrate is waived unless the party desiring arbitration notified the other party, within three (3) weeks after the Administration's Step II position shall have been received by the grievant and the AAUP, of its intention to seek arbitration.

D. *Appointment of Permanent Arbitrator*:

The parties hereby designate EVA ROBINS to serve as permanent arbitrator of all grievances arising under this Agreement. In the event that Miss Robins declines to serve in such capacity, or resigns, or is unavailable to hear a particular dispute, or otherwise cannot be reached for a period of two (2) weeks after the first attempt, an alternate arbitrator shall be selected for each arbitration pursuant to the rules of the American Arbitration Association, and the arbitration shall be conducted pursuant to the Voluntary Labor Arbitration Rules of such Association.

E. *Cost of Arbitration*:

The necessary expenses of arbitration, excluding counsel fees, shall be shared equally by all parties.

F. *Excluded Matters*:

Notwithstanding anything to the contrary contained herein, the following matters, which are governed by existing practices and statutes (for example, Personnel Plan, Faculty Constitution), shall not be subject to the foregoing grievance and arbitration procedures: disputes relating to termination or suspension of a tenured faculty member or of a nontenured faculty member during the period of a contract, appointment, reappointment, promotion, academic freedom, and tenure.

G. *University Grievance Committee*:

The provisions of the Personnel Plan relating to the University Grievance Committee shall continue in full force and effect with respect to matters within its jurisdiction thereunder. [This provision was inserted pursuant to Award (Case No. D-173-A) of Arbitrator Eva Robins, dated April 4, 1974.]

H. *Right to Initiate Arbitration and Settle Disputes*:

No faculty member covered by this agreement shall have the right to initiate arbitration under the provisions hereof, such right to initiate arbitration being limited to the AAUP and the Administration. In the event that any claim is made at any time by any faculty member against the Administration or the AAUP under the provisions of this Agreement, any agreement or adjustment made by or between the AAUP and the Administration with respect to such dispute shall be final and binding upon the faculty member.

[This sample grievance procedure taken from the Collective Bargaining Agreement By and Between the Administration of Adelphi University and Adelphi University Chapter of the American Association of University Professors, September 1, 1973 to August 31, 1976, Garden City, New York.]

Edward P. Kelley, Jr.

Negotiating the language of a contract, having come to an apparent agreement on issues, is a crucial step toward a constructive approach to contract and institutional administration. Only when the parties mutually agree upon the words to be used and meaning to be given to each clause in the written document can it be sufficiently flexible to cover a variety of situations and contribute positively to cooperative and productive relationships between faculty and administration. To protect the rights of the parties, a well-written contract can and ought to provide detail; at the same time flexibility, so essential to imaginative, artful administration, need not be sacrificed.

Contract language which is continually in dispute serves only to foster an atmosphere of distrust and dissatisfaction. This dissatisfaction leads to additional grievances, the bringing of charges

Writing Contract
Language to
Avoid Grievances

before an employment relations board, and future contract negotiations which defend positions by cataloging rights and procedural
detail. The mood of dissatisfaction and the resultant increase of
grievances are the seeds of "by the book," unilateral, or crisis management. On the other hand, when parties take a well-considered,
carefully drafted contract before their constituency, explain the
meaning of the terms, and then reaffirm their support of the agreement, an atmosphere of trust and mutual understanding is encouraged. Such an attitude provides the fertile ground upon which
imaginative, goal-oriented administration can grow.

The portions of the contract with which the parties should
be most concerned are those clauses dealing with the advancement
or retrenchment of personnel, preservation of academic freedom
and past practice, governance (where appropriate), the descrip-

tion of the grievance procedure itself, including arbitration, and, more recently, statements regarding equal employment opportunity and affirmative action. These areas of the contract are frequently the most difficult to administer. Consequently, they lead to the greatest number of grievances, often as a result of contract language which fails to fully integrate the intentions and desires of the parties.

It must be said at the outset, however, that even the most carefully constructed language written by a highly skilled labor attorney may still prove troublesome. When relations between faculty and administration are adversarial, unions tend to use grievance machinery and the contract language itself either as a vehicle to achieve those results they were unable to gain at the bargaining table or to keep the administration strictly within a narrow interpretation of the language. In an atmosphere of mutual trust, misunderstandings or misinterpretations regarding contractual provisions are often worked out in an informal fashion. The purpose of this chapter is not to propose contract language that is advantageous for union or management per se but to suggest language that may lead to fewer grievances.

Personnel Actions

Faculty, nonteaching staff, administrators, trustees, alumni, and even students have, at one time or another, taken issue with procedures, criteria, and alternatives concerning personnel actions. With the advent of unionization and collectively bargained faculty contracts, these difficult matters are brought to the forefront by virtue of a readily available, legally enforceable contract grievance procedure. In the face of formalized grievances, the institution may be forced to better define problematic language such as "just cause," "make every effort to find a suitable or equivalent position," "significant qualifications," and "ordinarily approve."

It may be valuable here to examine that portion of a contract or trustees' policy which sets out the criteria for evaluation for promotion, tenure, and renewal. The 1975–1977 contract between Western Montana College and the faculty union at that institution recites the following at section 9.100:

Qualifications and Criteria

    Promotion will normally be based on the following criteria. Weights specifically assigned thereto may differ depending upon an individual's duties and particular skills:

    1. Ability to teach effectively;

    2. Ability to conduct research effectively;

    3. Ability to keep up-to-date and to translate and disseminate knowledge in the appropriate professional field;

    4. Ability to stimulate individuals to high scholarly attainment and to develop leaders;

    5. Professional status, educational qualifications, and scholarly reputation;

    6. Potential growth and productivity;

    7. Capacity for cooperation;

    8. Contributions other than as a teacher and scholar to the welfare of the department, the College, the community of Dillon, and the State of Montana.

    Time in rank is also considered. . . . Merit rather than time in service is the overriding criterion.

    It is expected that a candidate for an associate professorship or a full professorship would have received the highest academic degree . . . appropriate. . . . There must be concrete and indisputable evidence of the candidate's dedication to the profession and above all the candidate should possess irreproachable integrity as a scholar.

There is a two-fold difficulty with this section of the contract. First, various items within the section itself are vague and therefore may be grieved again and again in order to get an interpretation satisfactory to the union. A number of questions could be raised here. In the second sentence of the section will weights assigned differ based on the kind of degree (Ed.D. or Ph.D.), program (elementary education or biology), or contribution to the mission (service courses or major courses)? Will the development of two state legislators and a town judge satisfy item 4? What evidence is sufficient to establish in an indisputable manner the candidate's dedication to the profession?

The second difficulty centers upon the exclusivity of the criteria. The parties to the contract are without specific instruction and interpretation as to whether or not all other criteria are excluded when some criteria are listed in the contract, that is, whether the university may take personnel action based on criteria not listed within the contract. One arbitrator answered in the negative finding that a denial of promotion based on criteria other than those contained in the contract was impermissible (Commonwealth of Pennsylvania and Association of Pennsylvania State College and University Faculties/PAHE [Pennsylvania Association of Higher Education]; J. Branschein, arbitrator, September 7, 1973; C. T. Whitmer, grievant). Another arbitrator decided differently on a similar issue stating that denial of promotion based on presidential ranking of all qualified candidates was not improper. The arbitrator concluded "that the qualifications as set down in the contract are a necessary, but not sufficient, condition for promotion" (Westchester Community College Federation of Teachers and Westchester Community College-County of Westchester, New York; M. Benowitz, arbitrator, May, 1976).

In view of conflicting decisions and the unsettled state of the law on these issues, the best suggestions that can be made are to (1) list *broad areas of qualifications* (such as effective teaching, competency in research, and university service) to be evaluated (to permit flexibility of interpretation that will adequately cover a great variety of individuals), (2) delineate *specific procedures* which faculty must follow in collecting and weighing evidence for each qualification before making a recommendation to the appropriate administrator (to minimize grievances resulting from lack of due process), (3) stipulate that each faculty recommendation be accompanied by a full statement of procedure, sources, and evaluation of evidence (to permit administrators to judge the thoroughness of process and accuracy of judgment), (4) specify the right of the administration to reject any recommendation on the basis of reasons including, but not limited to, insufficient evidence, failure to follow contractual procedures, or failure to follow administrative directives, such as limiting the number of promotions to be made, and (5) provide a method of appeal that retains final decision-making authority with the administration. These specifications follow accepted methods of scholarship in that they place ultimate faith in evidence and procedure. They also provide clear, acceptable means for administrative review, judgment, and action. It is also helpful to specify the administration's right to use recognized specialists from outside the university to assist in appeal procedures (especially for tenure, promotion to full professor, discipline, or retrenchment) and to state prior to the listing of qualifications that "evaluative criteria shall include, but not be limited to, the following" or that "the criteria listed are exclusive."

Another area with which administrators should be concerned is that involving discipline or discharge of professional staff. Traditionally, professional staff could be discharged during an appointment term only for "just cause," "good and sufficient cause," "proper cause," or upon some other equally vague standard. This type of terminology has been the root of many grievances. Under a collective bargaining scheme, it may be wiser to adopt an alternative method for dealing with removal, one which is more precise in defining those employee actions subject to disciplinary review. In this regard two suggestions are made: First, establish a corrective, or progressive, disciplinary model which sets out a range of offenses and prescribes the corrective action to be taken (warning, counseling, probation, or suspension without pay) for each successive offense ending in discharge where appropriate. Flexibility should be limited to those instances in which administration and union can agree in writing, in advance of any disciplinary action, and with the full written consent of the person involved. Second, it is generally helpful to eliminate the use of "removal for just cause" as an attempt at definition and replace it with some variant of the following: "Discharge—Dismissal of an employee, usually for some infraction of the rules or policies of the company [*trustees*], incompetence . . ." (Roberts, 1966, p. 78). It should be noted that most contracts negotiated in noneducational enterprises, fully list in the contract or posted work rules the grounds for discharge in order to reduce errors in administration and grievances by employees (see Chapter Twenty-One for further discussion of this point). This area is one in which colleges have tended to be vague and careless prior to unionization of faculty. As a result, some administrators waver between being indecisive or making harsh decisions based on indefensible grounds causing grievances, embarrassment, and loss of time and money.

A third area of concern should be those clauses having to do with retrenchment of faculty members. Does seniority as a "priority" factor in retrenchment limit the administration's decision-making authority about the needs and mission of the institution? At least one arbitrator has held in the affirmative. The case involved the following retrenchment clause: "When it becomes necessary to terminate the services of tenured members of the professional staff because of retrenchment, rank and years of service to the college will be considered as priority factors." The arbitrator held that the institution should retain a European historian over an American historian with less seniority even though the assignment would be to teach American history (Fulmont Association of College Educators and the Board of Fulton-Montgomery Community College, S. Shapiro, arbitrator, June, 1973). To provide the institution flexibility in administering policy and resources, such contract clauses should be hedged with some qualification such as, "In addition to these priorities, the institution will consider the priorities of government requirements (for example, affirmative action), program requirements (need for specialized teachers), and other factors relating to excellence and viability of the institution."

A second retrenchment problem concerns part-time faculty not included in the bargaining unit. In some instances, a clause is bargained requiring that when retrenchment is necessary "reductions in force shall first take place among part-time . . . faculty . . ." (Contract between Fairleigh Dickinson University and Fairleigh Dickinson University Council of American Association of University Professors Chapters, September 1, 1974 to August 31, 1976, p. 132). The difficulty here is that the unit determination made by the NLRB in the instant case recites the following: "For reasons set forth in our decision in New York University, 205 NLRB No. 16, we agree with the AAUP's position and will exclude all part-time faculty" (*Fairleigh Dickinson University*).[1] In view of the principle of exclusivity of representation which requires that an employer deal only with the certified agent about the terms and conditions of employment for *employees in the unit* and in view of a unit determination exclud-

[1]205 NLRB No. 101 (1973).

ing part-time employees, it is questionable, on technical grounds, whether or not an administration should negotiate the terms and conditions of nonunit employees. An administration which negotiates a retrenchment clause that covers nonunit, part-time employees may incur their anger, leading to unionization or a strike by part-timers, and, in addition, subjects itself to potential unfair labor practice charges brought before a labor board either by part-time employees or by a labor organization desiring to represent part-time employees. (It should be noted here that labor boards do not ordinarily entertain complaints from noncertified agents or nonunionized employees.) Should the part-timers unionize, however, it is almost certain that they would bring before a labor board a charge against the institution for violation of the principle of exclusivity. The appropriate labor relations board could be expected to issue a cease-and-desist order requiring that the employer discontinue negotiating part-timers' terms and conditions with the representative of full-time employees. In turn, it is probable that the retrenchment clause negotiated with the full-timers' representative would be voided causing further possible entanglement. Only if a savings clause had been earlier negotiated would the remainder of the contract be preserved. In any case, the union would surely demand renegotiation of a new retrenchment clause. Still another possibility is that part-timers, under ordinary trustee policies, could pursue an endless or insoluble series of grievance hearings upon the first attempt at reduction in force. To avoid these problems, the institution should negotiate the terms and conditions of unit employees *only*, leaving administrators free to handle the retrenchment of part-timers as it wishes in order to protect the viability of special programs (extension and continuing education) which depend heavily on the special knowledge of certain part-time faculty members. Administration's right to refuse to bargain conditions of nonunit employees has been fully upheld (Academic Collective Bargaining Information Service, 1976b, p. 2).

Academic Freedom and Past Practice

Academic freedom when defined as the right to full freedom in research and discussion of matters in the classroom that relate to the subject matter being taught needs no protection in a contract dealing with terms and conditions of a faculty member's employment. It is, or should be, accepted in the educational enterprise that academic freedom applies as soon as a faculty member steps on a campus, and it is one of the few uncompromisable absolutes recognized by the profession as well as by the courts. Collective bargaining, on the other hand, is grounded in quid pro quo and the art of compromise. A process which has as its life blood the give and take of compromise is and ought to be mutually exclusive of an uncompromisable commitment to academic freedom. Therefore, language dealing with academic freedom in a collectively bargained contract can only serve to diminish the esteem in which academic freedom is held and to reduce the effectiveness of collective bargaining as a dispute-resolving mechanism. Faculty unions will turn to any device to "win" a grievance, and a statement of academic freedom in the contract provides a handy argument to be used in support of almost any grievance related to nonreappointment, nontenure, or nonpromotion. If academic freedom becomes an important issue which the institution wishes to concede in some appropriate manner during negotiations, then the mention of academic freedom should be put in the preamble, with a statement in the grievance section that nothing in the preamble may be used for purposes of initiating or supporting a grievance.

Past-practice or benefits-preserved clauses also present difficult problems. The problems, especially in negotiating the first contract, center upon which past practices are to be preserved (items in the faculty handbook, trustees policies, administrative regulations, individual department policy or custom, informal campus policy). The traditions of higher education, including academic freedom and shared governance, may require that administrators not agree to a past-practice or benefits-preserved clause. Just as inclusion of academic freedom in a negotiated contract may reduce the dispute-resolving effectiveness of the bargaining relationship, so, too, can inclusion of a benefits-preserved clause inhibit the efficiency and effectiveness of the process by spawning grievances from a variety of extracontractual sources. The generation of an unknown number of grievances based on policy and regulations outside the labor agreement will negate the effectiveness of the contractual grievance procedure. Equitable, rapid resolution of differences arising under the terms of the labor agreement is one of the prime advantages of collective bargaining. This advantage will be sacrificed or greatly impaired if the grievance procedure becomes the avenue for any and all employee complaints, merit notwithstanding.

To avoid difficulties in institutional, contractual, and grievance administration, it is suggested that no past-practice or benefits-preserved clause be bargained. Rather, in an attempt to preserve equity while securing the traditional advantages of collective bargaining and contractual grievance procedures, the administration should bargain for cataloging within the contract all rights to which it will be contractually bound.

Governance

Some administrations have bargained governance guarantees into faculty contracts. Although the elevation of traditional shared authority to an enforceable contractual right is a laudable motive for contract governance, the way is left open for individual and union grievances over such things as program curtailment and, at some institutions, presidential selection. For example, section 14.18(a) of the Fairleigh Dickinson University contract (September 1, 1974 to August 31, 1976) reads as follows: "With respect to the selection of the President of the University, there shall be significant faculty participation in the Board of Trustees' search and three (3) members of the faculty shall be elected by the faculty . . . to advise on the selection of candidates." Section 15.22(b) of the same contract recites the following in defining a "contractual grievance." ". . . is a dispute regarding the proper interpretation, application, or alleged violation of this Agreement, in other than a faculty status matter. . . ." With little or no other limitation on grievances, it is arguable that an individual or the union could grieve the trustees' selection of a candidate if the three faculty members had opposed that particular individual, basing the grievance on frustration of the intent of the contract. The union could argue that when participatory rights are granted by contract, the grant of ineffective rights frustrates and contravenes the intent of the contract and the purposes of collective bargaining. Should an arbitrator uphold the grievance, the faculty would hold the power of veto over the trustees' authority to appoint a new president. The proper antidote is to refrain from bargaining these types of management

rights, leaving the trustees the right to invite the faculty to participate, as a matter of good will and collegiality, each time as the trustees
wish. If the negotiator feels a strong need for compromise, a qual-
ifying clause should be added to the effect that the trustees will in
no way be bound by the advice of the three faculty members.

In general, the purposes of collective bargaining—efficient
contract, grievance, and institutional administration—and the traditions of shared governance would be better served by a contract
and a grievance procedure which does not deal with traditional
faculty governance. The natural desire of faculty to increase its
participation in management decisions (nonmandatory subjects of
bargaining) are better satisfied through a noncontractual commitment to new or existing governance structures. The delicate balance of power in an institution of higher education is determined
by education law (charter) and by labor law. Education law provides
trustees with authority that is, in turn, limited by terms stipulated
in labor law. Trustees gain little, if anything, by compromising what
little final authority they have. This does not mean that trustees
should not be liberal in seeking advice and consultation on a *voluntary* basis. It does mean that their authority should not be unwittingly
and legally (by contract) reduced to the point where they no longer
have sufficient power to be responsible for their duties as stated
in the education law (or charter). Extracontractual arrangements,
as well as the contract, should clearly require commitments to the
goal of educational excellence by each of the parties. Attempts to
contractualize tradition, excellence, and the like usually serve to
overload the grievance procedure while reducing the flexibility
inherent in traditional governance.

Grievance Procedure Description

Leslie and Satryb have dealt with this subject in detail in
Chapter Eleven. However, the need for a tight, well-written, clear
grievance procedure which (1) precisely defines that which is grievable, (2) limits the number of steps to only those necessary to a fair,
equitable, and speedy final decision, and (3) protects the interests
of the institution, the individual and the union should be emphasized. Since it is the obligation of the employer and the employee

representatives to negotiate and administer the contract in a manner which discourages the filing of frivolous grievances, the following elements for a grievance procedure are suggested:

1. An informal attempt to resolve the grievance with union participation should be required.

2. Two formal oncampus reviews, the first by a midlevel academic officer and the latter by the chief executive officer or his designee, should take place.

3. A final review, either inhouse or by an outside arbitrator, that is binding upon the parties, should take place. When the final review is to be arbitration, arbitrators should be selected from a limited list established during contract negotiations and made part of the contract. This reduces time and conflict already generated during critically important grievances. An alternative procedure is to use an inhouse review panel described by the grievance procedure with a relatively constant membership to ensure integrity, reliability, and competence.

4. Access to the grievance procedure should be strictly defined through an exclusive list of grievable subjects. The list should set out with particularity those sections of the contract which are grievable and those which are not. In addition, the contract should explicitly state that extracontractual matters are not grievable. Where the grievability of a matter is questioned by the administration, the issue of grievability should proceed immediately to the presidential level and then to a referee designated by the contract to decide grievability questions. When steps and referees for deciding issues of accessibility, along with a limited list of grievable subjects, are all detailed in the contract, fewer grievances will be processed with considerably less time, expense, and emotion.

5. Finally, a parallel process should be bargained whereby an individual faculty member (union and nonunion member alike) or the administration may file grievances objecting to actions of the union. An informal attempt at resolution should be required. When informal steps fail, the grievance should be formally filed with and heard by a faculty committee. The second step of the formal procedure should involve an appeal to the union president or his designee. A final and binding step should include appeal to a campus-wide faculty-administrative review committee or to arbitration.

For further information the reader is referred to the contract be-
tween Wagner College and The Wagner College Chapter of the
American Association of University Professors, September 1, 1974–
August 31, 1977, pp. 57–59.

Equal Employment Opportunity and Affirmative Action

The issue of discrimination is one for the law and the various
state and federal agencies which specialize in the area. The obligations of equal employment opportunity and affirmative action
are not contractual. Commitments made in contracts serve only to
provide access to a grievance procedure which is neither designed
nor qualified for dealing with the complexities of discrimination.
As Leslie and Satryb have recommended in Chapter Eleven, a separate, extracontractual grievance procedure specifically designed
to meet Title IX requirements is the only meaningful way to deal
with charges of discrimination on the local level.

Conclusion

Grievance avoidance is best served by specific language on
issues of faculty privilege and more open language on issues of
institutional authority and responsibility. If this sounds biased
(which it is), it merely follows the nature and purpose of bargaining. Before bargaining, an institution holds all authority and resources. Negotiation is a process of giving some of its authority and
resources to faculty in return for services and peaceful relationships. It is only natural, then, that the contract be very specific about
what is given and very general about "everything else" to be retained.
Although vague language applied to management rights provides
flexibility for administrators, it merely fosters grievances designed
to seek interpretation and establishment of parameters when applied to faculty benefits. For example, some portions of the contract
may require institutional flexibility to assure the viability and quality
of the educational programs of the institution and to guarantee
the rights of other university constituents. Such contract clauses
preserve institutional authority and are not assumed to be open to
grievance challenge. Yet, a clause specifying benefits written in the

open language of "not limited to" provides a basis of grievance which may be settled by an arbitrator's award and which may, indeed, reduce the very flexibility which the institution intended to retain in the former clause. Thus, it is essential that the parties to a contract carefully review the language proposed for each clause and, in view of local conditions, decide whether the institution would be best served by flexible language fostering imaginative administration or specific language reducing the number of grievances and freeing the parties to direct their energies toward institutional goal attainment.

G. Gregory Lozier

13

❧❧❧ ❧❧❧ ❧❧❧ ❧❧❧ ❧❧❧ ❧❧❧ ❧❧❧ ❧❧❧

Although some sectors of higher education have maintained mild growth patterns in recent years, the rapid expansion of the 1960s has generally given way to a deceleration and even stabilization in growth of both enrollments and resources in the 1970s. In addition, austere budgets have become the norm in many states, and a process of fiscal and program consolidation is generally underway. According to Lanier and Andersen (1975), these conditions, compounded by soaring inflation and deep recession, have combined to indicate "massive evidence of widespread retrenchment in higher education" (p. 77). Colleges and universities, as have many other organizations in the public and private sectors, now face the prospect of personnel redistributions and retrenchment. These conditions, plus an accompanying decline in faculty mobility, increase the importance of job security since termination, whether

Negotiating Retrenchment Provisions

voluntary or otherwise, can have dire professional and economic consequences for those affected.

The chapter begins with an overview of the public positions of the AAUP, the American Federation of Teachers (AFT), and the NEA on faculty retrenchment. This overview is followed by an analysis of retrenchment provisions as contained in a sample of ninety-one collective bargaining agreements negotiated through 1975 in a cross section of colleges and universities with faculty bargaining units. The analysis explores the prevalence of retrenchment provisions in contracts, the relationship of these provisions to instructional level and type (two-year versus four-year and public versus private) and faculty agent, the methods prescribed for identifying a need for retrenchment, the order of layoff, notification requirements, recall provisions, faculty participation in retrenchment decisions, and the interaction of retrenchment provisions with affirmative action goals. These analyses provide the basis for some extended observations about faculty retrenchment and collective bargaining and for posing several questions to be considered by administrators faced with negotiating a collective bargaining agreement.

The Unions' Perspective

William Van Alstyne, past president of the AAUP, noted in 1971 that declining student enrollments and unavoidable conditions of financial stringency may lead to the termination of tenured faculty. In such cases, "Nothing at all will insulate adversely affected individuals from the hard prospect of unemployment" (p. 329). The NEA, the AFT, and the AAUP have treated the issue of faculty reductions from a national perspective in varying degrees of comprehensiveness. Of the three, the AAUP has provided the most comprehensive public stance with respect to the faculty retrenchment issue, and, therefore, greater emphasis is given here to the AAUP's position.

The NEA provides its affiliates with some guidance on the issue of retrenchment in a section on "Faculty Reductions" in its *Sample Master Contract for College and University* (Chesebrough and Encinio, 1970). In addition, the topic of "Reduction in Force" is treated more thoroughly in a draft statement on "Due Process and Tenure in Institutions of Higher Education" (National Society of Professors, 1973).

The AFT, according to Robert Nielson, head of AFT's college division, has not developed a national position statement on the issue of faculty retrenchment, but relies mostly upon local chapter initiatives and negotiated settlements to reflect the AFT's concern in this area. Through numerous conventions the AFT has developed positions dealing with various topics, such as academic freedom and the rights of faculty, peer involvement and professional control, and academic due process.

The AAUP first treated the issue of faculty terminations in Regulation 4 of the statement on "Recommended Institutional Regulations on Academic Freedom and Tenure" (American Association of University Professors, 1968), and subsequently revised it under the heading "Termination of Faculty Appointments Because of Financial Exigency, Discontinuance of a Program or Department, or Medical Reasons" (American Association of University Professors, 1975). According to Committee A of the AAUP, the current revision was "designed to provide more specific procedural guidance in cases resulting from an assertion of financial exigency and to distinguish between those cases and cases of formal programmatic or departmental discontinuance not mandated by financial exigency" (p. 329).

Under Regulation 4, the AAUP defines a bona fide financial exigency, for which an institution may terminate a tenured faculty member or a probationary faculty member before the end of a specified period of appointment, as "an imminent crisis which threatens the survival of the institution as a whole and cannot be alleviated by less drastic means" (p. 329). The Regulation posits four steps in responding to a state of financial exigency: (1) identification of the imminent or actual crisis, (2) response to considerations of educational policy and determination of where within the overall academic program retrenchment may occur, (3) identification of criteria for designating the individuals whose appointments are to be terminated, and (4) assignment of the responsibility for identifying individuals whose appointments are to be terminated. The AAUP recommends that faculty should be afforded a participatory role in the identification of the crisis and the designation or approval of the individual or individuals who will determine specific faculty terminations. It further proposes that considerations of educational policy and development of criteria for identifying individuals to be terminated should be the *primary* responsibility of the faculty or an appropriate faculty body.

The regulations also propose that terminated faculty members should have the right to a full hearing before a faculty committee. The issues to be considered in such a hearing roughly parallel the four steps of the retrenchment considerations proposed above. In such instances, according to the AAUP, the validity of the educational considerations and the retrenchment criteria per se shall be presumptively valid, providing that the faculty have held primary responsibility in these matters. However, the AAUP does not hold the same justification for a bona fide exigency and the application of retrenchment criteria, for which the burden of proof rests with the administration.

Other considerations regarding retrenchment under conditions of financial exigency include order of retrenchment (for example, nontenured before tenured faculty), provision for placing a faculty member in another suitable position within the institution, providing for appropriate notice or adequate severance salary, and the opportunity for recall should the retrenched position be reestablished within a period of three years.

On the matter of discontinuing an academic program or department not related to conditions of financial exigency, the AAUP guidelines suggest that such a decision should be "based essentially upon educational considerations, as determined primarily by the faculty as a whole or an appropriate committee thereof" (p. 331). The statement cautions against making such judgments on cyclical or temporary variations in enrollments, but rather should reflect long-range judgments regarding the institution's educational mission. Auxiliary issues, such as alternatives to termination and the rights to a hearing, correspond, with minor nuances, fairly closely to the AAUP's recommended procedures for termination based upon conditions of financial exigency.

Retrenchment Clauses in Contracts

This section explores retrenchment provisions negotiated by affiliates of the AAUP, the AFT, and the NEA.

The Sample

Retrenchment provisions in existing collective bargaining contracts provide one means for exploring alternatives for dealing with retrenchment issues under collective bargaining. Accordingly, a sample of ninety-one collective bargaining contracts was obtained from my personal files, from the files of the Center for the Study of Higher Education at The Pennsylvania State University, and the Academic Collective Bargaining Information Service (ACBIS). This sample includes seventy-eight public institutions of higher education and thirteen private colleges and universities, and represents fifty-nine two-year institutions and thirty-two four-year, multicampus institutions (which includes several two-year campuses at the City and State Universities of New York and the University of

Hawaii). The faculty bargaining agent affiliations for these ninety-one agreements are the AAUP in sixteen; AFT, fifteen; NEA, thirty-nine; merged affiliates, ten; and independent agents, eleven. (Since the agreements were negotiated prior to the dissolution of the NEA-AFT merger in New York State, these bargaining agents were included in the "merged affiliates" category.) In order to test the representativeness of these ninety-one agreements, a comparison was made of the sample distribution on institutional type, institutional level, and bargaining agent affiliation with the corresponding population distribution of colleges and universities with faculty contracts (Kelley, 1976). None of the subsequent chi-square tests of hypothetical proportions produced significant results. Accordingly, it was concluded that on these variables, the sample of contracts constituted a fairly representative sample of the collective bargaining agreements in higher education. Analysis in a later section of this chapter also looks at the distribution of these contracts by the effective year of the agreement. (The effective year of the agreement does not always correspond to the year of negotiation, since some contracts are retroactive.) On this variable there may not be as extensive a degree of representativeness, particularly with regard to the limited number of two-year institutions (three) analyzed for the years 1974 and 1975; however, there is no readily available population distribution by which to test this variable statistically for representativeness.

In addition to the key word *retrenchment,* relevant clauses were identified by such other descriptors as *termination, reduction, layoff,* and *financial exigency.* Overall, fifty-four (59 percent) of the ninety-one agreements examined contained some form of retrenchment provision. The corresponding percentages for four-year public institutions, four-year private, and two-year public institutions were 63 percent, 69 percent, and 56 percent, respectively. Analysis revealed no statistical significance in the distribution of contracts with and without retrenchment provisions by institutional level and type. (It should be noted that the sample of agreements did not include any contracts from private two-year institutions; however, as of February 1976 there were only two private two-year colleges with contracts.)

Similar conclusions were made regarding the relationship

between faculty agent and the incidence of retrenchment provisions. Of the fifty-four contracts in the sample containing retrenchment provisions, 75 percent of the contracts negotiated by the AAUP, 73 percent of independent agent contracts, 64 percent of the NEA contracts, 44 percent of the NEA-AFT contracts, and 33 percent of the AFT contracts contained retrenchment clauses. These data suggest that the faculty agents most likely to negotiate a retrenchment provision in a collective bargaining agreement are affiliates of the AAUP and the NEA or an independent faculty association, whereas AFT agencies (alone or in merger) are least likely to negotiate a clause dealing with faculty retrenchment. Analyses of these data were not statistically significant.

Another variable of potential importance is the effective year of the collective bargaining agreement. The frequency of retrenchment provisions in contracts increased substantially in 1972 from the pre-1972 period, from 38 percent (n = 6) to 62 percent (n = 16). In each of the three subsequent years (1973, 1974, and 1975) the proportion increased less dramatically—61 percent (n = 19), 70 percent (n = 7), and 75 percent (n = 6) respectively. Despite an increase in the proportion of contracts negotiated with retrenchment provisions from 62 percent in 1972 to 75 percent in 1975, these data do not portend a ground swell in attention to the issues of staff retrenchment and financial exigency in collective bargaining contracts. This conclusion may prove premature since severe budget constraints did not hit many of the institutions involved until 1975 and 1976. Settlements reached in 1976 and 1977 should be closely scrutinized. As to the relationships between the effective years of the agreements, institutional level and type, and faculty bargaining agent, there is no particularly notable transition over the years examined.

Criteria for Retrenchment

Of considerable concern to many faculty members and administrators is the basis on which the need for retrenchment is identified. Review of the fifty-four contracts containing retrenchment provisions revealed that the typical clause allowed for the implementation of retrenchment procedures in case of "financial considerations," "enrollment shifts," or "reductions in or eliminations of academic programs." Financial considerations were mentioned in thirty-nine contracts, program adjustments in thirty-three, and enrollment considerations in twenty-five. Eleven of the fifty-four contracts with retrenchment clauses either provided no criteria for instituting retrenchment procedures or made a general introductory statement, such as "in the event of a necessary reduction of staff."

In general, the responsibility for identifying the existence of conditions warranting implementation of retrenchment rests with the board of trustees or the president of the institution. The matter of faculty involvement in these considerations will be explored subsequently in this chapter. Although the initial decision that a retrenchment condition exists may fall to the administration, many of the agreements provide for administrative explanation and justification of the conditions warranting retrenchment and for involvement of faculty from the programs or of faculty members to be affected.

Several of the retrenchment provisions establish enrollment standards, student-faculty ratios, and other types of formulae for identifying retrenchment conditions. For example, in the contract for the Fulton-Montgomery Community College, the "Termination for Retrenchment" clause states that, "Tenured faculty will not be terminated for retrenchment resulting specifically from an enrollment decrease unless there is an accumulative reduction in full-time equivalent students of 10 percent or more below the base figure 1971 full-time equivalent students." At Oakland University, the "Over-Ratio Layoff" provision of the retrenchment clause stipulates that faculty retrenchment may be instituted when the actual full-time equivalent number of faculty exceeds by more than 20 the number of full-time equivalent faculty necessary to maintain a student faculty ratio of 21.3.

Since many of the earliest statements regarding faculty retrenchment use the concept of financial exigency and because of the publicity which the concept has received in several court cases, most notably Bloomfield College, it is interesting to examine the frequency and manner in which the term "financial exigency" has been used in collective bargaining agreements. In fact, the term *financial exigency* was found in only one of the thirty-three two-year college contracts, but appeared in thirteen of the twenty-one four-year, multicampus contracts. Many of the two-year college contracts refer to financial considerations, insufficient funds, financial adjustments, and decreases in revenues, but the avoidance of the term *financial exigency* is unexplainable from the limited perspective of the contracts themselves. Of those agreements using the financial exigency concept, few attempt to define it. The contract for Pratt Institute indicates that financial exigency must be demonstrably bona fide and fully explained and documented to the Institute faculty to the effect that unless the Institute effectuates the inherent economies, the viability of Pratt Institute is endangered. The agreement for Fairleigh Dickinson University stipulates that "The University shall not declare a state of Financial Exigency unless it is demonstrably bona fide. Financial exigency shall be defined as an emergency condition in which the University's continued existence is in serious jeopardy for financial reasons." The contract for the University of Cincinnati notes parenthetically that a financial exigency is "an imminent financial crisis which threatens the institution as a whole." Even in these examples, the subjective nature of the definitions remains.

Order of Retrenchment

In the fifty-four contracts reviewed which contain retrenchment clauses, "seniority-related" language was the most frequently observed retention criterion. Thirty-seven of the agreements cite *length of service,* typically in one's campus, college, or discipline, as the primary determinant of the order of retrenchment. Many of the agreements also require that nontenured, noncontinuing, or probationary faculty must be terminated before tenured or continuing faculty are retrenched (twenty-seven contracts), and nineteen agreements require termination of part-time or temporary faculty prior to full-time or regular faculty. When two individuals have the same status (for example, tenured and full-time), several contracts add academic rank, and even time in rank and birthdate, as the distinguishing qualifiers.

Many of the contracts contained language which indicated that the adoption of alternatives to retrenchment was preferable. Some of the alternatives noted include recourse to normal faculty attrition, providing an opportunity to adapt one's academic skills or retrain in another discipline, early retirement, or reassignment to another suitable position in the institution either with instructional or noninstructional duties. The contract for Fairleigh Dickinson University stipulates that before termination of a full-time faculty member may occur, a number of alternatives must be pursued, including development of a shared teaching load, reassignment, supplementation of nonteaching duties, shared teaching with other institutions, retraining, transfer to nonteaching position, reduced load with proportionate reduction of compensation, and early retirement.

In addition to suggesting alternatives to retrenchment, a number of the provisions indicated that when retrenchment is necessary, certain qualifiers are to be imposed upon otherwise strict standards of seniority. For example, eighteen of the fifty-four contracts with retrenchment provisions require consideration of the maintenance of a viable academic program and of the qualifications of the faculty to perform the necessary instructional duties. A typical statement is found in the Oakland University agreement, which states that layoffs shall occur in the prescribed order of seniority "subject to the ability of those remaining full-time faculty members to perform satisfactorily the teaching responsibilities assigned to the academic unit." The contract for Gateway Technical Institute provides that the following factors be taken into account: (1) the teacher's area of certification and academic training, (2) the teacher's seniority in the district, and (3) the teacher's past and potential contributions to the educational program.

In those contracts which contain both seniority-related standards and standards of educational merit for determining the order of layoff, the language used in the various agreements provides for interpretive flexibility. Some of the contracts seem to indicate that although seniority is the controlling factor, considerations may be given to the educational merits of the decision. In other contracts, standards of professional competence and maintenance of the academic programs are to provide controlling influence upon the retrenchment decisions, with seniority being applied as practical. Experience in the application of these combined criteria in retrenchment decisions bears watching.

Finally, ten of the fifty-four contracts containing retrenchment provisions did not stipulate the criteria for determining the order of layoff. Four of these provisions indicated that the order would be determined by some form of consultation, while the remaining six left such consideration to speculation.

Notification Requirements

Specific notification requirements for personnel affected by retrenchment occur less frequently in collective bargaining contracts for two-year institutions than for four-year institutions. In the former, thirteen of the thirty-three contracts reviewed contain no notification requirements, whereas only three contracts of the twenty-one four-year institutions are mute on this issue.

In sixteen of the contracts, the notification requirements are related to the faculty member's length of service with the institution (or, in some circumstances, with the current academic department) or some other condition of employment, such as tenure or continuing appointment status. The variable time parameters specified in these agreements, especially the thirteen contracts for four-year institutions, are fairly consistent with the guidelines for notification suggested in the AAUP policy statement on "The Standards for Notice of Nonreappointment" (American Association of University Professors, 1967). The longest notification requirements appear in the contracts for Fairleigh Dickinson University (seventeen months notification for tenured faculty members) and Wayne State University (eighteen months for tenured or continuing service personnel). In the remaining contracts the time specifications for notifying individuals to be laid off range from one month to one year, with a mode of three months or a March 1 or March 15 date. Four contracts indicated that these requirements are "to be determined," "to be timely," or "as soon as possible." Many of the other agreements with specified dates also indicate that the notifications should be timely and that the suggested dates are minimum periods of notification.

Two special provisions regarding notification requirements found in the sample of agreements deserve mentioning. Five of the contracts indicate that severance pay can be provided in lieu of appropriate notice. Under such an arrangement, a faculty member can be terminated even though the notification deadline has passed as long as the faculty member is provided fiscal compensation equivalent to the period required by the notification standards. A second distinguishing item in several contracts is the elimination of standard notification requirements when the cause for retrenchment is financial exigency; under such conditions the granting of "appropriate notice" should be substituted for such standards.

Recall

Only eight of the fifty-four contracts containing retrenchment provisions do not provide any reference to the establishment of some type of preferred hiring list or recall possibilities for faculty members who have been retrenched. There is considerable variability in the contractual language dealing with the recall of terminated faculty in the remaining forty-six agreements.

Thirty-six of the contracts stipulate a specified period of time during which a faculty member could remain on a recall list. These time periods range from one year to the age of retirement with the mode being two years (twenty-one contracts). In seven contracts, the time on the recall list is subject to contractual status or length of service at the time of retrenchment or both. In two contracts, the recall list time specification is for the duration of the agreement.

Forty-one of the recall provisions provide that recall should be based on the inverse order of layoff. However, thirty-two of these provisions stipulate that the recall must be consistent with academic needs, faculty qualifications, or both. Typical language in the two-year college agreement specified rehiring the faculty member for the same position held prior to retrenchment. In the remaining nine contracts for two-year institutions, no specifications of academic qualifications or needs are referenced.

A number of recall provisions stipulate more than the order and years of eligibility for recall. Twelve contracts indicate that upon reemployment, the rehired faculty member will retain his previous status with respect to employment benefits and years of service, that is, tenure, rank, and eligibility for sabbatical, and sick leave. Many of the recall provisions provide time parameters for notifying a faculty member that a position is available, and for the faculty member to accept or reject this offer in turn. The typical time frame is between fifteen and sixty days. One contract, that for Wagner College, allows the faculty member up to one year to accept or reject an offer of reappointment. Five of the contracts indicate that once a faculty member rejects an offer of recall, the college or university has no further obligations to that individual. In contrast, two other contracts indicate that the right to recall is not rescinded by failure to accept a reappointment, and the faculty member can remain on the preferred hiring list for the duration of the prescribed time limitation. The recall provisions for four of the contracts indicate that the faculty member is responsible for notifying the administration by some prescribed date each year that the faculty member wishes to maintain his name on the preferred hiring list; failure to do so causes removal from the recall list.

Faculty Participation

Specific provisions for faculty involvement in the development and implementation of retrenchment procedures were present in seventeen of the twenty-one four-year college contracts, but in only thirteen of the thirty-three contracts for two-year institutions. Twenty-one of the contracts in the sample provide for general consultation between the administration and the faculty or its representatives, with no further specifications regarding the scope of consultation. In other contracts, faculty participation is required in verifying the existence of a state of financial exigency (four contracts), in concluding that there is a necessity for personnel and program retrenchment (six), in developing alternatives (four), in determining the number of faculty to be terminated (two), and in identifying the criteria or order for termination or the specific terminations themselves (seven contracts).

In eight of the contracts containing provisions for faculty participation in retrenchment decisions, the proposals developed by the faculty or its representatives are in some measure binding upon the administration. At Temple University, a twelve-person faculty-administrative committee can make a final and binding decision for reasons of academic program qualifications and requirements, affirmative action goals, academic excellence, or early retirement in order to follow an order of retrenchment different from the general seniority guidelines provided by the contract. In the 1973–1974 contract for Bard College, the determination of the number of faculty members to be terminated is made by the union's executive committee, while the faculty senate, following approval by a regular faculty meeting, determines the particular terminations which respond most appropriately to the existing financial exigency.

Faculty involvement in retrenchment considerations is frequently accorded through the faculty union, its chief officer or executive committee, or personnel committees of the organization. This was more typical of two-year college contracts than those of four-year colleges. In other contracts, faculty experience and expertise is introduced through the academic department, division, or college, or through the faculty senate. In such instances (six in four-year institutions), the contractual language provides for the development of a special college or university commission through which faculty input is considered.

Affirmative Action Considerations

The point has been argued that collective bargaining can provide an additional level in the efforts of minorities and women to achieve parity with white males in their conditions of employment. There are a number of affirmative action related issues which are promoted by collective bargaining agreements, including the incorporation of nondiscrimination clauses and provisions for equal pay and adjustments of salary inequities. However, as Lussier (1975) points out, the former does little more than to reaffirm policy, whereas the latter, experience indicates, requires a strong coalition of women and/or minorities to press their demands upon both the union and the administration. In general, rather than assist affirmative action goals, unions in industry and the public sector have tended to accept and reflect the prevailing social climate and have typically served to institutionalize many aspects of present-day discrimination (Fratkin, 1975). For example, a strict seniority system ("last hired, first fired") as a standard for determining the order of retrenchment may be in direct conflict with the aims and purposes of affirmative action. Even when contracts include language which requires the ability to maintain academic integrity and to deliver the institution's academic programs, there typically is no consideration made for affirmative action goals. Of the sample contracts reviewed containing retrenchment clauses, only three, those for Central Michigan University, Temple University, and the University of Cincinnati make any special mention of the institutions' affirmative action plans when considering faculty retrenchment. In her overall analysis of the relationship between collective bargaining and affirmative action, Lussier (1975) concludes that "On the basis of contracts negotiated to date . . . it appears that the best friend of affirmative action is likely to remain federal legislation and the courts" (p. 10).

Retrenchment Issues

In his recent book *Faculty Bargaining: Change and Conflict,* Garbarino (1975) notes that, "As more institutions find themselves forced to reduce staff, the importance of policies on 'retrenchment' rises and provisions dealing with these procedures are appearing in agreements" (pp. 175–176). As we have seen, a significant number of organized institutions have already negotiated provisions for faculty retrenchment or reduction, but the retrenchment issue will probably become an increasingly important subject of negotiations for many institutions in the coming years. The review of existing retrenchment clauses in the previous section reveals that there are many issues involved in retrenchment considerations. In the concluding section of this chapter, five of these issues are discussed: retrenchment as a subject for bargaining; defining a condition of exigency; developing criteria for determining the order of retrenchment; maintaining academic program effectiveness; and determining the role of faculty in the process.

Should Management Negotiate a Retrenchment Clause, and, if so, How Comprehensive Should the Provision Be?

There is considerable support for the position that contingency planning in advance of crisis is preferable to "shoot-from-the-hip" solutions to exigencies (for example, see Furniss, 1974; Bowen and Glenny, 1976; and Finkin, Goldstein, and Osborne, 1975). Experience indicates that the implementation of extraordinary personnel procedures in a time of financial exigency is likely to arouse criticism and resistance on many fronts. However, such a conclusion does not independently justify the decision to negotiate a contractual retrenchment provision since other factors weigh heavily in such a decision.

One factor is the relationship of the institution's financial status to the decision of the faculty to adopt collective bargaining. If the college or university is already experiencing a state of financial retrenchment or if personnel reductions have been instituted, it is very likely that there will be strong pressures on the part of the faculty's representative to negotiate a retrenchment clause. The comprehensiveness of the union's demands on retrenchment is likely to be dependent upon previous faculty-administration relationships and the faculty's role in retrenchment considerations prior to collective bargaining. An institution in which the faculty's participatory role has been limited can anticipate greater pressures to negotiate a retrenchment clause with either extensive faculty influence upon retrenchment decisions or built-in constraints upon administrative freedom (such as adoption of objective criteria for retrenchment and formula-based procedures for determining the existence of a layoff condition).

A second and related factor is the model of negotiations which is adopted at the bargaining table. Bucklew (1974) distinguishes among three types of negotiations: (1) employment—negotiations are basically limited to issues such as wages, fringe benefits, and working conditions, (2) structural—negotiations are expanded to include procedural aspects of professional and governance matters, and (3) comprehensive—a broad scope of issues are negotiated in both policy and procedural terms. If the parties agree to a limited scope of negotiations in which a sharp distinction is maintained between employment conditions and professional considerations, a retrenchment clause, if negotiated, is not likely to provide for more than a requirement that the decision to institute retrenchment procedures necessitates the participation of faculty. On the other hand, adoption of the comprehensive approach to bargaining promotes the inclusion of extended procedural or policy retrenchment considerations.

Another factor is the visibility which both the administration and the union wish to give to the prospect of faculty retrenchment. Harris (1976) has suggested that although planning to establish priorities for growth is desirable, priorities for cuts stated in a public document can be a self-fulfilling prophecy. Although this appraisal may overstate the argument, both the administration and the union may find it more accommodating to agree to work jointly on retrenchment considerations at the appropriate time, but not in the context of the table negotiations. In addition, thought must be given to the adaptability of the procedures to all circumstances of exigency. An important consideration is the flexibility of the procedures, whether explicitly detailed in the retrenchment clause or developed independently of negotiations, to respond to short-term and long-term exigencies, federal, state, and local policy considerations, programmatic adjustments, and changes in student demands.

An important consideration in negotiating any issue is the

potential for misinterpretations of the contractual language. As discussed earlier, the national unions promote and recognize the necessity of external arbitration or litigation in resolving disputes arising out of the interpretation of contractual language. If explicit retrenchment procedures are negotiated, they should detail the steps to be initiated in a time of exigency, and provide appropriate protection for those classes of personnel involved in the retrenchment in a way which leaves little, if any, room for misinterpretation or challenge. Furthermore, explicit procedures, carefully written, limit the potential arbitrariness of external evaluators should the interpretation and administration of the procedures be challenged. On the other hand, the workability of contractual language is affected by the number and type of variables contributing to the exigency. *Maneuverability in times of crisis is essential.* Although there may be explicit language in a limited retrenchment provision requiring that the administration work with the union or its representatives, a realistic appraisal of the conditions contributing to, and of the means to deal with, the exigency must be able to pass the scrutiny of an external arbitrator. An example of a limited clause is provided in the agreement for Rutgers University. The Rutgers retrenchment clause, "Reduction in Force," states that, "Where the university asserts that, for financial or budgetary reasons, it intends to terminate an academic program, a number of faculty members, or to suspend promotions, it will present its plans to a joint committee, three to be chosen by AAUP and three by the university, serving fixed terms, for evaluation by that committee. The university agrees that it will give full and fair consideration to the recommendations of the committee prior to making its final determination." This kind of statement meets the basic expectations of consultation, yet retains flexibility for executive decision. It also leaves little room for an arbitrator to overturn a university's overall decision to retrench.

Finally, the prospect that most retrenchment decisions are likely to be grieved looms large. Employment terminations can have dire professional and economic consequences for those affected. Job security becomes an issue. Experiences at such institutions as Oakland University and the Pennsylvania State Colleges suggest that when the retrenchment becomes necessary, the unions will take every possible delaying action. Terminated faculty members and union officers are unlikely to be sympathetic to considerations of academic quality and program integrity. Their priority will almost always be full employment. This fact alone should be uppermost in the mind of any administrator attempting to bargain a retrenchment clause that will provide flexibility and relative immunity from negative grievance reviews.

When Does a Condition Warranting Personnel Retrenchment Exist,
and On What Basis Should Such a Condition Be Justified?

Despite the variety of treatments of this issue in existing contracts, the solutions may be categorized into two classes. The first and most prevalent approach is to develop contract language which supports initiation of retrenchment procedures on one or more of the following bases: insufficient financial resources, significant enrollment shifts or declines, and changes in instructional programs. Typically, little effort is made in existing contracts to define these conditions further. Such generalized language provides maximum flexibility for management, although usually subject to the advice and consent of the faculty or its representatives, to determine on what basis these conditions are justifiable. It is management's responsibility to provide documentation of the conditions warranting retrenchment, management's decision to initiate retrenchment procedures, and management's responsibility to terminate the retrenched faculty.

Whether or not the concept of financial exigency should be employed in retrenchment contract language is arguable. Few of the contracts currently using the term *financial exigency* attempt to define it. The courts are providing some guidance, albeit somewhat conflicting, as to what constitutes a situation of exigency (see Chapter Twenty-Two on retrenchment and administering the contract). Also, the AAUP is attempting to establish its special definition of the term. Since any grievant will attempt to persuade an arbitrator that some special definition helpful to the grievant's charges should prevail, it may be good judgment to omit from the contract any term that has been given such broad publicity and more than one definition. Until such time as the term is clarified further, one may assume that to declare a financial exigency requires extraordinary circumstances, a condition of crisis proportion before tenured faculty can be terminated. It may be more plausible, therefore, to use more general language such as "financial considerations" or "insufficient funds" which appear to take into consideration fluctuations in operating funds and cyclical variations in enrollments and require something less than conditions of emergency or crisis. However, such an approach may be opposed by a union and will no doubt require astute bargaining.

The second type of contract language for establishing a situation warranting personnel retrenchment can be classified as the formula approach. By tying retrenchment considerations directly to some formula-based criterion, the need to terminate personnel is determined by prior judgments. The basis on which retrenchment is instituted is documentable, heretofore mutually agreed upon, and provides clear parameters for making decisions. Existing formulas typically relate the retrenchment issue to enrollment considerations rather than attempt to tie the decision to budgetary conditions, and, accordingly, are usually effected before conditions of crisis are realized. However, despite the straightforwardness of the formula approach, it provides the administration little flexibility to meet special problems of affirmative action, quality control, or severe budget cuts imposed by factors other than enrollment (for example, budget cuts by the legislature). It is essential therefore, to negotiate procedural safeguards that will maximize flexibility in decisions relating to the specific people to be retrenched and will minimize the effects of grievance reviews.

Can Evaluative Criteria of Quality Be Substituted for Objective
Standards in Determining the Order of Faculty Layoffs?

It is argued that, to be effective, layoff or retrenchment procedures must establish some objective standards for determining the order of layoff and recall. Such standards reduce the impact of personal bias and the risk of procedural deficiencies and are less likely to invite extended litigation.

On the other hand, the objective standard most typically adopted, namely seniority defined as length of service, is an industrial sector principle which disregards the university's concept of excellence and may be unacceptable to higher education. Qualitative judgments are an inherent aspect of faculty personnel policies and practices. Since academic program quality is so intimately related to the quality of the faculty, quality control would appear to be contingent upon retention of the most qualified faculty, regardless of seniority status. A more careful analysis of the issue is required.

As Brown (1976) notes, seniority is comprised of several elements: tenure, rank, length of service, as well as qualifications. "But, of the various components of seniority, only length of service in the institution bears little relation to quality of performance" (p. 11). Rank implies merit, and tenure requires an exacting scrutiny of quality such that an institution is willing to commit itself to the individual for the remainder of his professional career. Furniss (1974) points out that whether seniority is a reliable indicator of quality "depends heavily on the care with which normal procedures involving individual evaluations have been established and administered" (p. 163). In the absence of such scrutiny, the overriding and inappropriate temptation may be to use the retrenchment conditions as a mechanism for instituting new evaluative procedures. Such untimely procedures are unlikely to be an adequate substitute for ongoing effective qualitative evaluations, independent of other considerations which are prone to distort the purpose of the evaluations.

A seniority system for determining the order of layoff may also come into direct conflict with certain public policies of the institution, particularly affirmative action programs. Accordingly, other considerations may inhibit the adoption of a seniority system as an appropriate means for determining the order of layoff. The next question deals with the issue of what constraints upon this standard may be appropriate.

Retrenchment offers little opportunity to initiate constructive academic reform, program review, and personnel evaluations. Such reviews and evaluations are almost bound to be hasty and the results subject to questions of integrity. Maintenance of effective academic programs under conditions of retrenchment is therefore dependent on previously existing programs of academic review, and documented instructional requirements and enrollment trends. It is not necessary, and probably not desirable, that such ongoing programs of review be specified in the collective bargaining agreement. What is critical is that these reviews, both programmatic and personnel, are occurring at all organizational levels, for all ranks, and for tenured as well as untenured faculty. Retrenchment clauses should recognize the importance of these reviews when retrenchment is being instituted.

There are additional means for reducing the potential impact of retrenchment on academic programs. A standard precursor to retrenchment is the implementation of nonpersonnel budget cuts. While across-the-board cuts in travel funds and departmental allotments may have the advantage of sensitizing the academic community to the institution's financial plight, a more selective approach to preretrenchment budget cuts may be preferable on at least two counts. First, the implementation of budgetary cuts in selected administrative areas may serve to protect those areas where the institution can programmatically least afford them. The latter programs, if and when financial conditions reach the stage in which retrenchment becomes necessary on a broad scale, may more likely survive the impact of subsequent retrenchments in budgets and personnel if they have not already been subjected to across-the-board cuts. Second, selective budget cuts at the preretrenchment stage, presumably based on an ongoing process of program review, will establish a precedent for dealing differentially with academic programs during periods of retrenchment.

Perhaps most vulnerable during periods of retrenchment are new and experimental programs. Although typically a financial liability for the institution in their infancy, many of these programs are responding to new enrollment markets and may potentially improve the overall resources of the institution. Frequently the faculty assigned to these programs have little seniority in terms of either their length of service with the institution or any other objective standards which may be applied. It may be important for institutions with such programs to develop contractual language which protects experimental and innovative programs, programs for the disadvantaged and minorities, and programs for adults. Even more generally, the anticipated future demand for each program may be a far more important consideration than current program support and enrollment. This should be recognized in any contract dealing with retrenchment to provide administrative flexibility in preparing for the future of the university.

How and When Should Faculty or Their Representatives Become Involved in Retrenchment Decisions?

Much has been written about the concepts of shared authority and the role and importance of faculty participation in decision making. It is not the purpose here to reconstruct the wealth of material on this topic. In summary, however, shared authority may be viewed as a continuum from codetermination by faculty and administration to collective bargaining. As one moves from codetermination to collective negotiations "the tenor of relationships between the faculty and administration changes from one of mutual influence and persuasion to reliance on codified, formal authority relations embodied in a legally binding agreement" (Mortimer and Lozier, 1972, pp. 4–5).

Under the principle of codetermination, the faculty is generally considered to have "primary" responsibility in areas of direct academic concern, such as the curriculum, course content, degree requirements, grading policies, admissions, and the selection and retention of academic personnel. Retrenchment decisions are regarded by faculty as being within their purview based upon their collective role in the selection and retention of academic personnel. Yet, labor boards generally see level of funding, number of employees, and hiring and firing as all being management prerogatives. Furthermore, considerations of financial exigency or other conditions warranting retrenchment typically go beyond the mere "hiring and firing" of faculty. Thus, according to the Carnegie Commission's report on governance in higher education (1973), "The cessation of growth calls for more flexibility in making readjustments in past patterns of operation; but faculty collective bargaining organization may mean more rigidity and more attachment to the status quo ante. Financial stringency often requires more centralized control of decisions affecting expenditures; but central control is also more suspect. These cross-pressures are illustrative of the general problem of the swirling crosscurrents affecting governance" (p. 10).

Inclusion of faculty in the retrenchment decision-making process may be justified on two bases. First, faculty participation is appropriate because of faculty expertise in academic programs and academic quality. Second, faculty participation is important in creating a balanced perspective and attitude on the part of those affected by the decisions. Thus, faculty members, as joint participants in the decision-making process, can play an important role in retrenchment considerations. But collective bargaining, with its delineation of faculty-administration responsibilities, its formalization of this relationship, and its legally binding constructs, establishes a considerable constraint upon traditional relationships. Although on some campuses these relationships have been sustained in some areas despite the presence of collective bargaining, it can probably be expected that in general the faculty will not be able to engage in codetermination and in collective bargaining on the same issues at the same time. The criticial nature of retrenchment decisions suggests that retrenchment may be an appropriate issue for defining the changing nature of the role of faculty under collective bargaining. For, as Naples (1974) suggests, "collective bargaining presents management with the opportunity to delineate areas of managerial freedom of action which were cloudy and unclear under traditional governance" (p. 59). Although these observations do not negate the arguments for including the faculty in retrenchment decisions, they highlight the constraints which collective bargaining poses upon the level of faculty responsibility called for in such documents as the AAUP's statement of faculty termination (American Association of University Professors, 1975).

The above discussion focuses primarily upon whether faculty have an appropriate role in retrenchment decisions. A related, but sufficiently distinct, issue is whether the administration as management is required to negotiate the faculty's role in retrenchment considerations. A distinction is made between mandatory subjects of bargaining (those specifically required by law under the rubric of "wages, hours, and other terms and conditions of employment"), permissive subjects of bargaining (those potential subjects which are neither required nor prohibited by law), and illegal subjects of bargaining (issues expressly prohibited by the controlling labor law). The distinction between mandatory and permissive subjects of bargaining should not be lost. Administrators must consider carefully whether issues which are permissive subjects, such as overall budget, organizational structure, and the selection and direction of personnel, should be negotiated at all unless some clear advantage to such a concession is realized by management. Although such a consideration should retain an appropriate academic perspective, seeking advantages and concessions is a recognition of the formalized employment-management dichotomy created by collective bargaining.

As noted above, the faculty in many colleges and universities have an established role in decisions with respect to academic considerations and faculty personnel policies. Schwartzman (1974) points out that authority in these areas has been afforded to faculty as faculty. It may be quite another matter whether this role is a mandatory subject of bargaining with the faculty as union, or whether it falls within the permissive subject category. "The mere fact that a subject matter has traditionally involved faculty participation does not convert the topic into a mandatory subject of bargaining" (p. 359). If demanded by the union, management may have an obligation to bargain the impact of managerial decisions upon working conditions. All other aspects of the retrenchment issue seem to fall within the permissive area of negotiations, making their negotiability subject to a host of considerations. Before entering into negotiations, the administration should develop an overall bargaining strategy and determine which model of negotiations (that is, comprehensive, structural, or employment negotiations) it wishes to adopt. There is an obvious interrelationship between these decisions and the issue of the negotiability of the faculty's role in retrenchment decisions. At one end of the spectrum, faculty participation under the employment negotiations model might be limited to negotiations of the impact of retrenchment upon working conditions; faculty would not be involved in the determination to initiate retrenchment procedures. Under comprehensive negotiations, a retrenchment provision might provide for faculty participation in preliminary budget considerations and analysis of an institution's financial conditions, in the decision to initiate retrenchment procedures, and in the determination of the areas, and perhaps individuals, to be affected.

Finally, Katz (1974), in a discussion of faculty participatory models, points out that under traditional models of governance, an enormous gulf separates the "primary responsibility" afforded faculty in areas of academic concern and the "final authority" vested in administrators and governing boards. However, the application of the final authority might also be dependent upon the model of participation adopted. The Carnegie Commission (1973) observes that the adoption of unionization may have a significant impact upon the growth of managerial authority. The governance report suggests that "The attitude may come to be that managers should manage and teachers should teach" (p. 44). Accordingly, many faculty members do regard retrenchment as the business of management, and they seek no role in the development of retrenchment guidelines and procedures, recognizing that if such provisions exist, the provisions will only be instituted sometime, somewhere, by someone, upon somebody. Such was the reaction of the union for the Pennsylvania State Colleges, which refused to cooperate with the state when the latter sought the union's assistance in developing guidelines for implementing the contract's retrenchment provision.

Summary

Five important retrenchment considerations are discussed in the preceding sections. First, the analysis considered whether retrenchment should be negotiated by management and how comprehensive such negotiations should be. The review, while acknowledging the need to prepare for conditions of exigency, emphasizes the importance of flexible contract language and procedures. Such flexibility may be best promoted by limited contract language.

Second, the concept of financial exigency and the difficulties in defining it before it actually occurs are noted. Although based on admittedly limited bargaining experience, it appears that negotiated formulas for identifying retrenchment conditions cannot overcome the harsh realities of being laid off. Establishing student-faculty ratios in a vacuum is quite another thing from terminating a faculty member.

Third, the discussion suggests that there are correlations between seniority and various indices of professional quality such as rank and tenure. To reduce the onus of a seniority-related order of termination, ongoing qualitative evaluations in the absence of crisis are advocated so that retrenchment decisions are not substituted for sound promotion and tenure reviews.

Fourth, the importance of maintaining academic program effectiveness and integrity is emphasized. Administrators must consider what impact retrenchment decisions will have upon academic program vitality. What role might a continuing procedure of academic program reviews have in supporting program effectiveness? Can selective, rather than across-the-board, budgeting cuts help stave off further retrenchment while protecting financially marginal but academically sound programs? How can the potential vulnerability of new and experimental programs caused by retrenchment decisions be reduced or eliminated?

Fifth, the issue of faculty participation is discussed. There is a difference between faculty-administration governance relationships and the codified and formalized employee-management dichotomy. Collective bargaining promotes new styles of management and imposes constraints upon traditional areas of faculty responsibility. Under a controlling labor relations statute, issues within the prior realm of faculty-administrative codetermination may be within the purview of "management's rights." There are many indications that retrenchment decisions are increasingly regarded, even by faculty, as the sole responsibility of management.

Every experienced administrator knows that the way an institution conducts its faculty and academic program evaluations, the ingenuity used in administering budgets and dealing with difficult financial decisions, and the diplomacy with which retrenchment is handled will determine to a significant degree the amount of turmoil through which an institution and its faculty will have to go. Yet, no optimal retrenchment clause for all institutions can really be proffered. By their very nature, institutions vary considerably, and good bargaining solutions will reflect the styles and concerns of institutional and union leadership.

Barry L. Hjort

14

It should come as no surprise to college and university administrators that students want to be included in the collective bargaining process. During the early 1970's when significant numbers of faculty members in public and private institutions began to look with real interest at collective bargaining as a tool to achieve their ends, college students were turning from protest and civil disobedience to more traditional political methods as a means of making their special concerns known. As state enabling legislation was passed to authorize faculty members to select bargaining agents of their choice, concerned students and their chosen representatives sought to have their voices heard at the bargaining table. Through adroit student lobbying efforts, the student interest in faculty collective bargaining is now recognized in public-sector enabling legislation in three states: Montana, Oregon, and Maine.

Enabling Legislation

Assume for the moment that your state has an enabling act which authorizes faculty collective bargaining or that a bill has

Involving Students
in Bargaining

been introduced in your state legislature and student organizations are pressing to be recognized as participants in the bargaining process through amendment of the existing law or legislative alteration of an introduced bill. What is your posture as regent or trustee, as a chancellor or commissioner, as a president or college or university administrator in the face of this effort? Do you resist the student lobbyists and possibly alienate an important constituent group of the academic community? What if the students are successful in spite of administrative resistance? Can they be won back in the course of the bargaining process or will their enmity die slowly? What if your trustee policy is to support student participation in faculty bargaining? How do you support student effort and to what extent in the legislative process?

Obviously, the answers to these questions will vary depending upon a variety of factors, many political, at the time they are raised. But for purposes of this discussion, assume that a conclusion to support student participation in collective bargaining has been reached in the appropriate deliberative process. How then should the right of student participation be properly expressed in the law?

Numerous theoretical models for student participation have been hypothesized (Bucklew, 1975), and three different working models of student involvement in faculty collective bargaining are now in the early trial stages of operation in Montana, Oregon, and Maine. The legal and practical differences are significant.

In Montana, which was the first state to authorize student participation in faculty collective bargaining at its public institutions, the Montana Student Lobby originally sought passage of two bargaining-related bills in the 1975 legislative session. The first bill would have guaranteed students a tuition rebate in the event of a faculty strike. This proposed legislation failed by a wide margin in balloting in the Montana House of Representatives. The second bill, which was extensively amended and then passed by wide majorities in both houses of the Montana legislature, amended the Public Employee's Collective Bargaining Act to allow students certain rights of participation when the board of regents or its designee engaged in negotiations with faculty representatives. The law is permissive in that it allows students to exercise the option to observe negotiations as members of the administration's table bargaining team.[1] They may participate in caucuses of the management team, meet and confer with representatives of both parties before negotiations actually commence, and meet and confer with the board of regents before it ratifies any faculty collective bargaining agreement. Student participants are enjoined by law to "maintain the confidentiality" of the negotiations. Under the Montana model, students are thus by law joined with the administration bargaining team for purposes of negotiation, even though as a practical matter, the interests of the students and the administration will not be congruent on all issues.

In Oregon, students achieved a status in faculty collective bargaining which was initially sought in Montana but which was rejected by the Montana legislature because of opposition to the proposal from faculty organizations and Lawrence K. Pettit, the Commissioner of Higher Education. The Oregon law authorizes students to participate in faculty negotiations as independent third

[1]59–1602 R.C.M. (1974).

parties.[2] Three student representatives are authorized to participate in negotiations at each of the eight Oregon state colleges and universities. Students are permitted access to all documents prepared by either party in the process and are allowed to meet separately with both faculty representatives and the administration. As in Montana, students are required to observe the same rules of confidentiality that apply to negotiators. Even though the Oregon students are not affiliated by law with either party in the bargaining process and are therefore independent third-party participants, they do not have the authority to approve or ratify any contract which is negotiated between the administration and faculty representatives.

In recently enacted legislation passed by a special session of the Maine legislature, University of Maine students were granted certain limited rights to participate in collective bargaining negotiations when bargaining is to take place between university representatives and either a faculty or a professional administrative bargaining unit.[3] Under the Maine act, the board of trustees is required to appoint three students to represent student interests in collective negotiations. Interestingly enough, the law also places upon the university the responsibility of considering and representing student interest and welfare in applicable negotiations with appropriate bargaining units. Student rights under the University of Maine Act include: (1) a permissive right to meet with the bargaining agent before negotiations commence, and (2) a mandatory right to be allowed to meet with the university bargaining team once negotiations have commenced and at reasonable intervals until negotiations are concluded. As in Montana and Oregon, Maine student representatives "must observe the confidentiality and other rules binding the negotiating parties in the collective bargaining process."[4]

The three operational models for student involvement in faculty collective bargaining provide a wide diversity of choice for administrators and others concerned with the adoption of appropriate legislation to authorize student participation in faculty col-

[2]O.R.S. 243.650 to 243.782 (1975).
[3]26 M.R.S.A. 1022(10) and 1024(4), (1976).
[4]26 M.R.S.A. 1024(4), (1976).

lective bargaining. At the one extreme is Oregon where students have independent third-party status in negotiations, and at the other end of the spectrum is the Maine law which closely circumscribes student rights and involvement in the process. Montana's law allows broad student participation in virtually every significant phase of the bargaining process but requires that students be affiliated with the management team.[5]

If your state is faced with the prospect of student involvement in faculty collective bargaining, the nature of enabling legislation to sanction that involvement will ultimately depend upon the political exigencies of the moment, the special concerns of the constituent groups involved in seeking to pass or defeat such legislation, and the legislative state of mind regarding students as a group and public-sector collective bargaining as a process. What should the administrative posture be in the preenabling-act stage given the above considerations? Clearly the answer to that question will depend upon what administrators and the governing board hope to achieve by including or excluding students. Deliberations should focus on at least such factors as (1) the extent to which it is desirable to have students involved in policy formulation, (2) the recent history of major student issues at institutions and the successful or unsuccessful resolution thereof, (3) the probable union position on student involvement, (4) the probable changes in policy and internal relationships if students are or are not accorded a significant role in the faculty bargaining process, and (5) the tactical implications of having students act as an independent third party in negotiations or as a nominal affiliate of either management or labor.

Student Preparation

Presume for the purpose of this discussion that the legislative hurdle has been cleared and that the institution or system is faced with the prospect of faculty collective bargaining with an added twist. Student representatives are now authorized by law to participate in some fashion in the process. What steps may students and administrators take to ensure that student representatives are

[5]59–1602 R.C.M. (1974).

properly prepared so that their participation in collective bargaining will be constructive and meaningful? The initial efforts should naturally be directed to organization and education.

It would be presumptuous on the part of any administrator to interfere with the students' establishment of their own form of organization for preparation for collective bargaining. If students have been sufficiently concerned with the advent of faculty bargaining to seek legislation authorizing their involvement, their student lobby group or existing student government will undoubtedly establish an organizational framework to effectively represent their interests. In a multicampus system, this framework may simply take the form of a steering committee made up of students from the affected institutions or an ad hoc group bolstered by members of the student lobby team. At a single institution, a student government subcommittee, specially appointed to oversee student collective bargaining concerns, may be the proper organizational model. Whatever the structure, some responsible student committee should be formed as soon as possible to make decisions and direct student participation from the outset.

Although it may be inappropriate for administrators to suggest the form of the student organization which will govern their participation in collective bargaining or for that matter to interfere in the selection of student table representatives, suggestions from administrators as to how to educate and prepare for the process should not be regarded by students as meddling or improper interference. The pedagogical function can be fulfilled in several ways. First, student attention can be directed to the considerable literature produced in recent years concerning faculty collective bargaining and its ramifications. The ACBIS and the Research Project on Students and Collective Bargaining are excellent sources of information for particular subjects with which students may be concerned. There are also numerous monographs which can serve as primers for the newcomer to the field of academic collective bargaining.

To provide an overview of how collective bargaining proceeds, an insight into the nuances of the process, a review of the legal constraints, and to make clear the responsibilities of the parties, the administration might suggest a jointly sponsored seminar for educational purposes. Such a study group should include presentations by representatives of the administration, any interested union organizations or associations, retained consultants and, if available, a student who has familiarity and experience with faculty bargaining. The diverse mix of viewpoints from such a seminar will hopefully coalesce to give interested students a broad grasp of some of the complexities of the process with which they are involved.

Prior to the commencement of actual negotiations between faculty and administration representatives, each party should make an effort to meet with student representatives to explain proposals, counterproposals, and other matters of general concern. In some cases, such a meeting will be required by law. If it is not, the administration and the union will do well to make their respective initial positions known to student participants, if for no other reason than to generate an initial feeling of goodwill. The maintenance of that goodwill is a significant factor in any collective bargaining negotiations to follow which involves student representatives.

Students will normally be left to their own initiative to develop issues, if any, for presentation at the table. Usually, significant student concerns will be highlighted by a general poll of the student body or a written solicitation by the student government for suggestions as to issues to be included in the student proposals. If the enabling act is silent as to the method for presenting student concerns to the negotiating parties and it is agreed that such issues will be concerned, the mechanics of getting student issues to the table should be worked out well in advance of an exchange of proposals by administration and faculty representatives.

The Student at the Table

Table Etiquette

The special provisions of enabling legislation will probably settle some of the questions of table protocol which must be considered in accommodating a third party in faculty collective bargaining negotiations. If the enabling act is silent on this matter or if negotiations are conducted pursuant to agreement of the parties, a myriad of questions are presented. For example: (1) how many student representatives shall be allowed at the table; (2) where shall they be physically located; (3) may students call a caucus and halt negotiations; (4) with which party are students allowed to confer when a primary party calls a caucus; (5) what happens if students breach the confidentiality of negotiations; (6) to whom may students relate progress of talks and critical issues without breaching confidentiality; (7) are there limits on the number of students who have a "need to know"; (8) may discussions proceed without student representatives present; (9) to what documents and information will student representatives be permitted access; (10) may students issue independent press releases on negotiations progress; (11) are students subject to unfair labor practice charges; (12) shall students sign and ratify the final agreement; (13) can students be bound as parties to observe the agreement if they do not sign and ratify; (14) what limits may be imposed on consultations outside the negotiating room or caucus room between student representatives and another party; (15) what is the student role after impasse or in the event of a strike; and (16) who bears the costs of student participation in the bargaining process (Shark, 1975, p. 10)? This is a small sample of the questions which are presented by student involvement and obviously there are no pat solutions which cut across all jurisdictional lines.

Because of the unique nature of tripartite collective bargaining, the setting of ground rules in a so-called prenegotiation agreement takes on added significance. Many of the questions can be settled by a comprehensive prenegotiation agreement which establishes the procedures to be followed in the bargaining process. If proper planning precedes the settlement of bargaining ground rules, many of the nettlesome questions of students and table etiquette will be resolved before they become bargaining stumbling blocks.

Working with Students

Assume that you are now at the bargaining table with a student representative whose role is well-defined. What are the implications for you as an administrator or as a member of the administration team, and to whose advantage, if any, will the student's presence be? The answer depends largely on the attitude of the participants. Students are, and can be, a powerful force in table negotiations and issue settlement. If they are treated in a less than forthright manner, ignored, or shunted aside, their reaction is predictable. If, on the other hand, they are regarded as legitimate participants in the process, their opinions sought, arguments weighed, and their proper role acknowledged, their reciprocity will generally be forthcoming. Establishing a good working rapport with student table representatives cannot be overemphasized. Timely student support of the administration position on a particular issue, and supporting arguments developed independently from a unique student perspective can prove invaluable. Whether the enabling act makes students an independent third party or affiliates them with the administration or with the union, the time and effort involved in seeking their understanding and support is well worthwhile. If the act affiliates students with the administration at the table, there is a strong advantage from the start. The subtle psychology of familiarity with administration positions and arguments, and the present state of institutional fiscal affairs will produce an ally at the table if handled with some degree of sensitivity. If the bargaining law provides students with third-party status, the cultivation of student understanding and support is probably made more difficult. Nevertheless, it is a task worth the undertaking.

Student affiliation with administration does not mean that the administration should pander to the student interest at any cost so that a powerful administration-student coalition presents a solid front at the table on every bargaining issue. Certainly a real diversity of opinion is healthy in the collective bargaining setting as in any academic context. Nor should the administration efforts to coopt student support be limited to actual table negotiations. The working relationship with student collective bargaining representatives must be established well before the parties get to the table and should continue through contract ratification and contract administration. Mutual respect and trust should be established over a period of time in order that students begin to regard the administration and the union as more than an extension of the ubiquitous establishment.

Student Issues and Demands

What kinds of issues can one expect student interest to center upon and what kinds of student demands can be anticipated? The list would seem limitless, but there are concerns shared by students at most institutions which may be affected by the advent of faculty collective bargaining (Shark, 1975, pp. 2–3). Some of these concerns are interrelated, and they will be accorded varying degrees of emphasis depending on the unique nature and history of particular institutions. Nonetheless, most of them will appear in some form or other in student collective bargaining proposals. Student concerns often include: (1) the possible impact on tuition and fees of increases in negotiated faculty salaries and fringe benefits; (2) the possible interruption of student educational progress in the event of a faculty strike; (3) the preservation and extension of student rights previously established by agreement with faculty, administration, and governing board; (4) the establishment of an effective student grievance mechanism; (5) an opportunity to sit as participants or observers on academic committees concerned with faculty tenure, promotion, evaluation, curricular structure, and class size; (6) the establishment of a faculty evaluation procedure that ensures faculty accountability and proper delivery of instructional services; (7) the establishment or refinement of methods of providing proper delivery of campus student services; and (8) a general consumer's interest in knowing in advance what a particular class, course, or curricular offering will be and having some reasonable expectation after enrollment of delivery of that product.

This list is not comprehensive and the necessarily abbreviated treatment does not permit examination of how individual issues should or can be treated in the bargaining process. However, at least in Montana, student bargaining persistence has led to faculty contract provisions which speak to most of the above issues (Collective Bargaining Agreement, 1976, pp. 19–20 and Northern Montana College Faculty Contract, 1976, pp. 8–11).

Brief mention should be made of how student issues come before the primary bargaining parties for consideration. In Montana, students are by law allowed to participate in caucuses as part of the administration's bargaining team, and although they are observers, student representatives have been physically seated with the employer's table team. To facilitate the process, student demands have been separately identified but presented with administration counterproposals when such proposals were submitted to the union for its consideration. In Oregon where students have independent, third-party status, some arrangement must be worked out to allow for the submission of student proposals to the administration and the union when the primary parties are exchanging their respective proposals. In Maine, there may be some uncertainty as to whether students may independently originate proposals in light of the legal enjoinder upon the university to consider and represent student interests in collective negotiations.

The last important question related to student involvement and faculty collective bargaining is what issues do students support and which party do they side with in bargaining? As a matter of enlightened self-interest, students vigorously support proposals they have advanced such as those enumerated above. It is my experience that they also tend to support broad student representation on academic committees, traditional academic freedom and affirmative action provisions for faculty, merit components in faculty salary structures, reasonable faculty working conditions, strong faculty accountability and evaluation provisions, and comprehensive faculty grievance mechanisms. Students tend to oppose reduced teaching loads, the granting of tenure and promotions based solely on years of service and time in rank without comprehensive evaluation, excessive across-the-board salary increases and expanded faculty fringe benefits that involve significant added cost to the institution. Students do not necessarily side with the administration or the union on a continuing basis. They frequently have an independent point of view on important issues and will, as one might expect, side with the primary party which advocates a point of view most closely approximating their own perceived self-interest.

Student Participation: An Assessment

Despite a good deal of initial skepticism on the part of observers, participants, and commentators familiar with academic collective bargaining, student involvement in the process has, in Montana, not only worked, but worked positively and constructively. Student involvement has resulted in the negotiation of faculty contract provisions which hopefully will serve all three parties well. As with any first contract effort, latent dissatisfaction lingers with each party over certain contract provisions. On the whole, however, all parties agree that student participation in Montana has added a beneficial dimension.

Positive Results for the Administration and the Union

A college or university administration can reap substantial benefits from having students closely involved with faculty collective bargaining. The most obvious immediate benefit is the development of close lines of communication among all three constituent groups. Unfortunately this kind of communication is frequently lacking on college campuses not involved in a collective bargaining process. If certain past management decisions have been perceived by students and faculty as having been made without their participation, and for seemingly irrational or illogical reasons, bargaining table confrontation can clarify the basis for those decisions. Moreover, the compromise settlement through negotiations of significant campus issues which involve students, faculty, and administration gives all participants a sense of being full partners in the operation of the institution. Dialogue between union and administration with students present gives the students a much improved understanding of the nature of crucial campus issues. The setting also presents an opportunity for students and faculty to thresh out matters which have long rankled one or both parties.

The second significant effect of student participation is that students are a positive force in the collective bargaining process, and having student support on an issue or issues is undeniably an asset to the primary party beneficiary. However, an asset to one party is clearly a liability to the other. A third benefit is the enhanced communications and is probably best characterized as an improved student understanding of how their institution works. The collective bargaining setting gives students an unparalleled opportunity to gain some insight into administrative decision making. After sitting through hours of negotiations, student representatives will know more about the institution's fiscal condition, its internal academic process, and the contemporary political, academic, and fiscal concerns of administrators and faculty members than any of their student government predecessors no matter how hard working. Although this view may be disquieting to some, it ought nonetheless to be categorized as a benefit.

A fourth benefit to the administration and the union is that the contract itself presents a vehicle for resolving student-related matters which previously required independent action. For example, federal law now requires that any institution which receives federal monies must establish a grievance mechanism for students.[6] A student grievance procedure that will satisfy the requirements of federal law can be developed and included in the faculty contract. So also may the requirements of the Buckley Amendment[7] concerning the handling and release of student records be formalized in the collective bargaining agreement under the section devoted to student rights. These are but two examples of matters which in the absence of collective bargaining would have required resolution by some other independent process.

Positive Results for Students

The Montana experience with student involvement in faculty collective bargaining demonstrates clearly that student goals, in the abstract sense of contract clause recognition, can be achieved through the bargaining process. Whether such goals are implemented in an operational sense as a result of contract recognition and student, administration, and faculty effort is a question which remains unanswered because of the relatively recent ratification of the contracts in question.

The provisions in the faculty contracts recently ratified at Eastern Montana College and Northern Montana College which relate to students touch on practically all of the contemporary student concerns outlined above. In Section 16.000 of the Montana Eastern Montana College Faculty Contract: 1975–1977, the student role and student rights and responsibilities are enumerated at some length. The parties all agree to recognize that students are a vital factor in efforts to maintain and improve the quality of education at the institution and that students must be included in the decision-making process. Students are given representation on all standing committees, search committees for the filling of both faculty and administrative positions, and any committee appointed to review and evaluate a faculty member or administrator. Faculty members must fully inform the students at the commencement of each quarter of the course description, requirements, and grad-

[6]20 u.s.c. 1681, 1682; 45 c.f.r. 86.8 (1975).
[7]20 u.s.c. 1232g, Family Educational Rights and Privacy Act (1974).

ing policy for each class. All parties agree to recognize and work cooperatively with student organizations and also recognize the rights of students as set forth in certain existing student documents. A comprehensive student grievance procedure is established which binds the student to any final determination if he elects to use its procedures. The union agrees to advise the president of the student governing body when a faculty strike is imminent. And last, students agree to recognize and abide by regulations setting forth their responsibilities which are listed in the current edition of the faculty-staff handbook. The students also made their opinions known on a variety of other matters. Their concern with institutional fiscal condition and the possible financial impact of expanded faculty fringe benefit provisions served as a substantial counter weight to faculty arguments addressed to across-the-board salary increases and expanded leave and sabbatical privileges. In terms of the Montana experience, student representatives were a strong moderating influence upon the bargaining proceedings. They were rational and objective, and their fresh perspective added significantly to the process.

Legislation Regarding Students

Montana

Section 59-1602

(Definitions) When used in this act: (1) "public employer" means the state of Montana or any political subdivision thereof, including but not limited to, any town, . . . or other authority established by law, and any representative or agent designated by the public employer to act in its interest in dealing with public employees; when the board of regents is the public employer defined in this section, the student government at an institution of higher education may designate an agent or representative to meet and confer with the board of regents and the faculty bargaining agent prior to negotiations with the professional educational employees, to observe those negotiations and participate in caucuses as part of the public employer's bargaining team, and to meet and confer with the board of regents regarding the terms of agreement prior to the execution of a written contract between the regents and the professional educational employees. The student observer is obliged to maintain the confidentiality of these negotiations. (As amended by Ch. 384, L. 1975, effective April 10, 1975.) [Taken from 51 GERR 3511 November 10, 1975.]

Maine

Section 1022 (10) In addition to its responsibilities to the public generally, the university shall have the specific responsibility of considering and representing the interests and welfare of the students in any negotiations under this chapter (as enacted by PL 1975, c. 603, Sec. I).

Section 1024 (4) Students

A. When collective bargaining is to take place between the university and the faculty or professional and administrative staff, the board of trustees shall appoint three (3) currently enrolled students who are broadly representative of the various campuses and who may meet and confer with the bargaining agent prior to collective bargaining.

B. During the course of collective bargaining, the student representatives designated under paragraph A shall be allowed to meet and confer with the university bargaining team at reasonable intervals during the course of negotiations, such meetings to occur at least upon receipt by the university of the initial bargaining proposal of the bargaining agent and before final agreement on a contract or any major provisions thereof. The students shall be bound by the same rules of negotiation, including, but not limited to, those regarding confidentiality, as the participants in the negotiations. [Taken from 26 M.R.S.A. 1022 (10) and 1024 (4) (1976).]

Oregon

Section 243

(Appropriate bargaining unit; exclusive representative) (1) When an appropriate bargaining unit includes [faculty], . . . the duly organized and recognized entity of student government at that institution may designate three representatives to meet and confer with the public employer of those members of the faculty and the exclusive representative of that bargaining unit.

(2) During the course of collective bargaining between the public employer and the exclusive representative described in subsection (1) of this section, the representatives of student government designated under subsection (1) of this section shall:

(a) Be allowed to attend and observe all meetings between the public employer and the exclusive representative at which collective bargaining occurs;

(b) Have access to all written documents pertaining to the collective bargaining negotiations exchanged by the public employer and the exclusive representative, including copies of any prepared written transcripts of the bargaining sessions;

(c) Be allowed to comment in good faith during the bargaining sessions upon matters under consideration; and

(d) Be allowed to meet and confer with the exclusive representative and the public employer regarding the terms of an agreement between them prior to the execution. . . .

(3) Rules regarding confidentiality and release of information shall apply to student representatives in the same manner as employer and employee bargaining unit representatives. [Taken from 51 GERR 4618, 4618(A) December 8, 1975.]

William J. Neff
John D. Forsyth

Most of the work of costing union demands, that is, the development of data, should be completed at least a few weeks prior to the beginning of negotiations. Initial calculations concerning a new or altered demand should not ordinarily be made in the presence of the union. Such activity is too time consuming, accuracy may be sacrificed, and it may lead to unnecessary disagreements. Costing at the table should be limited to showing the other party the cost of a given demand after the necessary costing has been completed away from the table.

The Costing Function

In most service organizations, including institutions of higher education, salaries and benefits represent the largest single cost in the employer's budget. These costs generally represent over 50 percent of the total budget and, in many cases, exceed 75

Costing
Union Demands

percent of the total budget. In addition, when considering faculty salary and benefit costs, most institutions of higher education spend over 50 percent of their total compensation budget for faculty salaries and benefits. Thus, the importance to the institution of accurate costing of the faculty contract cannot be underestimated.

Some initial concerns for the institution in approaching the costing function are (1) what are the objectives of the institution in the negotiation of a contract, and (2) who should have the responsibility for the costing function?

What Are the Bargaining Objectives of the Institution?

The need to have specific bargaining objectives is most important in the costing function as well as in the bargaining process. The bargaining team needs to know the priorities of the institution, especially in the area of expenditures. It is necessary to know the priorities of direct versus indirect salary as well as priorities among indirect salary items. The bargaining team must also know the economic parameters within which it must work. Once these are established, the team can construct alternatives which meet the institution's objectives and are equivalent in cost.

It should be noted that to have or maintain as a bargaining objective simply the minimizing of cost increases fails to recognize that minimizing salary and benefit costs is not only a function of bargaining power but also a function of how and where increases will be directed. For example, the institution's position on whether or not to provide a dental care plan may have long-term cost implications which are much greater than initially providing a plan which is totally, or nearly totally, paid for by the employees. Consequently, the institution must be able to determine not only how much more (or less) it will spend, but also a plan of priorities as to how the increase (or decrease) will be allocated. It is a mistake to be indifferent to how additional dollars will be spent because long-term costs may be much different from those originally envisioned.

Who Has Costing Responsibility?

It is important that the institution identify a person or persons who will have the responsibility and accountability for costing. In many institutions this is a shared responsibility between or among the business and financial offices, the records, data systems, and payroll offices, and the chief negotiator's office. Clearly the number of people involved should be kept to a minimum in order to ensure confidentiality as well as to minimize the potential for error. Final responsibility should be clearly assigned in order to ensure accountability and efficiency.

Whether one individual or several have the costing responsibility, the chief negotiator must be familiar with the data and the method of calculation since he must, at all times, be in the position to speak knowledgeably and with authority on any aspect of costing.

Data Development

In order to ascertain what the cost implications of a demand or proposal may be, accurate base data are essential. Inaccurate data yield inaccurate cost figures, which may, in turn, cause the institution to make errors in both its long-term and short-term decisions and in unjustifiable shifts in priorities. Negotiated decisions based upon inaccurate data are not easily reversed or modified once an agreement has been reached. Consequently, the institution may find itself living with unfortunate fiscal decisions for at least the duration of the contract.

Additional problems may be created by inaccurate data and cost estimates. Overestimates may lead the institution to a decision to face a strike because the cost of the proposed agreement appears to be greater than that which the institution wishes to accept. Conversely, if the cost figures are underestimated and agreement is reached to spend more money than is available for a particular service or benefit, the institution is forced to increase its revenues or to make cuts in services or benefits elsewhere in the budget.

Pitfalls of Costing

In attempting to cost the union's demands or the institution's own counterproposals, it should be recognized that not all costs are easily identifiable or easily converted to dollar figures. The institution should conduct a complete cost-benefit analysis on any proposal prior to incorporating it into a collective bargaining agreement. The costs may be economic, noneconomic, or a combination of both. The benefits may be positive, neutral, or negative.

Even when demands clearly have a dollar versus dollar relationship, negotiators must be conscious of the assumptions which have been made concerning those dollar figures. Erroneous assumptions in calculating costs or developing data may make the final decision less meaningful than trying to decide between extra dollar expenditures and flexibility in running the institution. Likewise, care should be taken to ensure that cost predictions made on past practices are realistic, that the delivery of educational services in the past reflects the anticipated delivery of educational services in the future.

Data for Costing

By and large, costing is a mechanical process if the required data elements are available. However, to conduct a meaningful cost-benefit analysis, it is necessary to have readily available accurate data representing a number of years. The lack of such data places the institution's bargaining team at a distinct disadvantage. The greater the number of assumptions that must be made during the course of the negotiations, the greater the likelihood that the resultant figures will be unrealistic. Moreover, there are instances in which the presentation of the facts may encourage the union bargaining team to modify an existing position. Consequently, the importance of the development and maintenance of a data base cannot be overemphasized.

The data necessary for the purpose of collective bargaining generally falls into either of two general categories: internal data and external data. (In this connection, see the tables suggested by Joseph Hankin, Chapter Eight.)

Internal Data

The advent of collective bargaining may or may not make significant demands on an institution's information system. If the institution has demographic data on members of the bargaining unit in machine processable form, the probabilities are that the informational demands of the bargaining team will pose only a minor burden. However, if this is not the case the demands of the bargaining team on the information system may often seem unrealistic.

The data base should include historical as well as current information. Data elements which may be necessary during the bargaining process and thus should be in the information system include: name and social security number, activity category (a code describing the activities that faculty typically perform, such as teaching, research, service, and administration), activity Full Time Equivalent (FTE) percentage effort (the percentage of each faculty member's time assigned to each function: teaching, research, committees), contact hours by course section, course identifier, section identifier, mailing address, appointment effective date, appointment expiration date, classification, organizational unit (that is, department), pay rate, salary grade, accrued hours sick leave, accrued hours vacation, awards and honorary degrees, earned degrees and certificates awarded (and dates awarded), military service, publications rating, special competencies, university chairs, enrollments in optional fringe benefit programs, physical handicap status, race, sex, citizenship status, original date of hire, and tenure code. Class sizes and trends in course and program enrollments may also be of value.

The combination of an adequate data base in machine processable form and the use of standard statistical computer programs should provide the institution with the information that is necessary for constructive negotiations.

External Data

A significant amount of information on faculty salaries and benefits can be obtained by contacting: (1) College and University Personnel Association (CUPA) and (2) American Association of University Professors (AAUP). However, it is usually necessary to examine information that is not collected by any national organization. A survey is often the best vehicle to collect such information. Decisions that should be considered prior to constructing a survey instrument include:

1. An institutional survey versus a joint survey with the union. Conducting a joint survey generally enhances the likelihood that the parties will be in agreement on the fact situations at the selected institution. However, the parties must agree upon the variables and institutions to be surveyed as well as actual survey construction. Approaching the union with a proposal for a joint survey prior to the beginning of negotiations may provide the institution's bargaining team with an interesting perspective of the union's attitude toward the institution as well as the bargaining process.

One of the potential problems that should be recognized as a possible consequence of a joint survey is that the results may create additional bargaining issues. Another problem might be that the parties are unable to agree on what should be asked or how the survey is to be conducted. If the parties cannot agree, the institution must be prepared to conduct its own survey well before negotiations begin. Sometimes it is beneficial to have an informal association of similar colleges to provide an exchange of basic data each year.

2. Institutions to be surveyed. It is necessary to consider carefully the institutions to be surveyed. Are the objectives to determine the existing fact situation at peer institutions, private and public institutions with similar enrollments, institutions with similar regional or geographic locations, or a combination of these or other factors? Each institution must answer these questions for itself.

3. Variables to be surveyed. The selection process of variables to be surveyed should include a comprehensive review of items the institution believes will affect its ability to attract and retain quality faculty, staff, and students along with items that are objectives of the institution during negotiations or are perceived objectives of the union. (In a joint survey the union will often clearly state its objectives.) Such a review should culminate in the selection of items to be surveyed.

Once these determinations have been made the actual construction of the survey should begin. It is important to note that the survey questions should be clear and concise and leave no room for misinterpretation. Throughout the process it should be clear to those participating that the president of the institution will send the results of the survey personally to other presidents. This personal approach usually assures a higher return of questionnaires.

Categorizing the Union's Economic Demands

Once the data is in order and the institution has received the union's demands, the next step associated with costing is to completely understand the demands. The union's demands, which the university should request be presented in writing, should be reviewed by the institutional personnel responsible for negotiations and costing. All questions raised by staff members should be recorded and later presented to the union for answers. No assumptions nor presumptions should be made as to what the written demands mean.

When the demands are clearly understood, the management team should establish general categories and assign each demand and any subparts to the most appropriate category. The reasons for this categorization are threefold—to break down the demands into their simplest factors thereby facilitating costing, to ensure that all factors are identified and thus costed, and to present costing data in an orderly fashion.

We propose the following general categories for purposes of illustration:

1. direct payments for salaries
   a. salary increase programs
   b. salary increases based on inflation
2. development of an employment standard related to salaries or salary schedules
3. indirect payments
   a. overload pay
   b. off-campus courses
   c. third-term payments for eight-, nine-, and ten-month appointments
4. benefit programs
   a. insured benefit programs
      life
      health (basic, major medical, drugs)
      dental
      optical
      disability (long-term)
      legal
      pensions (supplemental annuity tax shelters)
      travel/accident
      malpractice
      supplemental income protection
   b. statutorily established benefit programs
      unemployment compensation insurance
      worker's compensation insurance
      Social Security program
   c. University benefit program
      sickness and disability pay
      vacations
      holiday pay
      longevity pay
      jury duty and witness pay
      bereavement/funeral pay
      professional development days

tuition programs
consulting days
health service benefits
parking fees
employee discounts
terminal leaves
payroll deductions (union, credit union)
d. leaves of absence
paid leaves
  sabbatical leave
  military (short-term)
unpaid leaves
  personal
  educational/research
  medical
  union business
  government service
5. Academic work environment issues
a. class size
b. teaching/research/advising load
c. committee assignments
d. academic calendar
e. support facilities (office, laboratory, equipment)
f. support staff (clerical, technical, graduate assistants, graders)
g. data systems support
6. employment security issues
tenure, rank, promotion, and reappointment
nonretrenchment guarantees
7. union operations issues
a. data and information generation
b. released time for union business
c. pay for union officials
d. check-off for union dues

Costing the Union's Economic Demands

Once each union demand has been categorized and assigned to individual(s), the task of costing may proceed. Our discussion will follow the proposed categories as outlined above.

Direct Payment for Salaries

Salary increase programs will generally center around five main types and combinations thereof: (1) across-the-board flat dollar adjustments, (2) across-the-board percent of salary adjustments, (3) fixed-dollar or percent-of-salary step adjustments, (4) merit programs providing for flat dollar or percent adjustments, (5) Cost of Living Adjustment (COLA) programs.

It is important to recognize that in costing any of these programs, there are significant policy considerations to be recognized even when the costs are identical. We will raise some of these concerns in each discussion. All examples will be based upon annual increases and costs. (Note: Costing considerations of benefit programs are not discussed here, but on page 289.)

Across-the-Board, Flat Dollar Adjustments for the Bargaining Unit of Each Classification. The key variables are whether the union's demand reflects FTE's or individuals and the entire bargaining unit or by classifications. Assume that 800 members in the bargaining unit (200 professors, 200 associate professors, and 400 assistant professors); total bargaining unit FTE's of 700 (200 in professors, 175 in associate professors and 325 in assistant professors); the costing is as follows:

1. Suppose the salary proposal is $600 for each 100 percent appointment and proportional for fractional appointments

$ amount × no. of FTE's = total salary increase cost

$600 × 700 = $420,000

2. Suppose the salary proposal is $600 for each individual whether the employee is full- or part-time

$ amount × no. of individuals = total salary increase cost

$600 × 800 = $480,000

3. Suppose the salary proposal is $500 for each full-time (100 percent) assistant professor, $600 for each full-time associate professor, $700 for each full-time professor. Proportional increases for fractional appointments

$ amount for classification a × no. FTE's + ... +
$ amount for classification z × no. FTE's = total salary increase cost
($500 × 325) + ($600 × 175) + ($700 × 200) = $407,500

4. Suppose the salary proposal is $500 for each assistant professor, $600 for each associate professor, and $700 for each professor

$ amount for classification a × no. of individuals + ... +
$ amount for classification z × no. of individuals = total salary increase cost
($500 × 400) + ($600 × 200) + ($700 × 200) = $460,000

From a policy standpoint, it must be recognized that across-the-board flat dollar adjustments create a compression factor, the degree of severity of compression being dependent upon the distance between the lowest-paid and highest-paid persons in the bargaining unit.

Across-the-Board Percent of Salary Adjustments. The key variable is whether the language reflects a single figure for the bargaining unit or varying figures determined by classification. The costing is:

1. percent amount × total bargaining unit salaries = total salary increase

2. percent amount × total salaries for classification a + ... + percent amount × total salaries for classification z = total salary increase

Percent increases across the board will, from a policy standpoint, preserve the same relative relationship between employees' salaries.

Step Adjustments Through Fixed Dollars or Percent Increases. A step adjustment program (salary schedule) is based on a system whereby varying rates of pay are associated with different levels (steps). The levels are delineated by variables that are defined as relevant to the salary program, such as discipline, rank, training, degree, years of service, publications, and performance. The data elements necessary to cost the system are, of course, the particular variables used in its construction and the number of individuals placed at each level.

Step increase systems are designed to ensure regular increases through a salary range (or part of a range) over selected periods of time. These systems are based upon the philosophy that the value of an individual in a position increases in relation to increases in certain defined factors, such as length of service and publications.

Merit Programs. The costing of merit programs, even with good data and experience under the program, is at best difficult because assumptions must be made that past program experience will or will not reflect future experience. Consequently, there is a strong incentive to place a total cost ceiling on a merit program. This is generally accomplished by defining a "pot" of money to be used for merit increases or by defining a maximum average merit increase for the bargaining unit.

Without this ceiling or maximum, costs may be projected on past experience (making the assumption that certain factors will remain equal or constant). However, there is naturally the element of risk that an influential factor which was assumed to remain constant may change or not vary as projected. Conversely, although a ceiling, or cap, may ensure cost control on the program, the purpose of a merit program (recognize and reward superior performance) may be negated if the program is not properly structured or if the ceiling is too low to ensure sufficient monies to reward superior performers.

COLA. A cost of living adjustment (COLA) is typically a salary increase which is the direct result of an increase in the national or a regional Consumer Price Index (CPI). Generally, a fixed-dollar or percentage increase is assigned to each percentage increase in the CPI. Typically, COLA provisions allow for a limited or an unlimited increase. A limited, or capped, program may be approached in either of two ways: (1) consider increases in the CPI to a predetermined level after which further increases in CPI do not result in increased remuneration or (2) place a maximum on the amount of the increase. Under either program it is rather simple to cost the maximum liability.

For example, assume the proposed COLA clause calls for a special payment once annually of .1 percent of salary for each .2 of a point increase in the CPI. The maximum payment to be received is 5.0 percent. The CPI is at 140.0 and the projection for the rate of inflation 5 percent (CPI = 147.0) for the next twelve calendar months. The gross bargaining unit salary payroll is $10,000,000 annually.

Therefore, if (1) inflation is in fact 5.0 percent, the cost of the adjustment would be calculated as follows:

5 percent = cpi of 147.0 or 7.0 point increase (5 percent × 140 = 7.0)

$$\frac{7.0}{.2} = 35$$

35 × .1 = 3.5 percent

.035 × $10,000,000 = $350,000 (additional salary increased cost to institution).

(2) If inflation is at 12.0 percent the cost of the adjustment would be computed as follows:

12 percent = cpi of 156.8 or a 16.8 point increase (12 percent × 140 = 16.8)

$$\frac{16.8}{.2} = 84$$

84 × .1 − 8.4 percent (which exceeds the 5.0 percent maximum allowed)

.05 × $10,000,000 × $500,000 (additional salary increased cost to institution)

Unlimited or uncapped cola provisions theoretically leave the institution open to an unlimited liability and, as such, are impossible to accurately cost and, in most cases with a high rate of inflation, are difficult to fund. However, estimates based on the anticipated rate of inflation can be made, but those responsible for making such estimates should point out the risks to management.

In addition to the aforementioned concerns, there is the question of whether or not such increases should be incorporated into the salary base. This question is discussed under Special Considerations on page 288.

Development of an Employment Standard

A significant economic factor in costing a faculty collective bargaining agreement is the definition of a 100 percent, or full-time, appointment. This standard will establish the institution's expectations and include variables such as class contact hours, research, advising, office hours, committee assignments, and community service. In order to cost such a standard, it is necessary to know the status quo. Any reductions in time commitment expectations should be viewed as an economic gain for members of the bargaining unit and an increase in institutional cost requiring changes in budgeting.

Other Economic Costs

The compensation program consists of direct salary and indirect salary (benefits). So far we have discussed the costing of the direct salary program. Indirect salary in the form of staff fringe benefits represents an ever-increasing percentage of the total compensation program. Therefore, it is important that the bargaining team have a degree of sophistication in the staff benefits arena. Prior to bargaining, the office charged with the staff benefits function should brief the bargaining team with statistical analyses of costs related to the institution's existing benefits program. *It is important to note that changes in the direct salary program will often have an automatic cost impact on the benefit program,* such as retirement contributions, life insurance, and disability. Consequently, this interrelationship needs to be incorporated in the costing procedure.

Turnover Costs/Savings. It should be noted that discussion in this section has proceeded on the assumption that faculty turnover, or its net effect on costs, is negligible. This may not be the case. In costing proposals, one should analyze the turnover activity in the bargaining unit to be confident that the net effect is not a factor. Naturally, if turnover has been a factor in the past, a decision must be made as to how to deal with the future period being costed.

Turnover must be measured not only in terms of numbers of positions and frequency of vacancies, but also in terms of the level and salaries of the individuals leaving the bargaining unit versus the level and salaries of the individuals entering the bargaining unit. This should occur even when the net change in number of positions is zero.

For example, if employees leaving the bargaining unit are replaced with employees at lower salaries, then there will be a net salary savings. However, if employees who leave are replaced through internal promotions carrying salary increases while new employees enter at salaries equivalent to those who were promoted, the net effect of turnover may be zero or result in an increase in cost. Often unions seek policies that force administration to make internal promotions that allow little flexibility in making savings through turnover. *Negotiators must be aware that change in operational policies often costs money.*

Special Considerations.   In arriving at the total costs of any of these salary increase programs or combinations thereof, special attention should be directed to the long-term cost implications (beyond the life of the proposal being costed) as well as the cost during the life of the agreement. Specifically, the following concerns should be considered:

1. *Increases which are built into the base versus one-time payments which are not built into the base.*

Example: A one-year contract proposal which plans to distribute $100,000 (10 percent) in "new monies" would increase a $1,000,000 payroll base to $1,100,000 by the expiration of the contract *if the entire increase* is built into the base. However, if $50,000 is built into the base through salary increases and the other $50,000 distributed through a system which does not built it into the base, such as one-time bonus-type payment, the institution will have a payroll base of $1,050,000 (105 percent) rather than $1,100,000 (110 percent) at the expiration of the contract. In both examples, the cost for that one year of the contract was $100,000 (10 percent) plus cost of automatic increases in benefits.

2. *Increases which will accelerate the base payroll at a rate faster than the rate of funding.*

Example: Assuming all increases are built into the base, a one-year contract distributes $100,000 (10 percent of base payroll of $1,000,000) over the next twelve months in the following manner: 6 percent ($60,000) on date of implementation of the agreement; and 7.6 percent six months from date of implementation. Because the 7.6 percent will be paid for only the last six months of the contract, the net effect in that six months will be only 3.8 percent. The total monies spent (cost) for those twelve months will be approximately $100,000 (10 percent of the original base). However, the base payroll under that twelve-month contract will be increased by 14 percent over the previous year ($1 \times 1.06 \times 1.076 = 1.1406$). Indirect benefits will also increase automatically on the new base payroll.

Additional Payments.   In conjunction with the establishment of the standard of what represents a full-time, academic-year (eight, nine, or ten months) appointment (employment standard), it is necessary to develop a compensation schedule for services that may be required in addition to this standard. *The process of determining overload pay and third-term (summer) payments is directly related to the full-time standard and should be costed accordingly.*

Costing Benefit Programs

Today, more than ever, benefit programs are a significant percentage of the total cost associated with employing individuals. Consequently, great care should be exercised in an effort to accurately cost these benefits, recognizing that the dangers of hidden or underestimated costs are probably greater than in the costing of salaries.

For example, a change in a given benefit in either coverage or structure (that is, interrelationship of one benefit program to other benefit programs) may significantly increase the processing of paperwork, thus increasing administrative costs. A change in the coverage, structure, or contribution rates of employer and employee may considerably alter the participation rates in benefit programs which are optimal. This is especially the case when a benefit program is changed from an employer-employee contribution program to a program fully funded by the employer. Many employees choose not to participate in programs for which they share the cost. In this situation the maximum increase in this hidden cost would be the number of eligible employees not participating times the employer's contribution rate.

Insured Benefit Programs. Insured benefit programs such as life, health, prescription drugs, dental, optical, disability, legal, travel-accident, malpractice, and supplemental income protection are generally purchased on a group basis with monthly premium payments established on a per employee (and dependents) basis. These premiums are generally based upon the cost of usage of the covered group. Consequently, as the factors upon which the premium is based increase, the premium generally will increase. In costing these insured benefits, it is important to keep in mind the following questions:

1. Will participation in the insured plan be mandatory or voluntary for members of the bargaining unit? If mandatory, the total cost per employee will, naturally, have to be multiplied by the

number of employees in the bargaining unit. If participation in the insured plan is voluntary, the level of participation must be an estimate. Past experience with any present plans or similar plans, and other colleges' or universities' experience with the plans, will generally be helpful in this estimate. Consideration should also be given to any factor which might increase the level of participation, thus increasing the cost. One should also know carrier policy as to whether or not insurance rates vary with percentage of unit participation.

2. Will the premiums remain constant during the life of the labor agreement? If the carrier will guarantee no change, the cost of the benefit may be readily computed. *If the carrier cannot predict future premium rates, the institution should insist on a cap or maximum contribution* which it will make toward a given benefit program (even when present contributions fully pay the employee's premium). Costs to the institution may thus be calculated at the defined cap or maximum.

3. Will the demographic composition of the group remain constant? If it does, the cost implications will be minimal but if the composition changes, for example, if the group's average age increases, the life insurance premium may increase, or if there is an increase in the number of employees who subscribe to two-person or family medical coverage rather than single subscriber coverage, the premiums may increase.

It is worth noting that many of the insurance carriers of benefit programs will be in contact with the union representatives in regard to rates, coverage, premiums, and cost. It is thus essential that the institution develop reliable cost data so as to be able to respond to the union's data.

Statutorily Established Benefit Programs. Most institutions of higher education are required to participate in at least three employee programs which have been established by federal law, namely, Social Security, Worker's Compensation, and unemployment insurance.

1. *Social Security.* Increases in salary and other taxable income will have an increase in the institution's costs (salary increase × Social Security percent) up to the maximum taxable salary as established by statute. Naturally, if all employees in the bargaining unit are at or over the maximum Social Security salary, there will be no increase in costs. Total costs will then be calculated by

multiplying the number of people in the bargaining unit by the maximum contribution as established by statute.

2. *Unemployment and Worker's Compensation.* Unemployment and worker's compensation expenditures and associated increases should be available on a cost-per-bargaining-unit (job family) basis. This will facilitate the recognition of these benefits and their costs at the bargaining table.

University Benefit Programs. In this category we generally place the multitude of programs which represent a benefit to the employee and a cost to the employer, but these costs are not always as easily identifiable as in the case of insurance premiums or salaries.

Benefits such as sickness and disability pay, holiday, vacations, jury duty, and others which provide for income continuation when services are not being performed, can be costed once the employment standard has been established. The costs can be calculated for the bargaining unit as follows:

$$\frac{\text{Total number of hours of income continuation from a program}}{\text{Number of hours in employment standard}} \times \frac{\text{Average}}{\text{FTE Salary}} = \frac{\text{Total}}{\text{Cost}}$$

In programs where employees are not expected to use all the benefits earned, such as sickness and disability pay, the average usage for the bargaining unit should be taken into account in calculating costs. Likewise, if the absence of the employee generates costs associated with covering the employee's position (for example, substitute's pay, overtime, and overload) then these costs must be factored into the total costs. Tuition refund costs must recognize such factors as percent usage, paid release time, and any costs of covering the absent employee. Longevity pay programs must be costed on the projections of program eligibility of the members in the bargaining unit over the life of the agreement. Programs which provide for discounts or establish a maximum (such as parking fees) must be costed in terms of loss of revenue to the institution, assuming usage would remain constant.

Unpaid leaves of absence generally may involve two types of costs to the institution: (1) the costs associated with the employee remaining in one or more benefit programs during the leave and, (2) the costs associated with covering the absence of the employee such as overtime, overload, or temporary employment. In most cases this cost may be offset by the savings associated with the no-pay status of the leave.

Academic Work Environment Issues

A number of academic work environment issues are generally treated as part of the question of what constitutes a full-time equivalent employment standard. However, others such as support facilities, support staff, data systems support and class size should, if they are to be a part of the contract, be treated separately. Costing such demands is relatively straightforward provided the existing fact situation is known and understood.

Although clearly identifiable as having cost implications, employment security programs, such as tenure, retrenchment benefits, and severance pay, are among the most difficult subjects to attempt to cost. Guarantees of employment or promotion clearly obligate the institution to continue salary and benefit costs whether or not the services rendered (or not rendered) are still desired. As such, these costs may extend far beyond the monetary considerations of salaries and benefits for nonproductive or nonfunded positions and well into the organization's ability and flexibility to manage.

Union Operation Issues Data and Information Generation

Typically (although the laws in jurisdictions may vary) an employer must provide a union with requested data and information that are readily available and are necessary for purposes of collective bargaining. However, during the bargaining process the union will undoubtedly have demands for data that members of the bargaining unit believe are necessary to administer their contract, that is, name, department, fraction of full-time salary, rank, home address, and work address. The demands will often include a schedule showing when reports containing specific data elements should be produced. Cost implications that need to be considered include systems analysis, programming, computer time, overhead, and the time required to verify reports and respond to any resulting questions or criticism from the union. Some contracts contain clauses which guarantee the union access to specific data elements as long as the union pays the cost of obtaining the reports. This latter arrangement is, of course, preferable, especially since most unions can afford to pay the cost, and when they pay the costs, their demands are usually limited to essentials.

Check-Off for Union Dues. Most labor unions will seek a commitment from the employer to withhold the amount of union dues from members' paychecks provided the individuals have completed the necessary authorization. Such a commitment should be viewed as a service and economic benefit to both the union and its members. Cost implications that need to be considered include systems analysis, programming, computer time, overhead, clerical time to review authorizations and answers related employee questions. One method of limiting this cost is to include a clause which restricts the number of times an individual may change their check-off card status. Again, some contracts require the union to reimburse the institution for the cost of providing this service.

Released Time for Union Business and Pay for Union Officials. Paid released time is usually limited to specific events, such as vote on union officers and file and process grievances. Cost implications depend upon the amount of coverage that is necessitated by such absences.

Union officials may be compensated by virtue of their union office because union business constitutes such a large portion of their time that released time is no longer practical. Some contracts require that union members cover, without pay, those duties usually performed by union officials on released time.

Conclusion

A discussion on how to cost a contract or union demand would not be complete without a word of caution on the spillover, or ripple, effect which is generally felt in every institution which has a number of job families or bargaining units. The effect itself is generally described as the pressure felt through demands by other bargaining units or the expectation expressed on the part of nonunion employees for the same or better salary and benefit improvements agreed upon in the contract being negotiated.

Consequently, a prudent institution, when costing a demand made by one labor organization, will also cost and study the implications of the demand, should it be granted or agreed to, by all other employees of the institution. This will naturally give the institution an organizational perspective which is clearly necessary in developing and maintaining a long-range labor relations policy and position.

George W. Angell
Edward P. Kelley, Jr.

16

Of all the perplexing problems posed for colleges and universities by government and court rulings during the past decade, few have been as pervasive as those related to antidiscrimination. Unless approached with careful thought and planning, collective bargaining can exacerbate these problems. Most labor laws prohibit discrimination in areas such as selection of employees, discharge, discipline, salary determination, promotion, work hours, work assignments, work loads, office space, vacation, and holidays. In addition, an employer cannot discriminate against an employee because he is or is not a member of a union, does or does not perform union duties, attempts to organize a union, makes union campaign speeches putting management in an unfavorable light, writes articles for the union news releases derogatory to the employer, among other things. Discriminatory action on the part of an employer may result in an unfair labor practice charge be-

Avoiding
Discrimination Problems

fore the National Labor Relations Board (*Jubilee Manufacturing Company*)[1] or before the appropriate state employment relations board (*Office of Court Administration and Emanuel Trotner*).[2] A labor board has authority to shape a variety of remedies such as requiring the institution to reemploy the individual, ordering back pay, imposing fines or directing that other remedial action be taken. Orders from labor boards are legally enforceable through appeal to an appropriate court. Any college or university president facing the possibility of faculty unionization should seek the advice of a competent labor attorney capable of preparing directives for, and lecturing to, the administrative staff, any one of whom may commit an unwitting unfair labor practice and for which the employer is held liable (Holway and O'Donnell, 1974).

[1]202 NLRB 272 (1973).
[2]8 PERB 4504 (1975).

Prior to Negotiations

During Election Campaigns

Employers and unions have an excellent opportunity during election campaigns to reaffirm their support for equal opportunity in employment and benefits. Union officials should provide examples of ways in which women and minorities have benefited from membership in their particular union, both at the local and national levels. When such information is not available, employees have every right to request that the union provide it (*Pacific Maritime Association*).[3] When there is evidence that a local union seeking certification as the bargaining agent, or its parent union, has participated in discriminatory practices, either knowingly or de facto, the employer may bring such evidence to the attention of the proper administrative board (NLRB or state PERB). The employer should be careful, however, not to make public charges against a union unless there is a basis in fact, not to attempt to sway voters by making unfair statements about the union's willingness or capacity to serve minority groups, and not to direct statements at minority employees to the effect that they will lose benefits by joining a union. Such actions may result in a finding of an unfair labor practice, the setting aside of an election, and the certification of a union despite the results of an election (*Media Mailers, Inc.*[4] and *Boyce Machinery Corporation*[5]).

Unions, on the other hand, also have the right to point out, during the campaign, inadequacies or inconsistencies in the employer's affirmative action program or in past employment practices. If such discussions are not accurately and fairly stated, the employer may request the labor board to delay the election date on the basis that the union, through false representation of the facts, has made it impossible to conduct a fair election.

It is not too late after the election for the employer or employees to present to the labor board any serious evidence of union discrimination. Union discriminatory practices could lead to the

[3]209 NLRB 88 (1974).
[4]191 NLRB 251 (1971).
[5]141 NLRB 756 (1963).

imposition of a range of penalties including decertification (NLRB Rules and Regulations).[6]

Review of Current Policies and Practices

Prior to negotiating a contract, the employer could conduct a careful review of employment policies and employee data in order to identify possible areas of discrimination that can be remedied in the process of negotiating a new contract free of illegal implication. Many contracts contain a general clause perpetuating past practices, past policies, or past benefits. Unions generally prefer to include such clauses in order to avoid any possible loss of benefits. On the other hand, institutions usually wish to avoid such clauses because they are too ambiguous. Few people know what "past policies" may be hidden away in the minutes of trustees' meetings or in administrators' handbooks. Most institutions followed, some years ago, policies of admission, faculty selection, faculty promotion, among other policies, which today may well be considered discriminatory.

Membership on the Bargaining Teams

It may be helpful after all circumstances are considered, for the employer to appoint someone from the institution's affirmative action office to the bargaining team or to a back-up committee which reviews issues being considered at the bargaining table. Both the employer and the union should consider the feasibility of including women and minorities on their respective bargaining teams, if for no other purpose than to assure that all issues at the bargaining table are reviewed for avoiding discriminatory policies or procedures.

During Negotiations

Both the employer and union should be wary of negotiating separate subcontracts for special groups of employees within the same bargaining unit, lest such contracts be interpreted as evidence

[6]29 c.f.r. 102, 60(a).

of unnecessary or unfair practices tantamount to discrimination. In general, all members of a certified bargaining unit, should be covered by the same contract, and no clause in that contract should discriminate against any department, division, school, or class of individuals within that membership. This is one good reason for a medical or law faculty to have its own bargaining unit. To have special work loads or salary levels within a single contract that are not available to others with "equal" qualifications could be viewed as discriminatory. Such contract clauses held by a board or a court to be discriminatory could be nullified (*Blanton* v. *Southern Bell Telephone*)[7] subjecting both union and employer to further review and possible penalties. In other words, equal employment rights of an individual or groups cannot be lost through careless bargaining processes, an inequitable clause, or by unfair grievance settlements.

Good Faith Bargaining

The federal statute (NLRA) and most of the existing state labor laws require both parties to negotiate "in good faith." Should either party refuse to negotiate an issue related directly to strengthening equal opportunity employment practices (equal opportunity for employment, pay promotion, job assignments) it may be subject to a charge of an unfair labor practice (*Farmers' Cooperative Compress*)[8] before the board.

The Negotiation of Contractual Clauses

Preamble to Contract

A college or university may wish to include a statement to the effect that it is an equal opportunity employer and has approved affirmative action plans for future employment. The union may wish to affirm its support of the campus affirmative action plan. Both parties may wish to state that the negotiated agreement shall

---

[7]49 F.R.C. 16212 F.E.P. Cases 602 (N.D., Ga.) (1970).
[8]169 NLRB 290 (1968), enforced in pertinent part, 416 F.2d 1126 (C.A.D.C. [1973]), cert. denied 396 U.S. 903 (1973).

in no way interfere with the operation of the affirmative action plan. This would be especially important in terms of the later clauses covering retrenchment and layoff procedures.

Both parties benefit by a preamble stating that the union has a history of nondiscriminatory service and is, therefore, well qualified to provide equal representation for all members of the bargaining unit regardless of race, creed, sex, age, and other factors. Enforcement agencies and arbitrators scrutinize the contract and the histories of the union and the institution whenever a charge of discrimination is being adjudicated. An individual may lodge a charge of discrimination against a union or the employer for a perceived inequity resulting from lack of union support, such as, unequal representation, at the bargaining table or at grievance hearings, or from unequal enforcement of institutional policy or benefits by the employer and the union.

Appointments, Tenure, and Promotion

If a review of appointment policies and employee classifications has not been recently completed, the parties may wish to include in the contract a clause that requires a joint review with the stated purpose that both parties will work cooperatively to seek remedies for any policies and practices and for persons negatively affected by such practices that may directly or indirectly permit or promote discrimination. Such a review should pay particular attention to such areas as salaries, ranks, part-time faculty benefits, summer employment opportunities, antinepotism practices, and rigid adherence to questionable qualifications for appointments and promotions.

College Calendar

Calendar planning requires careful thought in order to prevent the favoring of one group over another. The parties may wish to negotiate a contractual clause establishing a joint committee to screen proposed calendars for discrimination in such matters as favoring certain religious holidays over others. Consideration should also be given to practices which establish vacation periods uncoordinated with local school holidays and thereby regularly exclude mothers from the work force. In addition, vacation periods which prevent students from obtaining equal opportunities for vacation jobs may be called into question in the coming years.

Grievance Procedures

The contract ordinarily should not establish a procedure for discrimination hearings, but if the parties decide to do so, the procedure should provide the basic due-process requirements of notice, hearing, and opportunity to cross-examine witnesses. Such a process should be separate from those designed for other types of grievances. Some universities and faculty unions (Agreement between State University of New York and United University Professions, Inc., 1974–1976) have refused to handle discrimination cases within contractual grievance procedures, citing the existence of Equal Employment Opportunity Commission (EEOC) and State Human Rights Commission procedures (Title IX, 1972 Education Amendments)[9] as being adequate. Sooner or later this approach will be tested in the courts if for no other reason than it tends to convey an appearance of disinterest. It seems to us that this is now a sound approach since each campus is required to have Title IX grievance procedures specifically to handle discrimination complaints.

Leaves of Absence and Health Benefits

Leaves of absence, hospitalization, and surgical plans should permit no special exemption from benefits (such as "no coverage" for pregnancy related disabilities) that may discriminate against a particular group of employees.[10] In addition, a denial of a leave of absence because of age (too young, too inexperienced, too near retirement) is, at best, questionable. Legitimate purposes for leaves of absence should be clearly stated together with criteria for judging the merit of applications for leaves. The process of awarding and denying leaves should also be stipulated in a manner that helps to guarantee fair and equal consideration of applications for everyone. Every effort should be made to assure women and minorities

[9]20 U.S.C. 1681 (1972).
[10]29 C.F.R. Chapter XIV, Part 1604, Sec. 9.

fair and equal representation on committees that recommend or approve such benefits.

Management Rights

A management rights clause may be used to further emphasize the employer's commitment to equal employment opportunity and affirmative action by restating the employer's intent not to discriminate in directing the work force, in transfer, in discipline, or in other management responsibilities. The clause may also refer to the institution's affirmative action plan and state the employer's intent to exercise its management rights in conformity with that plan.

Nondiscrimination Clauses

Some parties like to include in the contract a separate clause affirming both the institution's and union's belief in, and adherence to, the principle and practice of nondiscrimination. Such a clause, no matter how well intentioned, will not protect either party against a specific charge of discrimination (*Edmund A. Gray, Inc.*).[11] It does, however, apparently have two plausible virtues: (1) it may establish a general tone and atmosphere that encourage both parties and their constituents to seek out and eliminate unfair practices, and (2) it may encourage those people who feel they are being discriminated against to enter complaints and seek redress. To achieve these virtues, the clause should make reference to specific extracontractual, Title IX grievance steps that are designed to expedite the identification and informal processing of complaints without causing undue exposure or embarrassment to those who believe they may have a just complaint.

General Working Conditions

If the parties are really serious about abolishing and remedying discrimination, they may agree to establish a joint committee to study the nondollar working conditions of faculty. Such a committee should investigate whether or not there is discrimination

[11] 142 NLRB 590 (1963).

in assigning offices, types and levels of courses, off-campus courses, early morning and late afternoon courses, committee work, parking spaces, extra pay opportunities, student advisement, travel funds, clerical services, student assistants, and other benefits. This type of discrimination can have subtle deleterious effects and often exists as a matter of tradition rather than reason.

Part-Time Faculty

Part-time faculty members are commonly injured by traditional discriminatory practices. Largely consisting of faculty wives and husbands, women from the community, and others whose special talents are taken for granted, part-timers are often paid unusually low salaries. They may seldom be given opportunity for tenure, promotion, full-time employment, adequate office space, clerical help, and other benefits. If part-time faculty members are part of the unit, a special clause in the contract should deal adequately with this important segment of the university's human resources.

Past Practices or Benefits

As stated earlier, many contracts include a clause designed to preserve to the faculty all benefits prior to bargaining. Such a clause could inadvertently perpetuate past discriminatory practices especially where only part of the faculty enjoy certain benefits. Both parties may share the guilt of discrimination (*Greggs* v. *Duke Power Co.*),[12] but ultimately the university will bear the burden of responsibility. It would seem wise to specify that any past benefits that now appear to be discriminatory would not be preserved. It should also be made clear that any clause preserving benefits shall not be used by the union or management as a barrier to eliminating past discriminatory practices.

Personnel Committees

One of the more significant ways in which administrators and faculty members can help to eliminate discrimination is the selection of committees which make recommendations for ap-

[12]401 U.S. 424 (1971).

pointments, promotions, and salary increases. The contract could include a statement to the effect that in appointing or electing such committees, care will be exercised to see that women and minorities are given fair representation.

Personnel Files

An extremely sensitive area commonly subject to allegation of discriminatory practice has been the reporting and keeping of personnel records. The contract should bar any unnecessary records of irrelevant data such as one's marital status, political activities, religion, and social group membership. The contract should also provide open access to one's own files with full opportunity of adding to one's own file valid information and rebuttal of critical statements found therein. Data necessary for affirmative action reporting should be collected and kept by the affirmative action office rather than by the personnel office.

Recognition of Agent

In the clause whereby the institution agrees to give official recognition and the right of exclusive representation to a particular union, the union should, in turn, agree to represent equally and fairly each and every member of the bargaining unit regardless of race, creed, age, or sex (*Miranda Fuel Company, Inc.*).[13]

Retirement and Pension Plans

Where the law permits bargaining of retirement plans, the contract should provide, to the extent possible, equal costs to the participant, equal access to membership classifications, equal service requirements to quality for benefits, and equal benefits (EEOC Guidelines).

Retrenchment

If traditional union practices of "last hired, first fired" lower the percentage of employed women and minorities recently

[13]140 NLRB 181 (1962) enforcement denied, 326 F.2d 172 (C.A. 2, 1963).

achieved under an affirmative action plan, modifications of those practices should be considered (*Watkins* v. *Steelworkers*[14] and *Waters* v. *Wisconsin Steel*[15]). The contract could recognize the priority of affirmative action goals and may well establish a joint committee of the parties to review the required number of layoffs, the most appropriate departments for retrenchment, and the best means to achieve retrenchment with the least harm to institutional programs and affirmative action goals (Agreement between Temple University [of the Commonwealth System of Higher Education] and the American Association of University Professors, Temple Chapter, Philadelphia, Pennsylvania, 1973–1976). Although the U.S. Court of Appeals for the Fifth Circuit found that a layoff on the basis of seniority is not, in itself, an act of discrimination (*Watkins* v. *Steelworkers Local 2369*),[16] the Supreme Court has ruled that retroactive seniority may be awarded to individuals who can show that they were illegally rejected for employment because of their race after the effective date of Title VII (*Franks* v. *Bowman Transportation Co.*).[17] Problems surrounding layoff procedures are being litigated constantly and negotiators should seek guidance from the most recent court decisions available. White males are now challenging appointment and layoff procedures which favor women and minorities, and the results to date are somewhat inconsistent.

Salary Schedules, Merit Salary Increases, Promotions

The contract should omit all references to special groups within a salary schedule that may be construed as discriminatory. Differences in salaries and ranks should be clearly determined on the basis of distinguishable meritorious training or service attributes. Even though both union and employer agree to salary payments that are found to discriminate, courts have generally held that the employer actually benefits from lower salaries and therefore is liable for paying back wages and other penalties assessed by the court or administrative board (Regulations of the Depart-

[14]369 F. Supp. 1221 (D.C. La. 1974).
[15]F.E.P. Cases 577 (C.A. 7, 1974).
[16](C.A. 5, 1975), 10 F.E.P. Cases 1297.
[17]U.S. Sup. Ct. (1976) 12 F.E.P. Cases 549.

ment of Labor for the Office of Contract Compliance).[18] A union is generally not penalized unless it withholds dues unequally or otherwise benefits directly from discriminatory practices. Salary factoring on the basis of favored departments or schools consisting predominantly of white males while disfavored groups are primarily staffed by women and minorities is, of course, open to charges of discrimination.

Affirmative Action Plan Noted in Contract

The contract could well indicate that (1) there shall be an effective affirmative action plan in operation, (2) the plan shall be approved by the appropriate governmental agency, (3) the purpose of the plan shall be to assure equal employment opportunity, (4) the union and employer will jointly and cooperatively participate in plan review and revision, (5) the union will support the employer's efforts to administer the plan fairly, (6) the union and employer will negotiate any differences of opinion as to interpretation and administration of the plan in order to assure equity for women, minorities, and others, (7) the plan objectives shall not be unduly modified by job retrenchments, (8) complaints of discrimination will be adjudicated quickly and fairly in accordance with procedures established in this article, elsewhere in the contract, or established by the institution outside the contract (Agreement between Rider College and the Rider College Chapter of the American Association of University Professors, 1974–1976).

During the Administration of the Negotiated Contract

Fair Representation

Fair representation, required by most labor laws, is the direct responsibility of a union to see that its services (for example, in negotiating better salaries and working conditions, in reviewing and processing complaints and grievances, in assigning members to union committees) are managed and provided in a manner equitable to all of its members regardless of sex, race, and religion.

[18]29 c.f.r., Sec. 800.

The employer, however, also can be held liable if management condones unfair representation; therefore, it should take appropriate steps to assure that union officials, and others when necessary, be informed of reports or complaints that may lead to unfair labor charges, to litigation in the courts, or to hearings before human rights commissions. Failure of the employer to take appropriate action may convey the appearance of support for union discrimination (NLRB Rules and Regulations).[19]

Picketing and Strikes in Support of a Grievance

A union should, of course, help process a discrimination grievance, but it may not use concerted activities in support of a grievance while that grievance is being processed through the steps as negotiated in a contract under the NLRA (*Emporium Capwell Company* v. *Western Addition Community Organization*).[20] This is also arguably true of a contract negotiated under most state labor laws.

Grievance Procedure and Remedy of Discrimination

The range of grievances that may be pursued under a negotiated contract usually includes complaints of discrimination. Should a charge of discrimination be denied by the final arbiter at the final step, it does not preclude the grievant from pursuing the complaint through the courts or other means such as a human rights commission (*Emporium Capwell*). Nevertheless, the briefs prepared and the reasoning of the arbitrator are always important evidence to be considered carefully by the courts.

Undue delay in the processing of a discrimination grievance caused by urging a grievant to rely solely upon the internal contract grievance procedure and resulting in the grievant's failure to file a timely petition before an external enforcement agency may be found to be discriminatory in itself, compounding the potential charge against union or administration.

[19]29 C.F.R. 102, 60(a).
[20]88 LRRM 2668 (1975).

Liability of Employer for Employee Actions

Under the NLRA, the employer is responsible for discriminatory action against an employee or potential employee even when such action is taken as a result of recommendations by a committee of employees who are acting under the authority of a contract or of an institutional policy. Similarly, a union is held responsible for its illegal action or for failure to take steps necessary to prevent or remedy illegal actions, such as discrimination, even when such illegal action is recommended by rank-and-file members acting in accordance with contractual or noncontractual procedures (EEOC Decision 74-93).[21] A union or a college committee may, for example, recommend that a grievance charge involving discrimination not be processed through the contractual grievance procedure. Such recommendation does not relieve the union or the college from making a proper decision.

An Illegal Contract Provision

An unfair labor practice may also be charged against a party that attempts to bargain an illegal provision (including discrimination) within a contract. Should such a provision be included in a contract, it provides neither party valid reason for a discriminatory practice (*Blanton*). Rather, it may constitute evidence against both parties as to an act of discrimination.

Should an employer discover an illegal clause in the contract, and the union refuse to cooperate in correcting the clause, the employer may unilaterally change the conditions of employment to conform with equal employment standards (*Savannah Printing Specialties and Paper Products, Local 604* v. *Union Camp Corp.*).[22]

Affirmative Action Plan and the Union Contract

The faculty union should be invited to help revise the institution's affirmative action plan whenever the employer believes it

[21]6426 CCH EEOC Decisions 4132.
[22]305 F. Supp. 632 (S.D. Ga. 1972).

would facilitate future negotiations and avoid potential conflicts between the plan and the contract. This is especially important in designing the order of retrenchment and subsequent recall since the potential conflict exists between the seniority rights principle established in many union contracts and the commitments of the parties to the goals of equal opportunity through affirmative action (Executive Order 11246 as amended by E.O. 11375, Sec. 202). If the certified union is not consulted in preparing the affirmative action plan, it may reasonably initiate an unfair labor practice charge.

After an affirmative action plan has been established, it would be helpful to include in future negotiated contracts a clause supporting the plan and providing consultation procedures for adjudicating any future conflicts that may arise between the plan and other clauses in the contract. Such conflicts, when not satisfactorily ameliorated at the local campus level, are sometimes adjudicated by a labor board or by courts. Some existing case decisions indicate that affirmative action requirements will be given priority over seniority rights stipulated in negotiated agreements; others do the opposite.

Agency Shop

Sometimes an employer agrees to the union's request for an agency-shop clause in the contract. This means that all members of the bargaining unit must either join the union or pay to the union a service fee equivalent to union dues. This means that the institution must discharge any employee who refuses to pay the union fees. This type of discrimination has been upheld by courts (*Knight* v. *Minnesota Community College Faculty Association*).[23] Some states (for example, Hawaii and Montana) require it by law. However, a decision handed down on December 20, 1976, by the U.S. District Court, Eastern District of Wisconsin (*Nettleson* v. *A. O. Smith Corp.*)[24] denied a defendant's (employer and union) motion to dismiss plaintiff's (employee) claim under Title VII of the Civil Rights Act of 1964. In this case the employee seeks damages and an injunc-

---

[23]C.A. 8th Cir. (1976); Case #76-1051.

tion to forestall the employer's action to terminate employment, at the request of the union, for failure to pay union dues. The employee's refusal to pay union dues is based on religious grounds. The court held that "the plaintiff's Title VII rights cannot be eliminated by the agreement between the union and his employer." The court indicates that the National Labor Relations Act (NLRA) looks to the parties *en masse* and that "when an individual is in conflict with either of the two groups, Title VII is the predominate statute." Should the court ultimately find in favor of the employee in this case and should an appeal to the Circuit Court of Appeals for the 7th Circuit sustain the employee, the conflicting decisions among the circuit courts would require the Supreme Court to settle the issue of individual civil rights versus union security rights under the NLRA.

[24] 14 F.E.P. Cases 161 (D.C.E.D. Wis., 1976), cf. *Cooper* v. *General Dynamics,* 533 F.2d 163, 12 F.E.P. Cases 1549 (5th Cir., 1976); and *Yott* v. *North American Rockwell Corp.,* 501 F.2d 398, 8 F.E.P. Cases 546 (9th Cir., 1974).

Edward P. Kelley, Jr.
Frank C. Gerry

Twelve of twenty-four state laws enabling postsecondary education faculty to unionize narrow the scope of negotiations by defining management rights or prerogatives. The remaining twelve state laws and the NLRA which enables faculty at private institutions to organize and bargain collectively, do not specify the rights of management (Academic Collective Bargaining Information Service, 1976a).

Before proceeding further a definition of management rights may be useful. Roberts (1966), the Webster of collective bargaining, defined the rights of management in the industrial sector as "those aspects of the employer's operations which do not require discussion with, or concurrence by, the union or rights reserved to management which are not subject to collective bargaining. Such prerogatives or rights may include matters of hiring, production, scheduling, price fixing, and the maintenance of

Negotiating Management Rights and Other Special Contract Clauses

order and efficiency, as well as the process of manufacturing and sales" (p. 238).

In essence, the matter of management rights in higher education relates directly to the heart of the educational mission through reservation of institutional direction and control of resources, both economic and human, to the chief executive and the board of trustees (or the appropriate government in the case of public institutions). In preparation for negotiations, it is vital for the administration's bargaining team to possess a complete understanding of which issues are mandatory subjects of bargaining and which rights, powers, and functions should be reserved as areas of unilateral administrative authority. Such an understanding will serve to prevent the team from inadvertently "bargaining away" administrative rights essential to the effective operation and control of the institution (see Chapter Seven).

Prior to negotiations, a full review of relative case law on the scope of bargaining and management rights should be conducted. Additionally, the administration's bargaining team should give strong consideration to three contract clauses as vehicles for the protection of management rights. Those are (1) a preamble, (2) a zipper clause, and (3) a management rights clause.

A preamble is found in almost all negotiated agreements and may be employed by the administration to establish the tone of the bargaining relationship. This may be accomplished by delineating those areas in which the administration agrees to share authority and those rights reserved exclusively for management. For example ". . . while the United Faculty of Florida (hereafter UFF) as the elected bargaining agent, retains the exclusive right to negotiate and reach agreement on terms and conditions of employment for the members of the bargaining unit, and the Board of Regents (hereafter the Board) retains its rights, under law, to manage and direct the State University System, . . ." (Agreement between Board of Regents, State University System of Florida and United Faculty of Florida, 1976–1978, paragraph 2 of Preamble). For additional examples of contract preambles see Section I of the Contract Clauses presented at the end of this chapter.

Technically not part of the body of the contract, provisions contained in the preamble are not subject to grievance and arbitration. Being external to the contract, management rights included in the preamble may not be eroded by future arbitration decisions and are not subject to intense renegotiation. However, faced with a difficult case, an arbitrator may review the preamble to establish the intent and spirit of the parties when they fashioned the agreement.

Lest protecting management rights in the preamble appear to be the answer to an administrator's prayer, some management advocates strongly contend that the preamble alone lacks sufficient protection and force under labor law. In the absence of specific management rights in the body of the contract, an arbitrator may well ignore the "spirit of the parties" and render a decision abrogating rights considered essential to the managerial function.

Another contract commonly used to preserve management rights is the so-called "zipper clause." This clause attempts to make clear the scope of agreement between the parties. In its traditional form a zipper clause states that the provisions within the contract represent the sum total of the agreement between the parties and that all items not expressly addressed within the contract are outside the scope of the agreement and are reserved as management rights. There is little experience to date with employing the zipper clause as the sole protector of management rights; however, as later discussion will demonstrate, it is a valuable clause for management and should be given high priority by the administration's bargaining team. Examples of zipper clauses are offered in Section II of the Contract Clauses.

The final and, by far most common, clause employed to reserve managerial authority is the "management rights clause." Such a clause is designated to reserve for the administration the exclusive right to direct and control staffing, including the number of staff members, their assignment and scheduling, discipline, transfer, and discharge. Other rights that are often reserved by this clause include the number, location, and operation of campuses and extension centers as well as the right to alter and modify organizational structure and to extend, curtail, or discontinue operations partially or completely. It is suggested that the management rights clause also contain provisions for the reservation of the right to establish standards and maintain quality of performance, to establish rules for order, and the right to establish criteria for evaluation.

When drafting a management rights clause, an administration should maintain its breadth and flexibility of operation by stating that the enumerated rights are not all-inclusive but, rather, are exemplary. Further, as in the zipper clause, an administration should insist upon language that reserves all rights to the administration except those expressly limited or granted by explicit language in an article of the contract. For example, "Any of the rights, powers, authority, and functions the University had prior to the negotiation of this Agreement are retained by the University, except those expressly abridged by a specific provision of the Agreement. The University not exercising rights, powers, authority, and functions reserved to it or its exercising them in a particular way, shall not be deemed a waiver of said rights, powers, authority and functions or its right to exercise them in some other way not in conflict with a specific provision of this Agreement" (Agreement between the University of San Francisco and University of San Francisco Faculty Association, July 1, 1976 to June 30, 1981, Article 5.1, p. 4). Additional samples of management rights clauses can be found in Section III of the Contract Clauses.

Inclusion of a strong management rights clause in the negotiated agreement has several administrative advantages. First, the protection afforded management rights by such a clause is more specific than that of the preamble or zipper clause. As part of the body of the contract, a list of powers and rights may be expressly reserved to the administration. Secondly, the enumeration of exemplary management rights in the contract establishes useful guideposts for arbitrators, the courts, and labor boards as they review grievances and challenges. A well-written management rights clause helps to limit the neutral's jurisdiction and to prevent expansion of the agreement, especially when the contract specifies that the management rights clause is not subject to grievance. In absence of strong language and often because of it, an employee organization may seek to gain through the grievance and arbitration process that which it was unable to win at the bargaining table. In such situations, the management rights clause can serve as a firm guidepost for arbitrators as they attempt to find a basis in the contract to support the arguments of each party. In like manner, strong management rights language may be of assistance in cases before a labor board. For example, a management rights clause reserving the right to hire, fire, and determine staffing needs to the administration may be a strong defense in an unfair labor practice hearing where the bargaining agent is contending that hiring part-time faculty can only be done in consultation with, or upon approval of, the union (subcontracting may take work away from members of the bargaining unit).

A strong management rights clause also serves to clarify for subadministrators those decisions they have a right and obligation to render. The introduction of collective bargaining has often resulted in middle- and lower-level administrators being intimidated or feeling uninformed. Perceiving themselves to be excluded from the negotiation process but wide open to grievances on matters they do not fully comprehend, these administrators may become excessively cautious in rendering decisions. Inaction by this group of administrators or the excessive use of meet-and-discuss sessions with bargaining unit members may be translated into a surrendering of vital management rights. A strong management rights clause can serve to assure these administrators that they still have the authority to discipline, establish work rules, and make other decisions not influenced by the contract.

Lastly, a management rights clause may be employed by the administration to educate faculty and to discourage unnecessary grievances as to the authority of administrators. Subadministrators can point out to the faculty that the contract specifies managerial rights and that properly considered decisions are not in violation of the agreement but rather in accord with the authority reserved to the administration.

In keeping with the collective bargaining axiom that for every argument there exists a rebuttal, the negotiation of management rights is not without several disadvantages. First, some observers recoil at the very prospect of negotiating these rights. It is argued that unilateral rights inherent to management cease to be unilateral when submitted to the give-and-take of the bargaining table. To include management rights in the body of the contract is to submit these rights, powers, and functions to negotiation. A second disadvantage is related to the future negotiability of management rights. Some observers argue that a listing of the rights in the contract provides the employee organization with a target in subsequent negotiations. The union will argue that all rights listed in the current contract were placed there by the administration and are therefore negotiable. How a particular labor board would rule on such an argument would be difficult to predict.

The issue of negotiability makes it incumbent upon the administration desiring such a clause to secure strong, yet flexible, language during the first round of negotiations. It will prove to be very difficult and costly to attempt to recover in subsequent negotiations rights lost at the outset. An administration should take great care in drafting language that specifies the rights desired but does not limit future administrative options. The law asserting jurisdiction over the institution's bargaining process should be reviewed to discover if any rights are reserved by statute. Court and labor-board decisions on the subject should also be extensively researched (see Chapter Eight). The management rights uncovered by this research should be compared to those rights the administration feels it needs to operate the institution to achieve its educational goals. It may be that there is no need to negotiate a rights clause because the institution is already well protected by the statute and earlier decisions of the labor board.

Lastly, it should be remembered that administrative rights listed are exemplary and are not to be considered all-inclusive. Absence of such language may result in a loss of much desired and often required flexibility. As a general principle, the administration should be specific and limited in stating what rights, benefits, and privileges the institution grants faculty through the contract, and, in turn, very broad and unlimited as to what rights, powers, authority and functions it retains for itself. This procedure is in keeping with the nature of bargaining: give away as little as possible and keep as much as possible.

Other Clauses

Recognition Clause

Many, if not all contracts, contain a recognition clause wherein the institution recites its willingness to deal exclusively with the representative of the bargaining unit. The danger in bargaining this clause lies in the potential for expansion of the bargaining unit. If the recognition clause recites that the institution will deal only with the certified representative of the faculty or of the unit if the membership of the unit has been in dispute, the administration can expect grievances or petitions to the labor board to modify the unit composition based on the administration's assent as expressed in the negotiated recognition clause. The recommendation then, if a recognition clause is to be included in the contract, is to recite recognition of the agent as the exclusive representative of the unit *exactly as described by the order of the labor board*. Refusal to deviate or to bargain any other clause will not result in a charge of refusing to bargain in good faith since deviation in description of the certified unit would result in bargaining the terms and conditions of employment for nonunit employees (a nonmandatory subject of bargaining).

Access to Information Clauses

If this subject is broached at the bargaining table, it would be unwise to refuse to bargain it since board decisions generally favor the union's assertion that access to certain information is essential to its ability to bargain. There is a certain amount of information which the union must have to reasonably and equally represent members of the bargaining unit and which may not be available from other sources. Examples of such information are current rank, salary, and seniority breakdown which would only be available by polling the entire unit membership and in that form would not be official. Therefore, the institution should be prepared to bargain *limited* information access. The word *limited* is used intentionally since, in our opinion, there are sufficient grounds upon which to deny information except in the form in which the institution normally produces the data. Numerous grievance decisions in New York, Pennsylvania, and Michigan have supported institutional positions denying information except in the form in which it is normally available. However, an institution could bargain for payment by the union for costs incurred in producing information in the form desired by the union. Some unions will insist that they have the right to all information that the institution has. This type of demand should be resisted as being unnecessary to bargaining, costly to the institution, and a breach of the institution's right to privacy regarding certain matters (for example, memos and committee reports developed in preparation for negotiations).

Sabbatical Leave Clause

This subject, since it has an impact on terms and conditions of employment of faculty members other than those on leave, should be carefully negotiated. Since the ability of the whole department to provide the required number of quality course offerings may be substantially affected by the number and special knowledge of those on professional leave with or without pay, each department as a whole should have significant responsibility for screening all requests for leaves from that department. Final decisions, however, should always be reserved for administration, since only it has final responsibility for program excellence and

budget allocations. All clauses relating to leaves of absence should
be consistent with the institution's stated policy and plan for faculty development. It should also reflect the institution's concern for
excellence and the need for administrative flexibility in distribution of resources.

Our recommendation, then, is to require, prior to administrative decision, departmental review and recommendation of
all applications for professional improvement leaves including
sabbaticals, with a clear statement about the impact on departmental
staffing, program, and financial needs. In addition, departmental
recommendations should include a statement of how the absentee's
course and other responsibilities will be met by the remaining staff
and a description of the method of reporting upon the success of
the leave. Finally, in no event should the union have any veto or
approval authority over professional improvement leaves since
this is clearly a management function and a prerogative that does
not have to be bargained.

No-Strike, No-Lockout Clause

In private institutions bargaining under the NLRA and in
public institutions where the state law does not prohibit strike, such
a clause may have value in that contract enforcement could result
in penalties imposed upon the union in dollar or performance
terms, both of which will directly benefit the institution and possibly the students, who are, of course, most injured by strike or lockout. However, for public institutions in states prohibiting and
effectively enforcing the prohibition against strikes, such a clause
appears to serve little useful purpose to the administration. In
states where strikes are prohibited, a labor board or court reviewing
a charge of violating the no-strike agreement would likely turn to
the law rather than to a contract for direction as to conditions and
penalties appropriate to the case. Some college administrators have
become interested recently in preserving their own right to close
the college and lockout the faculty when the faculty threatens a
strike. The September 1976 lockout of faculty by the Community
College of Beaver County, Pennsylvania, appeared to be so successful in bringing the union to terms as to cause other colleges to consider similar procedures. (We do not recommend lockout but are

simply reporting it here.) Therefore, before bargaining a no-strike, no-lockout clause, management should carefully consider its own loss of flexibility and whether or not lockouts as well as strikes are prohibited.

Savings Clause

The inclusion of a savings clause should be determined by review of all that has been agreed to and upon the desirability of preserving the contract should one or more clauses be found illegal. The traditional savings clause reads as follows: "If any provision of this Agreement or any application of the Agreement to the parties of this Agreement shall be found contrary to law, then such provision or application shall not be deemed valid, except to the extent permitted by law, but all other provisions or applications shall continue in full force and effect" (Collective Bargaining Agreement between the Faculty Bargaining Coalition of Eastern Montana College and The Commissioner of Higher Education on behalf of Eastern Montana College, July 1, 1975 to June 30, 1977).

One problem that may arise concerning saving the contract centers upon the difficulty of determining what, if any, additional clauses are partially or wholly destroyed by virtue of a voided clause. The problem may be resolved to the satisfaction of both parties by using a designated referee to decide upon the validity of clauses should a dispute arise after the declaration of illegality of one or more clauses by a court or other appropriate agency.

Zipper Clause

This clause which recites that the agreement as written constitutes the entire negotiated settlement (thereby excluding extracontractual matters such as past practices, past benefits, trustees policies, and faculty handbook from the contract and grievance procedures) provides several advantages. Providing there is no past-practice or benefits-preserved clause in the contract, a zipper clause provides protection from: (1) attempts to negotiate traditional practices into the contract during the contract term, (2) grievances based on extracontractual matters, and (3) consideration of past practices by arbitrators when settling grievances. Formal negotiations, rather than grievance decisions or errors by subadministrators, would be required to modify or expand the provisions of the agreement. Administration's attempts to limit arbitral or judicial review to "the four corners of the contract" are substantially strengthened. In any event, no contract should be ratified without a clause which provides some finality to the terms of the agreement.

Term-of-Agreement Clause

The date upon which the contract will terminate is a factor which may greatly influence the tone and effectiveness of the next round of negotiations. Many contracts have set the expiration date as the last day of August which may result in summer-long postponements of bargaining and may increase the possibility of class interruptions caused by strikes or slowdowns resulting from the lack of a signed agreement. Thus, it is suggested that the parties agree to a contract termination date sometime in the spring in order that effective negotiations, when needed, may continue through the summer to reduce the likelihood of fall-term strikes.

Conclusion

Suggestions made in this chapter are intended to enhance the administration's effective operation of an institution by taking advantage of one or more of the opportunities offered through collective bargaining, by reducing the bases from which disputes arise, and by encouraging equitable and speedy resolution of those disputes which do arise. When the parties recognize that they have interrelated goals and that the needs of the parties are best served by amicable relationships, each contract clause will be bargained with more concern for institutional viability and excellence.

Contract Clauses

Section I: Preambles
Example 1: Preamble

WHEREAS, the intent and purpose of this Agreement are to provide to the Institute's student body career-oriented collegiate education at reasonable costs consistent with instruction and guidance of excellent quality, thus moderating the growing economic burden on students and their families, and to promote increasingly high standards of academic achievement in every phase of the Institute's special mission in higher education, and

WHEREAS, the intent and purpose of this Agreement are to promote and improve the quality and effectiveness of education at the Institute, the parties to this Agreement concur that these objectives can be materially achieved through the amicable adjustment of matters of mutual interest through the establishment of basic understandings relating to personnel policies, practices and procedures, and matters affecting other conditions of employment relating to wages and hours, and

WHEREAS, it is recognized by the parties that mutual benefits are to be derived from a continual improvement in the position of the Institute as an institution of higher learning, that the faculty is expected to advise in developing educational programs, and make recommendations to the President of the Institute, it being understood that final decisions on all such matters are solely within the jurisdiction of the Board of Trustees of the Institute.

NOW, THEREFORE, in consideration of the mutual covenants herein contained the parties agree as follows:

[Taken from the Agreement between New York Institute of Technology and The Council of Metropolitan and Old Westbury Chapters of the American Association of University Professors at the New York Institute of Technology, September 1, 1974 to August 31, 1977.]

Example 2: Preamble

WHEREAS, the Union has been designated as the bargaining representative by a majority of the full-time faculty members;

WHEREAS, the Board and Union have voluntarily endorsed the practices and procedures of collective bargaining as a fair and orderly way of conducting relations between the Board and the full-time faculty insofar as such practices and procedures are appropriate to the obligations of the Board to retain the right effectively to operate Prairie State College and are consonant with the paramount interests of the public and the students of Prairie State College;

WHEREAS, the Board, the Union, and the full-time faculty members are proud of the College's tradition of service to students and are dedicated to providing the students of Prairie State College with the highest caliber of instruction and individual attention and counseling to permit the fullest opportunity for individual and intellectual development;

WHEREAS, it is the intention of the parties to this Agreement to provide, where not otherwise mandated by statute, for the salary schedule, fringe benefits and conditions of employment of the full-time faculty members covered by this Agreement, to prevent interruptions of work and interference with the efficient operation of Prairie State College, and to provide an orderly and prompt method of handling and processing grievances;

NOW, THEREFORE, the parties agree with each other as follows:

[Taken from 1975–1977 Agreement between Board of Community College District No. 515, Counties of Cook, Will and State of Illinois and Prairie State College Chapter of the Cook County Teachers Union, Local 1600, AFT, AFL-CIO.]

Example 3: Preamble

The intent and the purpose of this Agreement are to promote and improve the quality and effectiveness of education at St. John's University, New York (the "University") and to maintain high standards of academic excellence in all phases of instruction at the University. The parties hereto concur that these objectives can be materially achieved by means of amicable adjustment of matters of mutual interest and through the establishment of basic understandings relative to personnel policies, practices and procedures, and matters affecting other conditions of employment.

It is recognized by the parties that mutual benefits are to be derived from continual improvement in the position of the University as an institution of higher learning; that the faculty is particularly qualified to assist in formulating educational policies and developing educational programs; that the University has responsibility to present and make available to the student body the kind and degree of learning that meet the highest standards of higher education; and that these objectives can be materially advanced by conducting uninterrupted courses of study. It is further recognized that the roles and responsibilities of the Administration and the faculty are interdependent in the determination and implementation of educational policy and objectives and require the broadest possible cooperation and the fullest exchange of information and opinion with regard to such educational matters. To meet these goals, the parties have endorsed in principle the general educational philosophy of the 1966 *Statement on Government of Colleges and Universities* (the "1966 *Statement*") of the American Association of University Professors and have incorporated certain specific provisions of the 1966 *Statement* into the Agreement.

Now, therefore, the parties hereto agree as follows:

[Taken from the Agreement between the Administration of St. John's University, New York and the St. John's Chapter of the American Association of University Professors–Faculty Association at St. John's University, 1974–1977.]

Section II: Zipper Clauses

Example 1: Zipper Clause

This Agreement constitutes the entire negotiated Agreement between the Commissioner, the Administration, and the Coalition and supersedes any previous regulations, faculty contracts, previous practices, or policies which may be in conflict with the expressed terms of this Agreement. This Agreement shall constitute the Master Agreement for all faculty members in the bargaining unit.

[Taken from the Collective Bargaining Agreement between the Faculty Bargaining Coalition of Eastern Montana College and the Commissioner of Higher Education as agent for the Board of Regents of Higher Education on behalf of Eastern Montana College, July 1, 1975–June 30, 1977, p. 19.]

Example 2: Zipper Clause

This document contains the entire Agreement of the parties. No provision or term of this agreement may be amended, modified, changed, altered, or waived, except by written document executed by the parties hereto.

[Taken from the Agreement between the University of Hawaii Professional Assembly and the University of Hawaii, March 1975 to June 1977, p. 24.]

Section III: Management Rights Clauses

Example 1: Management Rights Clause

This Agreement shall not constitute any limitations upon the College's ultimate responsibility for all matters concerning the College or upon the College's authority to exercise its rights and responsibilities except as specifically provided herein.

[Taken from the Collective Bargaining Agreement 1975–1980 between the Loretto Heights College and the Loretto Heights College Faculty Education Association, NEA, p. 23.]

Example 2: Management Rights Clause

The AAUP recognizes that except as hereinafter specifically provided, the operations and administration of the University, including but not limited to, the right to make rules and regulations pertaining thereto, shall be fully vested in its Board and the President and their duly designated representatives. Except as hereinafter specifically provided, nothing herein stated shall be construed as a delegation or waiver of any powers or duties vested in the Board or any administrator by virtue of any provision of the laws of the State of Delaware or the Charter of the University.

[Taken from Collective Bargaining Agreement between the University of Delaware and American Association of University Professors University of Delaware Chapter, September 5, 1975 to June 30, 1977, p. 3.]

Example 3: Management Rights Clause

Western has the responsibility and, subject only to the limitations imposed by the express and specific terms of this Agreement, the right to manage, direct, and control the University and its programs.

Western's existing rights, privileges, and responsibilities to manage its academic and nonacademic programs not specifically delineated by this Agreement shall continue in full force and effect. In the event that the specific terms of this Agreement conflict with such rights, privileges, and responsibilities, the specific terms of this Agreement shall be controlling to the extent necessary to resolve such conflict, provided however, that this Agreement shall in all cases be interpreted so as not to deprive Western of its legal authority to control all final decisions regarding its academic and nonacademic programs.

Except as limited or abrogated by the terms and provisions of this agreement, Western's rights and responsibilities include, but are not limited to, the right: (1) to hire all employees, to determine their qualifications, their compensation, and the conditions for their continued employment; (2) to terminate, promote, transfer, assign, lay off, and recall all such employees; (3) to establish, modify or abolish programs and courses of instruction, as deemed necessary or advisable by the Board; (4) to determine the University calendar, class schedules, hours of instruction, and the duties, responsibilities and assignments of faculty and other employees with respect thereto; (5) to locate, relocate, and remove its equipment and facilities; and (6) to control its property.

[Taken from the Agreement between Western Michigan University and the Western Michigan University, AAUP Chapter, September 20, 1976 to June 30, 1977, p. 5.]

Harold R. Newman

18

The seventeenth century English poet, John Dryden, in peevish temper wrote, "Damned Neuters, in their middle way of Steering, Are neither Fish, nor Flesh, nor good Red Herring." One should be cautioned that a neutral and a neuter are not at all the same thing. If a neutral is to be successful in his profession, he must be a decisive chap with a strong personality and be capable of influencing others. No one with a neuter personality could influence anybody. Neutrals have been important throughout history. Medieval popes mediated and arbitrated among warring sovereigns. Henry Kissinger travels the globe as a conciliator. My friend, Professor Maurice Trotta (1974), informs us that arbitration was used over thirty-five hundred years ago in Egypt and in Greece in the ninth century B.C.

Never has there been a time in the history of our country when neutrals have been in greater demand. Not only has there

Using Neutrals
to Help Settle
Impasses

been a tremendous spurt in the organization of public employees so that collective bargaining in the public sector is becoming as commonplace as bargaining between unions and management in the private sector, but we live in a time when priests and ministers talk back to bishops, tenants organize against landlords, prison inmates file grievances against guards and wardens, and to the utter shock and dismay of old soldiers, privates may file grievance charges against officers!

What is characteristic of each of these situations, whether at the labor negotiations table or in the churches, housing projects, the penal institutions, or the military, is that what is really being sought or discussed is *power sharing*. Unions do not permit employers to determine unilaterally the wages and working conditions of the members they represent. The clergyman, the imprisoned felon, and the army private have a common desire to have their grievances articulated and addressed. Indeed, with regard to the tenants' organizations, there may be an economic demand on the table for a freeze or even a rollback of rents. But whatever the issues and wherever the setting, there is a strong thrust taking place for decision-making *assisted by* an impartial individual or agency and an end to unilateral determination. According to a study by Professor Joseph Garbarino (1976), more than one hundred thousand faculty members in public and private colleges and universities throughout the country are now unionized. Administrators in unionized postsecondary schools should, therefore, try to accept collective bargaining as a normal fact of life. It should not be looked upon as a cross which administrators must bear. Those unfamiliar with campus life under a collective bargaining contract with the faculty may find themselves pleased and astonished to discover that dealing with one or even a few faculty union representatives on a wide spectrum of problems can be vastly less painful than individual negotiations with a variety of "self-governing" academics.

Every college or university administrator is familiar with that curious facet of academia known as "faculty governance." Certainly, it has been possible for institutions of higher learning to live with faculty-shared decision making on tenure, curricula, and promotions without serious consequence to the administration. The power sharing in faculty governance has, as a matter of fact, been sharply criticized by some of the leading advocates of collective bargaining in higher education as permitting administration to escape responsibility, for making faculty responsible for unpopular decisions, and for permitting the existence of weak management (Garbarino, 1976). In any event, power sharing through faculty governance is, of course, characteristic of post–secondary schools. Bargaining on the part of faculty union should not, as Dr. Angell has pointed out in Chapter One, create new and severe problems for college or university administrators. On the contrary, it should create opportunities for more effective administration and better faculty-administration relationships. Collective bargaining does not represent a diminution of administrative power for management. Indeed, it is a fair statement that what is not ceded to the union in the specific language of the collective bargaining agreement clearly remains with management. Administrators may be startled to discover that far from being weakened by the existence of a collective bargaining agreement, they may be embarrassed by their new-found management powers and responsibilities.

The techniques of negotiation and the matter of contract language are treated elsewhere in this book. However, it is inevitable that there will be some occasions when the parties involved in collective negotiations will be unable to agree and the assistance of the neutral will be required. The neutral or impartial may come in a variety of sizes and weights, but all of them fall into three general categories—mediators, arbitrators, and fact finders. Some professional neutrals are able to perform all three functions. Some prefer to work at two of the three and others to specialize in only one. But the work they perform is generally of enormous value to the parties in dispute and to the community where the dispute is located.

Who Are the Neutrals?

Neutrals involved in the conciliation or adjudication of labor disputes are usually generalists in the sense that they function in private industry and in the public sector and may be involved one day with mediating a strike in a textile mill and the next day with a dispute involving draftsmen and engineers working on an aerospace project. There are some neutrals who are considered to have special expertise in certain industries and professions and who are repeatedly called upon to resolve impasses involving printers or airline pilots, for example. Indeed, some of these specialists, usually arbitrators, are written into contracts as the specific umpires who will be called upon should disputes arise over the interpretation of the contract. (We shall discuss later the function of the arbitrator in contract interpretation as differentiated from the arbitrator's function in establishing contract terms.)

The labor neutral is seldom someone who has spent his professional life totally as an impartial. Many men and women who are nationally known as mediators or arbitrators worked earlier in their careers as union staff members or as industrial relations executives for large companies. Thereafter, they made a conscious choice to discard the advocate role and work full time as neutrals. This decision can only be made when the individual has met two basic requirements. The first is that he is truly a neutral and has no biases for or against unions or management. The second is that he has worn the sooty yoke of apprenticeship in labor relations long enough so that there is no question but that he is knowledgeable about labor law at the state and federal level, thoroughly understands the techniques of bargaining, grasps the mystique of wage rate setting and salary schedules, has better than a nodding acquaintance with economics, and has a good understanding of the structure of unions. Beyond these things, he must be endowed with the kind of personality and intelligence, sensitivity and drive that will enable him to motivate individuals and groups in specific directions and to be able to get their confidence after very brief exposure to him. This paragon must also be endowed with a good dash of ego. Certainly, a mediator whose ego did not demand that he get a settlement lest the continued impasse murder sleep or the arbitrator so diffident that the parties had no sense of security that whatever his award, it would be the product of sound knowledge and good rational thinking, should seek other vocations.

There are, of course, neutrals who have never been anything else. These generally fall into two categories. There are those who, after academic training, joined government agencies and obtained their experience representing such agencies, and there are, of course, the academics whose specialty is labor relations. There are teachers of collective bargaining and related courses in many of the institutions of higher learning in the United States who are just as famous as practicing labor neutrals as they are as academic theoreticians.

Let us examine the three broad categories of conciliation activity performed by neutrals.

Mediation

Repeatedly, when one is asked for a definition of what a mediator does, the response is something like, "It is a question of style." Sometimes, the reply is "mediation is an art and not a science." Both statements are true, but quite obviously they do not provide the questioner with a useful answer. The basic reason that mediation is always difficult to define is that the mediator works with almost no ground rules and in a rather unstructured situation.

Furthermore, since the mediator must have the confidences of the parties and he almost never keeps any notes, we must heavily depend on anecdotal reporting of mediators' experiences for information.

The mediator's function essentially is to assist the parties to achieve a *voluntary* agreement. In the words of an outstanding mediator, Theodore Kheel, "The mediator is a catalyst on a hot tin roof." They must believe that he is knowledgeable about the issues that separate the two sides. They each must believe that he empathizes with their problems. Finally, they must have the unshakable conviction that if they tell him something in confidence, it will not be communicated to the other side. The mediator uses a variety of devices to gain the confidence of the parties. By making simple verbal observations, he can, perhaps, at one and the same time show that he both understands the issues and empathizes with the problems the parties have with them.

One experienced mediator carries a standard lined yellow pad attached to a clipboard. During the negotiation sessions he will draw gargoyles, unicorns, and winged dragons on the yellow pad. He will not put a note down that has to do with the substance of the discussions lest the note should be carelessly left and devoured by an eager reporter or someone else who should best not see it. Mediators learn to keep all but the most complex matters in their heads.

The fact that my mediator friend is busily sketching does not mean that he is not listening very attentively. At some time perhaps, the union representatives will demand another paid holiday. "We've got to have Election Day as a paid holiday." The pencil which has hitherto drawn only mythical creatures now does some rapid calculation based on the total number of employees and their wage scale. "You mean," says my mediator friend, "you are talking $28,000." Both negotiating teams beam on him. The union's team knows he has grasped their position that there is a piddling amount of money involved, while management can tell that this is a mediator who knows the score and called attention to that outrageously astronomic demand for $28,000! But even after the mediator has gained his total acceptability with the parties, his work is yet before him. Theodore Kheel, whom I mentioned earlier, was involved in a very difficult impasse in which the employer was a public authority which had very little money to put on the table. Mr. Kheel recognized that the union constituency was rather superannuated. Many of them, therefore, would be very concerned about retirement pensions and health insurance. Mr. Kheel's strategy was to push the union hard to lower their pay demands (an immediate cost item to the employer) and to push the employer hard for substantial pension and insurance improvements (a deferred cost to the employer). It is precisely in this kind of situation that the question of confidentiality is so important. Suppose the union had said to the mediator, "OK, we'll take 4 percent across-the-board instead of the 6½ percent we have been demanding, but you have got to get us 100 percent family coverage on the hospitalization." The mediator without communicating to the employer that he had a scaled down union demand might tell management's team, "Look, I'll try like the dickens to get them to come off that 6 percent but you've got to give me something better on the pensions and insurance." He might then reverse field after getting employer concessions on fringes and lean some more on the union until he had pared their wage demands still further. Eventually, an agreement begins to take shape.

Seldom is the script as neat as I have described it, and it is never simple. Usually, there are a substantial number of economic and noneconomic issues on the table. One of the first tasks of the mediator is to try, by probing and by careful listening, to find out what issues are the really important ones to each side. There are almost always some things that are "throwaways." But always the mediator must keep in mind that there are substantial differences between aspiration and reality that he must educate each side to understand. The final agreement will not make either party totally happy. The mediator must take on the unpleasant task of deflating positions held dear by the negotiators for each side, or no agreement is possible. Like all other humans, college and university administrators and faculty negotiators can repeat certain positions at and away from the bargaining table with such frequency and vehemence that they come to believe that those positions are immutable and must be treated as Holy Writ.

Whether the mediator spends most of his time meeting jointly with the parties or has them separated for most of the time depends on a variety of factors. One, certainly, is the question of the bargaining climate. If negotiations before the mediator got on the scene had deteriorated to the point that shouted insults have been exchanged and really hard feelings had developed, it might require that the mediator keep the parties totally apart until the time for signing the memorandum of agreement. In other situations, as Kenneth Kressel (1972) has pointed out in his excellent study of mediation techniques, the mediator may deliberately have the parties confront each other even if tempers are high, because he believes the catharsis of a shouting match may be useful. Generally, mediators have the parties together and apart as the situation seems to require. For example, mediators who wish to work for one public relations board are required to pass a stiff and highly pressured Civil Service oral examination. One of the staff had been put through a simulated mediation situation by the oral examiners and was asked at one point what he would do if one of the parties then rose and stormed out. His reply was a classical delineation of what mediation is all about. He said, "I might get up and pull on their jackets and beg them to stay. I might fling my arms across the elevator door and say they could not leave, or I might just sit there and say to myself, 'Good, the other side had to see that.'" A classic description which demonstrates that mediation is ad hoc.

The most important thing to say about mediation, perhaps, is that it is to be preferred to all other kinds of neutral intervention and it is why, where statutory impasse procedures exist, mediation is almost always the first step. The other conciliation devices should only be used if mediation fails. Any individual knowledgeable about labor relations would say that the best agreement is one consummated by the parties without third-party intervention. Obviously, that is truly voluntary collective bargaining. The parties know more of their own specific situation than any outside neutral, no matter how skilled and knowledgeable, can possibly know. The parties have to *live* with the contract, while the neutral goes on to his next assignment. But the mediation process still affords the parties the opportunity to make their own agreement. The mediator is powerless to compel the parties to do anything. He has to rely on persuasion. Meanwhile, the parties are, in fact, continuing to bargain. That is why mediation is often referred to as an extension of collective bargaining.

Perhaps we should issue a word of caution at this point. The mediator is not likely to be particularly fond of college adminis-trators or, for that matter, of college faculties. He is a total pragma-tist. His only interest and, in fact, his only function is to assist the parties in getting a settlement of their dispute. The mediator sees no villains and no heroes—only two groups of people with prob-lems. If both institutional and faculty negotiators complain that the other side is unreasonable, he may or may not agree with either one. (He is unlikely to give his opinion.) But their opinion of each other is excess baggage he does not need and will not carry. Later, I shall discuss how to maximize the use of a mediator.

Arbitration

There are many kinds of arbitration. These range from the arbitration of community disputes to commercial arbitration in the world of business. But in labor arbitration there are only two categories—rights arbitration, which is sometimes called grievance arbitration, and interest arbitration, which is also known as contract arbitration. Rights arbitration involves the arbitrator in making an award in a matter arising out of an interpretation of an existing contract. For example, the arbitrator may be called upon to inter-pret what the contract language means with regard to a grievance, such as the denial of a fringe benefit to an individual or group of employees or a matter of discipline of one or more persons. Inter-est arbitration gives the arbitrator the responsibility for actually writing terms of a new contract. It is infrequently used in the private sector, and in the public sector it is generally used in cases involv-ing policemen, firefighters, hospital workers, or others whose du-ties involving public health, safety, or welfare would make any work stoppage unthinkable.

Arbitration is carried out as a quasi-judicial proceeding. Unlike the mediator, the arbitrator does not meet separately with the parties. He sits as a kind of judge and hears the testimony of witnesses, accepts evidentiary material in the form of exhibits and may receive briefs from the advocates after the conclusion of the formal hearings. When the arbitrator has completed reviewing all the evidence submitted, he will issue an award binding on the parties.

Fact Finding

Fact finding is a misnomer. The neutral who has been dubbed "fact finder" in a particular dispute discovers rather quickly after his arrival on the scene that the parties are well acquainted with the "facts." Suppose the facts are that the college endowment is low because of a misbehaving stock market. Further, that administration is finding that the cost of everything from fuel to heat the campus buildings to lab materials has risen astronomically because of inflation. He also finds that the faculty is hurting badly at the supermarket and the gas station and everywhere else because of higher prices, and that they are the lowest-paid four-year college faculty in the region. Student tuition was raised in each of the past three years, and yet the school is still in a very tight fiscal squeeze. After repeated attempts by teams representing faculty and administration, both sides agree that further negotiations would be useless. If the fact finder's function were only to delineate the melancholy facts described, how would the dispute be resolved? Obviously, it wouldn't be.

What then is the use of fact finding? The process has a variety of uses. In the first place, it permits the parties to have the real issues separating them to be illuminated. The need to prepare oral testimony and written data for the fact finder will automatically cause much chaff to fall off the bargaining table. Second, with regard to the "gut" issues as, for example, faculty salaries in the hypothetical situation I have described, the fact finder can separate reality from aspiration for both parties and suggest about where the settlement must be. Finally, and very important to the parties, the fact finder provides them with a "political" scapegoat. It is always necessary, following any dispute resolution, to obtain ratifications of the agreement. It is politically convenient for the negotiators to point to the fact finder's recommendations as being responsible for any proposed settlement. This is especially true if it has some aspects that their principals find hard to swallow. (Keep in mind that in almost no instance is a final agreement totally satisfactory to either party in a labor negotiation. It always represents a compromise.) It is convenient for the negotiators to say, "Well, we weren't too happy with that item on sabbaticals but the fact

finder, Mr. _____ , has had twenty years' experience as a labor
neutral and he had all the evidence before him. We felt we had to
go along." It is entirely right and proper that heat be directed at
the fact finder for his recommendations. One of the functions of
the neutral is to act as a lightning rod.

One more comment about fact finding. Fact finding reports
involving impasses at public colleges and universities will likely be
made public. State statutes covering public employee bargaining
usually so require. Therefore, despite the fact that the recommendations of the fact finder are not binding on the parties, there
is some considerable pressure on them to accept a document whose
recommendations and rationale have been disseminated in the
media.

Summary of Techniques

The best way to delineate differences among the processes
involved in mediation, arbitration, and fact finding is to examine
the powers of the neutral in each. The mediator has no power to
do more than point out areas of possible resolution of a dispute and
to use persuasion. The fact finder hears testimony and accepts
briefs, data, and other evidentiary material. But when the hearings
have been terminated and all the evidence has been given to the
fact finder, he can only write a report and make *recommendations*
for resolution of the dispute. Only the arbitrator can issue an *award*
enforceable in the courts.

There are often variations in the conciliation procedures
used. If a particular impasse seems almost intractable, there may
be with the parties' permission something known as "med-arb."
Here the mediator attempts to get agreement on all outstanding
issues, but if he should fail, he is permitted to act as an arbitrator
and make a binding determination on the issues that remain. Usually fact finding takes place after mediation has proved unsuccessful but if the parties need a fact-finding report for "political" reasons
or if it is deemed wise to illuminate the issues for the parties immediately, then fact finding may occur before any formal attempt
at mediation. Although arbitration usually involves but a single
arbitrator, some state laws and many contracts require tripartite
arbitration performed by an arbitrator representing the union,

one representing the employer, and a neutral chairperson. Sometimes, too, interest or contract arbitration may involve the arbitrator(s) being compelled to take the last best offer of one or the other party or, as a third alternative, the fact finder's report.

Flexibility in conciliation techniques is of such importance that it cannot be overstressed. Whichever procedures bring about settlements with which the parties can live comfortably are valid and must be used. Again, of course, at the risk of redundancy, we should stress that the optimum situation is for the parties to reach agreement without third party intervention and failing that, to settle in mediation. But no matter how conscientiously the parties may strive to do so, it is not always possible.

When Does a Neutral Enter a Dispute?

As we noted earlier, there are now approximately 100,000 faculty members in colleges and universities who are unionized. In 1970 the NLRB took jurisdiction over private colleges and universities whose gross annual revenue from all sources amounts to not less than one million dollars.[1] That means that such institutions are subject to the NLRA and the employer and the union are bound by the federal law to bargain in good faith wages, hours, and other terms of conditions of employment, the negotiation of an agreement, or any question arising under an agreement. Where a collective bargaining agreement is in effect, if one party wishes to end or change the contract, it must notify the other party in writing about the proposed termination or modification sixty days before the date on which the contract is scheduled to expire. If the contract is not scheduled to expire on any particular date, the notice in writing must be served sixty days before the time when it is proposed that the termination or modification take effect. Further, the negotiator must offer to meet and confer with the other party for the purpose of negotiating a new contract or a contract containing the proposed changes. Also, he must, within thirty days after the notice to the other party, notify the Federal Mediation and Conciliation Service of the existence of a dispute if no agreement has been reached by that time. The negotiator must notify at the

[1] 183 NLRB No. 41 (1970).

same time the state or territorial mediation or conciliation agency in the state or territory where the dispute occurred. Thus, private colleges and universities which meet the requirements for coverage under the NLRA are required, under certain circumstances, to obtain the assistance of neutrals when necessary either from the Federal Mediation and Conciliation Service, the state board of mediation (if the particular dispute occurs in a state where there is such an agency), or both.

Most unionized higher education faculty are, however, employed by public institutions. Here, the assignment of the neutral to an impasse in collective bargaining will depend on the particular statute covering public employee bargaining in the individual state in which the impasse occurs. Twenty-four states now have statutes covering some or all public college employees and have agencies administering such laws which are responsible for the procedures used to resolve collective bargaining disputes. These agencies ordinarily will arrange for the assignment of neutrals when necessary. In the event that an impasse occurs in a state in which there is no public sector bargaining law or if such law does not cover employees of post–secondary schools, the Federal Mediation and Conciliation Service would probably, at the request of the parties, provide for mediators and arbitrators as needed.

As a general rule, mediators are *assigned* to disputes by government agencies. Arbitrators are usually *chosen* by the parties. The method of choosing the arbitrator varies. Sometimes, the parties themselves jointly agree on an individual and simply communicate with him and ask him to serve. In other instances, a government agency or the American Arbitration Association (a public service corporation involved in dispute settlement) will supply a list of arbitrators to the parties. Union and management rank the individuals on the list in order of preference. The appointing agency then would designate the individual with the lowest score. A third method is that of striking names from an odd numbered list. The parties strike alternately until the one person left is designated. (This is the method used under the interest arbitration statute covering higher education arbitration in Maine.)

Choosing the Neutral

A major concern of the parties in a dispute in a higher education institution in the choice of mediator, fact finder, or arbitrator is whether he is competent to work in the unique setting that is a college or university. Government officials responsible for appointing mediators and fact finders (I am one) are always conscious of the fact that in conciliation, what is needed, to use an expression favored by our youth, are "different strokes for different folks." Simply put, some mediators do exceedingly well working with professionals. Others work more comfortably with pragmatic blue-collar workers who are concerned almost solely with salary and dollar-benefit issues. These neutrals prefer to be miles away from any bargaining table involving social workers, medical interns, or college professors. The mediator or fact finder assigned to a dispute involving a college or university is not likely to be someone who cannot tell ash from oak in the groves of academe. He may himself be a college professor (from another institution, of course!) of the labor relations specialist variety described earlier and should be assigned only if acceptable to administration. But even if he is a full-time mediator, he will almost certainly understand the language of the institution. Finally, one may be assured that he will possess those qualities described as essential to the successful mediator.

Arbitrators are, of course, chosen by the parties themselves. A list of names—five or nine or seven—may mean nothing, but the vitae of the arbitrators should reveal a greal deal. If the parties wish to use an arbitrator who is also an academic, the vita will be helpful. If they wish to avoid using an academic, by all means they should not choose one. (My own opinion is that the labor mediators and arbitrators who teach at the college level are an outstanding group of neutrals, and there has never been any reason to suspect that any of them are biased for or against other college faculty personnel. At least that is my opinion, and, perhaps, it is not shared by all administrators and union representatives.) The Federal Mediation and Conciliation Service uses a computerized assignment system for its arbitration panel. No arbitrator is likely to be assigned to an impasse at an institution of higher learning by the Federal Mediation and Conciliation Service who has not had good experience dealing with such schools.

Another method of learning about arbitrators is to use the monthly Summary of Labor Arbitration Awards published by the American Arbitration Association. There are separate summaries for arbitration in government and arbitration in the schools. One can read arbitrators' decisions in other cases. But it should be understood that an award in a case involving another postsecondary institution, though it may appear to have circumstances similar to one's own situation, may, in fact, be quite different.

It may come as a mild shock to college or university dons and administrators that an experienced mediator, fact finder, or arbitrator with no college education at all, might perform very effectively in a dispute in a higher education institution. William E. Simkin, Director of the Federal Mediation and Conciliation Service during the administrations of President John F. Kennedy and President Lyndon B. Johnson put a very low priority on formal education in connection with mediation skill and success (1971). I agree wholeheartedly with Mr. Simkin, but I am not prepared to bruise anybody's psyche on such an issue. If a Ph.D. is wanted as an impartial, ask for one.

It is really the responsibility of the parties to educate the neutral when he comes on the scene in any dispute. Every work place has its own bargaining history, special relationships, and special problems. Even if the neutral has worked in a score of collective bargaining situations involving colleges and universities, each particular situation is going to be somewhat different than anything he has experienced before. Both parties should point out special problems and nuances, the role of department chairpersons, for example.

The Neutral and Negotiations

In both private industry and public sector employment, in both the oil industry and school district negotiations, a union starts out by asking for substantially more than it expects it will finally have to settle for and an employer begins by being far more rigid and conservative than he believes he will have to be to get a settlement. This refers to both economic and noneconomic issues. There is no dishonesty or deviousness in the parties' doing this. If they were to begin from their bottom line positions, they would have no place to move. The "bargaining in good faith" required of the parties under the NLRA and under the state statutes governing public employee bargaining does not require giving the other side whatever it wants. It requires only that the parties come to the table with the intention of obtaining a settlement. Such intention is not affected by the parties initially taking positions that are unrealistic. On the contrary, we recall with pain an impasse which we were mediating some seven or eight years ago, when the good people on the management team for the college entered the room at the first session we had called and announced that they had $92,000 for pay increases for the faculty for the coming year. "There it is," said the distinguished chief negotiator for the college, "and the union can spread it over the schedule any way they like." That, in fact, was all that the college had to negotiate with. But despite the fact they had in sweet innocence told the truth, the union did not believe them. On the contrary, the union team felt that if the college had proclaimed that it had $92,000 for faculty salaries, it did, in fact, have vastly more. A strike was narrowly averted. There is little place for primitive Christians at the bargaining table.

In most negotiations there is a kind of ballet performed by the parties. They dance toward each other and away. Then they dance toward and away from each other again until they no longer dance away. If the neutral is present, he will direct each pirouette and the final pas de deux. As the parties dance toward each other throughout the ballet, information is exchanged. The information may be given thunderously or by innuendo. Positions are considered and reconsidered and "quids" are sought for "pro quos." Meantime, the neutral, if one is present, choreographs and conducts using "direct," "indirect," and "reflexive" strategies.

One can read *Hansard,* the official record of debates in the British Parliament, and after comparing statements made by outstanding members at the turn of the century and then reading *Hansard*'s reporting of exchanges in the House of Commons or the House of Lords day before yesterday on a related subject, come to the sad realization that the right honorable gentlemen do not move with speed and, perhaps, do not learn very much very quickly. (A perusal of the *Congressional Record* of seventy years ago and today would, I suspect, bring one to the same lamentable conclusion about our own legislature.) Colleges and universities tend often to move with the same glacial speed. Even when faculty and administration fundamentally agree on a necessary reform, it may be many years before all of the procedural minutiae can be overcome and then reform instituted. I know of one situation in which the college president despaired of ever persuading a slow-moving faculty senate to get around to formally agreeing that the system which required associate professors' tenure determination after only one year's teaching at the school was totally bad, and to agree to a change. After a faculty union was recognized and bargaining for a contract begun, the neutral assisting the parties to reach agreement was able in the space of twenty minutes to get a change in the tenure rules and to have it incorporated in the contract.

In Chapter Seven, George Angell dealt at length with the complex and very important question of scope of bargaining. One of the important functions of the neutral is to put this question into proper perspective. The neutral is not concerned merely with ascertaining whether, as a result of prior decisions by government agencies or the courts, a specific matter is or is not a mandatory subject of negotiations. Even if a subject is nonmandatory, but not prohibited, it may be one that management may be well advised to discuss with the union side for the information which may be derived. Further, such a subject may involve a demand management is willing to accept in place of a demand that management is not willing to accept but which does involve a mandatory subject or negotiations. The neutral can be most helpful in illuminating such possibilities.

From Joseph Hankin's excellent article on preparing for negotiations, which is Chapter Eight of this volume, you have come to understand the importance of preparation for bargaining. This cannot be overstressed. (Every mediator has a happy daydream that, in every dispute in which he is involved, the union and management teams have excellent quarterbacks and at least one team member capable of doing high school math so that economic items may be costed accurately. Alas, it is but a dream.) Once negotiations have begun, it is important to know when a neutral is needed and should be summoned.

When to Call the Neutral

This is a decision that cannot be made too hastily or too slowly. Nathan Cohen (1974), a member of the National Academy of Arbitrators and distinguished mediator and fact finder as well as arbitrator, has stated the following:

Assuming both parties desire to reach an equitable agreement and that both sides have settled or put aside non-essential demands, how can the parties best utilize the services of the third party neutral if they are still at loggerheads over items such as salaries, hours, work load, etc? First and foremost, the mediator or fact finder would expect that the parties have fully explored and understood their differing positions so that there is no question that an impasse exists. By exploration, I mean not only discussing the demands or responses as presented by the parties, but also discussing realistic alternative and fall-back positions. Too often parties agree with alacrity that the gap between the demands and offers is too broad to bridge and the services of a mediator are needed without any real effort to explore possible trade-offs or "quid pro quo's" from which settlements are reached. To seek third-party intervention too early before such efforts are made is to abdicate the responsibility the parties have to negotiate with each other and to attempt to reach their own meeting of the minds.

On the other hand, to explore endlessly and to call for help the night before a threatened job action or before the handing down of a unilateral executive determination leaves too little time for the neutral to rearrange his other work and personal obligations, let alone to familiarize himself with the issues and to explore and suggest new avenues for settlement which may be more acceptable to the parties. Proper timing of the actual intervention of the third party can result in the best utilization of the mediatory talents of that individual. Of course, even though the existence of an impasse may be defined by statute according to the calendar and the use of impasse procedures is governed by law, the parties should not abandon their negotiation efforts on the ground that time has run out. They may still meet by themselves to do what is necessary while the mediator remains available on call or is used for procedural guidance.

I have mentioned that the parties should be able to explore alternative or fall-back positions when they reach an impasse. This type of flexibility is essential to negotiations if one is not to paint himself into a corner with nowhere to go. Too often a union or an employer will refuse to consider what

*will happen if the other side is not amenable to accepting a
"final" or "unalterable" proposal or demand. When the bluff
is called and the proposal is effectively turned down, alternatives will have to be sought unless negotiations are to be
abruptly terminated. If one recognizes the interrelationship
between items such as salaries, working time, work load, staffing, holidays, vacations, sick leave, productivity, length of
contract term, etc., it should be obvious that the judicious
coupling and recoupling of items may result in a degree
of flexibility that obviates the need to take fixed dead-end
positions.*

Despite the fact that calling upon a third party for assistance
in a collective bargaining dispute seems sometimes to be a negative
step ("We should do it ourselves"), it is strongly urged that there
be no hesitance in summoning the aid of the neutral before an
impasse deteriorates to the point that the parties are no longer
bargaining meaningfully on the substantive issues before them.
Instead, they may out of frustration be involved in making highly
emotional evaluations of "bad faith," "bad character," or "stub-
bornness" of the other side. This exercise is wasteful at best. The
neutral, to be mediator, fact finder, or arbitrator, has a very constructive role to play *if he is needed.* The optimum situation, once
again, is one in which the parties come to agreement by themselves.
But this is not always possible. If impasse is reached, the neutral
should be summoned.

A Final Note

The most important fact to keep in mind about the role of
the neutral in the settlement of collective bargaining disputes is
that he is a well-prepared professional. He does not approach his
responsibilities in a mechanistic fashion nor will he seek to shape
and fit a settlement along lines that he considers "equitable" without regard to the needs and concerns of the parties. The mediator
will not substitute his judgment on how issues should be resolved for
that of the parties. The arbitrator and fact finder will do everything
possible to find solutions that the parties can live with comfortably.

The neutral who found himself in a single year with the responsibility for assisting a contract settlement at the University of Maine and at Reed College in Oregon, for example, would be aware of far more than the three thousand miles separating those institutions. One is a state university and the other is a private college. There are substantial differences in faculty, curriculum, student body, governance, geographic spread of campus, funding, and many other characteristics. He will be aware of these factors. The neutral is the servant of the parties, and whether in Maine or Oregon, their efforts should be to maximize the benefits available from his skills, his experience, and his determination to be of assistance in shaping a contract that can serve as the framework for a harmonious and cooperative relationship.

Colleen Dolan-Greene
Frank C. Gerry
Edward P. Kelley, Jr.

❧❦❧❦❧❦❧❦❧❦❧❦❧❦❧❦

Faculty strikes do occur. In fact, almost every academic term brings forth reports of threatened or actual faculty work stoppages someplace in American higher education. Since no one can accurately predict where or when a strike may occur, it is incumbent upon college and university administrators to prepare carefully a "universal" plan from which a constructive response to any potential strike may be quickly put into action. Such a plan requires an instantaneous marshalling of institutional resources in a manner unlike that in any other situation. To be of assistance in preparing such a plan this chapter will first briefly review common reasons for a strike, then consider the types of concerted activity a faculty union may employ, and lastly address the substantive issues in formulating specialized responses to particular situations.

Reasons for a Strike

Strikes do not just happen. It is always possible that an inexperienced union or management may not be able to avert a spon-

Responding Constructively
to Strikes and
Threats of Strikes

taneous strike arising from an unpredicted, emotionally charged event, but for the most part, strikes and other militant actions are designed by union strategists to attain specific goals and objectives about which management has usually been adequately forewarned (for example, several weeks of impasse). Begin, Settle, and Alexander (1975) isolated two major causes of faculty strikes. The first was "the perceived failure of the bargaining process to resolve faculty concerns which initially led to the institution of a bargaining relationship" (p. 5). Secondly, they found that in strike situations there existed among union leaders a perceived "loss of control and/or lack of control over those resources necessary for the acquisition or maintenance of professional status" (p. 6).

Each institution will have to evaluate which issues are most likely to trigger a strike by its faculty. Concerns motivating faculty unionism are often clearly enunciated during the organizational campaign and, if not resolved, may fester into infectious cause for strike. Additional faculty goals undoubtedly will arise at the bargaining table. The decision by a union to call a strike is the product of a complex social, economic, and political cost-benefit analysis. The employee organization must judge the importance of particular bargaining objectives in light of membership support, campaign promises, and its own available fiscal resources. If a strike or militant action is called, the administration should assume that the union has carefully weighed the possible consequences and firmly believes that such concerted activity will help achieve the bargaining objectives of the membership. Also, if the union has threatened militant action, the administration should assume that the union has the ability to carry out its threat. However, this may not always be true, since many organizers realize that the threat of a violent tactic may often be more effective than the tactic itself. The union's potential ability to carry out its threat should encourage the institution to develop a plan of action to protect the interests of the students, trustees, and nonunion staff during the strike period. By having a plan to meet the demands of the worst possible situation, the institution should be more able to respond effectively to any threat posed by the union. It should be stressed that there is no guarantee that a strike or militant action will be successful in attaining the goals of either the faculty or its organization. It is the responsibility of the administration to communicate this to the faculty, students, trustees, and administrative staff during the period of threats. It should also be pointed out that strikes can be very costly to the union as well as to the college.

In evaluating the immediate reasons for a strike and the union's current bargaining objectives, it should be noted that the long-range gains sought by the union often go beyond the momentary issues. As noted by Begin, Settle, and Alexander (1975), the Rider College faculty strike resulted in "the tremendous psychological change among the faculty from a feeling of frustration and powerlessness to a sense of accomplishment expressed by 'we did it'" (p. 76). This feeling of solidarity can be lacking prior to a strike and may be an important incentive in the union's decision to risk a strike even when only a modest economic gain is expected.

Walker, Feldman, and Stone (Chapter Ten) have reviewed administrative strategy for achieving institutional goals through collective bargaining. The goals and mission of the institution require equally careful review when developing a strike plan. If union demands have an exorbitant price tag or cause a significant and unacceptable erosion in the ability to manage and operate the institution, then there may be little alternative to meeting the strike with a force and determination necessary to defeat its purposes. In other situations, the disruption resulting from a strike may be more detrimental to the long-range institutional goals than further compromise on unsettled issues. In preparation for negotiations, an administration should formulate a realistic final position. This final position represents how far the administration will compromise to attain settlement. Faced with a strike, the administration may change those bottom-line positions. Collective bargaining tends to lack the certainty implied by bottom-line positions, and the administration may view its final offer with a different perspective when faced with an imminent strike. Many strikes can be averted with little loss simply by giving a little on one issue in return for a gain on another. This leads to an important concept. *A proposed strike can only gain substantial support among the faculty as a whole when faculty perceive the administration as being wholly unreasonable on some issue of major importance to them.* It should not be difficult to ascertain what that issue is and to offer one or more alternatives to the hard-line position offered by the union. This response is the first and most fundamental one which management can make. And the first page or two of the strike plan should be devoted to a procedure for finding and publicizing new alternatives. Nothing will more quickly take the steam out of a strike threat.

Types of Concerted Activities

The range of concerted activities which a union may undertake is constrained only by the imagination of its leadership. The nature and effectiveness of concerted activities and other tactics are often governed by the emotional strength and duration of issues prevailing in each local situation. Hence, since no two situations are alike, what is an effective union tactic at one institution may fail elsewhere. The following discussion of concerted activities should be considered exemplary rather than all inclusive.

Communication Campaign

The most subtle and frequently used tactic is a communication campaign. This activity may be employed to strengthen an organizing effort or to influence the direction of bargaining. Both on- and off-campus media can be used to articulate the union's position. Unions may attempt to curry the favor of local journalists in an attempt to secure an advantage with the newspapers. It also is not an uncommon feature of a communication effort to employ letters to the editor or even paid advertisements. A media campaign can be directed at a particular audience, such as the faculty, students, other employees, the general public, or the total community. The communication effort can also use more traditional academic campus forums. Incidental comments may be made in class lectures to inform students of the union's opinions and positions in collective bargaining. The existing academic governance structure (for example, faculty senate) can be employed to discuss, debate, or even filibuster a particular issue, and for that matter, any college or university committee can be employed in the same fashion. Additional forums which the union may employ to articulate its position include mass meetings, the student government, guest lectures, and teach-ins. A particularly sensitive forum is the student newspaper.

It is important that the administration monitor the tone and content of a union's communication campaign. Failure to respond may be viewed as a lack of administrative leadership and resolve. Even more damage may result by an effort to chase down every rumor and reply to every written or spoken comment. Nothing would please the union more. Short, factual, and well-placed responses will greatly assist in dispelling rumors and half-truths. In like manner, the tone of the administrative response is of vital import. A "paper war" with harsh comments from both sides is not only counterproductive to the purposes of each party but destructive to the institutional image. A constructive, reasoned response can do much to clarify the issues and might be the first time students and faculty have had an opportunity to understand the consequences of union demands.

Informational Picketing

A dramatic legal activity often used by a union is informational picketing. Pickets provide additional visibility to the union's position and may generate public pressure on the administration for settlement. Faculty members, other employees, and students may be recruited to join the picket line. Pickets may be placed off-campus for additional pressure. The union at a public institution may picket the governmental body responsible for appropriations or the body to whom the institution is administratively responsible. A union at a private institution may picket the primary contributors or any place that would provide exposure to its position. In absence of violence or disruption, informational picketing is legal in most jurisdictions.

Partial Work Stoppage

The most dramatic action a union can sponsor is the withholding of services. A partial work stoppage or slow down is often geared toward the institution at a particular point in time. For example, refusal to give final examinations, refusal to submit grades or to participate in the registration process may be especially annoying at a particular time. Partial work stoppages or slow downs that may be effective at any time during an academic term include not holding specific classes, cutting classes short, or devoting an entire period to discussing the union's position.

The complete withholding of service may occur without an official strike being called. On any one or on several days large numbers of faculty may call in sick or take personal leave. (Mass call-ins for sickness have been nicknamed the "blue flu" when police and firefighters are involved.) Even though this action may occur at a crucial time in the bargaining process, it is not uncommon for the union to plead ignorance. Management does have the legal right at its discretion to ask for justification of absence, and a first response to mass leaves may well be to maintain a record of those absent and require each employee to provide documentation for the claimed cause of absence.

Strike

A complete withholding of services with the union's open endorsement is a strike. This represents the union's demonstration of its ultimate political and economic muscle. It is possible to predict quite accurately when a strike is likely to occur from the tone of bargaining, the content of public statements, and increased pleas for solidarity, permitting valuable time for last minute review of plans and reminders to the administrative staff as to their precise responsibilities in event of a strike. The rest of this chapter outlines key issues for consideration in drafting a strike plan.

The Strike Plan

The college administrator facing a faculty strike for the first time may feel like Alice in Wonderland. Old relationships may be torn asunder, time will collapse and expand so that days seem like minutes and weeks like months. During a strike the campus environment often seems radically altered, and familiar scenery can appear as a whirl of motion. In a situation characterized by shifting positions and rapidly moving events, it is wise to have one's feet on firm, if not familiar, ground. The strike plan's prime function is to provide the administration with guideposts and alternatives because there will ordinarily be insufficient time to review options and formulate plans.

Development of a strike plan has an additional benefit for the administration. The plan's existence can be expected to have three sequential effects on the union and those it represents: anger, fear, and sobriety. The administration should allow time for all three reactions to occur. Knowing, although not specifically, that the administration is prepared for a strike may give a union second thoughts about "surprise" concerted actions.

Issues to Consider

Keeping the Institution Open

The key question in formulating a strike plan is whether the college or university will remain open if the faculty goes on strike—Oakland University in Rochester, Michigan has had two faculty strikes, one in 1971 and one in 1976. During the first strike, the administration closed the institution, that is, they had a lockout. Five years later the university remained open; faculty were encouraged to hold classes and students urged to attend. The first strike lasted two weeks, the second only three days. As in the case of union tactics, an administration's response may change to reflect new conditions.

The decision to keep an institution open will depend largely on the effectiveness of the strike in closing classes and in marshalling student and public sympathy. Preanalysis of this issue may include a review of who is in the bargaining unit, how many faculty are dues-paying members, and how many have voiced negative opinions about union activities. It is also important to know how many classes can be conducted by staff who are not in the unit, and how many substitutes are available and for how many classes. If any classes are, or can be, taught by administrators, support staff, substitutes, and part-time faculty not in the unit, an institution may decide that continuing all classes is a viable option. However, if the unit includes all full- and part-time faculty as well as academic support staff, then a well-supported strike may dictate the partial or total closing of the institution. Beaver Community College (Pa.) facing a possible strike at the opening of the fall term, 1976, decided that, rather than open school and risk the effects of a strike, it would keep the college closed until the faculty signed a new contract. From all reports, the administration felt that the move was successful in eventually settling the impasse. College was opened in October with apparently few negative effects on the institution. Thus, a lockout may be more effective before the fall term opens, but one example is insufficient evidence for a conclusion.

In evaluating whether to keep an institution open, the administration should not underestimate the effect of peer pressure on faculty who may consider not participating in the strike. Experience has proven that the institution should not assume that a large number of faculty will ignore the call to strike and continue to teach.

Because of these and other uncertainties, the administration should formulate a plan which contains an initial decision to remain open (if the term has already begun) and which provides a review of that decision at varying points in time, depending on the effectiveness of the strike. Keeping the institution open may demonstrate an administrative commitment to students, to education, and to integrity, favorably influencing both student views and public opinion. The disadvantage in closing after an initial decision to remain open is, of course, the impression that the institutional lead-

ership is breaking down under the pressure of strike. Thus, the
more appropriate course of action may be to use substitute teachers when administration can no longer carry the teaching load. For
a discussion of substitutes see pages 355–356.

The Strike Team

One of the essential elements of any strike plan is the appointment of key individuals to a strike team responsible for designing
and implementing a strike plan. This team, although relatively
small, should reflect the diversity of the institution's operations by
including chief or key administrators of the maintenance program,
student services, academic affairs, business affairs, and public relations. It is important to remember that members of the management bargaining team will not be available for strike-team service.
Hopefully, the bargaining team will be occupied at the table, and
if not, they must be ready on a moment's notice to return to the
table. In developing the plan and assigning responsibilities, the
administration must remember the fatigue factor. Tired people
tend to make errors. Every effort should be made to keep all members of the administration rested and alert. Food, sleeping cots,
changes of clothes, coffee, and other amenities should be provided
as needed. At no time should the administration appear unorganized, tired, or dishevelled. Family pressures and the resultant
impact should not be underestimated; therefore, plans should,
whenever possible, provide for reasonable blocks of time when some
team members can be at home, albeit on call.

Legal Action

With the exception of private colleges and universities, which
are covered by the National Labor Relations Act (NLRA), strikes are
generally illegal in higher education. However, Alaska, Hawaii,
Pennsylvania, and Oregon allow a limited right to strike. In addition, strike is permitted in Montana through court interpretation.

To determine the legal status of a strike and the extent to
which legislatively required impasse procedures have been followed, the college attorney should be consulted. An analysis of
legal restrictions should, however, be clearly listed in the strike

plan. The preceding chapter has addressed impasse procedures at length. At this point, it should be noted that a particular labor law may require the parties to exhaust the impasse procedures prior to calling a strike. In addition, if an institution desires to resolve a strike quickly, it may wish to suggest to union leaders that the parties submit the issues to binding interest arbitration. The advantages and disadvantages of interest arbitration should also be carefully listed in the strike plan. In addition, the strike plan should contain the legal opinions available to the institution. Managerial efforts to seek a court injunction ordering the faculty to return to the classroom have frequently been made without success. The necessary procedures to follow, together with the reasons most likely to result in an injunction, should also be catalogued in the strike plan. Although having some public relations value, efforts to enjoin the striking party have been largely unproductive. The request for an injunction may result in the judge ordering bargaining to continue within the confines of his chambers while the strike continues. In at least one situation (Oakland University, 1976), this decision by the judge led to an immediate end of the strike.

The objective of any strike is to disrupt and, if possible, to halt the operation of the enterprise in order to increase pressure on administration to compromise its bargaining position. Although academic strikes may generate tension and hostility as do industrial strikes, the nature of the educational endeavor presents some unique problems. Education is a labor-intensive enterprise whose product and consumer may be viewed as a single unit: students. It is difficult, if not impossible, for an administration to employ standard industrial responses to a strike. For example, if a strike is imminent, a college or university cannot speed up production to create surplus inventory to see it through the strike period. Students who view their education and career goals as being disrupted will not just wait on an assembly line to be finished when the strike is over. Experience has demonstrated that when education is interrupted by a faculty strike enrollment may shrink, through student transfer.

Since the immediate objective of an academic strike is to disrupt teaching, a strike plan should specify procedures to evaluate daily the strike's impact. From the outset, the administration should physically check each scheduled class to determine if it is being held. In addition, inquiry should be made as to whether class is being conducted elsewhere as a result of the strike. This action will provide an accurate reflection of the strike's effectiveness. Additionally, it provides an essential record for any subsequent action directed against individual striking employees.

Depending on the results of the classroom check, the projected length, and severity of the strike, a decision may be required about the hiring of substitute faculty, additional part-time faculty or permanent replacements. The ability to locate and attract qualified substitutes will depend in large measure on the complexity of programs offered, the types of classes to be taught, and whether or not a pool of talent is available. It is much easier to find substitutes for grade schools than it is for graduate schools. Geographic location will also influence the institution's pool of available and qualified substitutes. Institutions located in rural areas may find this to be a particularly strong constraint.

The strike plan must give careful consideration to the question of employing substitutes for striking faculty. Two distinct issues must be addressed. The first relates to the legality of employing replacements. The second is the desirability of such an action.

In *Hortonville Joint School District No. 1, et al.* v. *Hortonville Education Association, et al.,* the U.S. Supreme Court recently held that the school board acted within its rights by dismissing and subsequently replacing teachers engaged in an illegal strike.[1] The case, initially brought before the Supreme Court of Wisconsin, raised two central issues. Attorneys representing the teachers contended that failure by the school board to provide a hearing prior to dismissal constituted a violation of the employee's rights. Additionally, they contested the board's right to replace the dismissed teachers. The Wisconsin Court remanded the case to the Hortonville School Board to hold hearings on the dismissal of striking teachers. Subsequently, the Board held the hearings and upon completion dismissed the complaints of strikers. On appeal to the U.S. Supreme Court, the teachers contended their dismissal constituted a violation of their constitutional rights to due process under the Fourteenth Amendment. They additionally contested the employment of replacements. The Supreme Court held that, as illegal strikers,

---

[1] 44 L.W. 4864 (June 15, 1976).

the teachers could be dismissed without a hearing and that the school board acted in accord with Wisconsin law in the conduct of hearings which were held and subsequent dismissal and replacement of the strikers.

For private institutions of higher education and public institutions located in states granting the right to strike, the college attorney should carefully research this issue and see that the strike plan carries the essential cautions and recommendations. To date, it appears that most colleges would have the right to use temporary employees in an effort to keep the institution open. However, most state laws are unclear as to when and if the employer can convert temporary employees into permanent replacements.

Even if an institution is convinced it has the legal right to replace strikers, the plan should give extensive attention to the desirability of such action. The decision to employ substitutes will have serious political and economic implications. Substitutes may be subjected to verbal and physical abuse causing many to discontinue work after a day or two. This type of escalation of emotions may be detrimental to efforts at the bargaining table. In addition, should a later court or board decision order the college to reinstate replaced faculty members with back pay, the cost could be considerable. Alternative plans calling for the combining of classes, using nonstriking employees or instructional media and materials are somewhat less volatile means of keeping the institution open.

Relationships with the Board of Control

It is of vital importance that the board of governors be kept informed about the strike plan. In preparation for negotiations, the board should decide exactly how far it is willing to compromise. In both negotiations and a strike situation, the board must realize that the administration and its bargaining team need considerable flexibility in trading among dollars and issues. The preparation for negotiations and strike plan should anticipate union attempts to create distrust between the board and the administration. This is often done by publicly charging that the administration's bargaining team is not faithfully representing the will of the trustees. The objective of such tactics is to reduce the credibility of the administrative bargaining team and "smoke out the real decision makers." Because of such tactics, enough emphasis cannot be placed on the importance of having the board understand the bargaining process and be realistic in establishing a bottom line. If the board decides, for example, that it would take a strike rather than negotiate a salary settlement in excess of 5 percent, it will do immeasurable damage to the administration and future negotiations if two days into the strike it decides 8 percent is acceptable. This action plays directly into the union's hands since the objective of the strike is not only to destroy resistance to the immediate union demands but to create employer insecurity for all future generations. To "cave-in" will establish a pattern of bargaining that may assure at least an impasse with a threat of strike every time a new contract is negotiated. In addition, a "cave-in" clearly establishes the board rather than the administration as the party with whom to negotiate. This position weakens the administration in its daily work and encourages direct communication between union representatives and board members, usually leading to chaos.

Board members should also be made aware of possible attempts by the union to bypass the bargaining team by a request to meet independently with the board. Additionally, union members may attempt to call board members at home during a strike at all hours of the day and night in an attempt to plead their case. Clearly, such efforts are to be rejected. A complete strike plan should anticipate those events and provide strict board rules to guide members of the board and administration during a strike.

Relationships with Faculty and Other Employees

At the outset of a strike, the administration must remember that the faculty is legally and exclusively represented by the bargaining agent. The administration must assume that the union speaks for the faculty. However, neither party is a monolith, and many faculty members may not be in total agreement with either the strike or the bargaining objectives. It is important, therefore, to communicate with these people so that information furnished by the union does not go unchallenged. The strike plan should outline how the administration will communicate with the faculty other than at the bargaining table. The plan should also contain arrangements for special mailings and meetings as required. A simple, but helpful, detail is to decide in advance, when feasible, which groups to contact so that address labels may be prepared early. In like manner, the appropriate use of newsletters and personal contacts with faculty members who have continued to teach should be carefully thought out in advance.

Plans should also be made for the possibility of sympathy strikes by other unionized employees. Other unionized employees on campus will carefully watch how the administration responds to a strike. The institution should be open, honest, and totally factual in its communication with nonstriking employees. In all cases, it is wise to avoid communications that, by either tone or content, promote hostility or misinformation. Either may eventually lead to sympathy strikes.

Relationships with Students

In the planning stage and during a strike, the status of students often presents the most difficult problems. Students are likely to have differing opinions concerning collective bargaining and the strike. The administration should anticipate that the union will attempt to generate student support for its position. However, experience to date indicates that, while initially successful, union efforts will come to be viewed by students as an attempt to "use" them rather than to address their concerns. The use of students for purposes of political pressure should be avoided by both parties. It usually backfires.

Nevertheless, some students may actively side with the union and participate in militant actions. If a large number of students are inclined to use the strike as a means to attain student power or political change, the administration may wish to review institutional plans for dealing with mass militant student actions of the late 1960s. In the early stages student activists may tend to overreact to the situation. More often than not, overreaction will give way to a more conservative peer pressure as long as the administration restrains itself from making inflammatory responses to the activists.

Many students will see their educational career objectives threatened by the strike. The institution should publicly recognize those concerns and attempt to demonstrate to students that the administration is acting firmly and responsibly on their behalf. Informal meetings before and during the strike should be considered. As stated earlier, a strike plan should provide for the effective use of the Dean of Students and other student services personnel. The issue of grade-point averages and required course work may be of great concern to seniors and students considering advanced graduate and professional study. The administration should make it very clear that it will not tolerate academic retaliation against a student because of the student's opposition to the faculty strike.

The existence of resident students will further complicate matters. Many may be far from home and the strike plan should provide a method for addressing parental concern. In addition, the plan should examine the potential problem of sympathy strikes by food service and maintenance employees. If a decision is made to close the college, provisions must be made for a transitional period before students are able to leave. Advance plans should be made about how and when students will leave the campus. Those planning sessions could involve student leaders and discuss possible options for making up work, independent study, and the care and storage of personal belongings. Resident hall staff and student advisors may also be involved in this stage of the planning.

Any decision to close the institution should entail a projection of possible enrollment losses, increased attrition, and loss of revenues. If the institution is to be closed, plans must be made for possible tuition and housing refunds. The plan should be very clear as to how the institution will notify students and bring them back to campus in the event the institution reopens.

If the college is to remain open, a method of continuing food service and residence operations must be arranged. In the face of an effective and militant picket line, this may be extremely difficult. Unionized vendors and suppliers may refuse to cross the line while others may refuse delivery out of fear of personal harm. Plans should be made to escort needed supplies onto campus. In anticipation of a strike, an institution may plan to have a surplus of supplies.

Strikes lead to hundreds of telephone calls about every new rumor and one response is the establishment of a rumor control center. Oakland University established a "hotline" to receive calls about the strike. It is important that students be quickly and directly informed on changes of policy, what courses are being held, the status of their financial aid, and the like. In similar fashion, the strike plan should call for the publication of daily bulletins. Such publications should be dated and indicate the time of publication. It is always prudent to retain copies of all administrative communications to students, parents, faculty, alumni, and community. Additionally, copies of union publications should be collected, dated, and noted as to time of receipt. This material may be invaluable for planning responses, providing evidence before a labor board, or building a case to be presented before a court. It is also useful in making plans for future strikes.

Relationships with Administrative Staff

When a strike appears imminent, the strike team should be rebriefed about the contents of the strike plan. Lines of authority and responsibility should be reviewed. These meetings and the plan should address the appropriate role of the president. In preparation for negotiations and in the strike plan, the president's role and ability to function as the presiding officer of the institution should not be compromised. However, strict attention should be given to the delegation of authority so that each officer can carry out responsibilities quickly and effectively. As noted earlier, the administration cannot afford to be, or even appear to be, disorganized. Thus, a strike plan should specify who should provide authoritative answers to questions, especially in those areas normally handled by members of the bargaining team who may be working night and day trying to negotiate a contract.

The strike plan should also contain provisions for alternative modes of administrative communication. All members of the management team should be quickly and accurately informed of changes in the bargaining situation, the college's attempts at compromise, and the status of the strike itself. These provisions should not be dependent upon the usual telephone systems which may be either inoperable or jammed at crucial times. Special operators may be needed to keep lines open, and the telephone company's cooperation may be needed to establish new unlisted numbers, as well as for other services. Security officers, vehicles, and communication systems may be helpful at critical periods.

The concerns of administration members' families and the needs of individual management team members will need special attention. As noted earlier, food, cots, and other supplies should be provided. However, it may be easy in the heat of a strike to forget people's psychological needs. Rumors will fly, and charges, unfortunately sometimes of a highly personal nature, will be made. In addition, the skills and loyalty of the administrative support staff, such as long-time secretaries, should not be overlooked. They may have highly productive roles to play during a strike and calling on them in time of need may strengthen their ties to the administration.

Picketing

Informational picketing has been discussed earlier; however, the strike plan should outline the administrative and potential legal procedures to handle the pickets which accompany the strike. In major industrial strikes picketing is a mere formality or may be absent if management has decided to close the plant. However, if a decision is made to continue operations, the union is challenged to deter those faculty members and replacements who attempt to continue work. Additionally, the union may employ picket lines as a means of stopping vendors or suppliers from entering the campus.

Safety

The college should be prepared to protect the safety of all people who enter the campus during the strike. Coordination with campus security and local law enforcement officers is a key factor in providing a safe means of access and egress. Employees who feel physically endangered should not be required to enter the campus alone. Escorts and alternative entrances may be helpful.

Campus facilities and property should also be protected. If the institution has closed, the administration should be sure the campus is free of unauthorized visitors. Special care should be taken to protect costly and sensitive equipment, science laboratories, computer facilities and tapes, business machines, and other important resources. Additionally, if building and office keys have been regularly given to faculty, the strike plan should include quickly retooling all outside door locks. Conversely, if an institution remains open, access to the campus by strikers should be given attention. It may be unwise or unsafe to allow large numbers of strikers to congregate in certain places on the campus. This is a particularly sensitive question since the university ordinarily defends people's right to free assembly and free speech. To deny it during a crisis may be inflammatory rather than protective.

Maintenance

Two aspects of maintenance must be addressed in the strike plan. The first is plant operations and the second is hygienic maintenance. The physical plant office should be responsible for shaping this segment of the plan. Physical plant personnel have complete knowledge of the campus and those operations which must be maintained under all circumstances. During a winter strike heating equipment, water, water pipes, and the like may be damaged if not maintained at a minimum level. If the institution remains open, special plans should be made to protect areas vulnerable to interruption. The powerhouse, switchboard and phone service, and storage areas should be given special attention.

Plans for hygienic maintenance should address regular cleanup activities and the disposal of waste materials. Accumulated waste has often become a problem in situations in which other employees honor the picket line. The intensive use of supervisory personnel has been frequently employed to provide basic maintenance functions.

Physical plant managers should be required to provide the strike team with alternative plans for necessary maintenance from continued service by nonstriking maintenance personnel to contracting out services when and if necessary.

Auxiliary Operations

Many colleges and universities have an array of auxiliary functions that service and attract both on- and off-campus clientele. Included in such operations are conference and meeting programs, concert and lecture programs, theatre and sports events, medical and counseling programs. As part of a strike plan, responsibility and authority for appropriately rescheduling these programs should be clearly delegated to a special member of the strike team. Such programs offer the union an attractive forum for picketing, disruption, and enlisting sympathy. Additional attention should be given to the language of contracts for concerts, lectures, and conferences. Performing artists are well known for not crossing picket lines. Others will demand full pay regardless of conditions preventing performance.

Public Relations

The institution must designate *one* individual to speak for the college during the strike. The "one-voice" concept with public media is far more effective than a medley of administrative voices. A news blackout should be established for everyone in administration including the trustees and president. It is vital that the media obtain prompt and straight answers to their inquiries. If the existing public relations officer has a good relationship with the media, he may be assigned this duty. However, an institution should plan for possible media demands to speak with some "higher up" in the organization. If it appears the press officer lacks sufficient stature, an institution should consider appointing someone else as its spokesperson.

In all communications the watchword must be to play it straight. Establish a recognizable format and tone for administrative communications. Faced with wild and outlandish charges from the union, an institution's most effective response is likely to be a low-key, factual, and reasoned communication style. A reasonable, intelligent response helps to disprove the precise charges of unreasonableness which the union used to initiate the strike. In addition, paper wars are very difficult to win and should be avoided.

The strike plan should anticipate the need for a variety of news releases and responses to mail from concerned parents and alumni. A simple acknowledgment in response to mail from concerned persons may be prepared in advance and placed on mag card. Critical items in news releases may also be prepared in advance and be suitable for assembling into a finished product on very short notice. One must always remember that there will be little time to worry about format and elegance of communication once a strike begins.

Settlement and After the Strike

A good strike plan will always contain the elemental steps of "closing out" the strike period and reentering a period of normal college operation. There will be settlement, even if at times it appears impossible. For a smooth reopening of classes, careful procedures must be understood and followed by many people, each performing a particular service. It is wise to remember that despite the heat generated by a strike, the administration, faculty, and students must live together when it is over. Several institutions have deliberately decided not to attempt to score points during or following a strike by taking what the faculty might view as cheap shots or vindictive action. In like manner, attempts to set students against the faculty may make living under the settlement very difficult. No faculty likes to believe that it had to strike in order to achieve tolerable working conditions. Once over, a strike should be forgotten, and a reasonable attempt to reestablish good will and mutual respect will pay dividends.

The strike plan must address several important issues in this area. Lost classroom time will probably have to be made up. The use of vacations, semester breaks, and interim periods should be explored with faculty representatives. Agreement here can do much to heal wounds. Public colleges and universities should take great care in keeping state officials informed of all strike and settlement developments. For public and private institutions obtaining government aid on a student or credit hour basis, the impact of the strike on enrollments and funding must be considered as part of the strike plan. Early and continuing discussions with governing and appropriation agencies usually will elicit more cooperation and support than later isolated pleas.

In planning to make up lost classroom time, the administration should be careful to follow precisely the strike settlement and the law regarding retroactive salary agreements. Most state laws prescribe penalties for public employees who participate in an illegal strike. The institution should levy those penalties (usually withholding salary) in an even-handed way and encourage the union to seek, if it wishes, redress through appeal to the labor board. In general, a strike should carry some risk for the strikers. If an administration agrees to a retroactive salary agreement to cover time lost during the strike, it may be very difficult to convince faculty who worked during the strike that their efforts were meaningful or appreciated. This may have a damaging impact on future negotiations and strikes.

A strike plan should contain provisions for establishing working and if possible, friendly, relationships after the strike. Rumors about the settlement will be generated and other employees may view unionization as the only way to get ahead. News of the contract terms as well as the penalties assessed, should be spread quickly, broadly, and accurately. Public statements by administrators should contain no evidence of ill will toward the union or its leaders. Such statements should be short and businesslike to avoid, if possible, misinterpretation and lingering bitterness.

The strike will probably alter and unfortunately destroy some long-lasting relationships and mythology. The administration should not underestimate the residual tension and anxiety. The president and his staff will have to be unusually sensitive and adept in dealing with this development for months following a strike. One suggestion is to meet more often with union representatives and solicit their suggestions as to what can be done to normalize relations. The ability to accept union activities as part of the American tradition while eschewing "union-busting" attitudes and actions will do much to reestablish administrative leadership.

Lastly, a strike plan should recognize the need for rest and recreation for bargaining and strike team members. It is an exhausting and difficult experience. People will have voluntarily made endless ad hoc decisions that directly increased their work hours and work loads. Team members may have reached or exceeded their psychological and physical limitations. Compensation for such extraordinary service should be provided.

This chapter has attempted to assist administrators in planning for a strike. Many of the issues, behaviors, and responses discussed may violate some of the reader's cherished beliefs and values. If so, let us say frankly that we see no one perfect way of planning for or meeting a crisis. The suggestions herein derive from experience, research and, finally, sheer opinion. Hopefully, they provide alternatives to be considered, and as one prepares his own plan, details must be selected to fit the administrative personality and character of those responsible. As a summary the following outline of topics may be of some value in preparing a strike plan.

Topics to Be Included in a Strike Plan

Prestrike Activities

1. Appointment of a "strike team."
2. Compilation of a list of union behaviors that predict a strike on this campus.
3. Compilation of common causes of strikes at campuses similar to this one.
4. Establishment of a procedure for identifying the critical issues and shaping alternative bargaining proposals to reduce strike support among the faculty.
5. Establishment of a procedure for reviewing with governing boards and officials bottom lines as to critical union demands in the face of strike threat.
6. Establishment of a procedure for publicizing management alternative proposals to the union's demands.
7. Establishment of a procedure for warning trustees and appropriate government officials as to pending strike.
8. Establishment of a procedure for publicizing the existence of a strike plan.
9. Compilation of an up-to-date list of substitute teachers including administrators qualified to teach.
10. Analysis of which faculty members are likely to continue teaching during a strike.
11. Establishment of employer rules as to authority of bargaining team to act as exclusive agent for employer.
12. Establishment of an employer spokesman for publicity interviews during strike.
13. Compilation of advantages and disadvantages of interest arbitration.

Strike Activities and Management Responses

14. Management response to a union "communication campaign."
15. Management response to "informational picketing."
16. Management response to slowdowns.
17. Management response to a partial work stoppage.

18. Management response to a strike, establishment of (a/an):
   a. Procedure for determining effectiveness of strike each day.
   ·b. Procedure for determining whether or not to close college.
   c. Procedure for monitoring which classes are or are not in session each hour.
   d. Procedure for notifying faculty that each absentee must provide verification.
   e. Analysis of legal restrictions and penalties relative to strikes.
   f. Plan for publicizing restrictions and penalties relative to strikes.
   g. Legal options and procedures for institution to enjoin strikers.
   h. Legal restrictions for employing substitutes or permanent replacements for strikers.
   i. Advantages and disadvantages of substitutes or permanent replacements for strikers.
   j. Plan for keeping trustees and government officials informed about strike progress.
   k. Plan for keeping faculty, other employees, and students informed as to strike progress.
   l. Plan for neutralizing efforts by student activists to join or use the strike for self-interests.
   m. Plan for communicating with parents and alumni.
   n. Special arrangements to sustain food and shelter services during strike.
   o. Special arrangements for students should lockout be called.
   p. Plan for keeping detailed records of comprehensive strike records (news clippings, closed classes, union flyers, and other information.)
   q. Plan for sustaining morale of administrators under duress (especially members of the strike and bargaining teams).
   r. Plan for containing the actions of, and reactions to, pickets.

    s . Plan for safety of those crossing picket lines.

    t . Plan for alternative routing of traffic disrupted by pickets.

    u . Plan for controlling events peripheral to union mass meetings, such as unauthorized visitors, hecklers, student disruptions.

    v . Plan for maintaining or rescheduling extension classes, concerts, sports, and other events.

    w . Plan for determining how and when to levy legal penalties.

    x . Plan for communicating with members of classified personnel to allay sympathy strikes.

    y . Plan for protection of buildings and equipment.

Poststrike Activities

19. Establishment of a plan for publicizing, cooperatively with union, the settlement.

20. Determination of a method for resolving unsettled post-strike problems (for example, how lost classes will be made up).

21. Establishment of a plan for reestablishing friendly and open relations with the union.

22. Establishment of a plan for rewarding administrators who worked long overtime periods during the strike.

23. Establishment of a plan for readjusting budgets to reflect new agreement.

Part III

Once the contract has been ratified, the difficult task of maintaining day-by-day productive relationships between management and labor begins. Administrators and faculty representatives at the table were vigorous advocates, each arguing for policies that would be favorable to their respective parties. Each party negotiated the best possible agreement. Each made some gains. It is now their common responsibility to make that agreement work for the best interests of the parties and the institution as a whole. A spirit of fairness and integrity must prevail if the contract is to have meaning and value. But how can "advocates," after battling with each other week after week at the table, become allies in the pursuit of institutional excellence? Can it really be done? The horror stories far outnumber the glory stories, but cooperation can be achieved if each party believes it to be in the party's own best interest. The art of contract administration is built on the cornerstones of mutual faith and respect and an understanding that cooperation is far more difficult to achieve than a state of hostility. Don-

370

ADMINISTERING
THE CONTRACT

⬡⬡⬡⬡⬡⬡⬡⬡

ald Walker and his associates at Southeastern Massachusetts University discussed in Chapter Ten how these notions have guided negotiations at a public university. Walter H. Powell, a master practitioner of the art of contract administration at Temple University, discusses how these principles can be applied successfully in the everyday confrontations of labor relations (Chapter Twenty). Powell describes how the parties can build mutual respect and a determination to process decisions that will be fair to each faculty member and at the same time build institutional excellence.

Even when working relationships between faculty and administration are friendly and cordial, there occur more frequently on almost every campus two events which threaten this cooperation: arbitration and retrenchment. No matter how judiciously grievances are reviewed, sooner or later certain critical cases will be submitted to arbitration if for no other reason than to obtain an adjudication of interpretation of a contract clause. The most crucial cases involve discipline and discharge of a faculty member.

Ronald W. Bush, a former union organizer and now a contract administrator, explains the many operational details of administering a contract on which an arbitral decision hinges (Chapter Twenty-One). Arbitration cases must be presented extremely well, but the quality of presentation is limited by the care given to establishing and adhering to well-known, reasonable work rules.

Although Chapter Thirteen analyzed the content and underlying concepts of writing a viable retrenchment clause, there remains the incredibly difficult task of administering the various aspects of the clause under extremely emotional conditions, and doing it in a manner that meets conditions imposed externally by the courts. William M. Fulkerson, Jr., an officer of the American Association of State Colleges and Universities, has been monitoring since 1971 the difficulties facing institutions across the country as they have been forced to retrench services and staff. His office has become a focal point of inquiry and consultation for hundreds of administrators. Chapter Twenty-Two describes his interpretation of the landmark court decisions and how institutions can benefit from the reasoning behind those decisions.

Regardless of how well things are going, the parties know that negotiating a new contract is just around the corner. Caesar J. Naples who engineered several SUNY contracts and more recently the Florida State University System faculty contract, describes how a well-organized administration constantly prepares for the next contract by obtaining ideas, facts, and strategies from each grievance settled and from the ensuing impact on institutional operations. In other words, contract preparation, negotiation, and administration must be conceived as interlocking and mutually supportive aspects of a single master plan of operation.

Each of these artists of contract administration advises the establishment of priorities or goals through communication within the administrative team and among the administration and other institutional communities. Powell notes that the contract "represents the skeletal structure connecting the relationships between the parties, whereas the daily workings of the contract . . . become the flesh and blood giving body and life to the total relationship." Bush then suggests that the scope of arbitration be kept narrow in the initial stages of the bargaining relationship so that adequate "study and preparation" can be accorded this crucial step in grievance administration and so that the parties can "gain experience." Fulkerson follows with a statement that "guidelines for administering a contract specifying . . . criteria" [emphasis added] for personnel actions are essential to constructive contract administration. And Naples concludes that positive experiences in the administration of the first contract should lead to "goals and the boundaries of [bargaining] authority" and institutional mission, which should be reduced to writing and shared with the institutional community, where and when possible.

Walter H. Powell

20

It is my sincere belief that after faculty union officials and university management sign the terms of a new agreement, they stand should to shoulder vis-à-vis the rights and duties of faculty and administration. Management and union now have a common interest in getting full acceptability of the terms to which they have agreed.

Administering the Agreement

The essence of good labor relations is awareness of the magnitude and delicacy of the problems met in applying the labor agreement to the daily operations of the university enterprise. University administration is in an ambivalent managerial position when it agrees to use collegial governance as the instrument for administering a labor agreement. Shared governance and collegiality, al-

Making the Contract
a Beneficial Instrument
of University Governance

though a valued way of life in a university, often ignore sound personnel policies in such matters as the assignment of clear responsibility, the settlement of grievances, and the need to accept decisions derived through agreed-upon procedures (Duryea, Fisk, and associates, 1973).

The essence of contract administration within the collegial framework is, therefore, the building of mutual responsibility and support for contract administration. Joint responsibility is dependent on the understanding and maturity of union and management leaders. Fashioning joint responsibility is often a difficult task. For example, such simple terms as *employees* and *management* are an anathema in a university environment. Union members wish to maintain full professional status and prestige as faculty members, not as employees, and resent the term *management* as applied to the university administration. They do not want administrators to act as cold, businesslike managers, but rather as sympathetic, understanding colleagues. In spite of this, the building of a fair, objective relationship under a contract is a recourse to authority. Normally, faculty senates rarely invoke disciplinary measures. The character of the collegial relationship seldom brings about penalties or sanctions for overt violations or omissions. Yet the very lack of regular sanctions and rewards within a university may be the main deterrent to effectiveness and positive action.

The administration of the labor contract is primarily concerned with the settlement of all sorts of grievance issues, real and imaginary. The definition of a grievance issue, however, in its legalistic sense, is a breach of the agreement, and the final judgment as to the validity of the grievance charge rests solely upon a legalistic interpretation of the contract often by outside arbitrators called to campus for an impartial adjudication based on hard evidence. However, many issues are not arbitrable in accordance with contractual terms. Such issues should be heard by sympathetic superiors because the aggrieved must not only have an arena in which to exercise the right to dissent but must believe that those responsible for hearing dissent are motivated by a sense of understanding and fairness (Selekman, 1947, p. 85).

Seldom is the agreement so explicit that it will provide unmistakable answers to ordinary problems arising in the complex milieu of campus life. Often the day after signing the agreement, after months of negotiations, a new problem arises which had not previously been considered by either party. It can be addressed, redressed, disputed, ignored, or argued; but it is only the forerunner of the complexities of the daily relationship which will ensue. The labor agreement represents the skeletal structure connecting the relationships between the parties, whereas the daily workings of the contract and the handling of grievances become the flesh and blood giving body and life to the total relationship.

Exacting labor leaders often attempt to force through the grievance procedure issues which had failed at negotiations. Less mature middle managers, not aware of the pitfalls and potential costs, are likely to accede to the demands of the grievant and openly permit the whittling away of the rights and privileges so carefully guarded at the bargaining table. This improper handling of grievances can be costly in time, money, effort, and the effect on precedent for future bargaining (Selekman, 1947). In addition, the management of the contract requires constant vigilance, study, and clear-cut objectives as to the desired relationship between the parties. Unless the handling of grievances throughout the institution is consistent with the desired objectives, it will build ill will and bad morale among administrators and lead ultimately to costly arbitration cases.

Governance too often is confused with consensus, and neither process lends itself to concise decision making. When the mixture of collegial governance is coupled with a labor agreement, it usually leads to deadlocks and legalistic interpretations. A subsystem of legalisms is then projected as an answer to stalemates rather than as a solution to problems.

Good labor-management relationships are built by enlightened parties who are dedicated to the establishment of mutuality and harmony. This requires work and not just good will. Often, the starting point is a negative one, particularly at universities where confrontation and adversarial relationships have shattered the once pristine environment. Both parties are now dealing with legalized power factors, management in its acknowledged role as decision maker and the union as an organization with political clout.

Union-management relationships are contrived ones and must be established on mutual understandings and trust. To achieve a healthy working relationship will require attention to detail and the ability to understand the viewpoints of the opposing party. Understanding, in this context, derives from knowledge of political realism as much as from fact. Intelligent and responsive administration of the contract requires, therefore, an intimate knowledge of the political and power forces at work within the organizational structures of both the union and the university. Since the union probably came into being in an atmosphere of strife, antagonism, and hard feelings and since its motivation was built upon past inequities, indignities, and inattention, campaign rhetoric was strongly slanted against management, both as generalizations against practices and procedures and as specifics pertaining to individuals and individual weaknesses. Such rhetoric usually produces a residual anger and distrust among administrators (and some faculty members) which the contract administrator must understand and eventually overcome if the contract is to be administered in an even-handed manner.

The necessary transition from disagreement to agreement may also be fettered with difficulties arising from the negotiations process. University collective bargaining has engendered as much interpersonal animosity as the introduction of union negotiations in any sector of American society. Yet, it is hoped that affixing signatures to an agreement will be the basis for new behavior patterns even though strict adherence to any document or dogma at a university is fraught with all sorts of dissent. Uniformity is almost considered an interference with academic freedom. Nevertheless, there is need for consistent interpretation throughout the campus lest the university be torn apart by dissension. Intellectual differences of interpretations must be patiently, but firmly, resolved so that all colleges, all departments, and their union and management representatives may be thoroughly educated as to the intent, meaning, and interpretation of each contractual clause. Uniformity in approach as well as substance may well be the ingredient essential to good relationships.

To achieve this uniformity, management personnel must be trained in the subtleties of union politics, institutional policy, and grievance prevention. Normally, supervisors in a factory are brought together and given orientation seminars on methods of dealing successfully with the union and the new agreement. There is no such identifiable group of supervisors in the university. NLRB decisions vacillate between inclusion and exclusion of department chairpersons as members of the bargaining unit. Normal criteria for effective recommendations as to hiring and firing in industry do not fit the collegial model. Regardless of whether or not the department chairperson is included in the bargaining unit, he is the logical first step in grievance hearings.[1] The stated cause of a grievance may reflect on the behavior pattern of a department chairperson or it may relate to a single overt act or an omission or failure to act on time. If the department chairperson is both a union member and the first level in the administrative hierarchy, the ag-

[1] 193 NLRB No. 23 (1971).

grieved stands in a no-man's land, seeing his peer partly as shop steward representing his interests and partly as first-line supervisor representing managerial interests. This, the starting place for hearing individual (as opposed to class) grievances is logically the first-level supervisor; but universities have been most reluctant to designate the department chairperson as a supervisor.

There is no clear line of demarcation in determining interest or representation; faculty members are persistent individualists. In fact, this difference is an essential one between faculty and other types of collective bargaining. There is among faculty members themselves a considerable resistance to accepting these roles and these new relationships. Deans, too, are somewhat schizophrenic in that they, themselves, act, at times, as the spokesperson for their faculty and other times as representatives of the university.

Command and authority found in other aspects of our society seldom exist in the collegial structure of the university. A university is neither hierarchically nor administratively structured. Command and leadership are words of art describing levels of responsibility but subservient to the need to be a fellow scholar, a colleague, or a fellow faculty member. Whatever loyalties exist in this environment are generated by personal needs, and a higher level homage is paid to the discipline than to the institution. Unionization does not necessarily create dual loyalties when it identifies deans and department heads as logical steps in the settlement of complaints. It gives them new types of responsibilities. Many deans, however, are reluctant to accept new obligations and accountability for carrying out the new agreement because as grievances are processed, the dean literally goes on trial.

To assist the deans and the department heads in meeting their new responsibilities, it is necessary to introduce the contract, the reasoning behind it, and what went into it.

Training does not stop with the department chairperson and the deans. A reorientation task is necessary for the president, the provost, and all levels of administration. Such universal training and retraining in a university is a new phenomenon. Faculty enjoy bringing their complaints directly to the president. Now, he is no longer free to adjust grievances on an ad hoc basis. Collective bargaining ordinarily requires that the union participate in any and all settlement of grievances, and although an individual may process his own grievance, he cannot do so without the presence of union representatives.[2]

Grievances represent an extension of the bargaining process. It requires the president and other university officials to answer complaints according to the contract. Contract compliance interferes with the exclusivity of administrative decision making. Disputes which were previously sometimes disregarded now are fettered with short-time constraints and positive contractual duties.

One of the great difficulties in negotiating a new contract is that specific grievances are constantly being raised at the negotiating table. Clauses are written in response to specific complaints and often these complaints are so personalized that they are directed at the idiosyncratic behavior of one dean or one department chairperson. Thus, an attempt is made to write a contract that protects all faculty against that peculiarity in behavior of a single person rather than to write a broad principle to cover general faculty-administrative relationships (Levinson, 1976, p. 60). It is that type of behavior which must be very carefully addressed in training directors, deans, and chairpersons who act on behalf of the total institution as each administers the agreement. Some within this managerial group will resist all cooperative efforts with the union. Resistance to the sharing of powers with the union are usually steeped in prejudice, resentment, and often in the insecurities of one's own mismanagement. Weak, insecure management is not only a cause of unionization but is a continuing irritant to good relationships.

Roles for Each of the Parties

The very first job for all concerned is to meet the need of union officialdom, whether it be the executive committee of the union, the operational representatives, or, as more often called in the factory, the shop stewards, for clear uniform explanations of the new contract before real problems arise. Special communication techniques must be developed to help everyone understand the intent of new contract clauses. Although a great deal of effort may have gone into the writing of the clauses, those individuals

[2]29 u.s.c. 141 at Sect. 9a.

who were not at the bargaining table require detailed explanations of the intent behind each clause.

At Temple University, there was a realization of this phenomenon quite soon after the original negotiations had been completed. The understandings which had been developed between the chief negotiators would have to be interpreted and communicated to everyone on campus. The AAUP representing the faculty did have meetings with its executive committee, its members, and its occupational representatives from each of the schools. Similarly, the university through its chief negotiator spent considerable time with each dean separately and with the council of deans explaining all pertinent parts of the agreement. Probably the greatest effort toward achieving joint understanding of the agreement is that the two chief negotiators arranged a meeting for each school and college with all of the department chairpersons and all of the organizational representatives in that particular college. Then the two negotiators presented the contract as a common document, a document in which they had accord and agreement. The sense of the meeting was to explain what had been achieved rather than relate the difficulties of arriving at an agreement. In these sessions, everyone was allowed to question both negotiators and to explore the nuances of the agreement. This was done openly and publicly because neither party had anything to hide. It was felt and it is still felt that this type of joint presentation was far superior to any public relations release or self-seeking document on the part of either party.

The contract calls for at least one meet-and-discuss session each semester. During that particular session, problems are presented which may or may not be set forth in the contract. Often new negotiations take place either to amend the contract, bring into being changes which were not earlier contemplated, or to correct deficiencies which neither party had perceived when the agreement was originally written. The meetings have been most successful and their continuance almost assures a harmonious agreement built on mutual understanding.

A harmonious agreement is not a marriage of angels. Strong counterpositions and adversarial positions are taken in the defense of the rights of the aggrieved or of management. Settling faculty grievances in a judicious manner fair to all legitimate interests is an art rarely mastered (Satryb, 1976). Listening is a necessary condition preceding all grievance settlements, and the force and effect of the union contract requires university officials to listen and react thoughtfully to each complaint. Failure to adhere to the letter and spirit of the agreement now brings the collective reaction of the bargaining unit and not just the despair of an individual.

Due Process and the Grievance Machinery

Much of the rationale behind the organization of faculty has been a demand for due process. Probably no other term in American jurisprudence has been so misunderstood and so misapplied as the phrase *due process,* the right to a fair trial or the right to be heard through processes to which most people subscribe. Although there are many mechanisms similar to due process within collegial types of governance, the ultimate right to appeal to a neutral adjudicator has often been lacking and, thus, there is seldom a true terminal point for grievances in such governance. A negotiated contract ordinarily meets this criterion by providing a terminal point called *arbitration* (Committee for Economic Development, 1973, p. 60).

In its simplest terms, a grievance can be described as anything that bothers anyone. In many contracts, however, a grievance is limited to a violation of the contract. All kinds of rationalization for this narrow position can be made, but it will never meet the true concept of good human relations. Whether we call it counseling, psychotherapy, or just good human relations, the judicious handling of all complaints inside or outside the formal grievance steps is the only sound basis for sustaining good relationships. Responsibility for this cannot fall entirely on the administration since the union must accept obligation for weeding out the petty and inconsequential complaints prior to formal review.

The Union View of Grievances

Union officials frequently recognize that all complaints are not grievable. They might receive militant demands from their constituents which they might not wish to pursue. However, the union is a political body answering to its constituents in a democratic fashion and, to maintain member support, often must process unwarranted or unreasonable grievances. The question is whether a union can provide leadership without militancy.

To alleviate pressures of unwarranted grievances at Temple University, the AAUP established a unique Union Grievance Committee which enters the grievance procedure after being processed through the first two steps; the first step at the department chairperson's level, the second step at the dean's level, and the third step to the academic vice-president or his designee. During the period before it is taken to the academic vice-president, the union committee investigates the grievance and in reality tries the merit of the case to see whether or not a prima facie case has been established by the grievant. This act of leadership by the union has, in many ways, reduced the number of grievances. It has also provided a mechanism whereby much of the emotionalism has been stripped from the grievances and the grievance reduced to its bare essentials. The Union Grievance Committee often conducted such extraordinary research into the grievance that their reports were almost classic presentations of principle, procedure, and fact.

On the other hand, for management to simply declare that the matter is not a breach of the agreement and to stand rigidly behind its legalistic interpretation is counterproductive to good human relations. A common first reaction of a union is to embrace its own legalistic approach, and when both parties proceed within narrow confines of legalisms, formalization of grievance processing may rise to a point where almost everything will go through all steps of the grievance procedure and ultimately to arbitration. Too few administrators and unions are concerned with (1) reminding themselves of the underlying objectives of the grievance procedure, (2) selecting the best way to attain these objectives and, (3) maintaining the kind of relationship desired while achieving these objectives.

The very nature of a grievance procedure is not simply a matter of saying "no" to the grievant since it must be consistent with administration's overall philosophy as to the type of human contractual relationships it wishes to maintain. Although many college presidents and union officials would like to think that bargaining need not produce antagonistic relationships, most union-management procedures are essentially adversarial in nature. Both parties, however, must understand that adversarial positions are not necessarily a handicap to good working relationships. Much has been said in earlier chapters of this book about the drive for unionization among faculty members. This is still a difficult matter for university presidents to accept. Many of them would still like to consider the faculty senate as their private domain to aid, abet, and advise them in running the university. University officialdom has made many a senate into a sterile body, and the same officials are later surprised by the militant reaction of those who formed the union to attain freedom from their domination.

Dynamics of Grievance Processing

The handling of daily grievances is not too different from the normal complaints which the faculty wish to discuss with the department chairpersons, the deans, or the president. Usually, university officials are available to a faculty member at will. The unique change brought about by a formalized grievance procedure is the necessity of notifying the union and having the union in its official capacity act on behalf of the aggrieved. This daily relationship is dynamic, not static, changing every day in response to complaints dealing with such matters as promotions, change of assignment, classrooms, and hours. Grievance activity becomes the pulse indicative of the entire relationship between the parties. Since the relationship is affected by both internal and external pressures, successful grievance processing attests to the smoothness and the harmony with which the faculty and administration can meet new challenges together.

Grievance processing will also reflect accurately the behavioral relationships between the parties. Arbitrary approaches are set forth below as examples rather than as illustrations of pure systems. The areas of overlap are considerable, and each reflects a particularity of its own, distinguishable from the others.

Approach 1. A grievance may be approached legalistically only as a breach of a part of the contract.

Approach 2. A grievance is a request to correct a wrongdoing, a breach of contract, or an offense against an individual.

Apporach 3. A grievance is a manifestation of behavior reaction covered by the contract or simply an
uneasiness perceived by the aggrieved.

All three approaches deal with complaints which all too often
are handled shoddily through procrastination, indecision, and unnecessary delay caused by inattention to detail. Yet delay may be an
excellent tactic when used positively and sparingly, for example,
to provide time for lower-level administrators to resolve a problem
informally, or to let the union know it is not doing its job of screening out the trivia.

The timely handling of grievances is vital to good relationships between the parties. It is not uncommon to have specific time
limits for each step of the grievance procedure; and as each step in
the procedure progresses, those time limits should be strictly observed. At Temple, we have asked the union to file duplicate copies
of grievances simultaneously with the office of the academic vice-
president and dean of faculties. This is simply to provide a check
mechanism to see that the appropriate official responds with dispatch to all grievances at each step. If they cannot be handled in a
timely fashion, at least there is an attempt to extend to the other
party the courtesy of seeking approval of delays where warranted
so that the grievant does not feel distressed simply because there
appears to be no interest in trying to resolve the problem.

Sympathetic handling of grievances is as essential to good
relations as the timely handling of grievances. Considerate response
to another's feelings provides, without cost, therapy for release of
emotions; and whether it is the sense of injury, of injustice, or of
wrongdoing that creates hostilities, the validity or invalidity of a
grievance is frequently not that important to the aggrieved. Satisfaction often is simply in being heard. Grievances against the administration sometimes arise because of inexplicable actions such
as secrecy, failure to communicate with faculty, and untimely responses to questions or requests.

The proper background for handling grievances is to give
the parties an opportunity to discuss their rights and responsibilities
apart from the legalistic aspects of the agreement. If the administration approaches it in this way, it sustains the system of collegial juris-

prudence. Although new channels of formal grievances are established, there is no reason to foreclose traditional opportunity for parties to discuss their problems informally. The Temple model permits subcommittees on grievances to analyze all the facts and to ascertain whether or not the person has been illegally or unnecessarily deprived of expected rights or privileges. This broad clinical approach does place greater burdens on administrators since it calls for more hearings and a sensitive, humane approach to these hearings. Yet, it is the only way to ensure mutually responsive relationships capable of satisfying emotional as well as legal aspects of a case. Many subadministrators are not capable of handling emotional problems, and their search for absolutes becomes a hindrance to solutions. Good human relations require the university to provide trained labor relations assistance, not as a substitute for the academic chain of command but simply as a means to maintain objective attitudes, to lessen anger and resentment, and to dispel anxiety among faculty members.

Many times a grievance could be dismissed because of technical failures on the part of the union or grievant. Such a victory is shallow, no one is really satisfied, and tension for future grievances is created. Sympathetic handling of grievances is the essence of successful contract administration.

Due Process and Collegial Processes

Due process requires that each party have the right to file grievances. Management's aggressive position at the bargaining table is often controverted later by its reluctance to present grievances to the union. Maturity in labor relations allows management to take a constructive and positive stand on each issue and present demands as well as counter those of the union. Failure to present positions may increase the cost of operations and vitiate normal functioning of the contract. The same can be true of the grievance procedure. When management is dissatisfied with the functioning of the union or of the agreement, there is no reason why it should not present a grievance in its own behalf.

Faculty senates have long acted as collegial symposiums. Consensus is the rule and problem-solving the exception. This slow, tedious process is counterproductive to change. Time is seldom of importance, and although justice may ultimately triumph, it is often by happenstance rather than by design. In contrast, grievance procedures and meet-and-discuss sessions provide forums for immediate change. Bridging the two mechanisms is difficult but not impossible. Harmony between diverse faculty factions within the university environment can be achieved if the respective leaders of senate and union cooperate in resolving internal issues. Senators should be apprised immediately as to what is going on in union-management relationships and precisely what issues are mandatory subjects of bargaining. These subjects should not be agenda for senate meetings since the senate has no right to create dual unionisms by attempting to participate in those matters which are peculiarly union concerns. Governing these matters is the legal and unique responsibility of union and administration.

Establishment of a union raises a very serious question as to the future of a faculty senate even though there is no valid reason for disharmony. As a deliberative body, the faculty senate is not too different from the legislative branch of government. The responsibilities of debate, of searching for understanding, and of investigation are part of a lengthy process and properly belong in the forums of a senate rather than in those of union negotiations. Senates usually deal with matters of curriculum, planning, academic standards, and other matters outside those working conditions specifically enumerated in the union contract. Where conflict between senate and union does arise it usually is about what used to be rather than about what is. The power base for faculty action has shifted; the union as a political body may either preempt the faculty senate in pressures on the administration or join with it in a common purpose. At Temple, some members of the union power structure have also accepted faculty senate positions. This increases communication and diminishes union-senate conflict.

At some campuses unions and senates have not been able to delineate mutually exclusive but compatible roles. Friction between the groups can lead to serious disruption of normal relationships, and the administration should take steps that will encourage the two groups to work out their differences. It is essential that each party recognize the "territorial" rights of the other and refuse to perform overlapping functions. To do its part, the university must provide the same type of informational meetings for keeping the union up-to-date about university plans and action as it normally does for the faculty senate.

Communications

Undergirding good relations and efficient dispute settlement is a comprehensive, carefully planned communications system. Daily communications should be supplemented by periodic deliberative meetings. Twice a year the union and the administration at Temple meet in what we call a meet-and-discuss session; each party submits to the other party an agenda of those items it would like to discuss. There are no limitations on what can be reviewed but the meetings normally include (1) problems which have arisen under the contract, (2) grievances which are not breaches of the contract, (3) matters not discussed at the formal negotiations and on which some temporary relief or some negotiation is necessary, and (4) contract clauses which are troublesome to either party and may need interpretation or negotiation.

During the previous contract period at Temple, four different meet-and-discuss sessions were held. Many items were adjusted and actual changes in the grievance and arbitration procedures were established. Each change was constructive in building a better contractual relationship and reduced the number of demands to be resolved in negotiating future contracts. Other issues not involving change were brought to the attention of the administration, and an agreement was made to study each situation. Some of these issues did become the basis for union demands in later contract negotiations. In either case, the opportunity of discussing the problems in depth resulted in an atmosphere which gave each party a feeling of mutual understanding of the realities as perceived by the other and paved the way for immediate or future agreement.

Because of the openness of these meetings, we have had many informal sessions between formal meetings. Frequently, union and management representatives discuss problems and endeavor to agree on interpretation of particularly difficult clauses in the contract. Often, suggested interpretations are sent to the council of deans for its advice and reactions. Similarly, the union has presented to the faculty senate matters of interest to the faculty at large.

These interactions have created an atmosphere in which

both parties seriously try to solve mutual problems as they arise. Mutuality has become the theme, not in lieu of an adversarial stance but to find a common direction which can give the university a better working relationship in the interest of all. Harmony rather than disharmony characterizes the effort to make the agreement work.

Perhaps for the first time in the institution's history, faculty, administration, and all the attending support functions of physical plant will be faced with the necessity of obtaining higher productivity. For centuries, higher productivity has been a national goal, and in the private sector the right to introduce improvements to increase efficiency was an acknowledged responsibility of management. Managements with the most successful records have worked closely with their labor unions in creating labor-management committees, "Scanlon plans," and other joint efforts seeking an ultimate solution to each problem (Industrial Relations Research Association, 1975, pp. 1–3). Despite general affirmation of the necessity for increased university efficiency and effectiveness by union leaders, by the public, by faculty, and by administration, the affirmation often has a hollow ring, and resistance to change grows with increased union political clout. It is anticipated that increased faculty productivity will be one of the most pressing and demanding features of collective bargaining in the years to come (Industrial Relations Research Association, 1975, pp. 1–3). Yet there is little hope of reasonable resolution of this complex issue unless a harmonious working relationship among the parties exists. To attain and continue this kind of harmony, collective bargaining must join with collegiality and governance in guiding the operations of the institution.

Ronald W. Bush

The customary progression in the unionization of a college or university is that one or more issues arise that drive the faculty to consider unionization. The administration is immediately placed in a defensive position. Within a very brief time, the faculty and administration participate in an election, the bargaining agent is certified, and the faculty union immediately demands the commencement of negotiations. Negotiations take place over the next few months with management directing almost its entire energy toward satisfactory completion of negotiations. Upon ratification of the labor agreement, there is a general tendency for the college administration to "let down." At this point, the college administration often feels the worst is over and the college will be restored to its former operational structure.

The faculty union, however, is now placed in the position

Preparing for
Arbitration

of proving that these last few months of turmoil have been worth
the effort and that the union is worthy of faculty financial support.
The local faculty leadership will begin a campaign to test its powers
under the contract, usually by filing grievances. Suddenly, the administration begins to realize the possible consequences of the labor
agreement. Reviewing and trying to resolve grievances quickly
shows that the contractual obligation accepted by both the union
and the college has legal force and requires administrators to acquire new knowledge and skills. If contract administration in colleges and universities is to be effective, and if unnecessary grievances
are to be avoided, it is critical that the institution establish for college
administrators an ongoing training program in labor-management
relations, grievance processing, and conflict management. This
training program is essential for all levels of management. One

valuable technique is the use of union personnel as training agents. On a number of occasions, I have hired organizers from the various unions on a per diem basis to come into the institution and carry on a cooperative training program with management. The feedback from administrators taking the various programs has been excellent. The results demonstrate a lowering of the formal grievances and a better understanding by administrators of union actions.

It is also advisable that when a union is recognized on a college campus, if not before, the college establish an office of employee relations to guide and assist all levels of administration in implementing the contract and preparing for grievances. In hiring an expert to advise the management team and to assist the management team in contract administration, grievance handling, and negotiations, it is important to understand that qualified labor professionals experienced in higher education are rare and extremely expensive. It is a new position usually foreign to most colleges and universities and, therefore, careful review of a candidate's qualifications is critical.

Once the contract has been ratified, management soon realizes that many former administrative rules and customs are, in fact, contrary to the negotiated contract. At the same time, many colleges and universities find that the lack of written rules and regulations present special problems. As management attempts to administer the contract and to issue rules and regulations, union representatives will immediately challenge the right of the college administration to issue them. Faculty unions find it difficult to accept the fact that, regardless of collective bargaining, management has the right to promulgate reasonable rules and regulations to govern the operation of the institution and the conduct of the faculty in carrying out their assigned duties. The college administration may not, however, establish rules and regulations that are in conflict with a labor agreement, or that would be in violation of health and safety standards, or other applicable federal or state statutes. Faculty members under a labor agreement are expected to obey administrative orders, including reasonable rules and regulations. Failure to follow them can be grounds for the administration to institute appropriate disciplinary or discharge procedures. Should the union or its membership be in disagreement with a rule or regulation, it is the responsibility of both the union and its members to use informal discussions to get a change, and if not satisfied, then to grieve that rule or regulation as a violation of the contract or as a violation of "good faith" bargaining.

Historically, labor and management have accepted the negotiated grievance procedure in a contract as the heart of the contract. The grievance procedure makes the contract a living document primarily because it provides for the orderly resolution of disputes. Although arbitration has been generally accepted in labor-management relations as an ordinary terminal step of the grievance procedure, it is only beginning to gain wide acceptance in higher education. Most colleges and universities have very limited experience in the use of arbitration and, therefore, must be extremely careful in negotiating the scope of authority provided for third-party intervention.

When a college agrees to the use of arbitrators, it is important to establish working guidelines that will help the administration to meet the special problems inherent in arbitration proceedings. This chapter will discuss a set of recommended guidelines and some of the special aspects of arbitration that require special preparation.

I should state that I am a firm believer in arbitration for the resolution of grievances, and I also believe that the process should be restricted to the contract and be well understood by both parties. Used properly, it provides for the rapid resolution of grievances by well-qualified neutrals. It can also be a cost-saving as well as a face-saving device.

The parties should agree to use arbitration only as a "court of last resort." Every internal avenue should be explored before appealing to outside arbitration. This is not to say that either party should compromise what it believes the intent of the contract to be. Nevertheless, when arbitration is decided upon, each party should aproach it as each party would approach an appeal to the courts. Arbitration cases are usually won or lost on the quality of prior preparation. Inadequate facts and bad cases make for bad decisions and poor labor-management relations.

In addition to the usual preparations about who, what, where, when, and why, consideration should be given to the following recommendations:

Attorneys should be used sparingly. Unless the attorney is extremely well versed in grievance processing, there is a tendency to make the arbitration hearing too legalistic. Arbitration need not be set in a formal legal atmosphere. One purpose of arbitration is to allow the two parties to present a dispute to an impartial third party without being bound by strict legalistic principles such as the rules of evidence. It is to the college's advantage that a member of the administration be trained in presenting and arguing arbitration cases and that qualified labor management attorneys be reserved for complex cases that may call for the presentation of legal principles or that may ultimately be reviewed by a court. One argument against the use of attorneys is cost. The expense of an outside attorney can easily exceed that of an arbitration award.

Upon completion of the various steps in the grievance procedure and prior to arbitration, a thorough review of the grievance should be made. The individual arguing the case before an arbitrator must have a thorough knowledge of the grievance to effectively evaluate the strength and weaknesses of management's case. All too often, one side or the other is embarrassed in an arbitration hearing when evidence is brought forth that has not been presented at the lower levels. Potential friendly witnesses should be questioned, "Is there anything you wish to tell me that may come out in the hearing that could conceivably be embarrassing to the management position?" "Is there anything that the union may present that could have an impact on the case that we are not aware of?"

The threshold question in one of my recent arbitration cases was, "Does the faculty union contract carry over and protect adjunct faculty?" As the grievance proceeded through the various levels, it became evident that no agreement could be reached, and the issue would have to be resolved in arbitration. In preparation for the case, we were reviewing documents going back to the original contract, six years prior. Purely by accident, one of the staff came across a memorandum of understanding signed by the president of the union in which she explicitly agreed that the terms of the labor agreement did not extend to adjunct faculty. The memorandum of understanding was presented as admissible evidence at the arbitration hearing and the management case was won. Had we not taken the time to go back and review old documents, a very important arbitration case could have been lost.

Obtain a complete list of possible management witnesses. Each potential witness should be interviewed indepth before the arbitration hearing. Interviewing witnesses in advance of the hearing provides the college the opportunity to detect conflicting management positions and also to avoid embarrassment during the hearing. It is a good policy to rehearse with the witness all questions that will be asked while he is on the stand. Attempt to speculate what questions the union will ask in cross-examination and try to assist the witness in framing his answer. It is advisable that a witness not volunteer information not solicited. Many arbitrations are lost because a witness confuses the issue by providing unnecessary testimony. Also, one should assume that a hostile witness, when pressed, may lie under cross-examination. Therefore, one should not rely upon winning an arbitration case through cross-examination of witnesses. Arbitration cases are more likely won by well-prepared and well-coached friendly witnesses.

Study the collective bargaining agreement for several clauses that may have a bearing on the case. Particular importance should be placed upon such clauses as recognition, grievance, maintenance of standards, past practice, management rights, and union rights. It is not uncommon in higher education contracts to find two or more clauses in a contract addressing themselves to the same or similar issues, but with conflicting intents. This problem occurs more frequently in higher education faculty contracts than in industrial models. Such disparities can be used to advantage by either party, so do not rely on a single clause to win a point. *Study past contracts.* You may be able to determine the intent of the parties by tracing the development of a particular clause through prior labor negotiations.

Review federal and state statutes that may be in conflict with contract terms. Arbitration cases involving promotion, denial of tenure, seniority, work load, outside employment, discipline, and tenure may very well be in conflict with affirmative action legislation, fair wage and hour legislation, and general academic laws and regulations promulgated by the state legislature or the state board of higher education. In a recent case the labor agreement was quite explicit in what criteria would be used to evaluate faculty members for promotion and tenure. The legislature then passed a law which was in conflict with the labor agreement. The local board of trustees was directed by the board of higher education to implement the new standards passed by the legislature. The board, caught between the labor agreement and the directive from the board of higher education, implemented the new criteria as outlined by the legislation. The union immediately filed a grievance alleging violation of the union agreement. The arbitrator ruled in favor of the union by arguing that he (arbitrator) was a creature of the contract and could only look to the four corners of the contract and not be influenced by external considerations. The board was then forced to appeal the arbitrator's decision to the courts. The court found in favor of the board of trustees, thus making the recent legislation controlling. This was a costly exercise to reach what was an expected result, and may have been avoided, had the union and administration jointly requested an opinion of the attorney general or of a labor board counsel, prior to the evaluation.

Attempt to determine if custom and past practice will be an issue. Custom and past practice are often significant factors in labor-management relations. A past practice or custom is usually defined as a certain, but not always clear long-standing, mutually acceptable action which has been in existence over a period of time. This long-standing action on the part of either union or management can become an unwritten, but enforceable part of the labor agreement. Arbitrators are not in unanimous agreement as to what precisely determines a past practice; and, therefore, the issue is usually settled on a case-by-case basis. Colleges need to be extremely aware of what long-standing practices exist on the campus. College administrators often justify their actions by stating "we have always done it this way." This approach to collegiate administration, under a labor contract, can generate considerable embarrassment to the college and cost large sums of money. Arbitrators frequently but not always recognize management's right to control and direct the college and its authority to change unwritten conditions if they do not violate the rights of employees. Two recent arbitration cases involving past practice are somewhat amusing, but were costly to the employer. In one case, the union argued that the administration could not unilaterally stop providing free passes to the faculty for the football games; and in the other case, the union argued that the administration could not stop providing free coffee in the faculty room. In both cases the practice was long-standing, but not a written part of the labor agreement. The arbitrators ruled in favor of the unions in both cases and, thus, free coffee and free football tickets became fringe benefits without actual table negotiations. It is advisable that the college administration attempt to negotiate into the labor agreement that neither party will be bound by unwritten past practices or customs.

Draft a short brief prior to arbitration. Drafting a short synopsis of the grievance allows the administration to better organize its case, isolate the strengths and weaknesses, and further assist in framing the grievance presentation. The drafting of a brief is recommended purely as an organizational tool. Arbitrators can be influenced inordinately by a faulty or disorganized presentation of a case. Unless the issues are extremely complex, the parties should avoid costly prehearing and posthearing briefs as part of the case. Written briefs will be received by the arbitrator, but will seldom be accorded the same consideration as the evidence presented through the examination of witnesses. Lengthy, written briefs have a tendency to drive the cost of an arbitration case up, and the benefits may be questionable.

Research past arbitration awards at your institution and awards at other institutions that are similar in nature. Prior awards are not binding in arbitration. This is true even if the case is between the same parties and the facts and issues appear to be identical. An arbitrator is not bound to follow any rule laid down by his predecessor. Nevertheless, arbitrators are reluctant to issue awards that are conflicting or inconsistent with prior awards. It is, therefore, advisable to give considerable credence to guidelines handed down through prior arbitration awards. In a recent case involving a denial of promotion, we were able to argue that a prior award at the college involving the denial of promotion made it fairly clear that the administration had the ultimate right to promote those individuals it deemed worthy, and that the arbitrator had no authority to overrule that decision unless the administration could be proven to be arbitrary or capricious. The arbitrator, relying heavily upon the past award, agreed with the college's position and proceeded to expand the administration's decision-making authority in his award. This brings up a critical question when moving to arbitration, that is, do the parties have more to gain or lose by moving a grievance to arbitration? Many times an arbitrator will, in his decision, inadvertently expand the scope of the contract or restrict the powers of one party on issues that may not have been in direct dispute. If this can be predicted, one or both parties may become more willing to find a voluntary resolution of the issue.

Discuss the generalities of the case with other experts in the field. I never cease to be amazed at the insight colleagues can provide in preparing for an arbitration case. They can bring their experiences in similar cases, and thus assist with new insights and strategies. An excellent custom to establish is the exchange of arbitration awards among area colleges and universities. There are very few "unique" situations in contract administration. Therefore, arbitration awards from sister institutions can provide in-depth insight in preparing for an arbitration case.

In developing a checklist for arbitration preparation, I have intentionally left two complete issues for a more thorough discussion: the selection and appointment of an arbitrator and the arbitration clause.

Selection of an Arbitrator

The selection of the arbitrator may be as critical to winning the case as the evidence and documentation developed in supporting the college's position. The selection of an arbitrator should be approached with extreme caution. Selecting an arbitrator is like going to a doctor; if the symptoms appear to be that of a common cold, a general practitioner is usually sufficient. However, if the symptoms are of possible heart disease, the individual is wise to seek out a heart specialist. There is a limited pool of arbitrators experienced in the complexities of collegial life. The arbitrator selected by the parties should have the technical competence and background to handle the special issue before him. I cannot begin to remember how many times I have heard the parties say to each other after receiving the decision that the arbitrator "never understood the real issue." Remember that in arbitration the parties may be bound by an award that they never contemplated only because they were lax in selecting an adjudicator experienced in handling the special underlying causes of the issue.

The time spent in researching an arbitrator's background is never wasted. Before agreeing to an arbitrator, run an extensive check on his former experiences, his affiliations, and his reputation in the field. An arbitrator may be very acceptable for a police or clerical case, but totally unacceptable for a faculty arbitration involving such complex issues as tenure or promotion. Read some of his past awards. Are the conclusions and the award he recites within the frame of the grievance? Are they logical and straightforward? Is there a tendency to simply "cut the pie in half"? Does he lecture the parties? Is he a strict constructionist? Does he rely on other cases? Which cases does he quote? Many good arbitrators are eliminated because they have awarded the last five or six cases to one side or the other. It is always advisable to ask why. Make it a practice of checking with colleagues on both sides of the table about the reputation of an arbitrator before selecting or rejecting him. Experience has shown that the best arbitrators are praised consistently by both union and management. Arbitrators over the years develop characteristics and idiosyncrasies that become apparent to the practitioners. Some of the very best arbitrators I have had the pleasure of working with were employees of labor or management prior to becoming a neutral. This prior experience should not automatically eliminate them from consideration.

Appointing Agencies

The method of selecting an arbitrator is usually specified in the labor contract. The most common procedure in higher education is the naming of an outside agency which, upon request, will submit to the parties a panel or list of arbitrators. This list usually contains a panel of three or more names accompanied by a brief summary of their backgrounds and credentials. These names are selected from a larger pool registered with the appointing agency. The parties to the agreement then, independently or in cooperation, strike those names that are not acceptable to them. Should the complete list be unacceptable to both parties, then a second and, in some cases, a third list is provided.

The most popular appointing agencies are the Federal Mediation and Conciliation Service, the American Arbitration Association, and the various state agencies. Private publishing firms, such as the Bureau of National Affairs and Prentice-Hall, publish materials that provide advocates with more in-depth, biographical arbitration information. They also publish the complete texts of selected awards.

Ad Hoc Arbitrators versus Permanent Arbitrators

An ad hoc arbitrator is selected after a dispute arises, and his function is to hear the merits of the case and issue an award. His name is usually selected from a panel provided by one of the various agencies cited above. The parties are under no obligation to use him in any subsequent arbitration case. The ad hoc arbitrator concept is very popular when the parties first begin their labor-management relationship. The concept is also very popular when the number of grievances that go to arbitration is minimal. The advantage of an ad hoc arbitrator is that the parties have an opportunity to experiment on a case-by-case basis with various neutrals.

As the contractual relationship matures, there is a tendency to agree to a permanent arbitration panel or a permanent umpire. These are individuals selected to serve for a particular period of time such as the length of the contract. This permanent relationship avoids the time-consuming process of striking arbitrators for each case. If there is one umpire, he is used to render a decision in each arbitration case. If there is a panel, then an arbitrator is usually assigned on a rotating basis, but the same arbitrators hear the various cases during the life of the contract. A permanent arbitrator is usually a sign that the parties have reached a level of maturity in their relationship and feel comfortable presenting their cases to the same individual or individuals on a continual basis.

A permanent relationship allows the parties to forego the presentation of general broad background material in an arbitration case. The permanent impartial is usually familiar with the peculiarities of the institution, the past union-management relationships, the contract, and past agreements. A permanent umpire may also feel free to mediate rather than arbitrate a dispute.

I am a strong advocate of a permanent panel concept for higher education arbitrations. Once the faculty union and the administration have lived through a number of arbitrations and contract negotiations and have reached a reasonable level of sophistication in grievance processing, I recommend the concept of a permanent panel be written into the contract. Each institution should consider this concept around its own particular needs. A contractual provision for a permanent panel could be as follows: "Within thirty days after the date of this agreement, representatives of the parties to this agreement will obtain from the American Arbitration Association a list of arbitrators and will agree upon a panel of three arbitrators, obtaining additional lists if necessary. The parties will furnish the American Arbitration Association the names of the arbitrators selected. Thereafter, the American Arbitration Association shall designate one of said arbitrators to hear each grievance that may be referred to arbitration. This panel shall be in existence for the life of the contract."

A disadvantage of a permanent arbitrator is that there may be an initial tendency of the parties to rely too heavily upon the permanent arbitrator to settle disputes that may arise under the contract. His function may become more of a crutch than a last resource. There may also be a tendency of an arbitrator, if not carefully selected, to split awards. To retain favor with both sides and to avoid alienating one side or the other, he may feel the need to give each side a partially satisfactory decision.

A third concept gaining acceptance in higher education is the tripartite arbitration board. The tripartite board may be either permanent or ad hoc. The most common concept is for management to select one or more advocates, the union to select one or more advocates, with the selected advocates agreeing on a neutral third party to serve as chairperson of the tripartite board. The board is then empowered to hear the merits of the grievance and to render a final decision. The common understanding is that the majority will prevail. It does not preclude that a minority position may be issued recognizing that the minority report has no contractual force.

The advantage of a tripartite board is that it lessens the chance of an arbitrator handing down a decision that may be totally unacceptable to either party. It provides the parties an opportunity to influence a compromise and may lend more credibility to the award.

The disadvantages are that it is time-consuming and costly. The arbitration may be further complicated when the chairperson ends up mediating the issue in an attempt to get a majority opinion thus clouding the grievance.

Arbitration Clauses

An arbitration clause is that part of the labor agreement that provides for an impartial third party to arbitrate grievances that the parties themselves have been unable to settle in the early grievance steps. The arbitration clause can be extremely broad or narrow in scope. A broad scope clause allows an arbitrator to render a final decision on just about any dispute that may arise during the life of the agreement. This type of clause can lead to a great deal of misunderstanding and labor-management unrest. Very often the grievances that end in arbitration under a broad clause were never contemplated by the administration as grievable issues when the contract was negotiated. If a college or university has agreed to a broad definition of arbitration, it is advisable that they seek qualified assistance in attempting to limit the issues that are placed before an arbitrator. An example of a broad arbitration clause is as follows:

> If either the union or the grievant is not satisfied with the disposition of the grievance by the Board of Trustees, or if no disposition has been made within the time period provided in the grievance procedure, and it shall involve "an event which affects the condition of employment, discipline, or discharge, and/or alleged violation, misinterpretation, or misapplication of provision of the agreement or any existing rule, order or regulation of the Board of Trustees," it may within fifteen (15) days after receipt of notification of the decision of the Board of Trustees be appealed to arbitration.
>
> The arbitrator shall have no power to alter, modify, add to, or subtract from the provisions of this agreement. His authority shall be limited to deciding the disposition of the "event which affects the condition of employment, discipline, or discharge, and/or alleged violation, misinterpre-

tation, or misapplication of any provision of this agreement or any existing rule, order or regulation of the Board of Trustees" and shall be subject to, in all cases, the right, responsibilities, and authority of the parties. The arbitrator's fee shall be shared equally by the Board and the Union.

A broad grievance definition can lead to misunderstandings between the parties as to what is grievable under the contract. The administration will interpret grievances as being limited to the contract, whereas the union will tend to interpret the grievance machinery as the appropriate vehicle to resolve "all" disputes.

The administration probably will be very hesitant to submit issues to arbitration that are normally management functions—historically outside of a labor agreement. The natural consequence is that the arbitrator will be forced to first hear the arguments of the parties on the arbitrability of the issue at hand.

On the other hand, many contracts have narrow or limited arbitration clauses. The limited clause is beneficial to management in that it is easier to predict those issues that may be appealed to arbitration. A limited clause is as follows: "Any grievance or dispute which may arise between the parties involving the application, meaning, or interpretation of the agreement, but shall exclude any alleged understanding, practice, or other matters outside the terms of this agreement."

The arbitrator's function is to interpret the provisions of the agreement and to decide cases of alleged violation of such provisions. The arbitrator shall not supplement, enlarge, or alter the scope or meanings of the agreement, or any provisions therein, nor entertain jurisdiction of any subject matter not covered by the agreement. If, in the arbitrator's opinion, he has no power to rule on the issue submitted, the arbitrator shall refer the issue back to the parties without decision."

When negotiating an arbitration clause, it is advisable to take the following precautions: (1) Make the arbitration clause as specific as possible, stating precisely the particular subjects which an arbitrator may review and indicate that no other subjects are arbitrable. (2) If there are particular issues the parties do not want subjected to arbitration, specifically state them as being outside the province of arbitration. Examples of such issues outside of arbitration could be academic freedom, tenure, promotion, affirmative action, and governance. It is usually helpful to state that "only those subjects specified above shall be subject to arbitration. All others, such as promotion, tenure, and assignment of courses, are limited to grievance review by campus authorities as stated in the foregoing grievance steps." (3) A clear statement should be placed in the contract stating that the arbitrator shall not be allowed to supplement, enlarge, or alter the scope or meaning of the labor agreement. (4) Specific time frames should be spelled out in which the parties may appeal the grievances from one step to the next. This is of particular importance in appealing to arbitration. I would recommend that if a grievance cannot be satisfactorily settled, either the college or the union may appeal the dispute to arbitration within ten (10) days. (5) A specific provision should limit the types of awards which an arbitrator can make. Under no circumstances should he be permitted to award tenure or promotion, or to levy a fine against an individual. The contract might also set limits on money or appointment awards. As an example, the contract could say that "the arbitrator shall in no case make an award of more than $10,000 or extend a contract more than a period of six months." (6) A specific provision should be placed in the contract outlining the method of selection of an arbitrator. This will prevent disagreement on the validity of the arbitration selection process. (7) A clause should be placed in the contract limiting the time in which an arbitrator may render his decision. The general trend in higher education is to have the decision of the arbitrator rendered within twenty to thirty days of the hearing. This time restriction assists in expediting a resolution to the outstanding dispute. (8) A method of payment for arbitration costs should be specifically stated in the labor agreement. The general practice in higher education contracts is for the expenses and fees of an arbitrator to be shared equally by the college and the union.

Arbitration is one of the most critical concessions that the college can make to a faculty union. It should be done only after extensive research and preparation. Should a broad definition of arbitration be unwittingly accepted by management, it becomes extremely difficult to rectify that mistake in future negotiations.

Therefore, labor arbitration as the last step in the grievance procedure should be given a very high priority in terms of study and preparation. First contracts should always be carefully limited in order to gain experience.

William M. Fulkerson, Jr.

"A successful ouster of tenured professors by the undergraduate colleges of the large and widely known City University [CUNY] could embolden fiscally troubled administrations elsewhere and hasten the first notable breach in the previously inviolate tenure system.

What is largely undefined, though, is the gray area between financial exigency and academic freedom. Where does one end and the other begin?

But the fact that any tenured professor person in an instructional role may lose his job is an unusual development that is certain to have an unsettling effect on the academic world, which has come to take the security of tenure for granted" (Maeroff, 1976, sec. D, p. 13).

Mr. Maeroff's article appears to be an example of provincial-

Resolving
Retrenchment Problems
Within Contractual
Agreements

ism and delayed reaction. Many schools have already had to face the issues involving financial exigency and make hard decisions about retrenchment. It has been an expensive and painful process for individuals who receive the notice of dismissal as well as those who have had to make the decision and deliver the notice. Until 1971 most institutions had been taught and administered by people who had faced only the problems of growth. Institutional finances were based on formulas which projected growth, sometimes several years in advance. Thus, the problems of inflation, economic recession, and leveling enrollments was a new adventure not readily understood or appreciated by either faculties or administrators.

A study by the American Association of State Colleges and Universities (Fulkerson, 1974) revealed that only a handful of institutions had provisions for a declining economic base. Few institutions had procedures for layoffs or experience with fiscal exigency before 1972, and a common approach to the looming problem was nonexistent.

By 1973 court cases began to have an impact on the minimal due process required of institutions retrenching faculty because of fiscal exigency. In addition, collective bargaining agreements began to include retrenchment procedures different from those traditionally used before negotiations. The AAUP, ACE, Association of American Colleges (AAC), and the American Association of State Colleges and Universities (AASCU) began to study the issues as they related to their constituencies and sought to provide information and guidance in the policy and procedural aspects of the problem. A series of policies, articles, and books were produced through the associations. In 1971 the AAC published a "Statement on Financial Exigency and Staff Reduction." The AAUP updated its 1972 statement in 1974 and again in 1975 (American Association of University Professors, 1975). Todd Furniss of the American Council on Education has written several papers on "steady state staffing" (see also Fulkerson, 1974). These organizations have continued gathering and interpreting materials in an effort to establish some workable principles which will help the academic community cope with the continuing and increasing conflict over this important personnel issue.

At the same time, retrenched individuals in larger numbers have sought relief through the courts. Although 1975–1976 enrollments stabilized in most parts of the nation, the CUNY layoffs highlight the fact that there continue to be severe cases of financial exigency. The estimates of retrenched staff at CUNY alone range from 900 to 1,000 (*Higher Education Daily*, 1976; VanDyne, 1976). Some scholars have agreed that the population statistics indicate a student enrollment decline in the 1980s; others argue against that trend (Dresch, 1975a; Dresch, 1975b, pp. 239–247; Weathersby, 1974; Stampen, 1976; Mangelson and others, 1973). In either case, it does not appear that the available data could support a position that all institutions will continue to grow or to escape significant downturns. Studies in both public and private sectors reveal serious concerns about the future. Garland Parker (1976) illustrated the above point when he said, "This writer does not believe that enrollments will decline to the levels the demographic data of the traditional college-age groups would indicate, but they will do so in many, but not all, institutions. . . . There are leaner years ahead" (p. 12).

An executive decision to retrench employees raises a series of complex questions about the policies and procedures within the institution as they relate to fiscal exigency. Determining what part of the institutional community shall be affected and which individuals are to be retrenched constitute the crux of concern. The questions of appeal, conditions of layoff and recall, and other procedural aspects are extremely important in achieving fairness, but they do not alter the basic decision to retrench.

This chapter will identify policies and procedures which have passed the tests of legal scrutiny and describe how they may affect the mission of the institution.

Early Efforts to Retrench

In 1973 the AASCU received information from sixty-two of its institutions regarding fiscal exigency situations. Twelve released an aggregate of 134 faculty members that year because of retrenchment (Fulkerson, 1974). At that time fiscal exigency plans and actions within higher education institutions were relatively new and untried. The court cases resulting from that spate of dismissals have been helpful in defining and shaping many of the plans since devised. The following statement, rare in 1971, has now become quite common:

> *In the immediate future the University must deal with a series of budget reductions which will involve involuntary terminations of programs and positions. The magnitude of the economies confronting the University has been detailed in messages to the faculty last April, September, and December. These result from the state of financial exigency declared by the University on November 25, 1971, and by the State Board of Higher Education on December 17, 1971. In general, as you know, the crisis stems from shortfalls in the sources of funds in this biennium on which higher education operations depend: primarily, legislative appropriations, tuition and fees.*

> *Specifically, the University is now expected to effect reductions of $986,506 in the 1971–1972 budget and $977,427 in the budget for the 1972–1973 fiscal year. By direction of the State Board, the University is expected to make selection position reductions in, and redirections of, its academic programs (Fulkerson, 1974, p. 5).*

Such institutions have been, and continue to be, faced with tremendous stress and dissonance as they attempt to curtail expenditures within a value system that places priority on humane considerations for students, teachers, and staff. A review of several examples will provide some guidance in the preparation of policies and procedures.

Johnson v. *the Board of Regents of the University of Wisconsin*,[1] dealt with a situation in which thirty-eight tenured professors were dismissed for reasons of fiscal exigency resulting from reduced student enrollment and insufficient state support to maintain the then-current fiscal level. Judge Doyle outlined what he believed were necessary conditions in a dismissal procedure. He indicated that each plaintiff should be furnished with a reasonably adequate written statement of the basis for the initial decision to lay off, a reasonably adequate description of the manner in which the decision had been reached, and a reasonably adequate specification of the information and data on which the decision makers had relied when making the decision. Additionally, he noted that each plaintiff was to be provided the opportunity to respond.

A University of Dubuque decision provided a different type of instruction for an institution faced with fiscal exigency. First, it established that a declaration of fiscal exigency can justifiably be based on trend, which, if not reacted to, may demonstrate poor management by the administration (*Lumpert* v. *University of Dubuque*).[2] Secondly, the court said, "The Defendant was the contracting party and it is the financial condition of the entire institution, and not merely of some portion of its internal organization, that must be considered in determining whether a financial exigency

[1]377 Fed. Supp. 277 (1974).
[2]D. C. Iowa, 1st Dist., Law #39973 (1974).

existed to justify terminating Plantiff's contract."

Thirdly, the court provided a rationale for institutional determination rather than court determination. In fact, the judge indicated that the AAUP guidelines have no contractual standing in this case and that, "Defendant had to cut down in some one or more places and the determination of where that retrenchment should fall is strictly the province of the Defendant with no right of review in the court."

Finally, the court clarified the point concerning sufficient notice and defined lifetime contract as previously established by the Supreme Court. "Absent any consideration beyond the employee's promise to perform, a contract for permanent or lifetime employment is to be construed to be for an indefinite time, terminable at the will of either party. However, this right to terminate is subject to the restriction that the same may be done only on reasonable notice. The Plaintiff in this case was given over a year's notice of termination which was reasonable." In this instance, the court allowed dismissal based on its definition of a tenure contract, holding that fiscal exigency existed and one year's notice was sufficient.

The United States District Court for the District of Nebraska provides further instruction in acceptable methods of necessary termination due to fiscal exigency (*Levitt and Winger* v. *the Board of Trustees of the Nebraska State Colleges*).[3] The case suggests elements to be considered when the validity of the exigency is not contested. Conclusions of the court indicated that academic tenure rights do not guarantee an individual constitutional rights to continued public employment. Thus, demonstrated fiscal exigency is a sufficient cause for termination. [The court used the *Board of Regents* v. *Roth* case, 408 U.S. 564, 577 (1972) as a reference.]

The court commenting on the 1972 AAUP *Operating Guidelines on Institutional Problems Resulting from Financial Exigency*, stated that academic programming is of primary interest to the institution when it makes a decision to terminate an individual. Thus, programming can be a rationale for selection of particular individuals to be retrenched. Moreover, the court found that "The use

---

[3]376 Fed. Supp. 945 (1974).

of objective criteria in selecting faculty members for termination has generally been looked upon with favor by the courts when faced with substantially the same problem in desegregation cases."

The method used by Peru State College, Nebraska, involved a matrix of evaluations of all the faculty members as they related to the institutional programs. The President, with the two Deans "prepared a list of sixteen criteria on which faculty could be evaluated in order to verify the judgment made in deciding which faculty members would be terminated. This criterion was applied to each member of the faculty and consideration was also given to maintaining the most necessary programs at the college; and retaining those faculty members necessary for carrying on those programs." The court decided that the use of the objective criterion was fair and reasonable.

This case highlighted the necessity of establishing and following procedures prior to dismissal situations. Although the final program decisions may legally fall upon the administration, prior evaluations or established procedures would certainly be useful when it gets to the court. This will be more fully discussed in the next section of the chapter. As the Nebraska court said, "In the instant case, where lack of funds necessitated releasing a sizable number of the faculty, certainly it was peculiarly within the province of the school administration to determine which teachers should be released, and which retained." The court did not require faculty involvement in this case, but focuses on the validity of following an established procedure and an acceptable administrative function.

Finally, this court indicated that the manner of handling the situation was important as it related to the individual's future employability. The decision stated two principles of value: that as long as the actions taken neither alluded to cause nor alleged wrongdoing, there was no inherent detrimental effect in the dismissals, and that this action "did not in any way infringe any constitutional rights of either plaintiff" citing also *Perry* v. *Sinderman,* 405 U.S. 593 (1976).

Other institutions have had legal battles to determine the validity and legality of their procedures. Colleges throughout the country ranging from Western Washington to Emporia State, Mankato State, City University of New York, and Rutgers have had to face the problems of fiscal exigency and have had their share of headlines and court cases. Some have not been as successful as Peru State in their efforts to retrench. The situation involving the State Colleges and University of Pennsylvania and Bloomfield College in New Jersey are particularly instructive for those who wish to bargain legally acceptable retrenchment procedures and who want to avoid unnecessary entanglements.

The Pennsylvania schools have had difficulties in meeting their fiscal commitments for some time. They are under a bargaining agreement which has a retrenchment clause based on a declared fiscal emergency. The state had ordered retrenchment twice and reversed that decision both times by orders from the secretary of education. In 1974 an arrangement was made by the union and the state to forego the retrenchment even though the provisions and the need were agreed upon by the parties. The institutions were permitted to avoid retrenching faculty positions by instituting savings in other areas of the budget.

In 1976 a similar fiscal situation occurred, and this time the presidents were instructed to produce lists of individuals to be retrenched. Some of the institutions felt that accommodations might be made to avoid the layoffs, but they were ordered to provide the state with the list anyway. Again, the union was able to bargain directly with the state and was again successful in trading savings in budget expenditures for retention of all positions listed for retrenchment.

Two things evolved from this instance. Union and management were able to work out a special on-the-spot retrenchment agreement which provided for reduction of faculty, even where the contract specified no retrenchment procedure. Additionally, management, arguing for other methods of reducing expenditures, was able to follow the procedures written into the contract so that they would not be legally liable for failing to adhere to provisions in the contract (See Gershenfeld and Mortimer, 1976, pp. 61–63 and pp. 77–79 for a discussion of the state control of collective bargaining and how it affected the retrenchment under the contract between the State Colleges and University of Pennsylvania and the Association of Pennsylvania State College and University Faculties-APSCUF).

Bloomfield College in New Jersey has produced one of the

most controversial court cases relating to retrenchment (AAUP v. *Bloomfield College*).[4] The case has received wide publicity from the AAUP and the media because of the initial decision by Judge Antell and the apparent success of the appellate decision in favor of the AAUP (See Allshouse, 1975).

In this instance, however, the case provides important information in two areas. First, the court of original jurisdiction insisted that the burden of proof is placed on the institution to demonstrate that fiscal exigency exists. Judge Antell argues: "(1) that the Board's action be demonstrably bona fide; (2) extraordinary circumstances; (3) that staff expansions in other areas not be undertaken except in 'extraordinary circumstances.' " Second, the appellate court insisted that it was not the business of the court to tell Bloomfield how to manage its alternative fiscal arrangements.

> *In this vein, it was improper for the court to rest its conclusion in whole or in part upon the failure of the College to sell the Knoll property which had been acquired several years before in anticipation of the creation of a new campus at a different locale. The trial judge recognized that the exercise of the business judgment whether to retain or sell this valuable capital asset was exclusively for the Board of Trustees of the College and not for the substituted judgment of the court. Despite this, he engaged in an extensive analysis to demonstrate the potential ability of the institution to emerge from its dilemma by disposing of the Knoll property, thereby realizing substantial cash assets and relieving itself of the recurring financial loss involved in maintaining the same. Whether such a plan of action to secure financial stability on a short-term basis is preferable to the long-term planning of the college administration is a policy decision for the institution. Its choice of alternative is beyond the scope of judicial oversight in the context of this litigation. Hence, the emphasis upon the alternative use of this capital asset by the trial judge in reaching his conclusion that a financial*

[4]322 A.2d 846 (1974).

*exigency did not exist, was unwarranted and should not have
been the basis of decision.*

The Bloomfield decision illustrates the necessity for defining
fiscal exigency, for keeping the issue of burden of proof in mind,
for separating the issues of individual rights and institutional rights,
and for being as exact as possible in the details of the contract. The
next section will deal with guidelines to retrenchment and comment
on some of the consequences of those guidelines.

Guidelines to Making Retrenchment Decisions
with Contractual Agreement

The review of the court decisions provides a legal base for
proposing guidelines to those responsible for administering retrenchment agreements. Two simple, but fundamental, principles
applicable to contract management appear: avoid going to court
unnecessarily, but, if going, go with the procedural requirements
of the contract fully met. There is little that one can do at this point
about current poorly written contracts or contracts which contain
inherently weak legal standing. A suit involving a question of First
Amendment rights or some other constitutional issue cannot be
avoided if the allegedly aggrieved individual wants to pursue the
matter. However, appropriate due process and adherence to the
contract will prevent the case from being affected by the arguments
of procedural mismanagement.

Thus, this section of the chapter will discuss principles which
affect how the contract can be administered in light of the guidelines extracted from representative contracts and court cases.

Making the Decision to Retrench

Each contract, whether affecting private or public institutions, should define conditions for retrenchment. The more precise the specifications and requirements, the less likely there will
be argument over the conditions and the less room there will be
for misjudgment as to whether fiscal exigency exists or not. The
state of Wisconsin was successful in its determination that fiscal

exigency occurred. It was accomplished by declaration of the board and established as fact. Insufficient appropriations for operation at their then-current level was evident. Therefore, the board concluded that it would have to take action to remedy the condition. Other institutions have had a more formal approach to a working definition.

For instance, Bloomfield College in its contract with AAUP used a broad definition and the appellate court was able to find within it sufficient grounds for declaring fiscal exigency. "Financial exigency exists when the trend of the financial position of the College demonstrates that a fiscal crisis is imminent and that failure to retrench would seriously jeopardize the continued existence of the College. Financial exigency must be demonstrably bona fide, with the burden of proof being upon the Corporation" (Agreement between Bloomfield College and the Bloomfield College Chapter of the AAUP, July 1, 1975 to June 30, 1976).

This broad definition in the contract is followed by a listing of specific circumstances describing conditions for retrenchment:

> *In an attempt to clarify the meaning of the term* financial exigency *as used in this Article, the parties agree that the following set of circumstances, in any combination, may be indicative of that condition:*
>
> *(a) When total liabilities exceed total assets;*
>
> *(b) When current liabilities exceed current assets and the College is unable to secure additional funding;*
>
> *(c) When the College is unable to meet its financial obligations on long-term liabilities or covenants required of those obligations;*
>
> *(d) When enrollment projects of the New Jersey Department of Higher Education indicate a decline in enrollment of 8 percent or more in New Jersey undergraduate colleges, following a year in which enrollment in Bloomfield College actually declined by 10 percent or more;*
>
> *(e) When the College, excluding the Knoll property, has operated at a deficit of $100,000 or more for three or more consecutive fiscal years, subsequent to July 1, 1974, (a deficit exists when total incurred expenses exceed total actual revenues);*

> *(f) When the College, excluding the Knoll property,
> has operated at a deficit of $250,000 or more during the
> previous fiscal year (Agreement between Bloomfield College
> and the Bloomfield Chapter of the American Association of
> University Professors, July 1, 1975 to June 30, 1976).*

If the subject of tenure and the hiring of new faculty to replace the
faculty let go had not been raised, the problems of definition would
have been narrowly focused on the agreed upon determinants and
the judicial decisions may have been different. Thus, the first guideline is to secure a contractual definition of fiscal exigency according to the particular conditions and concerns of the institution.

The Nebraska case established that retrenchment decisions
are the prerogative of management. Given that assumption, the
objective is to be able to demonstrate that the decision was reasonable, if challenged. The manner of style of retrenchment and procedural detail is directly related to the amount of communication
and the degree of flexibility desired by the contracting parties. This
relates closely to the need for consultation and the degree of control vested in the faculty and administrators. The Nebraska case
contains contract language supporting the prerogative of management and the role of faculty. The contract sections are presented
here in reverse order for purposes of illustration.

> Section 2. *It is specifically agreed that the decision
> as to when retrenchment is necessary due to nonviability of
> programs, financial exigency, overstaffing, or by direction
> of the Legislature is reserved to management. When retrench-
> ment becomes necessary, the Board, the campus administra-
> tion, or designated representatives shall inform HEAN [faculty
> union] of the fact in writing by no later than the date affected
> faculty members are notified and provide HEAN with an ex-
> planation of the reasons supporting the management deci-
> sion to begin retrenchment. It is specifically agreed that the
> management decision that retrenchment is necessary due to
> nonviable programs, financial exigency, overstaffing, or by
> direction of the Legislature shall not be subject to the griev-
> ance and arbitration procedure of this contract. All other*

portions of this Article shall be subject to the grievance and arbitration procedure of this contract.

Section 1. *It is specifically agreed that whenever it appears that retrenchment is necessary due to nonviability of programs, financial exigency, overstaffing, or by direction of the Legislature, a faculty advisory committee shall be established on the affected campus to provide recommendations to the campus administration. In each instance the faculty advisory committee shall be established by the college president on the affected campus, the members of the committee shall be appointed by the faculty, and such advisory committee shall contain* HEAN *representatives. In each instance the faculty advisory committee shall provide recommendations to the campus administration on the areas requested by the administration and within the time limits established by the administration. It is specifically agreed that the faculty advisory committee recommendation shall be advisory only and that the final decision regarding the necessity and extent of retrenchment shall be reserved to management (Agreement between Board of Trustees for the Nebraska State Colleges and the Higher Education Association of Nebraska, June 1974 to June 1978).*

Thus, the second guideline recommends that the institution should attempt to negotiate a contractual clause that leaves the prerogative of declaring fiscal exigency and its extent in the hands of the administration. The clause eliminating the decision to retrench from the grievance and arbitration procedures is also a valuable asset to have in the contract since it clearly avoids a lengthy process which would still give the administration the final say within the earlier contract provision.

A third guideline from this contract involves the use of faculty and union representatives. They should be involved. The rationale and the extent of the involvement will be covered later in the chapter.

The Oakland University contract stipulates a calculation of student-faculty ratio and full time equivalent faculty for the purpose of determining any retrenchment action. Based upon that agreed upon formula, there is a clause detailing the manner of retrenchment.

> *Layoff may be instituted when actual FTE exceed by more than twenty the number of FTE required by Appendix D. The maximum number of full-time faculty members which may be laid off is given by the following:*
>> Actual FTE
>> minus   Actual FTE required by Appendix D
>> minus   twenty
>> minus   Number of overratio layoff noticed in effect
>> minus   The FTE credit calculated for laid-off, full-time faculty members *(Agreement between Oakland University and the Oakland University Chapter AAUP, July 1, 1975 to June 30, 1976).*

Although this formula does not give precise figures, it does illustrate the detail involved, reduces fiscal exigency to a definition controlled by specific conditions, and reduces the possibility of successful challenge by the faculty or the courts. Thus, if a university is on a strict funding formula, it may be advantageous to adopt an agreement detailing the conditions or circumstances which will not only define the existence of fiscal exigency but also determine the degree of action taken based upon a formula.

A review of other contracts revealed conditions requiring meet-and-discuss sessions with the collective bargaining agents and specifications for the types of response by the administrator in each case. One contract had two types of retrenchment provisions, one for fiscal exigency and one for extreme emergency situations. Each of these conditions called for procedures and timetables to provide as much due process and fairness as possible under the circumstances. Some of these conditions related to concerns outside of the definition and will be covered later.

This discussion has focused on the definition of fiscal exigency as it relates to preciseness of contract language. Obviously, the more precise the contract is in terms of measuring devices, the more accurately a decision can be made and defended, and the narrower is the ground upon which a union may challenge the retrenchment in court. However, it should be remembered that the more prescribed the procedures, the less freedom the institution has in determining when retrenchment is necessary. It may also limit the judgmental role of faculty. A fourth guideline may be derived from this discussion: the negotiator must always seek a balance between the amount of detail needed, on the one hand, to avoid ambiguity, indecision, and grievances and the amount of generality needed, on the other hand, to provide a basis for prompt and decisive action during emergencies that may arise from unforeseen conditions. No list of details can possibly include all the types of exigencies that may arise. Experienced negotiators, therefore, always work into the contract statements that recognize the right of management to take unusual measures in times of emergency or unforeseen conditions. Such a clause may be more easily included in the management rights section than in the retrenchment statement. Lacking this contractual right, administrators will need to fall back on legal precedents established in the cases cited. This is always tricky business since each case is unique, and case law can be used to support a challenge as well as to defend against challenge. In any case, the administrator must follow contractual procedures to increase the institution's ability to defend against grievances.

Deciding the Order of Layoff

The courts have indicated in the *Roth* decision that reasons do not need to be given for nonreappointment. This matter becomes one of contention, however, when an institution wants to make a decision based on areas other than institutional seniority. The burden of maintaining untenured staff while releasing tenured staff becomes very great. It is obviously much easier to base decisions on seniority. The simplicity of the mechanics, the avoidance of decision making, the alleged inherent good of experience, and professional commitment to tenure have led to some agreements which mandate seniority as the sole procedure for retrenchment. The arguments against seniority tend to deal with questions about subject matter qualifications of some tenured teachers, the inability to initiate and sustain new programs and ideas, the effect on affirmative action programs, the question of comparative competency of individuals, and the effect of retraining staff who are carrying a light student load while releasing some staff who have heavy loads.

The use of seniority has several variations from strict institutional seniority to programmatic seniority. The Pennsylvania State College contract (see Collective Bargaining Agreement Between Association of Pennsylvania State College and University Faculties (APSCUF) and the Commonwealth of Pennsylvania, September 1, 1974 to August 31, 1977) gives us an example of a seniority statement and the Temple University contract (see Agreement Between Temple University [of the Commonwealth System of Higher Education] and the American Association of University Professors, Temple Chapter, July 1, 1973 to June 30, 1976) offers an alternative that modifies seniority by several other considerations such as program effectiveness, academic excellence, and affirmative action goals (see Chapter Thirteen for more detail). Other contracts place priority on programmatic concerns and give little credibility to seniority. For instance, the Nebraska State Colleges contract specifically states that "Program viability shall be the controlling consideration in all instances (Agreement Between the Board of Trustees for the Nebraska State Colleges and the Higher Education Association of Nebraska, June 1974 to June 1978). In almost all of the contracts, the order of release specifies individuals who have been employed beyond the normal retirement age, temporary part-time, temporary full-time, regular part-time, regular full-time non-tenured, and regular full-time tenured. Even this type of apparently benign ordering may present serious problems to the administrator. Unless temporary and part-time employees are members of the bargaining unit, it is illegal for the union and employer to bargain their conditions of employment such as order of layoff. Secondly, if they are members of the unit, such a contract clause could be challenged on the basis of class discrimination (unequal protection). If the contract does have such a provision, it behooves the administration to lay off employees strictly in accordance with the provision in order to prevent a grievance challenge from a member of the unit, backed by the union. However, the administration should be aware that such an action may cause part-time employees to organize and challenge the contract. This is the dilemma which an administration must face whenever a contract has not been carefully bargained. Thirdly, laying off all part-time faculty may destroy special programs such as those ordinarily offered in extension and continuing education.

This section has established that there are several different ways of approaching retrenchment order. Some institutions have seniority as the controlling criterion, some have programmatic concerns, and some have combinations of both. Note that the institution which has a more precise definition of the order of layoff can make retrenchment decisions in a more impersonal and statistical way. However, it does remove value as a consideration, and reverts to, the basic question: Can the decision be rationally defended? More important to the courts is the question of whether the agreed upon procedure is fair to all concerned and was faithfully followed. The court presumes that the agreement was reached based on academic and institutional considerations.

Certain guidelines for administrators may be derived from this discussion. First of all, negotiators should shape contracts that violate neither the constitutional requirements of equal protection nor the limits of organizational privilege. Otherwise, contracts make it impossible for administrators to act with integrity. Secondly, it is advisable to place the final decision of layoffs in the hands of the administration, but with significant faculty input. Thirdly, when there is a reasonable doubt about the order of layoff, the contractual procedure and priorities should be strictly followed to avoid grievances and appearances of discrimination. Fourthly, when discriminatory procedures have earlier been negotiated, the administration should attempt, on the spot, to either renegotiate the procedures or to obtain union consent to deviate from the contractual procedures in order to avoid discrimination or program damage. As Ralph Brown (1976, p. 7) points out: "Furthermore, if faculty representatives are fully involved in the decisions that attend money crises, the decisions are more likely to be accepted by the faculty, if not by the victims, than at least by members of faculty hearing committees." Fifthly, the administrator must always be concerned about normal accountability. When the union is adamant about following contractual procedures even though it appears to be contrary to labor law or civil rights, the administration should seek guidance from the appropriate attorney general or labor board. Review by administrative judges costs little and gives the administration a firm base of action. Failure to act firmly, but judiciously, could injure the institution's capacity to maintain the respect and support of faculty, students, and the courts.

Finally, an institution committed to altering imbalances among its programs, faculty, and administrators is unlikely to do so through a seniority-based layoff system. Since the institution must maintain a degree of flexibility in shifting its resources, that is, to cut back in areas of less demand and increase where there is greater demand, it cannot accede to a union demand for purely mechanical means (for example, seniority) of deciding who shall be laid off and in what order. Thus, the sixth guideline on layoff procedure calls for retrenchment based on programmatic priorities as well as seniority considerations. Both are important and have been upheld in the courts. The final guideline is a reminder of the necessity to provide sufficient due process to meet constitutional requirements of equal protection, whether or not the contract stipulates it. Unions do not hesitate to take grievances to the courts charging the lack of due process, and courts have over and again ruled that civil rights cannot be denied on the basis of labor agreements. Thomas C. Fischer states that, "The present Supreme Court test of 'dueness' may be paraphrased as *fundamental concepts of fair play*" (1973, p. 2).

As noted in the review of court decisions, due process includes timely notice of termination, type of notice, request for a hearing or a reconsideration, jurisdiction of the hearing committee and the procedure and conduct of that hearing, assistance for individuals in finding other employment, and the recall provisions. Each of these areas has a wide variance within contracts. The timely notice options vary from the AAUP recommendation of one year notice to emergency ninety-day provisions. In each case the agreement is usually specific, as are most other procedural details such as notice by certified mail, the recording of hearings, distribution of transcripts, and the establishment of faculty development programs or employment assistance centers. Most institutions also provide for a recall of faculty on a need basis, up to three years following their separation from the institution. This provision is extremely important in supporting the rationale that the reason for separation is fiscal exigency. It is also important to realize that the constraints of seniority and program decisions apply equally to reinstatement since the choice of method will determine who will return to the institution first and whether or not each returnee will strengthen the university's program quality sufficiently to warrant reemployment.

Conclusions and Guideline Review

The chapter has reviewed court decisions, administrative actions, and contract clauses in order to suggest guidelines for administering a contract specifying retrenchment criteria and procedures. The guidelines are designed to provide the institution with a reasonable and legal approach that not only protects the rights of faculty members but also assures a sense of integrity and viability for administrators and institutions.

1. Make a thorough investigation as to whether or not the institution is facing fiscal exigency. If it does, express the terms of fiscal exigency in specific and workable language and communicate that decision to the entire academic community. If allowed in the contract, an announcement of a committee to investigate the existence of fiscal exigency may be helpful.
2. Explain the method of retrenchment as specified in the contract and how the institution plans to interpret the contract in order to protect the rights of individuals and the institution.
3. Indicate specifically how faculty will participate in making reviews and recommendations.
4. Explain how and to what extent the institution will allow for such factors as affirmative action and shifts in resource needs. Administer the contract as literally as possible. Deviations will be subject to challenge by the union and individuals. If there are good reasons for deviations a memorandum of agreement with the union should be secured in advance of administrative decision where possible.
5. Furnish each retrenched individual with a written statement describing the basis for the layoff.

6. Furnish the individual with a description of the process used in reaching the decision to lay off.

7. Provide each retrenched individual with the information used in the decision affecting that particular case.

8. Establish a mechanism enabling the individual to respond to the decision. (Hopefully the contract will have excluded fiscal exigency and the resultant retrenchment from grievance hearings and arbitrations. Thus, the appeal will be an internal one similar to ordinary promotion and tenure decisions.)

9. Provide timely notice according to contractual standards. Tenured and untenured teachers are usually treated separately. Adhere to deadline dates whether or not all of the information is in. A letter can always be rescinded, but failure to notify according to the contract stipulations usually creates costly arbitration and court cases along with expensive settlements.

10. Provide, where feasible, alternative training or assistance in finding other employment for tenured faculty facing layoff.

11. Make certain before laying off all part-timers first, even though it is in the contract, that part-timers are members of the organizational unit. If they are not eligible for union membership, the contract insofar as it establishes their conditions of employment is not binding. Review this matter with the union and work out a mutual agreement whereby programs (such as evening and Saturday courses) dependent on certain part-time teachers will be protected. If the union is uncooperative, seek guidance from the labor board or attorney general.

12. Provide for recall of faculty if the situation should improve. Remember that the decision was based on fiscal exigency and that it was not a dismissal for cause. Order of recall, however, should be determined on the basis of institutional and program need.

13. The mode and style of the final notification is extremely important. One president explained his method of notification and the reason behind it as follows:

Under no circumstances will the names and titles of the individuals to be laid off or retrenched be publicized by the College. I have given special consideration and thought to this particular problem. Layoff, or retrenchment, is a traumatic experience for any individual. However, research indicates that when friends and acquaintances are publicly notified of this occurrence, the trauma impact increases. Therefore, I have elected not to expose these people to this pressure by any action on our part, even though this may be construed by some as an attempt at concealment. Many persons affected may wish to inform their colleagues of the action. I am leaving this decision to the individuals' discretion, which is consistent with our practices in regard to the nonrenewal of term appointments of professional staff and nonretention of classified personnel after the probationary period ("Statement by President MacVittie").

The beginning and ending statements of this chapter have alluded to the trauma involved in retrenchment. The confusion and dissonance inherent when it occurs is tremendous. Individuals who have devoted their lives to pursuing an academic career and who have achieved a degree of security are faced with a situation which will throw them into a flooded academic market, or a totally new career situation, or perhaps unemployment. Barbara Malament describes her feelings in a recent article in the *Chronicle of Higher Education*. "I'm indignant because I came here voluntarily [in 1973], . . . I had just gotten a new contract at Yale. I was safe. I was not on the market. . . . I came here because I wanted to. One does want to work with people who grew up in New York. People who grow up with CUNY parents [her mother went to Hunter and her father to City College] grow up feeling very strongly about CUNY. Now to be kicked out without an academic judgment—by a computer or something tantamount to that—is outrageous" (Van-Dyne, 1976c, p. 7).

The formulation of the contract, as pointed out by Lozier in Chapter Thirteen, is the first important step. Fair and judicious administration of that contract is equally vital to the morale and well being of the institution. Following reasonable guidelines may enable an institution to accomplish the two primary lessons of this chapter: avoid going to court unnecessarily, but, if going, go with the knowledge that procedural requirements of the contract and constitutional rights of individuals have been fully accounted for.

Caesar J. Naples

23

❧❧❧❧❧❧❧❧

The bulk of this handbook is devoted to providing detailed information on every aspect of preparing for, negotiating, and administering the initial collective bargaining contract with a faculty union. Unquestionably, the trauma and pressure experienced by the institution and its constituencies following that first experience will leave their imprint on the participants. However, when the dust settles, when the wounds—opened or exacerbated during bitter electioneering, negotiation, and/or grievance resolutions—heal, thought should turn to the task of negotiating a second, or successor, agreement. This chapter provides some guidelines and suggests some considerations in preparing to negotiate future agreements.

The institution's bargainer can be sure that his union counterpart will keep in mind those demands which were dropped wholly or in part during the course of bargaining the current contract. They will, of course, be back on the table along with additional demands

Preparing
to Negotiate
the Next Contract

with the commencement of new bargaining. In this way, the union moves surely toward its goal of achieving the entirety of its initial package. Unless the administrator responsible for representing management's interest at the bargaining table begins early preparation for and anticipates the process of negotiating a successor agreement, he will again be reacting to the union demands from a weak, defensive posture. Happily, recognition of the importance of early planning for the next negotiations can provide an alert administration with significant advantages.

Having negotiated an initial agreement, the administration has already mastered most of the basic elements. A negotiating team has been identified, and it has learned the complexities of bargaining (how and when to caucus; good-guy, bad-guy; brinkmanship, and others). The governing board has had direct or indirect involvement in the bargaining process and the agreement has been ratified.

And although a disproportionately large share of the institution's resources were devoted to the initial process, it is over and will never again seem as strange or forbidding. By now the long-term relationship is beginning to take place. The electioneering period with its animosity and bitterness has ended. The administration (hopefully) has come to realize that faculty collective bargaining does not necessarily herald the absolute destruction of quality education. The union should become less paranoid since it has proved to itself and its critics that it could negotiate a contract, and many of its critics have either joined union activities or have gone on to other battles. This new stability on the part of the union usually provides the administration with a less desperate adversary. Finally, knowing that it can deal successfully in this new and different environment, the administration can begin to view the process of faculty collective bargaining as a means to institutional ends and not as an end in itself.

A careful look back is often the best way to begin to prepare for the future. While memories are still clear, a careful, candid analysis of the initial bargaining experience should be undertaken to identify the strengths and weaknesses of management's approach. A winning combination should not be changed, but a less-than-satisfactory one should be. Every precept in collective bargaining has its opposite and, often equally, valid counterpart applicable to slightly different circumstances. It is, therefore, a fundamental principle to keep what works in this most pragmatic of activities.

Additionally, virtually everything that has been said regarding preparation for bargaining the initial agreement has some application to subsequent negotiations. A review of the earlier chapters in this book will provide significant assistance in preparing to negotiate a successor agreement.

Identify Institutional Needs

A good place to start is with the projected needs of the institution. What will be the institution's short- and long-term posture, and will the future collective bargaining contract interfere, assist, or otherwise play a role in the institution's response to the anticipated problems? For example, a projected enrollment decrease coupled with a reduction in revenue might require the ability to reallocate resources, such as faculty positions, more quickly than normal annual attrition might permit. Does the agreement describe a layoff or retrenchment procedure which enables the administration to respond quickly and appropriately in such a situation? If not, the negotiation of such a provision might well be identified as being of the highest priority. Parenthetically, it is invariably easier to reach agreement on a layoff clause in the absence of a fiscal exigency.

Enrollment and economic resource pictures described by the long- and short-range planners may be seriously complicated by the tenure profile of the faculty. Does the high proportion of tenured faculty mean insufficient turnover to provide appropriate new perspectives brought by new minds? If so, serious thought might be given to negotiating early retirement options and other positive incentives to encourage current full-time faculty to relocate or to accept part-time status as the university attempts to build a more flexible employment structure. Additionally, existing benefits should be reviewed to determine whether or not they encourage personnel to remain on the university staff when their presence conflicts with university needs. What limitations or extensions of benefits can be negotiated to provide more management flexibility?

Academic program planners also identify trends and institutional needs and should play an important role in the preparation for bargaining a new contract. Apart from the foregoing considerations, changes in curricular offerings, changes in student interests, and other programmatic considerations may provide additional incentive to gain greater management flexibility in the allocation of limited resources. It would be a serious mistake to regard the process of preparing for negotiations—whether it be the initial or a subsequent agreement—as strictly a personnel or salary and fringe benefits activity.

Each administration should identify the current operating problems. Does management currently possess sufficient authority to manage? If the collective bargaining contract has left the administration with insufficient authority, the identification and recovery of that authority must assume the highest priority. One state system recently promised that no faculty would be laid off during the contract term. A different approach to employee security which might be more helpful to management would be to provide attractive benefits to those laid off, but nevertheless to preserve the ability to retrench staff and reallocate resources within reasonably short periods of time.

In dealing with the question of managerial authority, care must be exercised in identifying the causes of each problem. Often, more managerial authority is lost in the process of administering the contract than was negotiated away at the table. Unions are fond of asserting that unless the specific authority to do a particular task (such as to supervise or make rules) is allocated to management in the agreement, it can only be done by mutual agreement. By succumbing to such agreements, naive administrators create precedents difficult to change later. Unless management at every level is made aware of its authority (and responsibility) to exercise managerial authority, such authority will wither away. An equally great danger is the ennui borne of frustration which often besets the middle-level manager on a unionized campus. All the "action" seems to be at or near the president's office, and decisions made at the low and middle levels (departments and deans) are invariably appealed to, and settled at, the highest levels. Soon, the bypassed manager loses the incentive to make difficult decisions, preferring instead to let them be made higher up. *Not only* does this attitude deprive top management of its most valuable input, it also tends to destroy with detail the top managers of the future. Special care must be taken to ensure that this unfortunately common problem not be allowed to exist by scheduling frequent information (training) sessions and by ensuring that middle management has access to staff experience and support in carrying out its responsibilities.

Grievance review is an excellent device to reveal institutional problems. The most obvious indicator of problems is, of course, an inordinate number of losses in arbitration. Perhaps the contract language does not say precisely what was originally intended. In such case, the problem is easily resolved during the next negotiations (assuming, of course, that it is of sufficiently high priority to management and low priority to the union, or pragmatically, management is willing to pay a sufficient price for it). Another aspect of this problem is the possibility that management does not understand the provisions of the agreement and consistently takes action in contravention of the agreement. In such case, the solution is usually not to be found at the table but in internal communications.

Of greatest difficulty, perhaps, is the situation in which management refuses to accept the arbitrator's decision as precedent and commits the same type of infraction of policy. Such an attitude will guarantee a plethora of grievance arbitrations and a sure sense of animosity toward management for failing to follow the rules.

Finally, it may be helpful to keep track of all informal offers of settlement made during the course of processing a grievance and to compare them with the arbitrator's award. If the two are substantially different in a large proportion of cases which go to arbitration, the need for greater training in the handling of grievances is evident.

It is also extremely helpful to ask why the institution is winning grievances. Although it is somehow more difficult to learn from victory, a careful reading of the arbitrator's decision should provide useful information in this regard. Obviously, the most satisfying decision is one in which management's theory, reasoning, interpretation, and application of the contract is wholly accepted, whereas an award won simply because the union failed to prove an essential element of its case should be least satisfying and most revealing. Special note should be taken of especially helpful contract clauses which are frequently cited by arbitrators in sustaining management's argument. Needless to say, the retention of such language in a successor agreement should be an important priority.

The frequency with which a particular article of the agreement or a specific issue is grieved may indicate an important priority of the union which may emerge as a critical issue during the next negotiations. Frequently, a union will file repeated grievances over the same issue, despite earlier consistent losses, to attract members (either because the issue itself is important or to demonstrate its militancy), to harass the administration, or to create pressure at the bargaining table ("We will gladly withdraw all these grievances in exchange for management's acceptance of our demand"). In the first and second instances, discussion with the union about the underlying problem in a forum such as a meet-and-discuss meeting may help in resolving the issue. If this is done, the union may have no need to present the matter at the table.

A Contract Notebook

It is most useful in both administering an agreement and in preparing to negotiate a successor, to keep a notebook or file by contract clause and by subject. Any grievance decision or arbitration award which refers to, or otherwise has a bearing on, the item should be included in the file. Any articles, suggestions, or comments from any source, correspondence from employees and management, and good treatments of the subject in agreements negotiated by other institutions should also be included. In addition, any ideas developed during the course of living with the agreement concerning the particular item should be noted here. Such a file or notebook will be a primary tool in the development of management's goals for future bargaining.

All personnel or other pertinent institutional policies or rules which were not fully reviewed and satisfactorily rewritten prior to the original negotiations should be studied in the same manner as contract articles. Since most policies were not written to be scrutinized and interpreted by an arbitrator in an adversary setting, the language will often be found to be too general and imprecise for this purpose. Additionally, the interfacing of such rules and policies with the provisions of a collective bargaining agreement should be carefully monitored. Appropriate changes should be made either unilaterally or during negotiations, depending upon the circumstances. For example, in negotiations with its faculty union, the State University System of Florida proposed an extensive revision of the systemwide rules together with an invitation to negotiate the substance or the impact where appropriate.

Communications

Collective bargaining and the administration of the negotiated agreement, including grievance processing, is an unusual, esoteric, and therefore somewhat threatening activity to most university administrators. The process should be continually explained to them as it unfolds to ensure their most complete understanding. Accordingly, the administrator responsible for the collective bargaining program should make regular reports at staff meetings, provide ongoing training of management staff and be available on an ad hoc basis to individual managers when needed. In this manner, the process will become familiar and acceptable to them, and consequently, they will be able to provide greater assistance in successfully administering the agreement. Regular contact with academic administrators is an excellent way of explaining problems or questions about the agreement or the process. For example, deans who play a major role in the development of the academic calendar will question why holidays which are nontraditional in the academic context, such as Veterans Day or Columbus Day, are no longer available for classes. Questions of this type lead to better understanding by the deans who, in turn, have the opportunity to educate the negotiator as to their problems and concerns. In this way the collective bargaining program can be more closely attuned to the operations and programs of the institution. Instead of being an independent function, bargaining must become a process directed toward the achievement of institutional goals and needs. This priority is, unfortunately, too often reversed as collective bargaining is seen simply as a task to be performed and often as an end in itself.

In addition to an ongoing relationship to other administrators, a specially selected group of administrators should comprise the collective bargaining policy committee in preparation for bargaining. All areas of institutional activity should be represented at the highest level. This committee will effectively establish the boundaries within which management's team will negotiate. It will also make the effective recommendations about priorities and maintain the closest contact with the bargaining team during negotiations. The members of the committee must understand collective bargaining and how that process influences their own special area of responsibility. It is here especially that the regular continuous consultations described earlier pays its greatest dividends. Knowledgeable administrators, comfortable in their understanding of the process of collective bargaining, are much more helpful in that process than their less-involved counterparts. Discussions proceed to conclusion with a dispatch remarkable for academic institutions, and policies are determined which tend to be clear, precise, and germane.

Diminishing the Table Tensions

Good continuous communication with the union is essential to an effective program of contract administration and can reduce pressures which might ultimately complicate the bargaining process. The union should be able to contact a high-level administration labor relations spokesperson who can, in appropriate cases, resolve problems quickly and informally without resorting to time-consuming, formal grievance procedures. That administrator should be the one to whom responsibility for conducting the collective bargaining program has been assigned, and he should be of sufficient stature (inherent or delegated) to be reasonably successful in obtaining the cooperation of deans, directors, and chairpersons in resolving problems.

The longer problems fester, the more complex and difficult their resolution. If complaints are handled quickly, their resolution tends to be easier, and both the employee and the union will carry away a favorable impression of the administration. It is difficult (and, usually, unnecessary) to generate antagonistic attitudes at the table with such a history. Even the difficult problems are resolved more easily in such an ambience. Regular labor-management meetings, although a more formalized and structured activity, provide the same opportunity to solve problems.

The way grievance decisions are written can also have a direct affect on the negotiation of a successor agreement. In every case, management's response to a grievance ought to address the substantive issue underlying the difference of opinion which brought on the complaint. Although technical defenses, such as timeliness, must be raised to avoid waiving them, no significant grievance decision ought to be settled on such a limited basis. Not all lawyers can accept a procedural dismissal of a client's case by a court; so it would be unreasonable to expect a faculty member to derive much satisfaction or harbor much faith in the system when the decision addressing his grievance avoids coming to grips with the central issue. Grievances can be denied on procedural grounds, but I recommend that the discussion of the merits be prefaced by a statement such as, "While the grievance is denied for the reasons described above, a discussion of the merits may be informative." An employee who feels that his grievance received a full consideration on its merits is certainly more likely to accept such a decision than one who receives a curt, often unintelligible legalism such as "Grievant has failed to sustain his burden of proof. Grievance denied." A grievant who is not insulted by a denial is less likely to insist upon an appeal.

Important, too, is the dissemination of grievance decisions to all management levels. Studying the interpretations of how contract language applies to specific situations is a significant educational tool in assisting administrators in handling their daily problems. They learn the institution's philosophy of management and the skill of accurately reading the agreement. Furthermore, the feedback obtained from these administrators in response to grievance decisions provides an opportunity to keep the collective bargaining program in line with every level of management responsibility. For example, if the grievances are overly legalistic at a university which is attempting to strengthen the collegial relationships, the efforts are usually counterproductive.

The Expert Negotiator

The services of a professional negotiator who is knowledgeable and skillful in labor law, bargaining techniques, and higher education can be very valuable in most collective bargaining negotiations. Skilled and tempered by experience, he usually can avoid the personality conflicts and irrational disputes that often mark the bargaining process. His sense of timing, pace, and the ability to focus on that which is important saves time and effort and enhances the chances of a successful result. Knowing the case law determining the scope of bargaining can, in itself, save anguish and concern and often avoid protracted controversy because of the accompanying respect and credibility.

Conclusion

Finally, before the administration goes back to the table for another contract, it should have its goals and the boundaries of its authority written out as clearly as possible. Having clearly identified goals and prepared language simplifies the process immeasurably. Having language ready to offer at a moment's notice and being granted appropriate authority in advance of negotiations creates confidence, direction, and decisiveness. Internal misunderstandings among administrators are also lessened as they share in the prenegotiation deliberations and decisions. The new contract will not be a surprise, and the institution can move forward with confidence and unity.

Part IV

Wherever a state has permitted unionization of faculties, public colleges there have immediately asked several major questions. Should there be campus-by-campus bargaining or statewide centralized bargaining? Should there be a statewide master contract that covers only salaries and fringe benefits, leaving working conditions and governance matters to local campus bargaining? Should the governor as the public employer negotiate contracts with university faculties, or should the university's board of governors act as the employer? The answers to these and other questions will determine whether or not a campus can or will continue to be a self-governing academic community in which faculty, students, administration, and trustees share in policy making as well as in policy administration, or whether academic communities will become simply district offices representing the governor and legislature with almost all significant decisions being made in state political circles. We have been extremely fortunate in securing three

438

STATEWIDE
BARGAINING

⊂⊃⊂⊃⊂⊃⊂⊃⊂⊃⊂⊃⊂⊃⊂⊃

of the most experienced liberal educators to tell of their unique experiences relating to those key questions. Bargaining in the Pennsylvania State College and University System represents one of the best examples of successful centralized bargaining in the United States. David Hornbeck, former Deputy Secretary of Education in Pennsylvania tells the story (Chapter Twenty-Four) from the view of the central office. His lucid description of statewide goals and how they are being achieved through centralized bargaining will be an example of leadership to all interested in the advantages of statewide coordination of higher education. To balance this view, James Gemmell, President of Clarion State College in Pennsylvania, describes the effects of this same state-wide bargaining on campus autonomy (Chapter Twenty-Five).

Gemmell describes among other phenomena how the Clarion faculty senate was able to survive the pervasive authority and operations of a faculty

*union. In both Minnesota and Pennsylvania the labor law and case de-
cisions give unions the right not only to be the exclusive faculty agent for
negotiating "conditions of employment" but also to "meet and confer" with
administration on all management decisions. This created an overlapping
function with the senate which ordinarily is the faculty organ with which
administration consults about nonmandatory subjects of bargaining. As a
result of this ponderous situation, the Minnesota colleges decided to disenfranchise faculty senates. Pennsylvania colleges, however, decided to let
senates seek their own destiny. That Clarion's senate survived is a story
worth noting since senates in several other Pennsylvania colleges are now
inoperative.*

*In Chapter Two Martin Morand and Ramelle MaCoy, former and
current chief executive officers for the Association of Pennsylvania State
College and University Faculties (union) provide a third perspective. The
three chapters together provide the most complete analysis available of centralized bargaining in a single state. To complete the picture Lawrence
Pettit, Commissioner of Higher Education in Montana, describes perhaps
the most unique type of "centrally controlled" campus-by-campus bargaining in the United States (Chapter Twenty-Six). The unique factor here is
a blend of centralization and local autonomy achieved by using a bargaining
committee comprised of local administrators and chaired by a representative
of the central office (coordinating board). This type of bargaining may be
the answer to the problems posed by the two extremes, one in which a single
centralized contract is bargained by the governor's office (for example, the
State University of New York, SUNY), the other in which each college or university in the state bargains its own contract (for example, the public universities of Michigan). The former almost reduced the 30-odd campuses of SUNY
to branches of the state political system, that is, of the governor's office; the
latter system creates problems of whipsawing, great diversity in personnel
policies, lack of state coordination, and sometimes an inability on the part
of the campus to meet its negotiated salaries (for example, Wayne State
University in 1975).*

*Private colleges and universities will also be interested in the issues
posed. Should state contributions to private institutions continue to rise,
there may come a day when states will attempt to exert more centralized control over bargaining and management at private campuses as a matter of
equity and responsibility. In this regard, private institutions may find it to*

their advantage to deal with state governments in system-type units utilizing the state organization of independent colleges and universities as the primary political and management unit.

David W. Hornbeck

24

One is tempted when addressing issues of collective bargaining to sweep too broadly. There are, for example, two important questions which I intend to leave to one side in this discussion. The first is the fundamental question of whether collective bargaining is desirable in higher education. The second concerns the place of the strike in the public employee arena, particularly with reference to professional educators. These are significant and interesting issues of debate. But they are essentially irrelevant to my experience and to the topic of this chapter.

The Public Employee Relations Act of Pennsylvania (Act 195) is the primary source of the irrelevance. Act 195 answered both questions as it went into effect on October 21, 1970. It accorded all public employees the right to organize and bargain collectively including faculties in public institutions of higher education. It also granted a limited right to strike to these employees. Many people

Improving Educational Services Through Statewide Bargaining

⚭⚭⚭⚭⚭⚭⚭⚭

in Pennsylvania often talk of withdrawing one or another of these rights. In this state such talk is flailing at windmills. Collective bargaining is here to stay and, in this state, the limited right to strike will continue. I raise the question simply to suggest that the challenge here is to devote our intellectual and physical energy to the questions of how to make the process work rather than dwelling on what was or might have been. I recognize that some who will read this volume will not be operating in the same context and, further, they must seek advice on these prior questions. But once the context in which one must work is set, the essential challenge is to make the system work.

Preliminarily, let me say that I believe the topic I was asked to address is properly entitled "... to Improve Educational Services." There are some who feel such optimism is misplaced and would entitle the chapter "... to Prevent Deterioration of Educational Services." I believe collective bargaining can, indeed, be a tool for improvement.

Finally, to help set the parameters, I should point out that I write from experience with only one employer, the commonwealth of Pennsylvania, and within the commonwealth, the Department of Education. Within that context, I had four and one-half years experience of dealing with two contracts involving the 4,500 faculty members of Pennsylvania's thirteen state colleges and Indiana University.

When Secretary of Education, John Pittenger, and I came into office in January of 1972, negotiations between the commonwealth and APSCUF had been underway for a number of months and were within weeks of conclusion. Neither of us was experienced in the labor relations arena; we assumed, partly through indecision, that we should not intervene in the negotiations process in any substantial way since the process was in the hands of labor relations professionals. Moreover, we were of the view that collective bargaining should be limited largely to concerns focusing exclusively on wages and conditions of employment defined very narrowly. Educational matters should be excluded.

For nearly a year following the signing of that contract, we pursued the same general approach to the collective bargaining relationship. We took what the lawyers might call a strict constructionist view of the contract. By that I mean that if an issue was not directly discussed in the contract, there was no reason to discuss it. It meant that if any basis could be found in the contract for denying the claims of the union, we asserted that basis and denied those claims. It meant that if the contract did not say that something could or should be done, it was not done. As a matter of fact, neither the secretary nor I had very much contact with APSCUF at all. I think that it is fair to say that our own way of looking at the world also rubbed off on some of those who were responsible for dealing with the faculty at the local institutional level. A combination of our taking that position and others following suit had, as I look back, negative and very unfortunate consequences.

One of the clearest examples of that philosophy of a collective bargaining relationship was our reaction to grievances. I overstate it to some extent, but not greatly, when I say that in the first year when grievances reached the appeal level involving the secretary's office, we reviewed the materials submitted in a somewhat cursory way but, in fact, supported the decision of the president of the local institution. It is quite proper, even necessary, to support your managers. However, to follow their lead blindly can have serious consequences. It was the grievance procedure and its results which first led us to begin to reconsider our position. Toward the end of the first year, we found ourselves with a string of arbitration awards—seven, if I remember correctly—all of which were against us. To understate it somewhat, we thought those circumstances suggested a review of the way in which we were approaching labor relations. The culmination of that review is, I believe, represented in the second contract which we signed with APSCUF in October, 1974.

Before discussing the terms of the second contract that relate to educational improvement, I want to describe the process leading to that contract. The description will illustrate concretely the perspective on collective bargaining of one higher education employer more clearly than simply laying out a list of principles.

The first, and most crucial, decision was that—in contrast to the first negotiations—we, at the highest levels of the department, would be involved in the bargaining process. The secretary assigned the task of policy formulation, monitoring and overseeing the process to me as the Executive Deputy Secretary with instructions to keep him informed regularly. The secretary was quite clear that collective bargaining was one of a handful of issues facing the department that required our personal and continuing attention.

At the same time, having discovered the impact and potential impact of collective bargaining on the colleges, we felt it could not be left to the direction of persons whose primary concern was not education. Neither could we leave the formal process of negotiation to one without extensive labor relations experience. We felt that it was vitally important that the chief negotiator for the commonwealth be someone who had not only extensive experience in labor relations (including negotiations) but equally, and, perhaps more important, someone who understood the world of higher education and could speak the language of administrators and faculty alike. We were fortunate in finding such a person in Dr. Bernard Ingster. The choice of Dr. Ingster represented a significant departure from previous commonwealth practice in negotiations in that the particular department responsible for the employees involved in the negotiations selected the chief negotiator. The governor's Office of Labor Relations, which had conducted all other negotiations, was most cooperative and supportive in that decision.

The next major undertaking was the formation of something that we referred to as the Labor Policy Committee. This was a committee which I chaired on behalf of the secretary. Dr. Ingster, several people from our Office of Higher Education, and a representative from the Board of Presidents of the state colleges composed the committee. That committee began to meet in early September, 1973, some five months prior to the first formal negotiating session. Stated simply, if we were going to take this collective bargaining relationship seriously, we were going to be prepared. During the course of those five months, we solicited and received the advice of all fourteen campus presidents, people within the department, the opinion of people concerned with affirmative action, and others. We then spent days wrestling with the old contract. We considered proposed changes. We discussed our vision educationally for the state colleges and how the contract might relate to that. We argued. We wrote position papers. We did a statistical analysis of faculty ranks, wages, terms and conditions of employment in a host of institutions in neighboring states similar to our fourteen institutions. The result was a complete proposed contract representing the best thinking of which we were capable. It was that proposal which we placed on the table at the first formal negotiating session in January 1974.

That was another first in the experience of the commonwealth. The practice had been for the commonwealth to receive demands of the union in any given set of negotiations. Days, weeks, or months later, the commonwealth would react to those demands. By definition that meant the union in each instance established the baseline on all matters. By preparing ourselves we also happily began the negotiations with management's document shaping the initial conversation.

There were only two major areas for which we made no specific proposal. One was wages. We decided to limit the initial document to areas we felt directly influenced questions of educational quality. The other area was that of professional evaluation and development. There, however, we inserted a page in the proposed contract entitled "Professional Evaluation and Development," leaving the rest of the page blank. We did so to signal immediately to the faculty that we considered the system under the previous contract wholly inadequate, requiring substantial change. At the same time, it was important to tell the faculty we felt they must play a major role in what resulted. We had done our homework in that area. Indeed, we had prepared a full and specific proposal. But in an area of such sensitivity, we decided the homework we had done should inform our posture and conversation rather than represent our conclusions in the initial instance. Other than those two areas, every other major category was addressed.

At the first session, the commonwealth team and APSCUF's team decided to try to reduce the adversarial nature of the relationship to a minimum. We began by calling the negotiations conversations. Frankly, that kind of dialogue was possible because APSCUF had also been taking its responsibility seriously during the time the commonwealth had been preparing so arduously. We found from the beginning that the commonwealth and the faculty were coming together with a wide range of shared concerns. These revolved around issues of teaching excellence, rising costs, quality institutions, and the future of the state colleges. That common ground sustained both parties throughout the negotiations and allowed us to conclude the negotiations on the last day of August, 1974 without the intervention of a third party in any form—no mean achievement in itself.

In addition to the chief negotiator, the commonwealth team included two vice-presidents from the colleges. One was expert in administrative matters, the other in academic affairs. The team also included two persons from our Office of Higher Education, the Chief of the Division of Labor Relations in the department, and two representatives of the governor's Office of Labor Relations. The chief negotiator and I were in constant contact with one another. We met with the team. The Labor Policy Committee met to consider new developments. The background work we had done placed management in the position of being able to respond quickly and constructively to initiatives of the union. The contract that resulted faced issues of economic reality. It addressed specifically issues of teaching excellence. It involved a considerable measure of faculty participation in helping to shape thinking leading to decisions.

Before turning to the provisions of the contract related directly to educational improvement, let me comment on the manner in which we dealt with economic factors. Economic reality was addressed in two major provisions. One of those was the wage package for the first year which called for a 4 percent across-the-board increase in salary. We all, of course, know that in these inflationary times such an increase was hardly extravagant. And it was a tribute to the faculty that they considered such a settlement during a period of financial crunch in the institutions an investment in the future of the state colleges. On the other side, economic reality was further addressed by the commonwealth's pledge to retrench no faculty member for the academic year 1975–1976. That extended by one year a previous pledge of one year to a no-retrenchment policy which had resulted then in an agreement by the faculty to assist in helping management shift 5 percent of the colleges' resources to new priorities. We felt that it was very important that faculty, the administrations of the colleges, and the Department of Education were taking many new initiatives related to the quality of education and teaching excellence in our institutions.

To the same end, we left determination of wages in years subsequent to the first to a rather unusual mechanism in the event that the commonwealth and APSCUF were unable to agree to a wage package. The issue would be submitted to an arbitration panel. The panel would make a final decision subject to a ceiling that would be determined by the pattern of wage settlements between the commonwealth and the other unions representing other commonwealth employees. We decided to employ that mechanism for wage determinations in order to avoid having serious disagreements over wages influence and possibly destroy our mutual interests in giving primary attention to educational issues. The result has been that wages for the second year of the contract were raised 3.83 percent across-the-board and for the third year, 4.0 percent across-the-board. In the spring of 1976 when these wages were established, we agreed to extend the mechanism of the arbitration panel with a ceiling to decide the issue of wages for the next two years. In addition to these increases, each faculty person would get an average increase of approximately 1.9 percent per year due to state law regarding increments. The latter is not part of bargaining, but even if that is added to the contractually granted increases, the result is a lower settlement than nearly any other in the United States during that period of double digit inflation.

Let me turn now to the provisions of the contract directly related to teaching excellence and educational quality. There are four areas which I highlight as meeting the criteria. The first, because it holds the most possibility for long-term influence in improving educational quality through teaching excellence, is the area of professional development and evaluation. As I pointed out above, this was one category in management's proposal which was left open-ended. Without going into great detail, the previous evaluation procedure consisted of a process by which each nontenured faculty member was observed twice each year, and each tenured faculty member was observed once. A written critique was subsequently shared with each faculty member. In addition, there was a reference in the first contract to an evaluation being prepared for the nontenured member yearly. The same was to occur for the tenured member every three years. There were no criteria. The process in most instances was not taken very seriously. A reference in the first contract to student evaluations went almost wholly unobserved.

The contract signed in 1974 called for the creating of a six-person committee to draft a new evaluation procedure. The committee consisted of two college presidents, two members named by APSCUF, and two members named by the secretary of education. The contract specified that the new process had to receive four votes of the six members and these had to include at least one vote from each of the three categories of membership. Upon receiving such a vote, the new evaluation program would automatically replace the old one.

These elements of the contractual provisions are significant. First, the parties agree to argue after the contract was signed on the substance of the new procedures. In doing so they were recognizing the importance of evaluation and the inadequacy of the old system. Second, management recognized the importance of significant faculty participation in the decision. Third, the two secretary's appointees were from outside the system (a former dean from Franklin and Marshall College and a faculty member from the University of Pennsylvania Law School). Thus the contract was used to reach out for advice beyond the bounds of the colleges themselves.

The committee worked extremely hard for over a year. They spent at least one day on each of the fourteen campuses plus many additional meetings among themselves. The result at this writing is largely untested due to the delay in the final report that resulted from the thoroughness of their work. But most agree, I think, that much can be expected if the new procedures are implemented in a good-faith manner and supported by the union and administration equally.

In brief the new procedures called for the following:

For nontenured faculty a "faculty colleague" will be assigned to each. This person will assist the nontenured faculty member in meeting instructional and noninstructional responsibilities, in meeting departmental and collegewide established criteria for desired performance, and in becoming acquainted with professional opportunities.

The nontenured member will develop a statement of his understanding of the mutual expectations including the areas of performance and growth in the area of instruction, intellectual growth and development, professional service to the college, and professional service to the community. These statements are to be reviewed within three months and then annually.

Tenured faculty members are evaluated every five years or more often if necessary. A primary basis for the evaluation is a written statement by the faculty member covering the four areas of professional growth and development, intellectual growth and development, college service, and community services. In each instance the statement will reflect on the previous five years and will suggest areas for change and improvement.

A system is also laid out by which student evaluation will play a role. The department chairperson is specifically charged with seeing to it that a responsible evaluation instrument is administered concerning all faculty. The specific use of the results and the requirement that they be given "full consideration" is contained in the new contractual language.

Finally, a department Development and Evaluation Committee is selected in each department to oversee the implementation of the process. The committee discusses all evaluations, written statements, and the statements of mutual understandings with the faculty members involved. One of their primary responsibilities is to assist every faculty member to take advantage of developmental opportunities as there is an underlying assumption that every faculty, no matter how good, can improve.

The second provisions of the contract relating directly to teaching excellence and educational quality are the ones relating to promotions. In this area, like that of professional development and evaluation, the contract called for the establishment of an ad hoc committee composed of two members appointed by APSCUF, two college presidents, and two others appointed by the secretary of education. They were to call a meeting of representatives of the fourteen institutions who would describe the existing procedures and promotion policies at each college and make recommendations for improvement. After deliberation, the committee was charged with developing a set of guidelines to assist each college in preparing a new statement of promotion policies and procedures.

The state colleges and university are, as many similar systems in other states, former privately controlled normal schools. They were made teacher colleges in the 1920s. In 1961 the legislature designated them as state colleges with a view toward broadening the curricular offering. That was done, but it has only been in the past four years that the number of graduates in any given year, trained as teachers, dropped below the number who had pursued a different discipline.

This brief historical digression shows that until relatively recently many appointments to the faculty were made initially at the associate professor and full professor rank. This was done to compete with other institutions of higher education which paid more and had the "reputation" of being more prestigious schools. The result is that more than one-half of the faculty occupy the two upper ranks.

In addition, practice had led to a situation in many departments across the system in which longevity was the primary criterion for promotion. By statute, minimum qualifications are set forth designating the minimum number of years required and degrees held to be *eligible* for promotion. Few who achieved the minimum were denied promotion. This situation was one which APSCUF and the commonwealth sought to alter.

Under the contract, in addition to the minimum statutory qualifications, criteria for academic faculty promotions now include: (1) effective teaching, (2) fulfillment of professional responsibilities, (3) mastery of subject matter in discipline, (4) contribution to the college, and (5) continuing scholarly growth. The guidelines developed by the ad hoc committee then gave substance to those general criteria.

The guidelines called for the statement from each college to provide that teaching effectiveness is the most important criterion. Further, the statement had to be explicit in identification of the *evidence* acceptable for the purpose of making the appraisal of effectiveness. The evidence had to include, but was not limited to: (1) student evaluation, (2) quality of course syllabi prepared by the candidate, (3) reports of classroom visitations, and (4) quality of course examinations and paper assignments. The guidelines specified that conclusory statements could not be considered as evidence.

The evidence for "subject matter mastery" had to include at least: (1) the number and quality of publications as measured by reviews, citations, outside referees' evaluation, and the stature of publishers, (2) invited papers delivered, (3) testimony of experts in the discipline or related disciplines, (4) consultantships as measured by the number and professional importance, and (5) the terminal degree in the discipline.

Evidence concerning "continuing scholarly growth" had to include: (1) graduate work beyond the terminal degree in the discipline or in a related discipline, (2) attendance at workshops, institutes, or short courses, (3) participation in organizations advancing a professional field or discipline, (4) development of new scholarly or practical insights as a result of systematic investigation, and (5) development of a course based upon original concepts that demonstrate new possibilities of the discipline.

Evidence for evaluation in the area of "contribution to the college" must include: (1) significant contribution to college committees, (2) specific individual assignment, (3) significant contribution to departmental committees, (4) significant contribution to college governance, (5) significant contribution to student organizations or activities, (6) development of proposals that help the college, and (7) participation in community work in a professional capacity that brings recognition to the college.

The fulfillment of "professional responsibilities" is met by: (1) preparing for and meeting assigned classes, (2) conferring with and advising students, (3) holding office hours at least five hours per week spread over at least three different days, (4) evaluating students fairly and reporting promptly on student achievement, (5) participating in group deliberations which contribute to the growth and development of the students and the college, (6) accepting those reasonable duties assigned within the fields of competence, and (7) attempting to preserve and defend the goals of the college, without being restricted in the right to advocate change. Indeed, failure to meet these entry professional responsibilities, the committee said, would preclude further consideration for promotion based on the other criteria.

The guidelines were more expansive allowing each college to add criteria. They required each college in its statement to differentiate the "characteristics associated with the designations of" the academic ranks. That is, the evidence for assistant professor was not to be as stringent as for full professors though each of the several categories had to be met. Further, the guidelines called for specific attention to affirmative action in promotion policies.

The guidelines were accepted by the secretary of education. The colleges, through a variety of committees prepared their statements in accord with the guidelines and submitted them to the ad hoc committee for review. Acceptance of a statement from a college by the ad hoc committee was necessary before the college was allowed to promote anyone. Several colleges received immediate approval. Some changes were required by the committee in some statements before they were accepted. Today, all have been accepted and are in place at the fourteen institutions.

The third provision of the contract relating directly to teaching excellence and educational quality is the provision for Distinguished Teaching Awards.

At the state colleges, one device which was used in the past to reward meritorious performance was something we referred to as merit increments. Over the years the merit increments had, I think most would agree, deteriorated into a process in which a primary consideration was whether a particular faculty member had gotten one the year before or the year before that and whether that faculty member's turn to get one had come up again. The distinction that should have been associated with merit increments was for all intents and purposes nonexistent. The new Distinguished Teaching Awards take place at two levels. At the local campus level one, two, or three awards may be granted each year depending on the size of the faculty at the individual campus. Faculty members submit proposals to a committee composed of administrators, students, and faculty from other distinguished teaching institutions. The proposal lays out what the faculty member proposes to do by way of demonstrating teaching excellence and will pinpoint the evaluation process the faculty member suggests will reveal whether he has done it. When a faculty member is admitted to candidacy for a Distinguished Teaching Award, he then will do whatever has been proposed. At the appropriate time the local campus committee will evaluate performance. Some faculty may not have completed what they had proposed. Another group may have completed it and thereby be eligible to receive a certificate of teaching distinction but not the final distinguished teaching award. Finally, one faculty member from each of the three smallest colleges, three faculty members from each of the three largest, and two from each of the remaining eight colleges may receive the teaching award itself which will be worth $2,500.

In addition to the local selection, those receiving the Distinguished Teaching Award may become candidates for one of ten statewide awards which will be given on the basis of a selection committee at the state level consisting of three appointees of the secretary of education, a president of a local college, a president of a local APSCUF chapter, and a president of a local student association. Anyone selected for one of the state-level awards will receive an additonal $3,500. A faculty member, thus, would be eligible to receive a one-time $6,000 award if he were successful at both levels. The cost of this merit award system will be one-third to one-half of the old system. The difference will be expended on other educationally related problems to which both APSCUF and the commonwealth can agree.

,   During the first year of operation, there were several problems which the union and the commonwealth had to solve. One was to reward the work and effort of the faculty member whose approach to teaching is not what one would normally call innovative. It was possible for the process to deteriorate into a gimmicky orientation. Fortunately, this did not happen. Several steps were taken to avoid it. First, we strongly encouraged faculty operating in a "traditional" way to apply. Second, we allowed students, peers, or others to nominate faculty at the first step. Third, the teaching experience did not have to take place wholly after the proposal to the committee. That is, a faculty member could submit evidence of teaching excellence based on a course or program or other learning opportunity that had been underway for some time.

However one came to the attention of the local committee or whatever the teaching methodology, the faculty member still had to lay out the criteria on the basis of which judgment could be made of teaching excellence. The result in the first year was twenty-eight awards at the local level and eleven state awards with two of the latter being a shared award. Most agree that the quality of the work of those chosen was truly outstanding. That gave additional impetus to the second round which is, at this writing, underway. In addition, an analysis has begun of the various approaches to teaching used by the award winners. We hope that over time the commonwealth and the union will be in a position to describe some elements of teaching excellence that will assist others.

The fourth provision of the contract relating directly to teaching excellence and educational quality is that related to tenure. Here again, at many of the schools and in many of the departments, longevity was the primary criterion for receiving tenure. Moreover, longevity itself was not very burdensome as it was only three years.

The contract called for another ad hoc committee (Tenure Commission) composed of two union members, two members appointed by the secretary of education, and two college presidents. The Tenure Commission was instructed to "issue an advisory report that will include a description of current practices and decisions in the tenure area, recommendations for improved practices, and suggestions that may be used by the president when he/she makes tenure decisions." In contrast to the provision relating to promotion, evaluation, and Distinguished Teaching Awards, the product of the Tenure Commission is advisory rather than mandatory.

The first step which the Tenure Commission took was a survey of the colleges to identify current practices. The returns from the colleges suggested very strongly that almost all of those eligible on a time basis for tenure are granted tenure. In a very few instances a few departments recommended against the grant of tenure, but these recommendations were not followed by the collegewide committees. When asked to characterize the minimum standard for tenure and given a five-point scale from "exceptional performance" to "candidate is likely to create problems" most responded that "the candidate must show promise of average performance of professional responsibilities." Also most tenure recommendations resulted from a majority vote with no minority views attached. Equally infrequent was the collection of evidence and reasoned statements in support of a positive recommendation. But with negative recommendations a full statement was forwarded to the collegewide committee. In terms of evidence, classroom observation was, as in the old promotion procedures, given the most weight. There was little mention of reliance on evidence which might indicate mastery of subject matter, scholarly growth, contributions to the department and the college, or other criteria.

There follows in the Tenure Commission report a series of statements of what tenure should be. First, it pointed out that

> [*T*]*enure is not appropriately granted to a faculty member merely because he/she has done nothing wrong during the probationary period. . . . Second, every tenure decision is a statement by the institution about its future. . . . Third, the decision to grant or withhold tenure cannot be reached (ineluctably) from some litmus test. . . . Fourth, it follows that participants in tenure decisions should be prepared to evaluate candidates in terms of institutional standards and goals. . . . Fifth, the institution should state, insofar as it reasonably can, the grounds it will use to reach a judgment. . . . Sixth, statements, aspirations, goals, and policies are guidelines for judgment; but they do not obviate judgment, and judgment in tenure decisions is unavoidable. . . . Seventh and finally, the difficulty and subtlety of judgment in tenure decisions in no way relieves faculty members of the professional burden of making such decisions seriously and on relevant grounds. . . .*

The commission went on, in some detail, to make recommendations concerning, among others, identification and definition of a position to be filled; procedures for recruitment and appointment; criteria, evidence, and judgment in evaluation; content

of a tenure recommendation; and the roles of the various participants. At this writing the advice given by the Tenure Commission
is too new to determine its impact. Given the baseline data summarized and the nature of the advice, it is, however, readily apparent that improvement can be expected with faculty and management
cooperation. Since both played decisive roles in offering the advice,
the cooperation may be expected.

The four areas which I have reviewed represent the most
significant categories of the contract that influence educational
quality and teacher effectiveness. However, there are four other
provisions of the contract which are also important and have various effects on the educational program.

One for which both the commonwealth and APSCUF have high
hope is the Educational Services Trust Fund. In the wake of the
first contract, signed in 1972, the federal Cost of Living Council
disallowed the payment of 1.4 percent of the negotiated wage increase for one of the years involved. The commonwealth and APSCUF
jointly appealed the decision, asking if the money were used for
the benefit of the colleges and not for individual faculty in the form
of wages, could it be paid. The council agreed that was appropriate.
The Trust Fund thus came into existence. It is administered by
six trustees, three from APSCUF and three from the commonwealth. Its purpose is to fund programs, projects, and activities
jointly agreed to, which will contribute to teaching effectiveness,
improvement of the quality of education at the colleges, and fac-
culty development.

Considerable care has been taken in the formulation of funding criteria. To date, there have not been many grants. Until very
recently, the cloud of retrenchment hovered over the system as the
commonwealth had to meet a project deficit of $16,000,000. A year
ago termination notices were sent to eighty-two faculty members.
Ultimately, we were able to meet the deficit in other ways including
the wage settlement for this past year of 3.83 percent. But while
facing retrenchment, the Trust Fund was not active except in ways
related both to retrenchment and the purposes of the trust. In
several instances, for example, grants were made to faculty for retraining which will enable them to shift from areas from which they
would have been retrenched (low priority) to vacancies in higher
priority areas.

Now plans are underway for the full development of the Trust Fund. Two items bear mention, I think. First, the trustees are reaching out for advice from the campuses through a statewide conference this past spring and followup meetings on each campus. Again, the view is that faculty and local campuses are vital to change. If they are involved in the process, lasting change becomes a possibility. Second, the trustees are giving careful consideration to an Academy for Excellence in Teaching, an ongoing place as well as idea where attention may be given to improving teaching quality. One possible ingredient of such an effort may be the inclusion of the recipients of the Distinguished Teaching Awards as permanent Fellows of the Academy.

One might reasonably ask whether a one-time 1.4 percent wage increase will sustain such efforts. The answer is obviously no. One of the possible sources of sustained income for such activities will be money associated with the new promotion guidelines and the Distinguished Teaching Awards. In each instance the new program is less expensive than the old. The new promotion guidelines have yielded fewer promotions and the Awards cost substantially less than the old merit increments. To demonstrate that we were advocating the new provisions because of their educational merit rather than cost savings, we agreed that we would spend the residual amount in one of two ways. If APSCUF and the commonwealth can agree, the money will go to either the Trust Fund or a similar vehicle with similar purposes. The alternative is to distribute the residual among the faculty. With approximately 4,500 faculty and $200,000 per year in the kitty, that would be less than $50 per faculty member, hardly a sum on which to retire. Thus, the commonwealth hopes the former alternative will be adopted.

Still another provision which deserves attention is state-level "meet and discuss." During the course of negotiations, the language of some items in the first contract was carried over into the second contract, or only minor modifications were made. Yet they were areas in which both parties recognized continuing complex problems which affect the entire system. They included questions of retrenchment, affirmative action, independent study, work load, overload, summer employment, and retirement. We resolved to continue to discuss those items and others that will occur of a major policy nature in monthly meet-and-discuss sessions between APSCUF and the department.

The first contract had provided for meet-and-discuss sessions on the local level but not the state level. On the basis of two years of experience, the value of meet-and-discuss has been demonstrated many times. The best example was the issue of retrenchment. It came as no surprise that we were unable to agree. However, we met during a period of less than a year more than a dozen times to discuss the issues involved. Indeed, the commonwealth shared its proposed retrenchment procedures with APSCUF before implementing them and made some changes based on their comments because we thought they were right. Those discussions, I think, demonstrated to APSCUF that the commonwealth had grave concerns as to the impact of retrenchment on both the individuals involved and on the quality of the educational programs affected. That sort of understanding allowed the wounds of retrenchment to be less severe and the healing process to be a swifter one. The fact is that in the collective bargaining relationship (as with nearly everything else associated with human interaction) honesty, candor, and openness to others tend to breed respect that will see two parties through the worst of times and allow constructive activity in the best of times.

A third activity that has been very much a part of the collective bargaining relationship here is the planning activity. The redefinition of mission in the colleges has been a major priority of the department. As I outlined above, a substantial majority of the graduates of the colleges were trained as teachers until very recently. Education remains the single largest area of concentration with just under 50 percent of the graduates. The teacher oversupply, the need of commonwealth students for increased relatively low-cost liberal arts and other noneducation opportunities and the need of the commonwealth for graduates in other human service, public administration, business administration, health service, and other areas led the commonwealth to seek to redefine the thrust of the colleges.

With diminishing real dollars available, that meant shifting resources. What to shift, what new missions to pursue and related questions were not going to be answered quickly. And without some faculty support, dollar and management shifts probably would not occur at all. That meant participation, not edicts. The first step was a Statement of Mutual Understandings reached in 1972 in which the commonwealth agreed to a moratorium of one year on retrenchment and APSCUF agreed to help shift 5 percent of the colleges' resources from previous areas of expenditure to new ones. Following that, we agreed that all local planning commissions (one per campus) would have substantial APSCUF participation and that a state-level planning commission would be organized to advise the commissioner of higher education and the secretary of education on the redefinition of mission. The state-level planning commission (known as the 4-4-4) was composed of four persons from the department, four presidents, and four APSCUF leaders. They met regularly to examine a wide range of far-reaching questions related to the future of the system.

The results have not been as dramatic as some of us would have liked. Nevertheless, each college has been assigned at least one new mission. At least half of the institutions are pursuing the new missions with real vigor including following through with shifting resources to pay for it. This has actually taken place in less than three years with one of the years being consumed with the energy and emotion associated with retrenchment. In the world of education where change sometimes is glacierlike, the movement over the last three years has been gratifying.

The department has felt that the quality of the state colleges has been unfairly questioned. We feel that each of the fourteen can become institutions of real distinction. The institutions can be much more a system than they are now. Each institution can and should develop at least one area of such expertise that they achieve a national reputation in that area. Some may develop more than one. But each should have at least one thing which leads someone in any part of this nation to know that it is necessary to go to Slippery Rock or Clarion or West Chester or Cheyney or whatever in order to be fully informed in the particular area which is each college's area of real distinction. Difficult problems or rising costs and potentially dropping enrollments are going to continue. Significant new trends in higher education must be faced such as the number of minorities that should be admitted as students and employed as faculty and administrators. Ways must be developed in which the colleges become less sexist in employment and in the orientation of their academic programs. Differentiated missions must be provided to meet student, commonwealth, and regional needs. The kinds of initiatives which are implied in that range of objectives is not going to be achieved through fiats from the Department of Education or from the presidents of the institutions. It will require cooperation from the faculty.

I believe collective bargaining can assist in maintaining excellence and provoking change. It can help accommodate initiatives which come from many directions. To make that so, however, one cannot approach the issues in a cursory or ad hoc manner. A number of things have to be at work.

The process has to involve participation by managers at the highest level. In the instance that I have outlined, the secretary, the executive deputy secretary, the commissioner and the deputy commissioner of higher education, and the presidents of the institutions have to give time, thought, and energy to labor relations.

It is essential that there be much preparation and planning leading up to any negotiating session as was done in the Labor Policy Committee.

The kind of time and energy that has been given to implement that agreement must continue during the life of the agreement. One of the serious mistakes that people engaged in labor relations sometimes make is giving little or no attention to the relationships between the employer and the employee between contract negotiations. That always seems to lead to a new set of negotiations in which there are as many as 200 or 300 or 400 outstanding problems which in turn have to be dealt with at the bargaining table. Most of those issues could be solved prior to the time that a new contract needs to be negotiated.

That leads me to the principle of flexibility. A contract is a contract is a contract. At the same time, if either the union or the employer views the contract in an absolutely rigid way, solutions to many problems will not be forthcoming. There is one view of the collective bargaining relationship which reflects the view that the secretary and I originally took. That view reads the contract in the narrowest fashion possible. There are problems that arise in any contract which were not foreseen by those at the table when the contract was negotiated. It is essential that the parties be in a position to sit down and talk to one another and arrive at reasonable solutions to the complex problems that face us all. In the course of doing that, the manager need not give up what some hang on to in a somewhat religious way—that entity called management rights. In fact, reasonable solutions to complicated problems represent in my view the exercise of management rights. By and large, I view the collective bargaining process as a process that can and should be devoted to problem solving. The problems facing higher education today are probably more difficult than they have ever been. Rigidity and narrowmindedness have no place in that kind of world.

Finally, if one is to justify participation by people at the highest level; if one is going to prepare and plan extensively; if one is going to approach collective bargaining as a problem-solving process and be flexible, there is one other necessary ingredient. One must view the faculty as partners in this enterprise. One should embrace the concept of participation, not fear it. One should do everything in his power to provoke trust rather than distrust. Until such time as the faculty are viewed as allies and, following that, respond as allies, we will not have the kind of relationship that will result in the achievement of the goals often mutually held. In any human endeavor, where there are vested interests and strong opinions held, the development of a trust relationship is an arduously difficult task. Both sides have to work at it. Both sides are in the position of having to maintain a position, yet be sensitive to the position of the other party. It takes skill, sensitivity, and a masterful exercise of the art of compromise in order to achieve the best which is possible out of such a partnership. Both sides are going to make mistakes. But if those mistakes constantly lead to the drawing of rigid lines, the relationship is in trouble and higher education is in trouble as a result.

I have tried to set out in these pages the basic principles which in my view are necessary to make collective bargaining a tool to improve educational quality. I have done so through describing the experience in Pennsylvania. At the risk of being redundant, it might be helpful to summarize the several principles:

1. Management at the highest levels should be involved in a direct manner.
2. Management should carefully determine its own goals through thoughtful planning.
3. Management should take initiatives in negotiations, participating in establishing the baseline point of departure.
4. Management's chief negotiator should be someone who speaks the language of faculty and administrators and is not simply a labor relations "hired gun."
5. That level of management directly concerned with education should direct negotiations as well as contract administration.
6. Significant faculty participation is necessary to meaningful change in the educational quality and, thus, must participate significantly in shaping the changes.
7. Sound systems of faculty evaluation and development, promotion procedures, tenure judgments, and other recognition mechanisms are among the most important factors influencing educational quality, and they can be improved through collective bargaining.
8. The adversarial nature of negotiations should be reduced to a minimum. Previous contract administration is the single most important factor in determining the tone and character of negotiations, but the ground rules of negotiations and the speed and wisdom with which management can react to union initiatives is important also.
9. Management's negotiating team and its planning process should include persons who must administer the contract on a daily basis.
10. The economics of a contract is not one-dimensional. For example, job security may be more important than wage level, particularly during a time of tight money or significant program changes.
11. Parties should seek to be imaginative in negotiations. Higher education collective bargaining is sufficiently new that no one has all the answers. Such devices as the ceiling-bound arbitration panel and the Educational Ser-

vices Trust Fund described above will not be found in many handbooks, but they work for us. You will discover similar problem-solving devices.

12. Although emphasizing the importance of the union and management working together, the collective bargaining relationship can be skillfully used to include good advice from persons from other institutions of higher education in the effort to improve educational quality.

13. A structured setting such as meet-and-discuss is vitally important to contract administration as a forum for airing and finding solutions to problems.

14. Planning for significant educational change can be made constructively a part of the collective bargaining relationship. Educational initiatives will no longer be accepted when handed down from on high. Cooperative effort between management and faculty is vital.

15. Contract administration is at least as important as negotiations and must be approached flexibly if the inevitable problems following the signing of a contract are to be solved.

16. Partnership with the faculty does not demean the role of management for good managers. Only the weak manager or administrator will fear participation. The cooperation is not always tidy, and one often has the urge to issue the edict but it will not work. I think a high level of partnership does work.

One can adopt the rigid narrow view of collective bargaining. Some continue even to pretend it does not exist. One can embrace the strict constructionist perspective of a contract. One can limit discussion at the table to wages and the traditional trade unionist view of hours and conditions of employment. And maybe someday I will write a chapter in another book and urge you to take such a view. But we pursued another approach with some success. I think that the good will of employer and employee alike can use the relatively new collective bargaining relationship to solve problems in higher education. It can help improve the quality of education and provoke better teaching. It can help lead to retraining rather than retrenchment of faculty members to meet needs that regions of the commonwealth and the commonwealth as a whole present to the world of higher education daily. The collective bargaining relationship can assist in the design of programs which meet the needs of minorities and women. The relationship can support the concepts of differentiated missions within a system of institutions that are marked by distinction. The risk is great; the stakes are high. But if the commonwealth and APSCUF succeed, the commonwealth and the students of this commonwealth will be the winners and that, when all is said and done, is what I hope we are about.

James Gemmell

~~~
⊱⊰ ⊱⊰ ⊱⊰ ⊱⊰ ⊱⊰ ⊱⊰ ⊱⊰ ⊱⊰
~~~

The concept of local autonomy in public colleges and universities is under attack today. The assault from one direction is led by quantitative-minded analysts whose preoccupation is with accountability, productivity, and cost-benefit analysis narrowly tailored to alleged manpower needs. From another flank, the attack is led by people who are new to the academic scene—negotiators, arbitrators, mediators, and state labor relations officials—whose knowledge of collegiality is likely to be fragmentary, whose familiarity with academic freedom may be only marginal, and whose potential is great for altering the traditional mode of governance in higher education.

The purpose of this chapter is to discuss strategy for containment of this two-pronged assault. The assumption is that considerable local autonomy and the responsibility it makes possible within a multicampus system of public education are good things

Protecting Campus Autonomy and Responsibility Within Statewide Bargaining

and that they can and should be protected. No doubt some readers will reject that view, and prefer alternate strategies. Nevertheless, I shall adopt it as my premise, describe what needs to be protected, and move to a consideration of strategy that can be employed to stem the erosion of campus autonomy that has accompanied statewide bargaining. When appropriate, I shall cite some of the serious lessons that I and other presidents have learned by (1) not taking action, (2) taking the wrong action, (3) not acting soon enough, and (4) not uniting to exercise what authority we had left. (My general thesis is that presidents must unite and exert concentrated power—much as faculties do through their unions.)

The reader should understand that I do not approach the subject without prejudices, and that I have held them so long that they now appear to be my considered judgment (Gemmell, 1975). I am a college president who spent most of his professional career

in the classroom and consider those days among the most rewarding. Having served as the impetus for development of a strong
faculty senate at my own institution, I continue to believe in broad
faculty participation in the governance process while administering a college where no more than one-third of the faculty voted
for unionism but were swept into it by virtue of statewide balloting. Obviously these facts should be considered in evaluating what
I have to say about campus autonomy.

Case for Campus Autonomy

Corwin and Edelfelt (1976, p. 28) define autonomy as the
discretion a person has to choose among already fixed alternatives, as distinguished from power, which is the ability to establish
alternatives. When one speaks of campus autonomy, what specifically is it that needs protection? Institutional autonomy is nothing
more or less than academic freedom at the institutional level; it is
the right of an academic institution to pursue its development with
a minimum of external restraint, wherever that course may lead,
just as academic freedom for the individual is the right to pursue
knowledge without unwarranted interference. Donald R. McNeil
(Western Interstate Commission on Higher Education, 1976) has
defined legislative involvement as "unwarranted interference when
it impinges on the academic integrity of our institutions; when decisions of governance, institutional management, academic policy,
program planning, admission requirements, faculty duties and
other related issues are not made in the halls of ivy, but in those
of the legislature."

Decentralization with diversity has been the historical basis
of our noble experiment with education in a democracy and is
needed more now than ever. What facts support this conclusion?
Americans have always regarded a college education as a vehicle
for upward economic mobility. Until recently this employment-
oriented philosophy of education went unquestioned in the United
States because there were frequently more white-collar jobs available than college graduates to fill them. Unwittingly, admission
officers sold college to new recruits as an investment with an economic payoff. Likewise, college presidents argued persuasively for
higher appropriations on the grounds of economic utility: higher

earnings for college graduates would automatically yield increased tax revenues to the state. This, of course, was a serious mistake and is an example of presidents taking the wrong action. Instead of defending public higher education as a right, the leadership in academia concentrated on putting a graduate on the moon. With that accomplished, the leadership set out to purify the environment, to cure cancer, to banish poverty, and to develop new sources of energy. In the meantime the space program has been curtailed drastically, the Vietnam conflict has ended, and an economic era characterized by unemployment and inflation has set in.

Belatedly, higher education has recognized the tactical error of choosing to justify its existence with the promise of better jobs. When jobs did not always materialize, critics of higher education everywhere questioned the value of going to college. Whether or not it is justifiable, taxpayers and legislators alike perceive educators as failures who misled them and squandered their revenues. They have retaliated with budget cuts and incessant demands for more accountability which, in turn, have led to greater centralization of authority over public colleges and a concomitant diminution of campus responsibility.

How should we respond to the predicament? Clearly one of two things must happen—either the law of supply and demand will operate to reduce the number of college graduates, or an increasing number of students will go to college for reasons other than employment. Of the two, the latter is so preferable that we have a strong obligation to promote it. But if large numbers of students are going to be attending college for reasons other than employment, then our institutions will have to undergo radical change. No one can be sure what that change will be—probably change in curriculum and structure, perhaps change in the professoriate and the clientele (already we see the average age of college students changing). Constructive change, however, is only possible under conditions of freedom; constraints are always conservative.

Thus far, the trade union models of collective bargaining borrowed by faculties have served as a constraint on change in higher education. The best hope for adaptation of the trade-union models to one more clearly attuned to change in higher education lies in the restoration of some degree of lost autonomy to the local campus. Given the highly centralized nature of collective bargaining and the extent to which it has led increasingly to extensive state-level involvement in institutional operations, this will be a difficult task. The goal is worth the effort, however, because each public college will serve its special constituency better if it can exercise reasonable control over its own destiny.

Administering a public college these days is a "Catch 22" proposition. Any good college president can cite dozens of ways in which operations on campus could be more efficient, but bureaucratic requirements intervene. At one hearing before an appropriations committee of the Pennsylvania legislature, for example, I testified that due to centralized purchasing requirements it had cost my institution $16 to purchase a $1 plastic bucket for the chemistry department. Paper work and administrative costs ate up the difference. When a state fiscal officer admitted this was no exaggeration, the legislature granted a bit more autonomy in purchasing to the local campuses.

On another occasion, tight control wielded by the state personnel office prevented campus presidents from replacing full professors on leave with people at a lower rank. Due to the intricacies of the control method used, to do so would have necessitated the addition of a new position number to the state's complement of workers, and that would have provided ammunition to political opponents in the upcoming elections. These are examples of mistakes made by central offices or agencies of state government.

Whether we condone such practices or not, it is not realistic to expect central offices of state government to voluntarily abdicate their authority over public colleges when ultimately they are held responsible for them by legislators who have little sympathy for the collegial approach to campus governance. Central officers who must deal regularly with legislators often feel the pressure to act without delay, and the political storms which swirl about their offices are not easy to weather, especially if there is little support from the field. To survive political attacks, central officials need support from campus presidents. To achieve political goals (budget reductions, better management, and so forth), central officers depend on campus presidents to make the necessary changes with the least loss of educational quality and the least negative publicity throughout the state. It follows, therefore, that central officials must give local presidents greater autonomy (flexibility) in choosing alternatives as to where, when, and how the changes shall be effected.

The lesson for presidents in this regard is that those who seek to protect campus autonomy and responsibility must accept the dependent relationship between the two. Only in that context will it be productive to talk about the "proper" locus of responsibility, or a workable division of responsibility, between local and central management. Can we agree that the "proper" prerogatives of the central office relate to level of funding, broad programs to be offered, broad ranges on salaries, ranks, and numbers of students and faculty, and that the prerogatives of the campus president relate to organization, resource allocation, and personnel decisions, or is some other division more appropriate?

The secret of adaptability to changing needs is *flexibility* with built-in structures to retain the basic characteristics of the enterprise—whether it be the operation of a college, a church, or a unit of government. The element of control is essential in any statewide system of higher education, but it must be exercised in such a way that it provides motivation for each of the colleges to use its local decision-making authority in a way that is consistent with overall goals. The issue is not who has power and authority, but the way in which control is applied. *Motivation* is the key word. Central agencies of government must provide incentives or disincentives to adopt behavior patterns that will lead to the accomplishment of desired objectives. For example, if campus presidents believe that their views go unheeded and that collective bargaining agreements have been made without their involvement, they will resent their reduced status and will vent their frustrations by criticizing the agreements and grudgingly implementing their provisions. A partial solution to the problem rests in effective involvement of local campuses before negotiation decisions are made, even if this means that the ultimate decisions are not exactly what the state officials orginally envisioned.

Considerations Prior to Bargaining

When statewide bargaining becomes inevitable for a particular group of institutions, one of the crucial issues will be to decide whether all matters are to be bargained at the state level and if not, which issues are to be handled locally. Bargaining for the Pennsylvania State College and University System followed the first pattern. Before negotiations began, the faculty bargaining agent suggested that the contract leave room for some issues to be settled on an individual-campus basis. This request was motivated by the problems stemming from the disparity in working conditions among the colleges. The union negotiators foresaw difficulty in obtaining statewide benefits and conditions which were at least as desirable as those of the most favored institutions.

Where a contract item might represent an improvement for some colleges, and a loss of benefits at the others, the faculty at the "losing" colleges would be understandably distressed. To avoid this problem, the union proposed to leave certain issues to local negotiations and campus representatives were directed to seek the support of the presidents for this point of view. The union people argued that forcing each campus to give up its local practices with respect to such things as tenure, credit for laboratory supervision, or maximum teaching loads would bring about statewide mediocrity and would roll back advances which had been achieved without collective bargaining.

This view at first had some support from the presidents, and when negotiations began the bargaining agent urged the state to accept the concept at the negotiating table, but the state vacillated. Ultimately the presidents united against local campus negotiating, out of fear of being whipsawed, and the state stood by this position. This was the turning point on centralization and the key to the loss of campus individuality and autonomy which has accompanied collective bargaining at the Pennsylvania State Colleges and University. In retrospect this appears to be another example of presidents taking the wrong action.

The union was correct in its perception that a master contract which detailed virtually every aspect of faculty-college relations would supersede earlier campus policies and outmode the previous working relationship between the faculties and the presidents. Although the union foresaw and lamented the loss of campus autonomy, it was also anxious to avoid the internal problems which any loss of benefits would entail. Had the union known at the outset that it would achieve a contract settlement which, with the exception of a few relatively minor issues, would match or exceed the best existing conditions, it is questionable that the issue of local bargaining would have been advanced with the same fervor.

The Pennsylvania presidents were probably wrong in opposing local negotiations. By their opposition they unknowingly gave up much of the institutional freedom which they had gained from the so-called State College Autonomy Act (Act 13 of 1970). Although they were motivated, in part, by the evident difficulties and potential pitfalls which local negotiations would bring, it may be that their concern for self-preservation outweighed their concern for autonomy. The presidents have decried the loss of flexibility and the increasing centralization of power which have accompanied collective bargaining. But they have done so seemingly without recognizing where the crucial turning point occurred and the contribution which they made to this outcome.

There are important lessons, therefore, to be gleaned from the Pennsylvania experience by those who wish to learn what can be done in advance of bargaining to protect campus autonomy within a statewide bargaining unit. *Lesson 1:* Without disputing Shakespeare's logic that "the play's the thing," it is interesting to note which actors were seeking independence and from whom. In a survey conducted by Lozier and Mortimer (1974) who asked the faculty to state their motives for supporting collective bargaining, local campus administrators did not emerge as the villains. The enemy turned out to be the legislature and state government who were castigated for failing to respond "to the needs of either the Pennsylvania state-owned institutions or the faculty of these institutions" (p. 105).

That disenchantment with local campus administrators was minimal was a predictable finding to anyone familiar with the Pennsylvania situation. Throughout the 1960s, campus presidents in cooperation with their faculty associations had labored with marked success in elevating faculty salaries, encouraging faculty participation in the governance process, diversifying the curriculum, reducing teaching loads, building the necessary plant, and securing needed equipment. But as the 1960s ended, administrators and faculties alike sensed that the locus of general decision-making authority was shifting from departments to campus administration, from the campus to a statewide board, and from the statewide board to the state budget office and the state legislature.

When it became obvious that the state agencies and the legislature were more than a match for campus presidents and their governing boards, the faculty concluded that a countervailing force was needed to offset the power of the state bureaucracy. Consequently, they opted for a bargaining agent which could exercise the necessary clout in dealing with the adversary.

The shift in authority from the campus to statewide negotiators is reflected in numerous provisions of the Pennsylvania State College and University contract. For example, tenure policies previously were developed independently on each campus, usually by faculty committees, and adopted by action of the trustees. Tenure is now detailed by the bargaining agreement and no local policy determination is permitted. Faculty evaluation procedures are prescribed in detail by the agreement, as well as the number of students a faculty member may accept for independent study. These are areas in which local autonomy has been curtailed.

The authority of campus presidents has been circumscribed by other provisions of the contract. Where previously the president had discretionary authority over exceptional salary increments, merit awards to faculty members are now handled largely by faculty committees and include participation by off-campus members. All candidates for faculty appointment must first be recommended by the department faculty. Former faculty members who accepted administrative assignments and now wish to return to teaching duties are subject to department approval. Summer contracts must be issued by a specified date and work load is limited by strict contract provisions. These are examples illustrating ways in which campus presidents lost their prerogatives to hire, fire, and to allocate resources.

Determining the Unit

Bargaining in a statewide system of colleges and universities is no sport for amateurs. Formal, legal negotiation is much more than debate. In a debate each side is polarized and tries to defend its position with logic as strongly as possible. In collective bargaining, depending on what is at stake, more than logic determines the outcome. In many cases, the ability to exert political pressure is at least as much of a factor in winning as logic. For example, under the particular law enacted in Pennsylvania, a logical case for excluding department heads from membership in the bargaining unit was made—the law clearly excludes supervisory personnel. The logic was set aside, however, when the lieutenant governor persuaded the college presidents to drop their opposition to inclusion of the department heads in the faculty unit in exchange for a pledge that the union would abandon its efforts to include administrative personnel. This is an example of presidents failing to unite to exercise what authority they had left.

Subsequently, and without the approval of campus presidents, the state agreed to the formation of a second unit representing administrative personnel. Thus, the union achieved its objectives through political influence rather than trusting its case to logic before the state labor relations board. *Lesson 2:* Beware of all who come bearing gifts. Assumed advantages can be turned into nightmares through naiveté and inept bargaining. Academic integrity, not political expediency, should dictate an institution's position on the issues, and it will probably take a unified group of presidents to successfully fend off political pressures often exerted indirectly through central office staff.

The decision to include department heads in the bargaining unit has had unfortunate consequences for the colleges. Traditionally, academic deans have appointed department heads; but under the Pennsylvania contract, heads are elected by the department, do not owe appointments to a dean and, hence, can be cavalier in their treatment of the dean. To meet their responsibilities adequately, deans need to have a line function in the exercise of authority, but they lack such authority under a structure in which department heads are elected and may be recalled by their colleagues. When the department head is included in the bargaining unit, he is no longer an extension of the dean's office, but rather the focal point for expression of faculty views. The only power base such a department head is assured is political, and this is a shaky base indeed. Frequently, unresponsive department heads are forced out of the leadership role, and "shadow chairpersons" emerge to name the tune to which their departments are already dancing. In such an environment, resistance to change intensifies, even when survival depends on it.

One of the most serious losses is the right of the department head to exercise some discretion in the management of a department. An example is found in the twelve-hour teaching load mandated in the Pennsylvania contract. Everyone knows, of course, that one set of twelve hours is not always equal to another twelve hours, and in the past a department head might vary the load from one person to another in order to maximize the efficiency and quality of the department. This right of management initiative and supervision has been lost in Pennsylvania. Under unionization, twelve hours has become, however artificially, a rigid mechanical determination for one and all.

To overcome the artificiality and inflexibility of a rigid mechanical work-load requirement, a different contract clause needs to be bargained. This would appear to be a contract matter better left to local agreement, since faculty and management would benefit from that approach. The parties in statewide systems should have enough courage to experiment with that approach, because neither party is happy with rigid teaching loads mandated by statewide contract.

When it comes to faculty recruitment, a department head under the Pennsylvania contract has very little to say because hiring is subject to approval of the departmental faculty, so the head is deprived of another means by which direction for the department might be provided. Even the department itself has lost much of its other discretionary powers under the contract. Prior to the agreement independent study was, by unanimous choice of several departments, an integral part of the academic program and voluntarily engaged in by the faculty. The contract has destroyed all that by setting independent study apart as something distinct from the curriculum of a given department, by mandating extra compensation for faculty members involved, and by leaving it to the discretion of management officials as to whether or not it shall be offered. Such special opportunities for students give the institution its vitality, yet are likely to be the first to go when dollars are tight. Should the colleges ever find it necessary to discontinue independent study for reasons of fiscal stringency, many fine academic programs will be seriously affected.

Lesson 3: Keep department heads out of the bargaining unit. Failing in that, however, the vacuum that results from their inclusion in the unit might be partially filled by providing the dean with an associate dean who assumes the traditional supervisory function of the department heads.

Reference has already been made to the early discussions between the state and APSCUF concerning which employees should be included in the initial faculty bargaining unit. All supervisory employees with the exception of department heads were excluded. Those excluded were assistant deans, directors of counseling, financial aid, placement, public relations and others, comprising approximately 10 percent of the college's professional employees.

During contract negotiations with APSCUF, salaries were frozen for nonunion as well as union professional employees. When APSCUF succeeded in negotiating a 35 percent increase in compensation over a three-year period, the "supervisors" moved to organize for bargaining, and APSCUF agreed to represent them. The state argued that it had a "deal" with APSCUF not to organize other supervisors if department heads were included. The labor board ruled that no such "deal" existed because at the time it was made APSCUF had no standing to enter such an agreement. Thus, APSCUF was free to organize the "supervisors" and the state was neatly finessed.

A protracted series of attempts ensued to separate "supervisors" from the management officers of the colleges. State attorneys concluded it would be best to negotiate the matter with the union. Campuses were directed to submit a list of key management officers with the idea that the balance of nonorganized employees would form a second bargaining unit. Somewhere along the line, the idea of a supervisory unit faded and was replaced by a second faculty unit, known as Unit II. Since the Unit II membership list was a negotiated one, it contained numerous anomalies. For example, at one college the head of the department of student teaching was in the original faculty unit (Unit I); at another the director of student teaching was in management. Directors of athletics started out as management officers, moved to Unit II, and then to Unit I—if they wished.

By permitting about half of the original Unit II titles to move into the original faculty unit (Unit I), the state won acceptance of a contract that was far less favorable economically to the remaining employees. The blow to campus morale in general and to the remaining Unit II employees in particular was shattering. Promotion ceilings were imposed on the latter by administrative fiat, totally ignoring their original employment expectations. The colleges inherited a "sweetheart" contract benefiting some 5 percent of its professional employees. The union deserted the remaining unfavored Unit II members, perhaps due to the small size of the unit and to the low proportion of union membership within it. Certainly no great credit for the fiasco reflected on either the state or the union, whose respective negotiators appeared to be more concerned with issues of centralized power than with serving all employees with equity or preserving the integrity of each campus. *Lesson 4:* Presidents need to unite sufficiently to influence decisions significantly.

Some of the disparities of the Unit II contract ultimately were removed during subsequent renegotiation, but lower salaries and promotion ceilings continue in effect for those employees. During the entire episode, campus autonomy suffered serious erosion. Management officers, who are barred from organizing, also absorbed some "lumps." The state clamped a tighter control over their appointment and compensation by creating a system of appointment levels which divorces all future appointees from faculty status. After flirting with the idea of withdrawing tenure and sabbatical leaves from incumbents, the state eventually "grandfathered" them. By a simple stroke of the pen, Pennsylvania has succeeded in creating a situation of unequal pay for equal work—one for incumbents and another for replacements—a situation bound to attract the attention of defenders of equal rights and nondiscrimination.

Negotiating the Contract

Collectively the Pennsylvania presidents represented substantial experience in higher education and an array of talent which was largely ignored in the initial bargaining by the state. That mistake can be avoided elsewhere by making certain that the team is led by people who are familiar with the ethos of higher education. During the first contract negotiations for the Pennsylvania State College and University system, the state's team was headed by a Philadelphia lawyer who had little or no experience with higher education, whereas the union's team was headed by a seasoned negotiator with experience in the Garment Workers' Union. The negotiating sessions convened in Philadelphia—an apt place to articulate a declaration of independence.

After eight months of negotiating, during which the garment worker deftly wrapped the colleges in layer upon layer of textile language and the Philadelphia lawyer became more and more hopelessly entwined, a contract emerged which has been described by some as "a landmark in the annals of labor-management relations" (one could wonder in what sense) and by others as "a disaster in terms of campus autonomy."

Barely a week passed following signing of the contract before the faculty senate in one of the fourteen colleges voted itself out of existence, abdicating its role in governance to the union. The contract had weakened the senate by a redistribution of authority and responsibility for a number of important policy matters including those pertaining to hiring, evaluation, promotion, tenure, and dismissal of faculty members. Specific contract language provided for establishment of committees in most of these areas to advise the management of the college. The senate concluded that its former governance functions had been usurped by the union and decided to withdraw from governance.

The reaction of faculty senates to the advent of collective bargaining varied elsewhere in Pennsylvania. At Clarion State College, where a strong tradition of faculty senate involvement in governance had prevailed and where no more than one-third of the faculty had voted for the union, a different result ensued. In a strategic move, the local union leadership designated the committees of the faculty senate to represent the union in the policy areas already enumerated as well as in the all-important area of the curriculum. So far this marriage of convenience has prospered and the prognosis for continued bliss appears favorable.

Not all the unfortunate consequences reported in the Pennsylvania case can be attributed to the decision on unit determination. Some were the result of mistakes made during the contract writing stage. Even faculty members lament these developments and contend that a union, by its very nature, can not legitimately be concerned with the quality of education since its legal responsibility is to bargain with respect to "conditions of employment." They argue that the union has no business concerning itself with institutional quality except when quality happens to be associated with a faculty benefit. They resent the tendency of faculty unions to try to take over faculty committees, such as a faculty senate committee on courses and programs of study, and to limit membership on such committees to dues-paying members, though obviously there are well-qualified, non-dues-paying members who could serve such a committee very well.

Though such developments are regrettable, the union has also done some very good things. It has dramatically increased faculty salaries in Pennsylvania, and most faculty members very much approve of that. If society wants faculty members to be professionals, then they must be provided compensation similar to that of professionals in other fields. Unionism has also reduced administrative arbitrariness in some quarters, and all of us must approve of that. But gains usually involve some cost, and the price for these gains has been unusually high.

Lesson 5: In those states where enabling legislation is still contemplated, efforts should be made to restrict the purpose of unionization to improvement of faculty compensation and working conditions, and to prohibit the creation of a dual administration and the subordination of educational quality to union power. For those states in which unit determination is still a live option, the costs of the Pennsylvania decision to include department heads are worthy of study. Even those in the contract-writing stage may negotiate contracts that define merit as the basis for salary increments, promotions, and tenure and require management officials to exercise line functions in these matters, as well as in the recruitment of faculty, selection of department heads, and curricular change. Only in this way can the public be assured that quality of the academic process will be protected, that needed flexibility for change will be maintained, and that an adversarial relationship between faculty and management will be minimized. Before unionization, the public could demand the resignation of a president when quality of the institution was unsatisfactory. Under rigid contracts negotiated by central officials under political pressure, the firing of a president may become meaningless, since a new president may be impotent to effect change.

Summarily, it can be said that Pennsylvania has a statewide bargaining system that does a poor job of encouraging campus initiative, local uniqueness, or campus pride. All of these are products of reasonable campus autonomy. The failure can be traced not so much to the phenomenon of bargaining itself as to the manner in which the state chose to carry on the process (1) under the direction of negotiation leaders whose skill and experience was less than that of their union counterparts, (2) without the direct involvement of the management of the institutions where the collective bargaining agreement must be administered, (3) with a kind of ongoing negotiation that establishes a complexity of rules and regulations that amount to state-level rules and regulations in academic matters, such as evaluation and promotion, again with very little representation of the management who must administer and enforce the agreed upon system.

Though centralization was evident before the Pennsylvania colleges ventured into collective negotiations, it cannot be denied that the highly centralized nature of negotiations in the Pennsylvania system has led increasingly to more extensive central state level intervention in college affairs. Though such intervention may forestall economic disaster for weak institutions by reserving sufficient funds to pay negotiated salary and fringe benefits, it denies other institutions the opportunity to engage in serious reformation and experimentation.

Defenders of higher education should heed this "clarion call" by taking the offensive as recommended at the ninth conference of the Western Interstate Commission on Higher Education (WICHE) to forestall further politicization of the university and to reverse the trend toward centralization of power, people, and educational opportunity. Lee R. Kershner (Western Interstate Commission on Higher Education, 1976) was right in urging restraint by those faculty, students, and staff who risk loss of campus autonomy by taking their grievances directly to the legislature and the executive. *Lesson 6:* If campus autonomy is to be protected, faculty and administrators alike must resist excessive detailing of campus organization and operation through the collective bargaining process.

Administering the Contract

The greatest protection for local autonomy is strong and fair administration of the negotiated contract at the local level. In the approach to contract implementation, attitude is of vital importance. The task is to transmute what happens into something viable and productive. A labor contract has a legal status that differs from that of other contracts which are usually binding and final. A bargaining agreement is not so tight. It comes to be interpreted and understood in the process of administering it. Learning to live with it calls for accommodation on both sides.

Administration of a labor contract will be affected in important ways by the language of the contract itself. Since this is treated in detail in Chapter Twelve, the comment here is restricted to the potential impact of contract language on campus autonomy. The Pennsylvania contract language, for example, fails to recognize local internal mechanisms for faculty governance, such as the faculty senate. It provides very limited provision for peer judgment in grievance and dismissal proceedings. The right to a dismissal hearing by one's peers is not stipulated, thereby leaving it to a succession of administrative officers and, ultimately, an arbitrator who may or may not be qualified to cope with complex academic issues to determine whether "just cause" does, in fact, exist for the action taken. *Lesson 7:* The language of a contract should be drawn with care if erosion of basic due-process protection is to be avoided.

Like other legal documents, some labor contracts are written well, and others carelessly. There can be honest differences of opinion as to interpretation of its terms. When disputes arise which cannot be resolved directly by the parties involved, the grievance procedure outlined in the contract will be invoked. Unfortunately, nobody really understands the impact of grievance procedures on academic processes.

Lesson 8: To protect the integrity of the local campus, every effort should be made to resolve disputes at the lowest possible level. It helps to start from the premise that if an employee thinks he has a problem, then, in fact, he has a problem. One should try to get at the facts—what has been violated, who has been discriminated against, how, when, and where? A climate should be established in which the grievant is encouraged to suggest appropriate remedies. Most grievances can be satisfactorily resolved at the local level. In some cases, however, state officials have interfered with that process. In Pennsylvania, for example, when grievances arose over eligibility for promotion, presidents were instructed to reject the grievances, though some presidents believed that the relief sought should be granted. In such cases, presidents are being compelled to act against their best judgment. If a willingness to accept local solutions to problems can be developed, faculty members will be less prone to seek the intervention of external parties, and in the process institutional autonomy is strengthened.

Experience in administering statewide bargaining agreements is quite sparse, which lays all generalizations open to question. It does seem fair to conclude, however, that primary responsibility for administering the contract should rest with local campuses. Wherever a central office has tried to do the job (in Pennsylvania, for example), local campuses have been unable to get timely answers to disputed items of contract interpretation. Consequently, campus presidents have had to act on disputes without knowing in advance if their actions would be sustained if appealed to higher levels. Occasionally a president has been assured of such support only to see it evaporate later. This does not, of course, connote perversity in the nature of central office personnel. The office, with good reason, might wish simply to avoid lengthy litigation. Nevertheless, a serious communication gap exists and efforts to close it have thus far been unsuccessful.

Since it cannot be refuted successfully with any substantial history, I will argue that campus harmony is more likely to prevail when major responsibility for contract implementation is left to the local campus. For local contract administration to succeed, however, faculty and administrators must be willing to accept local solutions to campus problems without resorting to higher authority. Sometimes the most ardent supporter of campus autonomy will turn to higher authority if dissatisfied with a local decision. That is, a faculty member may petition an administrative officer or a faculty committee for a certain action, and if not successful may then seek to reverse the campus result by exerting political influence to obtain legislative or executive intervention at the state level.

The faculty union has been disposed to such appeals during its early years in Pennsylvania. The formation of campus planning commissions is a good example. Each college was instructed by the central office to form a representative committee to develop detailed plans for campus program development. The colleges proceeded to do so in a variety of ways. On some campuses the faculty union was involved in selecting committee members, and on others it was not. The differences in approach related to local governance procedures which existed prior to collective bargaining and also to the degree to which campus union leaders and administrative officers were accustomed to cooperating.

The campus union leaders who were not satisfied with their involvement protested to the state union leaders who then obtained a memorandum from state officials which directed in detail the formation of campus planning commissions, to include the right of the union to select a portion of the membership. This memorandum was issued to the college presidents without prior consultation and clearly demonstrated both a union willingness to use political leverage in seeking certain goals, regardless of the impact upon local autonomy, and the cavalier manner in which state officials entered into such operational details as the appointment of committees. *Lesson 9:* If statewide prescription is to be avoided, campus presidents must find acceptable ways to involve the local union in the decision-making process.

Campus administrators, for their part, have not been above using real or imagined state directives as an excuse for failing to meet some requests from individual faculty members or the faculty union. This, of course, weakens campus autonomy. *Lesson 10:* There should be a vigorous attempt by local college administrators to rectify injustices at the onset of a contract. When a local administration stands by and makes no effort to rectify problems, it is beginning to lose its autonomy by default, and the process will expand. Local management can also lose autonomy by choice by hiding behind the contract, rather than pursuing it vigorously and fairly. Equitable and just treatment for all is the goal that should be pursued by both union and management. If such practice can be established, it will tend to protect campus autonomy.

Contract implementation activities, such as the meet-and-discuss forum, should be structured to permit local issues to be dealt with locally. *Lesson 11:* Those issues permitted at the state level should relate to clarification of existing contracts and should not be new or unresolved bargaining goals of either party. State policies should be kept as broad and nonprescriptive as the contract will permit. If, for example, state financial support for the college must be reduced, the colleges should be given wide latitude in determining their response to this condition. They should not be told, *in detail,* how to reduce expenditures through personnel cutbacks or other devices.

Take the case of retrenchment, which is treated in detail in Chapter Thirteen. Great claims have been made as to the effectiveness of recent union bargaining in Pennsylvania to prevent the retrenchment of eighty-two faculty members. The fact of the matter is that the state was able to retract the retrenchment order because it was based on assumptions that never came to pass. The campus presidents knew that the central office assumptions about enrollments, income, and expenditures for their institutions were inaccurate, but the central office rejected their arguments. In time, the presidents proved to be correct. There are many people who doubt that the state ever really intended to retrench but instead was using retrenchment as a bargaining ploy. The central office, of course, denies that allegation. If that was the case, the union may have precipitated the problem, rather than having solved it.

As a consequence of the agreement reached in Pennsylvania, the fear of retrenchment has been laid to rest for another two years. Some valuable time has been bought for the faculty, but the agreement is more palliative than substantive because it failed to deal with the basic issue—the legitimacy of the goal of nonretrenchment. Everyone knows that the labor market is changing and that higher education is undergoing alterations. Adjustments in staffing are needed to accommodate change and will continue to be needed in the future. There ought to be an orderly manner in which this issue in higher education can be approached that provides reasonable protection for those affected—the faculty members, the students, the institution, and the taxpayers. A rational application at the local college level supported jointly by faculty and management should help to avoid statewide mandates and, in the process, preserve a measure of campus autonomy.

As decisions occur in a statewide bargaining unit, the central office should be prepared to state clearly the objective sought and permit the colleges affected, first to participate in the state's decision-making process and then to choose a path to the desired objective that best fits the institution. In this way the interests of campus vitality and pride can be advanced.

Lawrence K. Pettit

26

Diversity has been a cherished characteristic of American higher education. We hold to the tenet that those in charge of the educational program on a campus are most likely to know what is best for that particular institution. We assume, moreover, that the plural interests of society are served best by variety in higher education as well as in other social institutions.

The principle of shared governance is central to college and university procedures for good reason. Faculty have always been considered professionals for whom it is inappropriate to prescribe rigid working hours or detailed accountability requirements. By definition they are experts in special fields, expected to contribute to the growth of knowledge as well as perform dedicated service in the classroom. Some are more productive scholars and teachers than others and theoretically are rewarded for recognizable merit through peer judgment leading to more rapid promotion and larger salary increases. Collectively, the faculty are given responsibility for academic management. They set the scholarly tone of the institution and determine requirements for admission, passing, failing, honors, and graduation. In these matters

Bargaining Educational Diversity in a Centralized State System

they have traditionally brooked little interference from local administration, let alone distant bureaucrats in the state capital.

When higher education functions in an economy of plenty, meeting the expectations of its students and others by providing the essential educated citizenry and trained manpower for society, there is little reason to expect that the traditional way of carrying out these duties will become suspect. But an economy of scarcity, in concert with changing societal and political conditions, usually sets in motion two forces which threaten the tradition of institutional autonomy. First, the society which supports higher education will ask difficult questions about cost effectiveness. At the risk of squeezing the soul out of campus life, external managers and decision makers shift the meaning of accountability, recasting it in terms of cost accounting, and require a centralization of administrative function and authority.

Second, faculty in search of economic security turn increasingly toward collective influence, both formal and informal. In the 1970s unionization of faculties on some 500 campuses has forced institutional management to the bargaining table. In a multicampus institution, centralized bargaining can easily and quickly erode campus autonomy and vitality. This chapter will describe the Montana approach to centralized bargaining, designed to protect campus autonomy and simultaneously meet requirements of statewide governance.

There is little question that public colleges and universities are going to be increasingly answerable to a central authority off campus. The question is no longer whether that will occur or whether it should. The distinction we need to make is whether or not central authority is essentially an educational figure, answerable to a higher education governing board, selected in a manner similar to the way in which campus presidents are selected, and of sufficient educational perspective to identify with the higher education community. That is, will authority be centralized in the office of a chancellor or commissioner of higher education, or will authority be lodged in the political branches of government? In the latter instance campus autonomy would be threatened not by a higher educational authority, but by a governor's budget officer, the director of a state department of administration, the legislative audit office, a legislative fiscal analyst, a state department of education which is part of the executive bureaucracy, or some other non-higher-education entity. In the interest of logic we need to distinguish between the two. The loss of autonomy in the first instance, by definition, is preferable to the loss of autonomy in the second. As a matter of fact, strong centralized higher education leadership can function as insulation or protection for the campuses by thwarting attempted assaults on their integrity by political decision makers. Collective bargaining poses perhaps the most serious current threat of political intervention in higher education. For example, bargaining in several eastern states has greatly increased the role of political agencies in determining the character of state colleges and universities. Such action appears to have occurred more by thoughtlessness than by design. As a result faculty representatives face more political office holders than educational administrators or trustees across the table. Three or four years ago it was obvious that campus autonomy was being eroded, but the effects of bargaining were not clear. For example, "Institutional autonomy and diversity have undoubtedly been declining during the last decade or two in both the private and public sectors, as governments at all levels have imposed a wide variety of controls over higher education, particularly as part of the price institutions must pay in accepting more and more assistance from public treasuries. It is too early to say that collective bargaining is contributing to this decline" (Carr and VanEyck, 1973, p. 284).

The most critical question, then, is who conducts statewide bargaining on behalf of public colleges and universities? We must also address the question of whether or not campus autonomy should be protected in a multicampus system. At the risk of appearing nonacademic, I should point out that there is a public responsibility to operate a multicampus system in the most efficient, cost-effective manner. Some central authority must be charged with ensuring fiscal accountability through uniformity in accounting and financial reporting procedures. Moreover, in a time of scarce resources, it seems essential that some central authority be charged with continual program evaluation to guard against unnecessary duplication and to ensure that through intercampus exchange of resources, programs can be enriched while duplication is simultaneously prevented. Additionally, in order that there be a *useful* dialogue between the higher education system and political decision makers, it is essential that a central authority prescribe and implement a uniform manner of retrieving, analyzing, and presenting data. Other considerations of central coordination or governance must be preserved, for example, the determination of what programs exist at each institution and the allocation of resources among institutions.

Juxtaposed to these needs are the benefits of preserving campus autonomy in such matters as employment of faculty and nonacademic staff, determination of merit for pay and promotion, program degree requirements, and so forth.

The key, as in any system, is to find the proper mix of centralization and decentralization, or unit autonomy and system integration (Long, 1976). As Adam Yarmolinsky writes, "[T]here is no inconsistency between effective management through large systems and decentralization of major responsibilities to the local level" (1976, p. 74). In the hands of creative and alert administrators, bargaining may be used to attain or maintain this critical balance.

Is it possible to protect campus autonomy with the advent of faculty collective bargaining? There is no longer a single campus point of view, if ever there was one. Faculty collective bargaining has been primarily motivated by economic considerations, that is, to negotiate higher compensation levels and greater economic security. But many faculties have perceived that the bargaining process can become a method of protecting traditional faculty prerogative in a system of shared governance. These faculty members have the goal of locking in decision-making procedures which force local administrators to acknowledge an expanded faculty role. Collective bargaining thus may have created, for many institutions, a conflict model wherein the faculty turns to external authorities to further its economic objectives and simultaneously protect local decision-making prerogatives. In such a situation, the faculty continually must balance campus autonomy on the one hand and improved conditions of employment on the other.

The administrative point of view, as another component of the campus interest, is somewhat different. Although very few college or university administrators believe in low faculty pay, they virtually all hold strongly to the notion that the institution should be able to determine and promulgate its own priorities within broad state requirements. There is an administrative interest, too, in the preservation of merit as the chief ingredient in the formula for allocating rewards (and deprivations) among faculty. A pay scale based only upon across-the-board increments imposed by some external authority negates the local administrative prerogative of making merit judgments. There is a more basic (and, perhaps, selfish) motivation for local administrators to protect campus autonomy in bargaining. If authority patterns and reward structures, along with decision-making procedures, are negotiated between the faculty and some external authority, the role of the local administration may be reduced to ceremony. Surely that bargaining model constitutes an attack on a campus president's sense of efficacy and esteem.

A central authority for higher education, be he called chancellor, commissioner of higher education, or whatever, is beset with countervailing objectives of centralized authority and the preservation of a certain degree of campus autonomy. (I shall use the term *commissioner* here as it corresponds to the situation with which I am most familiar.)

A statewide commissioner is a person without a constituency who straddles that area where politics and academia intersect. He must represent his campuses and champion their interests in the political arena. He is viewed in that role by political decision makers as a spokesperson for the college and university community. In their eyes he is an *advocate,* and his entreaties, therefore, must be balanced by the contrary demands of others. Yet, in his relations with the campuses, he must represent the public, protect the taxpayers' interest, implement mandates of the legislature and the governor, act as spokesperson for a lay board of trustees, and balance the interests of the various campuses, thereby reaching decisions that are seldom satisfactory to any particular party. In such a milieu, a commissioner cannot function with any degree of effectiveness unless he has the resources and impulsion of explicit centralized authority.

Yet it is in the commissioner's interest, also, that each campus have a certain degree of autonomy. His primary responsibility is to preserve the strength and quality of higher education within the system of campuses over which he presides. To the extent that strength is found in diversity (and nearly all of us still believe that) he is impelled to preserve the diversity, freedom, and uniqueness of each campus. From a purely tactical point of view, moreover, the more diverse the institutions under his jurisdiction, the more flexibility the commissioner has in adjusting the claims and demands of the various campuses in order to achieve policy of greater systemwide benefit. In the same vein, greater diversity and autonomy allow the commissioner more latitude in explaining decisions which on the surface appear to favor one campus to the detriment of one or more of the others. To pursue that point, the inevitable diversity in any collection of institutions, from important research universities through an essentially four-year teacher's college, requires the preservation of campus autonomy in order to allocate resources in a manner compatible with differences in character of institution and disparities in faculty credentials.

Finally, it is in the commissioner's interest that there be a degree of campus autonomy sufficient to provide that someone on the campus may be held accountable for faculty quality, academic programs, fiscal integrity, and student affairs. In the absence of such presidential authority, the commissioner and the governing board are faced with the impossible task of administering such matters directly from the central office.

The interest of the regents or trustees in the issue of campus autonomy and its relationship to collective bargaining is similar to that of the commissioner's and, in most respects, cannot be construed as separable from his. He is their agent, and they share his need for a manageable system of campuses. They, too, have a stake in maintaining diversity in an effort to optimize the seemingly contradictory values of expanded opportunity (access) and furtherance of high quality. From their perspective and from that of the commissioner, diversity is essential, but the diverse campuses should complement one another and fit together in a coherent pattern. The first requirement assumes campus autonomy. Achieving the second will necessitate cooperation and some loss of campus autonomy. How does faculty bargaining affect this balance? Or more specifically, trustees should ask what the various effects of different *models* of bargaining on the balance between campus autonomy and system integration are. That should be the central question of our discussion.

Collective bargaining in a multicampus system can pose a threat to campus autonomy. The extreme situation would be one in which a common contract is negotiated for all campuses with a rigid lock-step salary and promotion schedule which does not allow the flexibility to take into account considerations of merit and marketability. If such a standard contract resulted in the graduate faculty at the state universities being compensated at the same level as an essentially nonresearch teaching faculty at a teacher's college, regardless of wide disparities in scholarly productivity and professional credentials, then it would be not only a threat to campus autonomy but an assault on academic tradition. "Many of the early students of collective bargaining have concluded that bargaining will have a negative impact on faculty salary differentials and merit increases and even on selectivity in promotions and tenure grants" (Carr and VanEyck, 1973, pp. 266–267). Even in the absence of a single contract or single bargaining agent for all campuses, local autonomy to some degree is sacrificed insofar as the negotiating authority for management is located off campus. When the commissioner has responsibility for bargaining on all campuses, the president and his administrative team suffer some loss of autonomy. That loss is compounded if the negotiating authority for management is not the commissioner of higher education, but rather, a representative of the governor's office or some other political functionary.

To some extent, however, bargaining can help to bring about greater cohesiveness and reason in a multicampus system, that is, ". . . collective bargaining may become a principal means for bringing a strife-torn academic community back to a welcome condition of stability" (Carr and VanEyck, 1973, p. 1). Say, for example, over the years an irrational pattern of faculty compensation has grown up in a multicampus arrangement so that there is little or no systemwide correspondence between compensation and professional merit, even though there may be fairly rational historical patterns within one or another campus. A single bargaining agent and a single contract, *if it is negotiated successfully in this respect,* could establish a salary scale that does link compensation to professional merit and does bring about greater equity within the system. This would be achieved at the expense of some loss of campus autonomy. If autonomy is enhanced by the means of negotiating separately on each campus in a multicampus system, then it is possible that an irrational pattern may be elaborated. This is particularly a danger if bargaining takes place first or only at those institutions at the lower end of the scale in faculty quality and if salary levels are negotiated at those institutions beyond that which can be met at the other institutions with whatever resources remain.

From what or whom, then, should campus autonomy be protected in a multicampus system? The first answer is *government* at all levels. When nonacademic authorities negotiate with faculty unions, the result is clear diminution of campus autonomy and a constriction of the administrative function on campus. This can be attenuated or elaborated depending upon the scope of the bargaining. The argument on behalf of such a bargaining model is that those responsible for providing the appropriation are also responsible for negotiating the salary level and attendant economic benefits. That argument has some merit if the bargaining can be restricted to broad salary and economic considerations. But even then, nonacademic bargainers from the governor's office or some other political structure are in unfamiliar territory as they contend with the technical matters of professional credentials, merit, and institutional differences in presuming to negotiate a systemwide pay scale for faculties. As the scope of bargaining is expanded, the danger is that external political authorities will endeavor to impose an inappropriate, bureaucratic model of technical work conditions on academic communities in exchange for the model of shared governance vital to the purposes and methods of higher education.

Yet some campus autonomy must be sacrificed for the net effect of bargaining to be an advantage rather than a disadvantage. I have addressed above the requirements of rationality and the preservation of academic tradition in the establishment of faculty pay scales. I have also noted above the requirements of coherence, efficiency, and cost-effectiveness within a multicampus system. At its best, bargaining in a multicampus system can be used to bring about needed reforms. It can be a tool to be used in the interests of returning a directionless grouping of campuses to an academically sound system which is administered in the interest of academic quality. It is conceivable that a commissioner (or chancellor) in charge of systemwide bargaining can bring such a system about.

The argument, in short, is that bargaining by an off-campus authority can be salutary if that authority is a centralized higher education authority and not a representative of one of the political arms of government.

Complete campus autonomy in bargaining within a multicampus system could, in fact, be chaotic. The major consequence of that model would be a reduction in the efficacy and authority of the consolidated governing board. Similarly, if each campus were free to negotiate its own contract, a clear temptation would be to expand the scope of bargaining, using faculty negotiations as a means of legitimizing decisions which countermand policy designs of the trustees and the commissioner. It is not unthinkable in such a circumstance that both sides of the table would work in collusion on some issues to thwart the off-campus centralization of authority.

The Montana Experience

The Montana process of centralized bargaining, with the chief executive of the multicampus system having a representative at each campus negotiation, is unique. With barely over one year's experience, we may offer some indications of how this model works to preserve both the necessary characteristics of local autonomy and those of statewide governance.

The Montana University System is organized into two complex, multipurpose universities, three smaller four-year colleges, and a college of mineral science and technology. The new constitution, which took effect July 1, 1973, created a board of regents with a high degree of constitutional autonomy and authority. Under Article X, Section 9, the regents have full power and authority to manage, govern, and control the university system. The constitution provides further that the regents shall designate a commissioner of higher education and determine his duties and term. The commissioner serves as a single executive head of the multicampus system. He is not regarded as part of the governor's administration, but is appointed by and responsible to the board of regents. Higher education virtually constitutes a fourth branch of government in Montana. The regents, and therefore the commissioner, by statute also have supervisory and coordinating authority over the state's three community colleges, all of whom receive state stipends.

By law, the commissioner of higher education as the agent of the board of regents is responsible for all labor negotiations for the Montana University System. In the nonacademic sphere this involves dealing at present with thirty-eight different bargaining units organized into sixteen unions. Faculty have organized for collective bargaining on three of the six campuses. The NEA affiliate (Montana Education Association) has organized the faculty at Northern Montana College and Western Montana College, both of which are essentially teacher-training institutions. At Eastern Montana College, once a teacher's college, now a more comprehensive institution, the faculty agent is a coalition of the AAUP and the AFT.

On March 8, 1976 faculty at the University of Montana turned down collective bargaining by a vote of 230 for no agent and 191 for AFT. The AAUP, which was eliminated narrowly by the AFT during the first round of voting at University of Montana, has petitioned for an election at Montana State University. There has been little visible activity with respect to faculty bargaining at Montana College of Mineral Science and Technology.

At the outset of faculty bargaining, the commissioner of higher education petitioned for the establishment of a single bargaining unit for faculty at all six campuses. That motion was opposed by faculty on all campuses and was denied by the Board of Personnel Appeals.

That decision, coupled with the statutory language, led to a new experiment in statewide collective bargaining: The statewide governing board has responsibility for bargaining, but must bargain separately with faculty at each campus. From the point of view of protecting campus autonomy, this was fortuitous as the idiosyncratic concerns of each campus, associated with its basic (and unique) character, are more routinely taken into account. Thus, faculty bargaining proceeded on the three campuses separately. Each table team consisted of a member of the commissioner's staff (usually a labor attorney) as chief negotiator for management, assisted by a local campus team which always included the chief fiscal officer and the chief academic officer. By law the students have been represented in the process at each campus also (See Chapter Fourteen).

The process of bargaining separately on the various campuses may be said to protect local autonomy first by retarding a strong impulse toward centralization and integration in areas where such a trend usually causes some apprehension. The systemwide budgetary effects, for example, are (1) a disruption in the trend toward interunit salary equity, and (2) a disturbance in planning a budget cycle. Although the principle of prebudgetary negotiations is sound, it assumes that negotiated levels of compensation can be reached in sufficient time to allow the constituencies on both sides of the bargaining table to form a coalition in the legislature to secure appropriations adequate to fund the contract. Problems arise because it is not possible to control the pace of negotiations, and consequently it is not easy to keep the negotiating cycle and the budget cycle in phase. The problem becomes particularly acute in a multicampus system where budgeting for the system must await completion of labor negotiations on one or more campuses.

There are other budgetary effects as well, which do not bear directly on the issue of campus autonomy, but merit attention—first, the diversion of staff time and financial resources to the effort, and second, the impact of the salaries and associated benefits which have been negotiated. We have computed a price tag for the negotiating process at Eastern Montana College alone at about one-twelfth the commissioner's annual administrative budget. The drain on the commissioner's office budget has been enormous, as there was no special appropriation to accompany the new bargaining responsibility. Yet the cost appears minimal compared to costs reported in more populous states.

Negotiated salary levels have had a predictable effect on campus budgets. A close analysis of the operating budgets reveals that the bargaining campuses have an imbalance between salary expenditures and operating expenditures. Salary increases on those campuses have been negotiated at the expense of supplies, equipment, books, travel, and other items necessary to sustain a quality program.

A second problem inherent in bargaining with three institutions in a six-campus system concerns maintaining common terms, conditions, and privileges of employment. Partially because of a system of planned diversity with an attendant high degree of campus autonomy, each campus experience has been different. For that reason the faculty perspective regarding problems and remedies will differ from campus to campus. Additionally, the perspective of the bargaining agents will differ. A Montana Education Association bargaining agent will perceive conditions of professional employment rather differently from an AAUP or an AFT agent; yet, where there is a single governing board for all institutions, there is considerable merit in striving to bring about some uniformity in the conditions of faculty employment, and the commissioner's spokesperson at each table permits an avenue to bring about this uniformity as rapidly as feasible.

The obverse problem involves table tactics. Simultaneous, but separate, bargaining disposes the faculty agents to whipsaw management by using the benefits negotiated on one campus to escalate the demands on another. The logical product of whipsawing is a group of contracts each of which incorporates the most favorable position, from a faculty point of view, on each topic that has been a subject of bargaining on any campus. Nonetheless, whipsawing can be controlled to a great extent by the central office spokesperson at the table.

The problem of maintaining common salary schedules and ensuring equity between bargaining and nonbargaining institutions could become the most troublesome. Perhaps it is not yet an established axiom, but my intuitive judgment is that the most professional faculties, who would deserve the highest average level of compensation in a system based on merit, are precisely those who are most chary of bargaining. Insofar as the faculties which do bargain are successful, particularly in a context of scarce resources, the resulting salary differentials may invert the distribution that merit would suggest. One check on this is to negotiate a "penalty" for failure to possess a terminal degree. For example, our contract with the faculty at Eastern Montana College has two salary tables, one labeled "With Doctorate" and the other "Without Doctorate." For a full professor with twenty-five years' experience, the difference can be $4,500. Here again the commissioner's representative at the table constitutes a check and can strive to negotiate local conditions to fit into a conscious systemwide pattern.

There is no doubt, moreover, that bargaining is a countervailing force to system reorganization. In the last three years Montana has begun to move toward emphasis on collaborative degree programs and shared resources between and among campuses. Particularly at the graduate level we have directed that programs, wherever possible, be conducted jointly, not only to reduce duplication, but also to enrich programs. We have begun to evaluate a dozen or so models for restructuring the six-campus system. This year the regents adopted a recommendation of the commissioner that Western Montana College merge with the University of Montana. An intercampus committee is at work to recommend integration procedures. The faculty at Western Montana College is organized for bargaining. The faculty at the University of Montana is not. Furthermore, if the University of Montana faculty were to organize, it is a certainty that the Montana Education Association would fare poorly in the selection of a bargaining agent; yet the Montana Education Association is the near-unanimous choice as agent at Western Montana College.

Bargaining may thwart efforts for providing faculty representation at the level of the commissioner's office and the board of regents through an interunit faculty council. That body now is made up of elected faculty delegates from the various campuses, including the chairperson of the faculty senate or his counterpart on each campus. There is considerable emphasis given to coordination between the interunit faculty council and the various senates.

Bargaining may have an impact insofar as it (1) results in a displacement of the faculty senate by the bargaining agent on each campus as far as effective faculty decision making goes, and (2) results in sufficient variations among campuses in the definition of faculty-administration relationships so as to render unfeasible any effective interunit faculty body designed to relate directly to the commissioner and the board of regents.

There is no doubt that the president's role in systemwide decision making is greatly reduced with the onset of bargaining between separate faculties and the state higher education authority. But regardless of what model is used, the president's authority seems destined to be modified by the bargaining process. His general administrative discretion may be reduced. His influence over the establishment of priorities is attenuated. Carr and VanEyck (1973) observe that, "Collective Bargaining may, even under the best circumstances, complicate the lives of presidents (and provosts and deans) and make their jobs more intolerable than many chief executives have found theirs to be in recent years" (p. 256). Campus autonomy is at least threatened to the degree that the role of the president, as campus spokesperson, is weakened.

Within a multicampus system, the process of faculty bargaining on some campuses is going to have an impact on non-bargaining faculty. At some point, the latter may feel compelled to organize for bargaining in order to protect its interests within the system. In a case of financial stringency, where either cutbacks are required or increases in salaries for all systemwide faculty are not possible, and a legal interpretation gives precedence to negotiated contracts over other forms of obligations so that the organized faculty receive salary increases and the nonbargaining faculty do not, we should expect that the latter would probably organize.

To increase coordination we have attempted in Montana to create a centripetal force through the use of a statewide policy team for faculty bargaining. This group consists of three members of the board of regents, the commissioner of higher education, one president, one academic vice-president and the commissioner's chief legal, academic, and fiscal deputies. It is important that either the president or the academic vice-president on the statewide policy team come from one of the campuses where the faculty is not organized for collective bargaining. This ensures that the process of negotiating at any one campus will take into account the impact the decisions will have on the nonbargaining campuses. During negotiations the table teams meet occasionally with the statewide policy team to discuss systemwide ramifications of issues which they are confronting at the table. If it functions well and if the negotiating teams are able to carry out their directives, the statewide policy team could be the device to turn collective bargaining from a disadvantage into an advantage for the system as a whole. It should act in the interests of equity among all campuses, including those which are not involved in faculty bargaining. Although this may be a minor blow to local autonomy, it is not necessarily a negative factor from the campus point of view.

It may be too early to assess the impact in Montana of collective bargaining on institutional autonomy. In any event, the commissioner's assessment is bound to be somewhat different from that of a president or a faculty. A confounding factor is that bargaining has occurred simultaneously with a new statewide governance structure for higher education and several important actions, such as the implementation of uniform accounting, a continual review of programs, which reflect a greater centralization of authority and consequently pose some threat to institutional autonomy.

To some extent, bargaining, because it has been conducted separately on the various campuses, has served to retard budgetary reform, perhaps justifiably, which was designed to have the effect of bringing about greater equity and coherence in the system. Such reform necessarily would be accomplished through the exercise of more concentrated authority in the commissioner's office at the expense of campus autonomy. Thus, a decentralized model of bargaining may become a valid counterbalance against a perhaps too rapid trend toward centralization of authority. Each reader must form his own normative judgment about that.

We have acted consciously to preserve institutional autonomy in several ways. The local table team includes, in addition to the commissioner's representative(s), campus persons designated by the president. In addition to the statewide policy team whose task it is to view the systemwide implications of what goes on at the table, there is also a *local* policy team (separate from the table team) on each campus where bargaining takes place. The local team is designated by the president. The statewide policy team, by including an outspoken president and an academic vice-president, ensures that the campus perspective will be represented. Still, the final authority for the management team is with the board of regents and their agent, the commissioner of higher education. It is not unlike the traditional system of shared governance on a campus where faculty, students, and others share in the decision making, but ultimately the president is responsible.

The protection of campus autonomy in the context of faculty bargaining in a multicampus system is linked to three important variables. First, is there a single consolidated *governing* board or, instead, a *coordinating* council superimposed on several boards? If there is one governing board, losing autonomy to that board through bargaining is not a radical departure from the natural order of things, since the board is the legitimate single authority generally. In a tiered situation where there is a coordinating council in addition to separate governing boards, the loss of campus autonomy is more deleterious. Second, is there a single bargaining agent for faculty on all campuses, or is bargaining performed separately on each campus? A single agent would normally result in a greater loss of autonomy by the campuses. Third, who bargains for management? If it is the commissioner of higher education, chancellor, or other person, the loss of autonomy is at least inside the higher education system. On the other hand, if the bargaining agent for management is part of the governor's executive establishment, then the loss of autonomy is outside the system and likely to be more harmful to the academic enterprise.

All of the results are not in yet for Montana, but I believe we have struck a fairly good balance in attempting to preserve a high degree of campus autonomy and still serve the needs of the governing board and the commissioner of higher education as they engage in the early stages of faculty bargaining on some, but not all, of our campuses. Perhaps the most valid analytical posture to assume toward the relationship between campus autonomy and bargaining at this point is to conceptualize a dynamic process. Accommodations are still being made. The parameters of adjustment are still being tested. In time, after investigating a few years' experience in several states, we should be able to describe and compare with some authority a set of bargaining models and assess their effects not only on campus autonomy, but on a full range of dependent conditions.

Part V

*N*o matter how well or how poorly negotiations and contract administration are progressing, they force almost everyone in the institution to reassess objectives and operational processes. When a union exists to represent faculty, should there be a faculty senate? Should a president consult with a senate? About what? Another worrisome matter is finance. How can the additional costs of bargaining be managed? Can the processes of collective negotiations be improved? Can relationships between union leadership and administration be reformed after years of adversarial confrontation? Above all else, the question that bothers a campus executive is whether or not a president can really preside when by law the faculty has legally formed its own organization and elected its own leaders.

President Joseph J. Orze, also a certified and practicing arbitrator, provides a sanguine, but pragmatic, analysis (Chapter Twenty-Seven) of appropriate relationships vis-à-vis senate, administration, and union. Vice President Neil S. Bucklew, who master-minded labor-management

502

NEW OPPORTUNITIES
FOR LEADERSHIP

❦❦❦❦❦❦❦❦

relations for many years at Central Michigan University and who has been commissioned by the ACBIS in Washington, D.C. to make the first comprehensive survey of the costs of academic collective bargaining in a single institution, shares with the reader his insights as to costs and how to manage those costs (Chapter Twenty-Eight). William R. Walworth is a college personnel administrator who handles faculty contracts along with those for service personnel unions. He sees the need for improving and coordinating union negotiations through institutional self-study.

The book ends, as it starts, in a call for leadership that transcends personal and private interests. President Leland Miles, who inherited a faculty strike threat before he even assumed the presidency of the University of Bridgeport, discusses the impact of faculty unionization on other university constituencies together with some thoughts about perspective, responsibility, and unity.

Joseph J. Orze

27

The college or university faculty which elects a collective bargaining agent as its exclusive representative, whether knowingly or not, has voted at the same time for a change in the ecology of its institution. For some, the process of change will be gradual and barely perceptible. For others, it will be as rapid and drastic as the impact of a blizzard. For all, it will be different, possibly better, maybe worse; but it will never again be the same as it was the moment before the vote in favor of a collective bargaining agent was tallied. There may be no physical changes in the institution and none in the composition of the faculty, but the academic environment will be altered, and the faculty's relationship with it, individually and collectively, will be redefined.

The most significant change will be an increase in the formal faculty influence over campus decisions. Other changes may include a shift in administrative roles and postures in relation to the

Working with
the Faculty Senate
in a Bargaining Context

faculty, a tendency toward centralization of administrative decision making, the formalization of communications between faculty and the administration with a gradual atrophy of informal lines of communications, and the development of an increasingly adversarial relationship between faculty union leadership and the administration.

The key to all changes is the formally contractualized power which collective bargaining brings to a unionized college or university faculty. It is faculty power with a legal imprimatur, which is new to both faculty and administrators who must live and work with it.

Prior to faculty collective bargaining in colleges and universities, faculty power was unevenly distributed within most institutions and exercised primarily through departments. Strong departments exerted the most influence in academic decision making through dominant roles on faculty committees, leadership in the faculty senate, and a generally more aggressive approach to their interactions with the administration. In the sense that they called attention to themselves in a variety of ways, meritorious or not, such departments received disproportionate shares of space, equipment, travel money, new positions, and other operating items. In prestigious institutions in which almost all departments had this kind of influence based upon their academic strengths and in which the institutions had ample resources for them all, we had the best examples of what has historically been known as faculty power.

Faculty senates functioned quite well in such a setting. As the representative body of the combined faculties of an institution, the faculty senate advised the president and the administration regarding academic policy. The strength of its influence, the combined faculties' power, often was instrumental in the final administrative decision at which it was directed. For a college or university whose faculty collectively possessed such advisory power, the faculty senate appeared to be an ideal democratic instrument to deal with matters of policy which had broad institutional implications while maintaining departmental powers to influence the administration in its allocation of resources and other departmental matters. It is no surprise that faculty senates have historically been considered strong and effective bodies on campuses of the nation's most prestigious private, independent colleges and universities and at its large, strongly research-oriented public universities.

At less prestigious schools, especially in the public sector, a tradition of a strong and effective faculty senate would more than likely be the exception and not the rule. It is at institutions such as these that faculty collective bargaining has made its strongest inroads into postsecondary education. This is clearly illustrated by the fact that of the 482 unionized campuses in the United States as of February 1, 1976, 416 (86.5 percent) were public institutions with 305 (63 percent) of them being two-year colleges, predominately community colleges, and approximately 20 percent being former state teachers' colleges or emerging universities (Kelley, 1976). Faculties at such colleges and universities recognized collective bargaining as a way of formally influencing campus decision making and voted for unionization as a vehicle for having their voices heard and heeded regarding the affairs of the institutions of which they were a part. Collective bargaining became synonymous with faculty power on the unionized campus, and to faculties un-used to working with it, the effects were often heady.

Whereas most faculty senates are advisory bodies whose influence is limited generally to matters of academic policy and governance, the influence of the faculty union is that of an equal partner in a bipartisan decision-making process, and the scope of its influence is as broad as it can convince the administration to let it be, but in no instance less than what enabling legislation said it must be. Decision-making entitlement represents real exercisable power, and it is this factor more than any other that marks the distinction between the influence of a faculty senate and that of a faculty union on a college or university and its functioning.

The Legal Powers of the Union

Contractualized faculty power is not limitless. It has clearly defined minimum boundaries stated in the enabling acts of the various states which provide for faculty collective bargaining. These minimum boundaries include the mandatory subjects for bargaining which must be negotiated in good faith if either the union or the administration wishes to bring them to the bargaining table. The most common mandatory subjects for collective bargaining, faculty and other, are wages, hours, and terms or conditions of employment. Wages and hours are self-explanatory and readily understandable as mandatory subjects. Terms or conditions of employment are ambiguous. From a union point of view, everything which is not covered by wages and hours is a term or condition of employment. From a management point of view, only what cannot be defended as a management right and must be included for negotiation is a negotiable term or condition of employment. It often takes a neutral third party, such as the national or state labor relations board, to clarify what terms or conditions of employment must be negotiated. Therefore, there is no consensual agreement as to what constitutes terms or conditions of employment for all unionized faculties or even for all states.

Although the scope of bargaining is treated at length elsewhere in the book, it must be emphasized here that the legal powers of the union extend only to the mandatory subjects for collective bargaining that the administration must negotiate with it. The union has no legal right to bargain for anything beyond these mandatory subjects. Whatever additional powers the union may gain at the bargaining table can only be achieved if the administration is willing to share one or more of its managerial rights with the union. The administration controls the scope of negotiations, and, in so doing, it determines the actual limits of the legal powers of the union. As indicated previously, unions will attempt to extend the scope of bargaining as broadly as employers will allow them to, but the employer always has the right to say no to any nonmandatory demand for negotiation. Should a nonmandatory demand be brought to the table by the union, the employer can reject negotiating it and retain the managerial right to take unilateral action on the matter as he may desire, or he may agree to extend the powers of the union by negotiating the demand.

A word of caution and advice is needed. Once a subject has been bargained, it is almost impossible for an employer to remove it from subsequent negotiations if the union insists upon retaining it. Therefore, unless there is a sound, well-researched, and carefully considered reason for doing otherwise, the best posture for an administration to assume, especially for a first contract, is that only mandatory items will be negotiated with the union. Such a posture respects the legal domain of the union while allowing the administration the choice of sharing those powers it may elect to share with the faculty whether it be through a faculty senate, the union, or some other representative body of the faculty.

The Legal Powers of the Faculty Senate

Historically, faculty power has been concomitant with the faculty's credibility as an advisory body. When faculty made decisions about institutional policy, it was because administrative authority was delegated to a representative faculty body. The responsibility, authority, and accountability for running a college or university rests in the collective hands of its governing board be it public, private, elected, appointed, county, state, or otherwise; thus only through the delegation of its powers can a board allow persons, such as its chief executive officer, or groups, such as the faculty senate, to share in its management functions. Prior to the advent of faculty collective bargaining, faculty did not possess legal, contractualized, decision-making power regarding the management of the school of which they were a part. However, faculty did possess certain legal powers generally limited to matters of academic standards, policies, and procedures and generally exercised by a representative body such as a faculty senate either through the charter of the college or university which stated the role of the faculty as an advisory body in academic matters or through various policies of the board of governors or trustees. In addition, the president of the institution, acting as the board's chief executive officer, could delegate to the faculty certain powers delegated to him by the board. The legal powers of the faculty senate normally can be found enunciated in the constitution of the senate and the faculty handbook of the college or university where it functions. With their acceptance and approval by the board of governors or trustees, they become legal documents of the institution, a part of the board's policies for the institution to live with and by.

As advisory bodies, faculty senates have traditionally exerted their strongest influence in academic areas, such as the setting of standards and policies for admission and retention of students, grading and academic regulations, graduation requirements, honorary degrees, academic awards and related academic concerns. In addition, they have served as the forums for faculty debate on campus and extracampus issues ranging from censorship of campus publications to the ideological stance the institution should take regarding space exploration and research. Their concerns have ranged from the concrete to the philosophical, and their influence as advisory bodies has shown as much variance. Their traditional role as advisors on academic matters to the administration is one that would greatly expand the scope of bargaining if it were allowed to be assumed by the faculty unions, and yet, academic matters are too much within the legitimate realm of faculty concerns to allow them to become administrative prerogatives. Some representative faculty body must concern itself with academic matters, and it makes great sense to have such matters identified as the primary domain of the faculty senate. This still leaves a lot of room for debate as to where curriculum committees, academic calendars, faculty personnel recommendations of various sorts, and other, not-so-easy-to-define, academic-related, yet possible working, conditions can best be dealt with. These and many other "grey" areas within the traditionally shared or permissible-for-negotiation milieu become the negotiable items. Sometimes the

union, the senate, or, possibly, an agreed-upon group or structure
outside of either organization becomes responsible for curriculum
review and approval at the department, school or division, and college or university levels.

In addition to gaining its legal powers through the charter
of the college or university, a faculty senate can achieve legal status
on a campus through inclusion in the collective bargaining agreement between the faculty union and the board. At Southeastern
Massachusetts University a faculty senate existed prior to collective bargaining and has continued in operation in the seven years
since. Union and senate leadership was often interchangeable,
and though there was a period during which the senate almost dis-
banded, it is operating today with a clearly defined mission which
is included as an article within the faculty collective bargaining
agreement. The article delineates not only the objectives of the
senate, but it also includes its constitution, its membership, and the
method of members' election, particulars on meetings and standing committees, and procedures for senate recommendations. The
entirety of the article had previously been worked out as an agreement between the faculty senate and the president of the university with input from others on campus as well. Its inclusion in the
union contract can be viewed as potentially beneficial or harmful
depending upon one's affiliation and point of view. The verdict,
as the senate president expressed it to me, was dependent upon
the good will and cooperation of the union, the senate, and the administration. In his words, "Procedures are fine, but the people
involved are more important" (telephone interview with Dr. Ronda
DiPippo, July 19, 1976). There had been concern on the part of
the senate leadership that the senate would be assimilated into the
union, like a committee, but this development did not take place.
Only time will tell how well such a senate will be able to function
and retain its identity within the contract and by itself outside the
union.

Some Observations

Although the specific advantages and risks of the Southeastern Massachusetts faculty senate's inclusion within the collective bargaining agreement are unknown at this time, some observations can be made regarding the placement of a faculty senate

or any reference to it in a collective bargaining agreement. From the vantage point of many varied professorial ranks, two levels of deanships and the presidency of a college as well as having negotiated faculty contracts and being active as an arbitrator and conciliator, I see no advantage for a faculty senate or any reference to it to be included in a collective bargaining agreement if it wishes to maintain its identity as a separate and distinct faculty body. The risk is great. Since a collective bargaining agreement is a contract between an employer and a union, everything that is included in it is legally under their joint purview. A senate or reference to it which is written into a contract can also be written out and thereby make the senate's future existence either doomed or precarious. As it has been proposed that there are no advantages to the inclusion of a reference to a faculty senate in a collective bargaining agreement, it is proposed that there is only one risk. It has been stated before, but it needs reinforcement. Everything that is included in a faculty collective bargaining agreement is legally under the joint purview of the administration and the union. There is no identity for personnel matters outside of the contract.

The Faculty Union/Faculty Senate Relationship: Three Possibilities

In Massachusetts, when the state college system was negotiating its first contracts with its member colleges' faculties, it was nonpermissible to bargain over salaries. As a result, to provide substance for the negotiations as well as for philosophical reasons, the system introduced governance to the bargaining table and thereby greatly extended the scope of bargaining for its future negotiations which occurred after the passage of the 1974 comprehensive public employee collective bargaining law which made wages a mandatory subject. The introduction of governance to the bargaining table has major implications for a faculty senate on a unionized campus, because it legally places the senate's turf in academia within the province of the union as the legal and exclusive representative of the faculty. The term "exclusive representative" is a common one in the recognition clauses of most faculty collective bargaining agreements. The idea of exclusivity creates a steady expansion of union concerns, a "creeping expansionism" (Kemerer and Baldridge, 1975, p. 149), which, when coupled with an administration's willingness to bargain the structures and processes of campus governance, can be the end of a faculty senate.

The studies that Kemerer and Baldridge have done on faculty unionism indicate the "prognostications abound about the future of senates in the face of union encroachments. Some are unclear, some are hopeful, but most are pessimistic" (1975, p. 50). Though pessimism may be the dominant mood on campuses which are facing or will soon face this issue, faculty unionism does not automatically signal the demise of a campus' faculty senate; however, it is almost a certainty that the ground rules for their coexistence will enunciate changes in the role of the faculty senate so that it will not conflict with the prerogatives of the union. Garbarino (1975, pp. 141–151) suggests that there are three basic relationships which may evolve between faculty unions and senates: competitive, cooperative, and cooptative.

It is difficult to imagine the benefits of a situation in which a faculty senate and a faculty union would interact in a competitive relationship. To be competitive, each body would have to have equally strong support within the faculty to vie for participation in the campus' decision-making processes. The likelihood of such equally strong support is slight, particularly where the union has contractual rights as the exclusive bargaining representative of the faculty. Should such equally strong support exist on a campus, the implications of turf referred to previously will grow in importance and intensity. While the dispute rages, the institution will suffer, unable to proceed with its ongoing business, unchallenged by one body or the other. If a contest should develop between a faculty senate and a faculty union, it is a strongly shared conviction that the result would be in the union's favor and the almost certain demise of the senate. (Gershenfeld and Mortimer, 1976, p. 49; Kemerer and Baldridge, 1975, p. 142). I think competition can be healthy and desirable in the business world of free enterprise, in athletics and possibly in affairs of the heart, but it has no place and can only be counterproductive in the governance and functioning of a college or university.

If the point of view that competition is not an appropriate relationship for a faculty senate and a faculty union can be accepted and if Garbarino (1976) is correct in his suggestion of three basic relationships for the two, let us investigate the implications for working constructively with a faculty senate in instances where the union elects either a cooptative or a cooperative relationship. The union determines the relationship, if any, which will be developed with the faculty senate because the union has a contractual relationship with the administration; and in a competitive situation, the union would have to be favored to win over the senate. Since it presents the fewer alternatives in terms of a successful coexistence of a faculty senate and a faculty union on a campus, the feasibility of a cooptative relationship will be investigated first.

When something is coopted, it is preempted, appropriated, or seized for oneself before others (Morris, 1969). In this sense, a cooptative relationship of a faculty union with a faculty senate can have only two possible alternatives. (1) The union can replace the senate and thereby have it abolished, or (2), it may selectively elect the areas of concern which it will assume and those it will leave for the senate; in the process, the union does not abolish the senate but sufficiently emasculates it to suit the union's purposes. Either way, in a cooptative relationship the union will assert itself as the dominant force in faculty decision making. This fact is vividly illustrated by what happened to the faculty senates in six of fourteen state colleges in Pennsylvania as the result of collective bargaining. Two senates were abolished and four others were described "as playing little or no role in decision making" [and performing] "little more than service, forensic and/or social functions." (See Gershenfeld and Mortimer, 1976.) In the Massachusetts state college system, faculty representatives in the campus governance system are selected by the campus union as a result of bargaining over governance. The senate with its elected representatives which existed prior to collective bargaining has been replaced by a multi-level tripartite governance structure in which the faculty representatives are appointed by the union.

Obviously, cooptation is not a viable means for working constructively with a faculty senate in a collective bargaining context. If the possibility for doing so exists, it will have to be predicated on the existence of a cooperative relationship between the faculty union and the faculty senate. The senate is generally not equipped to compete with the union, nor would it be in the best interests of the institution for it to do so. It will be emasculated or abolished should the union elect to coopt its functions; therefore, it must cooperate if it is to coexist with the union and contribute to the vitality and general welfare of the college or university.

Developing a Cooperative Relationship
Between the Union and the Senate

If true cooperation is to be developed between the faculty union and the faculty senate, the ground rules for its becoming must be established and clearly understood by both bodies and the administration. Although it is generally the best practice to have collectively developed ground rules so that they will be understood and effectively implemented, one must first identify the legally mandated scope of the union's bargaining by studying the enabling act under which it gained recognition and any court or labor relations board decisions which may relate to it when considering the ground rules for union and senate cooperation. Such a study enunciates the previously discussed mandatory subjects which must be bargained with the union. Undoubtedly, the union will view these mandatory subjects as the minimum boundaries of their concerns and will look upon all permissible subjects as potential items for the bargaining table. Bear in mind the concept of "creeping expansionism." It is in the broad realm of permissible subjects that the possibility for union-senate cooperation exists. Herein are included the variety of administrative responsibilities and authorities delegated to the faculty senate and academic committees, which can be broadly translated as the institution's collegiality, as well as those areas which have been retained as management rights.

In what may prove to be a landmark decision for academic collective bargaining at the collegiate level, the New Jersey Public Employment Relations Commission (PERC) in response to a petition brought before it jointly by Rutgers, The State University and the Rutgers Council of American Association of University Professors decided that

> there is no reason why systems of collegiality and collective bargaining may not function harmoniously. [The decision identified both collective bargaining and collegiality as concepts which] deal generally with the employer-employee relationship. [Collective bargaining does so by means of a formal statutory process, while] collegiality is essentially a system that has developed historically at the University and at many other similar institutions throughout the country

> *whereby certain functions generally performed by management, both public and private, are either shared with, or even entirely delegated to, groups of faculty members. [In its decision, the Commission emphasized that] the fact employee involvement in management functions is an historical reality at the University does not raise a given issue to the level of a "grievance" or a "term and condition of employment" if it is not otherwise so, [and] the University is free to continue to delegate to collegial entities whatever managerial functions it chooses, subject, of course, to applicable law (PERC No. 76-13).*

The Rutgers decision indicates the legality of the administration working with nonunion faculty groups on campus. In 1974 the State of Montana passed a higher-education collective bargaining act which specifically addressed the faculty senate/faculty union question in no uncertain terms with language that stated that collective bargaining shall not interfere with "the right of the faculty senate or similar representative bodies of faculty, or the committees thereof, from consulting with and advising any unit administration concerning matters of policy" (Kemerer and Baldridge, 1975, p. 142). The fact that it is permissible does not necessarily mean that it is possible or desirable. Only the particular chemistry of an individual campus can answer that. A history of good intrafaculty relationships and general faculty satisfaction with the processes for addressing academic issues would be of paramount importance to the feasibility of an administration working with a faculty union as well as other faculty groups, including a senate, in the decision-making processes of the institution. A faculty senate's productive coexistence with a faculty union depends a great deal on whether or not the senate, the union, or both perceive the senate as having a scope of interest which encroaches upon, or interferes with, the union's perceived scope of interest as well as its statutorily defined scope of bargaining. Stress is again placed upon productive, effective coexistence of a faculty union and a faculty senate, because although it may be legally permissible and even personally desirable on the part of some administrato to have both a union and a senate on campus, it may be functionally detrimental or even destructive if an atmosphere for cooperative coexistence does not exist or cannot be developed within the faculty. If it does exist or there are indications that it may be developed, the administration, with the president in the role of prominence, must diplomatically lead a tripartite effort to establish the ground rules for campus decision making that lies outside the mandatory scope of the union and that respects the legitimate concerns of all parties including the nonnegotiable rights of management which cannot be shared with either the union or the senate.

The ground rules should not only establish the scope of involvement in campus decision making for all parties, they should include the structure and processes for doing so. Although it is not the subject of this chapter, attention needs to be paid to the concerns and roles of students in campus decision making. It would be prudent to have student involvement in the ground-rules effort to address their concerns and contribute to the development of a total campus governance and decision-making system. As one of the three major constituencies of a college or university, students need to be actively involved in the development and implementation of the decision-making processes which will affect them. The wise president will insist on student involvement at the grass roots level of any ground-rules development. Without student involvement, a vital element in effective campus communications has been ignored, and the chances for effective implementation of any agreements have been reduced when they could have been strengthened. Aside from the mandatory subjects for bargaining between the union and the administration, there are no absolutes regarding the special domains of either a senate or a union. As noted earlier, even what is mandatory varies from state to state, and some schools, such as Central Michigan University, have chosen to limit bargaining with their faculty unions to only what is statutorily required, while others, such as Southeastern Massachusetts University, have used collective bargaining to virtually restructure their institutions. In between the two extremes are unionized campuses where the union domains exhibit the design consistency of a patchwork quilt, some repeated patterns but with a great deal of diversity.

The specifics of what shall be included in the agreed-upon domains of the faculty senate and the faculty union will depend upon several factors including the past history of performance by the faculty senate, the mandatory subjects which the administration must negotiate with the union, and a shared commitment to developing a conducive environment for a productive and effective senate-union coexistence. Once the roles of each are clearly defined, understood, and agreed upon, the administration, and particularly the president, will need to work diligently to ensure that effective lines of communication and interaction are established and used to achieve the harmonious functioning of collegiality and collective bargaining that the Rutgers PERC decision felt was possible. Care should be taken to address appropriate concerns to the appropriate body, respecting the boundaries of each. If there are concerns or issues of a general nature which do not specifically fall within the province of the union or the senate, the president should not hesitate to confer with union and senate leaders jointly to gain their views and to help him plan, act, or react in situations where this joint counsel could prove beneficial. If the special concerns of each organization are respected and dealt with properly, the president can use joint conferences with the leadership of both groups to strengthen their interrelationships as well as to provide himself counsel. In fact, periodic meet-and-confer sessions just to share concerns and ideas can be important to the development of the environment for effective coexistence on the campus.

The campus president is the most important person in the development of an effective cooperative working relationship between the faculty union and the faculty senate and in establishing the overall climate for personal and group interaction on the campus. The attitudes projected by the president are reflected in the attitudes of his administration and reacted to by faculty, students, staff and extracampus people. The president's role is a critical one in developing positive attitudes for effective cooperation, for opening and using lines of communication which flow freely throughout the campus, for overseeing the implementation of policies and agreements, and for generally serving as a mediator and catalyst for gaining the most effective cooperation among people and groups that is possible. Through his personal relationships with student and faculty leaders, the president sets the tone for their interrelationships. Realizing the variations in areas of responsibility and other concerns of individuals and groups, the president must work hard to respect the special concerns and domains of each. Of course, this sensitivity could and should be extended to include the student senate, the assembly of administrators and any other groups and persons.

A Point of Emphasis

Stress must be placed on the need for the president in a leadership role to coordinate the development of processes, procedures, and timetables for the implementation of the union contract, the senate's role in campus governance and decision making, the students' role, and the interrelationship of them all. Too often, agreements are considered to be completed once they have been ratified. Nothing could be further from the truth. In reality, an agreement just begins once it is reached and from then on careful attention must be paid to its effective implementation (Orze, 1974, pp. 15–17). This can only be realized if everyone involved understands the union contract and the senate's constitution. When little attention is paid to the development of such an understanding, it is to the detriment of institutional unity and purpose. The president must be a leader in this effort.

Comments and Suggestions

The chapter began with reference to a change in the ecology of a college or university as the result of collective bargaining. It has considered the scope of bargaining from both a union and administrative viewpoint and has emphasized the dominant influence of the union in the development of any possible relationship with a faculty senate. We investigated Garbarino's (1975) three suggested modes of such a relationship, and we concluded that if coexistence were possible it would have to be in a cooperative relationship. The need to develop ground rules for such a cooperative productive coexistence, with the president in a leadership role, led to the formulation of possible roles for each organization which emphasized academic affairs for the faculty senate and the mandatory subjects of bargaining as the minimum scope of the union with tripartite negotiations recommended to further define the roles of each. The reader may wonder whether or not it is possible to develop an environment conducive to the productive coexistence of a faculty union and faculty senate on his campus, since the article obviously emphasizes the dominant role of the union in the determination of any relationship with the senate that might be developed. The emphasis was not meant to dissuade the reader, but rather, to make him recognize the problems inherent in working constructively with a faculty senate in a collective bargaining context. The senate has a vital role to play on campus in representing the faculty regarding academic standards and policies. The role is too important to the educational viability and vitality of the institution to allow its abdication or to permit other than a representative body of the entire faculty jurisdiction over it. The challenge is to create the environment in which the senate can perform its role effectively in harmonious coexistence with its union counterpart and thereby readjust the ecological balance of the institution. To help achieve this, the following suggestions are offered:

1. As a starting posture for collective bargaining, limit negotiations with the faculty union to mandatory subjects only.
2. Clearly define the domain of the faculty senate focusing upon academic concerns.
3. Respect the specific domains of each organization.
4. Develop open lines of communication throughout the campus and its constituencies.
5. Establish a representative faculty union/senate steering committee to deal with nonunion-nonsenate concerns and also to share ideas and viewpoints. *Include students.* Their voices and views are important and necessary.
6. Meet with the joint steering committee as well as the leadership of the individual groups on a regular basis, not just to solve crises.
7. Give special attention to the implementation of agreements. Work at making them work by establishing the necessary procedures, processes, timetables, and personnel assignments to accomplish the task.
8. Build strong positive personal relationships with union, senate, and student leaders. The group relationships will reflect the personal relationships.

Neil S. Bucklew

Academic collective bargaining represents a significant cost factor for an institution of higher education which has adopted this decision-making model. These costs are primarily institutional or organizational and that is the focus of this chapter. However, there are costs other than administrative that are important and worth special note.

One continuing expenditure is the cost of being informed of the impact of bargaining even when one's particular university is not organized. Collective bargaining has enjoyed a rapid growth pattern in higher education during the past half decade. Over 300 institutions of higher education with about 500 campuses are now unionized. The growth pattern is stable, and decertification (moving from union status to nonunion status) is extremely rare. Contemporary university administrators are required to stay abreast of collective bargaining developments as an aspect of being compe-

Controlling the Costs
of Bargaining

tent managers. Not all institutions will unionize, but the potential is clearly evident. The cost of general administrative awareness is considered in more detail in the chapter that follows.

Another cost consideration to keep in mind is the cost of benefits or services not realized because of the presence of collective bargaining activity. Collective bargaining is a process that demands and uses resources and energy. This is in addition to the costs stipulated in the contract; these are processing costs. For each such expense, it is important to remember the possible alternate uses to which these resources could have been allocated. These alternate uses are denied. This represents a real cost of collective bargaining. The cost may be a computer program dedicated to costing contract demands instead of an improvement in the computer-based registration process. It may be a series of bargaining team preparation meetings instead of a series of student advising confer-

521

ences. The list is infinite. These processing costs represent a significant indirect impact; they are services not rendered or potential not fulfilled.

A preliminary observation about the cost of bargaining settlements versus the cost of these matters associated with nonunionized campuses is in order. Do the costs of negotiated faculty wage settlements exceed those of institutions where compensation is determined in a different manner? Traditional analysis in the private sector indicates that the answer is basically affirmative in the short run, but the difference is not significant over the long run. Public sector analysis has not been as clear. There has only been limited study of this question in the context of academic bargaining in higher education. Robert Birnbaum in a study reported in 1974 at the Second Annual Conference of the National Center for the Study of Collective Bargaining in Higher Education found that the salary levels of unionized schools exceeded those of comparable institutions that were not organized (Birnbaum, 1974). A later study by William Brown and Courtenay Stone for the Association of California State University Professors arrived at a different conclusion (Brown and Stone, 1976). Their study found no significant difference between the salary patterns of unionized and nonunionized institutions. They concluded that there was no evidence of general gains in compensation for unionized faculties as compared to nonunionized faculty. But many people question the validity of these studies suggesting that additional study of this basic question is needed. One final comment on costs other than basic organizational factors is important. Not all of the costs associated with collective bargaining are new or incremental. In some ways collective bargaining is simply a new way to deal with matters that are already being considered through established processes. The subject matter of bargaining is not new; only the process. Therefore, in considering costs of collective bargaining, it is important to remember that there are already costs associated with determining these matters.

These random observations on the cost of collective bargaining may assist in analyzing this important new phenomenon of higher education. The focus of the review that follows is the administrative or organizational cost of academic collective bargaining. These costs will be considered in the context of different stages of collective bargaining: the periods prior to unionization, during an organizational period, during collective bargaining negotiations, and the period of contract administration.

Stage One: The Period Prior to Unionization

Although academic collective bargaining will not extend to all institutions of higher education, it is clear that many universities will adopt this decision-making system. Universities will find it necessary to stay current. This will involve the maintenance of basic reference material regarding academic collective bargaining. The costs involved are not prohibitive, and many of them can be accomplished through institutional membership and use of resources currently available through higher education associations.

Relative to managing this cost, it should be noted that the dollar expense is not lost once unionization, bargaining, and contract administration have commenced. Rather, the materials produced become valuable library resource material which can be continually updated at modest cost.

Orientation of University Administrators

One way of staying current is to assure that university administrators who have a policy role in the institution are well oriented to the policy implications of academic collective bargaining. Attendance at special conferences will be one way to introduce university administrators to this phenomenon. Several organizations have annually sponsored special subject conferences on academic collective bargaining. They include the CUPA and the National Center for the Study of Collective Bargaining in Higher Education (NCSCBHE) at CUNY. Most of the national conferences in higher education now include special sessions on academic collective bargaining. This allows university administrators to develop an understanding of academic collective bargaining as part of their general pattern of conference attendance. Some institutions of higher education have used consultants as a way of accomplishing this general orientation. This has the advantage of orienting the administration of a university as a team. The resource person or persons used as consultants can also tailor their presentation to the particular circumstances of the university involved. Names of consultants can be obtained from the NCSCBHE at CUNY or from the Academic Collective Bargaining Information Service (ACBIS) in Washington, D.C.

In dealing with tailor-made consultant programs, an administration would be well advised to shop around since some organizations and their programs may be keyed to industry or to elementary-secondary education. In addition, there may be times of the year when services are least costly. Finally, two or more institutions could join together in sponsoring a program and thereby spread the cost. (Note: For a detailed analysis of procedures and devices for educating staff see Chapter Six.)

Reference Materials

Another form of general information on academic collective bargaining is general reference materials. In addition to a series of special articles on this topic, there have been approximately a half dozen general survey books. The more standard book references are: Carr, R. K. and VanEyck, D. K., *Collective Bargaining Comes to the Campus,* Washington, D.C.: American Council on Education, 1973; Duryea, E. D. and Fisk, R. S. (eds.), *Faculty Unions and Collective Bargaining,* San Francisco: Jossey-Bass, 1973; Garbarino, J. W. and Aussicker, W., *Faculty Bargaining: Change and Conflict,* New York: McGraw-Hill, 1975; Kemerer, F. R. and Baldridge, J. V., *Unions on Campus: A National Study of the Consequences of Faculty Bargaining,* San Francisco: Jossey-Bass, 1975; Ladd, E. C. and Lipset, S. M., *Professors, Unions, and American Higher Education,* Berkeley, Ca.: The Carnegie Commission on Higher Education, 1973; Tice, T. N. (ed.), *Faculty Power: Collective Bargaining on Campus,* Ann Arbor, Mich.: Institute of Continuing Legal Education, 1972; and *Faculty Bargaining in the Seventies,* Ann Arbor, Mich.: Institute of Continuing Legal Education, 1973.

The ACBIS maintains reference materials for administration in higher education. The materials include special topic papers, collective bargaining contracts, and other related materials distributed at little or no cost to institutions.

A special form of reference material is contract survey studies. These services provide examples of contract provisions under major topic headings. The University of Hawaii and West Virginia University have both developed contract clause finders or contract content analysis studies.

The NCSCBHE also maintains a very extensive contract locater service. This computer-based system provides extensive contract provision materials that would be of use to most institutions involved in negotiations and to individuals involved in research in this field. Additional information can be obtained by contacting the National Center office. Some institutions would find it helpful to obtain actual contracts from unionized universities. A list of institutions with contracts can be obtained from the ACBIS or the NCSCBHE.

Administrations will also find it useful to become familiar with the general labor relations reference materials that are probably already available through their campus libraries. These reference services are maintained by such organizations as Prentice-Hall, Commerce Clearing House, and the Bureau of National Affairs. The reference materials cover a wide range of collective bargaining materials including current events, grievance arbitrations awards, and labor law.

The activities and resources described above represent the kinds of information available to university administrators who are interested in maintaining a general awareness of academic collective bargaining activities. Most of the services and resources noted would not represent significant cost consideration. The information is either free or available through conferences and services already maintained as part of the ongoing operation of the campus. Some of the reference materials and consultant arrangements would represent a cost factor. In most cases, however, the cost of maintaining a general level of information is minimal and well within the scope of a university intent on understanding a major phenomenon affecting policy and practice in higher education administration. The cost range of the conferences and reference materials needed at this stage will be $5,000 to $7,500.

This nominal cost would probably be easily recoverable through savings at smaller institutions and through administrative training and advancement budget lines at larger institutions. In addition, modest grants may be available from local industries generally interested in managerial improvement of all sorts and from the federal government. A final suggestion at this very early stage, with contract negotiation and administration at least a year away: a high-ranking administrative official could be encouraged to take a full year sabbatical leave at half pay to study the union movement in higher education at a law or industrial and labor relations school. By sharing this person's load, the institution will realize a savings of half salary. And, when this person returns bringing an employment relations capability within the administration, substantial savings will be realized in avoiding the hiring of a new administrative officer to handle employment relations.

Stage Two: Organizational Activity

The decision to adopt collective bargaining is made by the faculty through a secret ballot election usually administered by a governmental labor board. This decision is normally made after a period of organizational activity and campus debate. The administrative cost associated with this stage begins to assume a level of some significance. The cost factors in this stage can be broken down into the period of the unionization debate, administrative preparation for an election, and the certification-election process itself.

There is normally a period of general debate as faculty evaluate the advantages and disadvantages of unionization. It is during this period that certification petitions are normally circulated. There is an increasing tendency for the university to be an active participant in the debate by sponsoring speakers, by preparing written background information to assure that faculty are fully aware of the policy implications of unionization, and by circulating factual information on collective bargaining, such as copies of pertinent articles and examples of contracts from other institutions. Faculty are interested in the opinion of key administrative officers on this topic. This requires careful attention to assure a well-stated position that is a fair and valuable contribution to the debate. Such programs could be funded either through a special trustees' grant, a special central office appropriation, or as a justifiable faculty development expense.

In most campus settings the debate has been sponsored by several faculty groups or committees. The university usually makes materials available but refrains from directly underwriting the advocacy aspects of these faculty efforts. The cost of developing quality resource material and making resource persons available is obviously determined by the amount of effort undertaken by the administration. The pattern is for more extensive involvement by the university, and this obviously results in increased cost at this stage. Costs are justified on the premise that institutions believe it is crucial to assure that faculty members are fully informed before exercising their right to vote on this matter.

Coordination of University Involvement in the Debate

In addition to the cost of participating in the debate over unionization, the university during this stage also finds it necessary to undertake certain organizational or institutional commitments with clear cost implications. At this stage the university has to establish a structure for the administrative coordination of its involvement in the unionization debate and the certification process that might follow. At a minimum, there is a need to designate a coordinating officer. This individual will have to be relieved of most other assignments, and other university policy-making officers will need to be available for the extensive planning sessions that occur during this period. It is reasonable to estimate the need for approximately one-half of the administrator's time at an annual cost of $15,000 to $20,000. A budget for resource persons, materials and printing, and so forth must be established because the materials normally are distributed widely and the cost involved is not minimal. Normally, there is a telescoping of events into a short time period, and many cost factors are exaggerated because time does not permit more economic approaches. However, where faculty senate educational budgets, faculty development lines, and special program lines are sufficiently flexible and where the administration has taken an "educate the entire community" approach, these cost burdens may be shared among various sections of the budget.

Legal Assistance

Most universities during this period find it necessary to arrange for special legal assistance. Few university attorneys have specialized knowledge or experience in labor law, and it is often necessary to obtain the services of an outside labor attorney during this period of time. Because higher education collective bargaining is a new phenomenon, many experienced labor attorneys will not be fully aware of the distinctive features of the university as an organization. This means that extra time must be given to orienting the labor attorney to the university setting. This will involve the time and effort of senior administrative officers of the university as policy questions are explored with the labor attorney. Legal issues will begin to surface during this debate period, and it is imperative that competent legal advice be available to the university. For example, there are certain prohibited practices during the period of a campaign and election, and the university will need to be fully aware of these prohibited activities. In addition, the certification process itself is a technical undertaking and the availability of legal assistance is a requirement, not a luxury. The cost in terms of administrative and faculty time is immeasurable. Legal assistance will probably be the one most significant cash cost factor during the organizational stage of unionization. The need for 500 hours of legal assistance is a reasonable expectation and the cost could easily range between $12,000 to $20,000, plus expenses.

The legal assistance becomes crucial if the organizational campaign proceeds to the certification level. This means that a formal petition for recognition has been filed and that a union is seeking exclusive bargaining-agent status. This petition signals the formal beginning of a certification process that has a series of cost impacts.

Certification Process

Once the petition is filed, the labor board will announce a hearing to consider the petition. The university will normally wish to be represented by counsel at this hearing. (See Chapter Four for a detailed review.) Are faculty from the professional schools included in the bargaining unit with other faculty? Are department chairpersons included in the unit? Are academic administrative support staff to be included with instructional faculty? These are not only questions of academic policy but also legal questions of unit appropriateness. Determining a position is a question of academic judgment and legal interpretation. The process of determining the university's position can be time consuming and costly. It may involve the development of job descriptions and the implementation of special organizational studies and survey information. It is unlikely that the university will have to add staff for these activities, but it will be necessary to forego many other services and administrative responsibilities in order to give the necessary attention to these items. There is, however, a justifiable way to spread the expense and to derive benefit in more than one area. For example, the planning and development of job descriptions, organizational studies, and staffing surveys will provide invaluable information necessary for the institution's affirmative action plan. In addition, much of the information gathered could be used in institutional and departmental long-range planning.

Once the hearings on unit and related questions are concluded, an election is ordered and supervised by the labor board. The actual cost of the election is basically underwritten by the board itself. There will be certain cost factors in the election that must be assumed by the university. This would include the maintenance of polling places, the development of voting lists with addresses, the posting of election notices, and the designation of election observers. These costs are required but not extensive.

The major cost during the organization stage involves legal assistance and a series of one-time-only costs as part of the organizational debate. A great deal of the administrative cost is normally assumed by the reassignment of administrative staff and the foregoing of other projects and services because of the press of the administrative activities. If unionization is selected, however, a series of basic administrative costs must be assumed.

Stage Three: During Collective Bargaining Negotiations

If the faculty elects unionization, there are a series of general organizational changes that must be considered by the institution. Some of the special assignments and arrangements that were instituted on a provisional basis must now be made permanent. Additional modifications must also be instituted as the university develops an administrative structure for handling academic collective bargaining on a full-time basis.

Administrative Organization for Collective Bargaining

The university must establish a university office responsible for faculty collective bargaining. In some cases this will involve the assignment of a major new administrative responsibility to an already existing officer. In many cases, however, it will mean the establishment of a new office to be headed by a senior administrative officer. This office will be responsible for representing the university in the full range of collective bargaining activities including preparation for negotiations, actual negotiations, and contract administration. The direct salary of a senior administrator to head this office will normally range from $25,000 to $40,000. Clerical support and other staff assistance can mean a direct expense approaching $75,000 to $85,000.

The office will be headed by an executive officer or director. Most institutions seek an individual with some combination of academic administrative experience and first-hand collective bargaining knowledge. This combination is not common, and many institutions have found it necessary to pay a premium price for the employment of such an individual. In many cases it has been necessary to reassign an administrative officer of the university and to supplement the individual with outside consultants and legal assistance for a period of time. The cost associated with the administrative officer involved often represents a new administrative expenditure. An alternative does exist. Recall the discussion concluding the stage one section of this chapter in which it was suggested that at an early stage a high-ranking administrator could be encouraged to take a sabbatical leave to prepare for an employment relations function. That person could, upon return from leave, take over as director of the employment relations office.

Another cost associated with the establishment of a permanent office for faculty collective bargaining involves legal assistance. The need for ongoing legal advice and guidance does not end with the certification process. In fact, it is only beginning. The university will probably find it necessary to employ a competent labor attorney or enter into a retainer for such service. If the decision is to employ a labor attorney, the cost will not only be the salary of the individual but the necessary support for that office. This will include the maintenance of a labor law library that is more specific than the resources normally maintained in university libraries. The cost associated with establishing a permanent university office and organization for faculty collective bargaining are both immediate and incremental. The impact of this cost could be reduced by hiring a young, but competent, attorney-administrator well before union organizing efforts begin. The person hired could serve as a presidential or vice-presidential assistant and thereby become familiar with institutional structure while preparing him as well as the institution in the law and employment relations.

In addition to the creation of a new administrative office, there will be an increased level of demand on established administrative units in the university. Existing offices and services will find that collective bargaining represents a demanding and impatient master. In some cases the need for service because of the advent of collective bargaining will increase by such a magnitude that additional staff will have to be added. The impact will be felt across the university, but those offices that will receive special pressure include the academic administrative offices (including deans), the office of institutional research, data processing, the university business office, and the university personnel office. Collective bargaining is a decision-making process. The decisions that are made are reduced to written terms and form a binding contract on the parties. It is, therefore, necessary to prepare for negotiations in an extensive manner. Information and studies (see Chapter Eight) become the backbone for significant policy questions that ultimately undergird the bargaining positions of the parties. This means that the offices noted above will have increased pressure to undertake studies, to become involved in committee work, and to participate in other preparation processes in negotiations. In addition to participating in the preparation activities, designated members of these offices will serve as bargaining team members. When negotiations are in full force, there is normally only limited time available for the participants to carry out other responsibilities. The cost factors of these increased administrative pressures on various university offices are great and should not be underestimated. The demands involve the development of information bases both inside and outside the university and the undertaking of various special studies as a background for the preparation for negotiations.

The negative impact of this preparation upon time and costs should not be overemphasized, however. Some enlightened administrators have said that the positive impact of unionization in this regard has been to force information gathering and planning necessary to good administration much of which had been neglected in the past since no critical need was evident.

Information Bases

The university will find it necessary to have detailed and documented information regarding faculty members and various personnel practices. This would include extensive information on individual faculty members. At a minimum it would normally be necessary to identify appointment status (regular or temporary), tenure status, rank, department, school, employment date, work load, fringe benefit options, and various historical information. In addition to individual faculty information, it will be necessary to maintain appropriate comparison data with other institutions. This will include salary comparison and fringe benefit comparison studies. In addition, basic personnel policies and practices will need to be compared in a wide range of areas including appointment, reappointment, tenure, promotion, work load, and class size. Given the subject matter of bargaining, various special studies should be undertaken, such as tenure projections, rank by rank projections, and affirmative action data. These are all examples of the kind of information bases that must be developed and maintained for collective bargaining purposes. In most cases it will be necessary to obtain computer-based capability. The cost of obtaining the capability includes software, and in some cases, new hardware. In all cases a real expense that must not be overlooked is the cost of maintaining accurate information in the data pools.

Preparation Process

Collective bargaining negotiations require extensive preparation. The development of information bases described above is only a starting point. The university will need to designate a preparation team which may or may not be the actual bargaining team for the institution. The coordinator of the preparation process will probably be the administrative officer selected to head the university's office on collective bargaining. The preparation team will be responsible for the full exploration of the upcoming negotiations in an attempt to identify bargaining positions for the university. The development of bargaining positions will involve the consideration of a range of policy questions, and in that regard the preparation team will have to consult with the policy officers of the institution. In some cases this will involve special preparation sessions with the board of control as well. The time necessary to adequately prepare for collective bargaining is very extensive. The process of preparation is intensive and costly. Because the outcome of negotiations may be the most significant cost factor in the budget of institutions, it is imperative that adequate preparation be undertaken. Although the costs are great, they will not be as great as the cost of inadequate planning and preparation.

Negotiations

Even the most detailed preparation must eventually give way to the actual negotiations. The major cost of the negotiations is the time of the participants. Again, the cost needs to be considered in light of options and services not pursued because of the involvement of the parties in the collective bargaining process. There are some expenses associated with bargaining location and other logistics, but these are normally modest. In most cases it is possible to identify meeting space at the institution which does not include rental expense. The actual schedule and duration of bargaining differs with each setting, but it is safe to generalize that the first negotiations are likely to be extensive.

Costing takes on a special role at the negotiations. It is important for the parties to be able to present the cost impact of their demands or positions in a clear and persuasive manner. This might involve special printouts, special studies, or other information which carry a cost tag. Another aspect of costing during negotiations is the capability to assign a cost factor to the various proposals and demands. In some cases the parties are able to identify a costing methodology to be used during the negotiations. In any case it will be necessary to have thorough information bases for purposes of costing proposals. It is not uncommon to have a computer-based costing system so that new proposals can be costed and their impact understood in a minimal period of time.

An inherent part of negotiations is communications. Both parties have publics to keep informed. This involves printing and mailing costs and the development of information releases. The costs may not be extensive but they are common. Costing takes various forms in the negotiations process. It is important to be able to cost the fiscal impact of governance proposals as well as cash demands and to present proposals in a persuasive manner that clearly identifies the cost impact of the demands. It is also important to maintain communication processes as part of the negotiating activity.

There are costs involved in *not* reaching an agreement. If an impasse occurs, it is necessary for the parties to eventually resolve the difference. This might involve the use of a third party mediator. There is normally little direct cost to the parties if the mediation services are provided by governmental units. Fact finding, a more advanced form of dispute settlement, is usually more costly. In these cases the parties present their position to a third party through a hearing system. The party then renders an advisory judgment designed to overcome the impasse. The university would find it necessary in most cases to use an attorney in these hearings and the cost of preparation can be extensive. One form of impasse resolution is a strike. The cost implications are significant and beyond the scope of this chapter. It is sufficient to note that the cost to the university must be measured in more than economic terms.

There are also costs involved in reaching an agreement. Once a table agreement has been reached, the parties normally have to go through a ratification process. For the university this ratification process is not likely to carry extensive direct cost. The table agreement must be presented to the senior administration and board of control of the institution. The most significant ratification costs are those of the union. The table agreement has to be redistributed in some manner to the faculty of the campus and a ratification election held. The direct costs of the ratification process for the union are carried by the union, but the institution is normally anxious to provide support at this stage of the process. Once the contract is ratified, it must then be printed and distributed as a collective bargaining agreement. It is not uncommon for the parties to share in this expense. The costs associated with this stage of the process do not end with the printing and distribution of the contract. A collective bargaining agreement is a dynamic instrument that requires contract administration.

Stage Four: Contract Administration

The major form of contract administration is through the contractual grievance procedure. This procedure allows faculty to raise questions of interpretation and application of the agreement through the filing of grievances. The grievances normally proceed through various administrative steps to a final binding interpretation system known as arbitration. The university office responsible for collective bargaining is also responsible for representing the university in the grievance-arbitration system of the contract. The time involvement in a grievance can be great. The arbitration process represents a third-party hearing system quite similar to the traditional judicial process of our society. Most universities use an attorney in arguing their case before arbitration. As in all hearing processes, there is a great deal of preparation cost attributed to each case. It is common for the parties to split the cost of the arbitration process. Under most collective bargaining agreements of higher education, there has been a minimal number of arbitration cases. Nevertheless, each case does represent a significant direct and indirect cost for the institution. The costs of preparing an arbitration case, legal assistance, and the direct cost of the arbitrator can easily range from $3,000 to $6,000 per case.

James Begin (1976), in a five-year study of grievances at Rutgers University, estimated the average cost per grievance (those not settled informally) to be in excess of $50,000. Rutgers involves a large number of people in its collegial-type grievance reviews, which no doubt increases costs. Nevertheless, the figure is probably accurate and negotiators should be aware of costs inherent in the procedures they negotiate. A short, three-step grievance review may be as fair and effective as a long drawn-out series of "committee" reviews and appeals procedures. It is certainly more economical.

Contract administration involves activities other than grievance-arbitration. It is common for the contract to establish various study committees and administrative committees during the life of the agreement. These committee assignments represent another form of resource use by the institution.

Collective bargaining is a cycle. Contracts begin and end and new contracts must be developed. Although actual negotiations of a particular contract may cease, the ongoing preparation never ends. Once collective bargaining has been selected, it is not likely that faculty will choose to return to a nonunion mode of decision making. The cost involved in preparation, negotiation, and contract administration becomes an ongoing expense of the institution. As such, it becomes extremely important for the university to be aware of the cost impact of collective bargaining and to learn to manage these costs in a way that assures informed and effective collective bargaining in the total context of efficient university operation.

Cost Checklist for Academic Bargaining
(at a moderately sized single campus)

Stage One
General Information on Academic Collective Bargaining

Activity	Estimated Time	Estimated Range of Cost
Prior to Unionization		
Orientation of University Administration		
Special conferences and workshops	4–6 people 100 hrs/yr	$ 2,000–3,000
Regular conferences in higher education	4–6 people 100 hrs/yr	2,000–2,500
Consultant(s) to the campus	12–15 people 120 hrs/yr	600–800
Reference Materials		
General reference books on academic collective bargaining	na	100–200
Special studies or services (e.g., contract clausefinders)	na	100–500
General labor relations reference services	na	200–500
Subtotal		$ 5,000–7,500

Stage Two
Organizational Campaign

Activity	Estimated Time	Estimated Range of Cost
Coordinator of University Involvement in the debate	1 person 1,000 hrs/yr	$15,000–20,000
Unionization Debate Materials and resource persons	na	2,000–4,000
Legal Assistance (retainer)	1 person 500 hrs/yr	12,000–20,000
Certification Process Petition	na	
Hearing on bargaining unit	1–3 people 200 hrs/yr	5,000–15,000
Election	2–4 people 100 hrs/yr	2,000–4,000
Subtotal		$36,000–63,000

Stage Three
Unionization

Activity	Estimated Time	Estimated Range of Cost
Administrative Organization for Bargaining Administrative office and support staff	2–4 people/4,000–8,000	$35,000–85,000
Legal Assistance	1 person/500	12,000–20,000
Impact on existing offices	na	3,000–4,000
Information Bases Individual faculty information Comparison information Special studies Computer-based information	1–4 people/500	5,000–6,000
Preparation Process Preparation team Policy development	4–8 people/1,000	10,000–15,000
Negotiations Team and logistics Costing of demands Impasse Communication Ratification	4–8 people/1,000	10,000–15,000
Contract Administration Grievance/arbitration Contract committees	1–4 people/2,000	25,000–40,000
Subtotal		$100,000–185,000
ESTIMATED TOTAL COST RANGE		$141,000–255,500

William R. Walworth
George W. Angell

To be fully understood, collective bargaining must be viewed in its broadest context. It is a day-to-day evolutionary relationship between employer and employees requiring skill and diplomacy in cooperative negotiation, administration, interpretation, and enforcement of a legal contract. This requires flexibility, imagination, diplomacy, and fresh approaches to the resolution of complex issues. But unfortunately, patterns of negotiation and contract administration often stagnate and become rigid, defeating the very purpose and meaning of the term *negotiation*. It is the purpose of this chapter to suggest a method whereby the parties can voluntarily and cooperatively seek new insights into their bargaining behavior with the hope of easing tensions, improving relationships, and using the total bargaining process as a positive force for institutional excellence. That method is self-evaluation.

Historic Perspective

Voluntary self-evaluation and accreditation of educational institutions are well-established traditions in American higher edu-

538

Improving Bargaining
Processes Through
Self-Evaluation

cation. Over the years accrediting teams have visited colleges and universities to help assess the quality of staff and programs for the purpose of improving institutional effectiveness in achieving their stated goals. The team visit is scheduled by invitation and always follows an institutional self-study. This process has provided an opportunity for an institution to enlist the expert help of the finest leadership in a geographical region at low cost.

Two common types of evaluation services are currently available. First, those designed by a regional accrediting commission to review overall quality of the total institution, and second, those of the specialized accrediting agencies, such as the National League for Nursing, each of which restricts itself to reviewing a single specialized academic area. Collective bargaining processes, however, have been consciously omitted from review by regional accreditation groups, such as the North Central Association and the Middle States Association of Colleges and Secondary Schools, possibly to avoid an unfair labor practice charge against the institution since accrediting associations are largely dominated by administrators. Yet those who have lived with bargaining know that it permeates every aspect of institutional quality from the establishment of purpose and priorities to the quality of students, faculty, and programs. By omitting the processes and effects of bargaining, accreditation agencies may be sounding their own death knell. Deprived of significant accreditation review, institutions pushing the frontiers of faculty bargaining are obliged to develop special means for evaluating and improving the bargaining processes they use. To be successful, negotiations must be cooperative. It follows that evaluation of its effectiveness must be jointly sponsored by management and union. This in itself is a break from traditional accreditation procedures which have been generally designed and controlled by one party (institutions control regional accreditation; narrow subject matter specialists control program accreditation). It is little wonder that these separate efforts, one controlled by the employer, the other by employees, have been fraught with bitter adversarial relationships, each body fighting for its own existence. However, knowing the value of neutrals, parties to collective bargaining can develop a new rigorous program of cooperative self-evaluation assisted by neutrals which eventually may offer a source of new vitality to the accreditation movement as well as to the bargaining process.

Organization for Self-Evaluation

Rationale for Organization

Bargaining conditions at every institution of higher education are sufficiently unique to warrant different approaches to self-study and self-evaluation. Some institutions have only nonacademic unions, others have both faculty and nonfaculty unions. Some institutions have kept a tight rein on whipsawing, holding all unions to approximately the same level and types of benefits; others have been unable to control the bargaining, especially when there have been different loci of table negotiations for each contract. Some administrators have little or no difficulty in working with civil-service employee unions but run into vexing problems in dealing with faculty unions or vice versa. Thus, self-evaluation should be designed to meet a specific objective (for example, how to improve bargaining processes and relationships between the employer and _ union) or to meet a broad objective (for example, how to improve working relationships and employee programs among the several unions and the employer). The latter is complex and always open to the quick withdrawal of one or more parties because of concern as to the preemption of issues for future negotiations. Thus, we are less optimistic about attempts to join representatives from several unions in a single self-evaluation effort even though the problems of personnel administration may be sufficiently irrational and irritating to warrant the effort. By and large, unions which have bargained unique benefits want no part of any effort that appears to be directed at equity or uniformity.

The administrator who wants to bring about equity or more uniformity is better advised to seek it at the several bargaining tables, one at a time. If the magnitude of the problems warrant it, the institution could give "uniformity of benefits" top priority in the coming negotiations with each union. Here, the institution's hand could be strengthened by a report from the regional accreditation association to the effect that differences in employee benefits are creating difficulties which ultimately affect the quality of the educational programs. Diverse benefits in union contracts simply will not, in and of themselves, be of sufficient interest to attract union cooperation for a self-evaluation program. Faculty members, for that matter, never have considered "technical difficulties" for administrators as a subject worthy of their time or consideration.

Employee Units

For whatever type of evaluation system devised, units will have to be considered in terms of broad categories. Each of the groupings may encompass more than one union contract depending upon their stages of collective bargaining and their willingness to cooperate. Again, initial efforts at self-evaluation should probably be limited to one group since lack of common aspirations will certainly be a major obstacle to simultaneous multigroup evaluations. First is the *instructional group,* including full-time teaching staff, part-time teaching staff, teachers' aides, and paraprofessional aides to the teachers. All those involved directly in the classroom setting should be involved in one group, if possible. The second group is *support services,* including staff assistants, technicians, secretaries, clerks, maintenance personnel, food service personnel, and others who support instructional or administrative personnel. This is the area most likely to have several subgroups under separately bargained agreements. The third group includes *administrators* who shape and administer operational policies, hire, fire, and generally meet the specifications of NLRA for supervisory-administrative personnel. The fourth group consists of *student, part-time employees*. There is little question that in the next few years they will be bargaining in one form or another, especially in the area of fringe benefits and general wages, hours, and working conditions. Even if the institution does not bargain directly with the total student body, it will be required to handle student employee relations under some kind of written agreement.

Finally, come the people who serve through *contracted services*. These people are, in the strictest sense, employees of the institution. An institution must consider this unit when assessing the effects of the total bargaining process since it may be looking for recommendations to continue and perhaps expand certain contracted services or to absorb part of them into other services. A good example is the security force. Some believe that this should be a contracted service while others think that on-campus security personnel is a more economical and controlled approach.

Intragroup Benefits and Services to be Studied

Within each group, support programs are interwoven in some way. They constitute an integral part of the total program of employee relations and should be evaluated if a true picture of policies, practices, and procedures of the institution is to be produced.

The first important area is *fringe benefits*. Not only are there benefits that have been agreed to by the institution but those which have been dictated by federal and state legislation. Examples are state retirement systems, unemployment compensation, and Workmen's Compensation.

Next in importance may be the *inservice training* programs. Many institutions and organizations are now being called upon to train their present employees for advancement in the organization or to retrain them for new positions and new systems as existing jobs and programs become obsolete and are phased out. Whether or not we accept the philosophy that management is to be responsible for the employee both at work and at recreation, it seems clear that legislation is moving in that direction. Sometime, perhaps soon, institutions may be called upon to assist staff members in their adjustments to happy and meaningful lives as a part of a comprehensive employment relations program.

Included in the next area are *advertising, recruitment, testing, evaluating, hiring, and firing* of personnel. All are complicated by new requirements for equal opportunity, affirmative action, and Title IX of the 1972 Education Amendments.

Safety and health is another major area to be considered. The *William Steiger Occupational Safety and Health Act of 1970* is having a tremendous impact on public institutions. Local labor agreements and governmental regulations are each attempting to dictate more rigid safety standards for schools. Health standards and improved productivity go hand-in-hand. With employees' health being of prime importance to the employer, health services will become a major area of responsibility in the years to come as schools become involved in national health plans.

The general area of *recordkeeping* and personnel files that meet government as well as contractual and fair labor standards must also be evaluated. Examples include applications, leaves of absences, resignations, disciplinary procedures, and other forms too numerous to list.

The *contracts*, as documentary evidence, offer a rich source of information for the evaluation. Contract language, the nature of the grievance procedures, management rights clauses, employee participation in governance, and so forth all shed light on the relationships among the parties, their goals, and their aspirations.

Finally, legislative, executive, and judicial bargaining processes must be evaluated.

Legislative Processes

Negotiation is the legislative process by which the parties share in developing certain policies, procedures, and practices of the institution. Management and labor together need to look at all contracts, agreements, and institutional handbooks and assess them in light of the purposes and effectiveness of the total institution. This does not imply that evaluators should be proposing language changes, additions, or deletions as this infringes the rights of negotiators. Self-studies and outside evaluators, however, can look at the agreements and discuss them in light of factors that influence the effectiveness with which an agreement may be administered. Just as important for evaluative purposes is a review of problems and obstacles at the last negotiation sessions. Examination should center upon meet-and-discuss sessions which might facilitate later negotiations, subjects for negotiations, agreements on publicity and the question of student involvement in negotiations.

Some would say that neither the contract nor the process can be evaluated without influencing future negotiations, thus committing an unfair labor practice. Done cooperatively without infringing individual member rights, neither party is likely to commit or charge an unfair practice. If, for example, the evaluation program has the support of the president and the board of trustees, the evaluating team could certainly make useful recommendations about managerial processes. If the study shows that a significant number of employees felt unable to adequately voice their concerns to their union about issues discussed at the table, for example, the evaluation team certainly could suggest that the union seek alternatives and provide examples for better communication with membership. Since neither party has to accept recommendations resulting from evaluation, there would be little base for an unfair labor practice charge by either party. Indeed, the evaluation may provide significant agenda for the next round of bargaining in a spirit of understanding and cooperation. In addition to helping the parties identify their own and the other's strengths and shortcomings, the evaluation may help them clarify relationships to unorganized groups. For example, the last group to organize usually is middle management. An evaluation team certainly could help the parties understand the concerns of, and possibly the need for better communications with, or even informal negotiation with, this group.

Executive Processes

The administration of contracts may be considered as the executive function in collective bargaining. Union and management leadership each carry heavy responsibilities for seeing that the contract is fairly and professionally administered. For example, the question may be raised as to whether the administration is requiring its first-line supervisors to become a functional part of the grievance procedure or whether it is encouraging all decisions to be made at the last level of the grievance procedure. On the union side the inquiry might focus on whether the union submits grievances which are clear and to the point or which are so vague as to misinterpret the root cause or principle involved in the grievance. Both sides have a responsibility to train and to instruct their people in labor relations to a degree that will enable them to fully understand the agreement and the commitments made by both sides. Bringing an in-house self-evaluation team together may be the first time the institutional parties have taken the time to sit down together and look at how effectively or ineffectively the agreements are being administered.

Judicial Processes

The final process to be evaluated is judicial: the interpretation and enforcement of the agreement. The evaluation should determine whether the parties have done all in their power to come to a fair interpretation and resolution of thorny issues or whether everything is being bitterly contested as grievances on a win-lose basis all the way to an arbitrator. An outside evaluation team can help to isolate the precise nature of the adjudication problems especially when the employer has failed to train its grievance-review officers in the practice of fair judicial reviews. In the long run, the evaluation procedure should help institutions to effectively settle their own disputes in a manner which builds better working relationships based on mutual respect and confidence.

The Internal Evaluation Team

Each party would be responsible for selecting its members of the inhouse self-evaluation team. Each institution would determine what general pattern or grouping would be desirable. Usually, a team of five to ten people will emerge as an efficient group to plan and conduct the institution's self-study of its bargaining processes. Each union would appoint at least one representative to the team, which, in turn, could be cochaired by a management representative and union representative who are respected and well informed about the institution's labor relations program. Other team members could be, for example, a faculty member, a student, an administrator, and a trustee all selected by mutual agreement between management and union. There are at least four aspects of a self-evaluation worth consideration:

1. management evaluating its own performance
2. management evaluating union performance
3. union members evaluating management performance
4. union members evaluating union performance

Management must extend an invitation to the unions to join them in the self-evaluation process or vice versa. If union representatives are not receptive to the idea, then management may wish to proceed with the first two aspects alone, share the results with the unions as best it can, and hope that union people will see the advantages of having input into the procedures. Going it alone, however, is a risky business since it seldom provides a comprehensive data base or the cooperation essential to changing attitudes and operational procedures. Any evaluation must be carefully planned to avoid union suspicions and unfair labor practice charges. The institutions may have to go through a mini self-evaluation once so that confidence can be developed for a subsequent study which would include all four aspects of the evaluation. Another confidence builder is to agree in writing that the results of the evaluation can in no way be used against either party in arbitration or a court suit.

Study Guides

One effective tool in conducting a self-evaluation is a set of pertinent questions directed at those who are affected by bargaining at each level. Each institution should develop its own questionnaires in view of its unique problems. There are, however, distinct advantages in having the outside evaluators (or agency) develop the questionnaires on a "neutral" basis after examining the issues as presented by each party. In the latter case each party on campus should be allowed to supplement the questionnaires with ideas, materials, and questions agreed upon by the internal team. The main job of the internal evaluation team would be to administer the questionnaires to a representative sample of employees and administrators, to study and interpret the results, and to send a full report to the external visiting team which will conduct its campus interviews on the basis of this report. Following are a few sample questions of the type that may be useful in conducting an evaluation at an educational institution:

For Union Members

1. How do you feel about your negotiating team?
   a. Is it sufficiently concerned about each member's welfare? Yes _____ No _____ Don't Know _____
   b. Is it sufficiently concerned about the success of the institution as a whole?
      Yes _____ No _____ Don't Know _____
2. Does your union conduct meetings to explain the proposed changes in your contract prior to ratification?
   Yes _____ No _____ Don't Know _____
3. Does it conduct inservice sessions after ratification to explain the total contract?
   Yes _____ No _____ Don't Know _____
4. Do you know who your union steward is?
   Yes _____ No _____ Don't Know _____
   a. Is he available when you need him?
      Yes _____ No _____ Don't Know _____
   b. Is he helpful when you request help?
      Yes _____ No _____ Don't Know _____
5. Are your union dues reasonable for the services you receive? Yes _____ No _____ Don't Know _____
   If no, how much should they be? _____
6. Does the institution conduct inservice training programs to help employees improve in their jobs?
   Yes _____ No _____ Don't Know _____
7. Does the administration have sessions with employees from time to time to discuss what is happening at the institution?
   Yes _____ No _____ Don't Know _____

8. Do you think there is sufficient cooperation between the union and administration?

Yes _____ No _____ Don't Know _____

9. Does the union grievance officer (committee) respond sincerely and effectively to member complaints?

Yes _____ No _____ Don't Know _____

Make suggestions _____

_____

For Members of Negotiation Teams

1. How many people are on your team at the bargaining table? _____

Is each one selected on the basis of specific qualifications?

Yes _____ No _____ Don't Know _____

2. Do you think your team commands the respect of the union employees?

Yes _____ No _____ Don't Know _____

Of administrators?

Yes _____ No _____ Don't Know _____

3. Does your negotiating team present those proposals that represent the thinking of its rank-and-file members?

Yes _____ No _____ Don't Know _____

4. Do you have the opportunity to participate in informal sessions with the other team?

Yes _____ No _____ Don't Know _____

With other unions on campus?

Yes _____ No _____ Don't Know _____

With student groups?

Yes _____ No _____ Don't Know _____

Make suggestions _____

_____

5. Do you believe that the current contract as a whole advances the educational mission of the institution?

Yes _____ No _____ Don't Know _____

If not, should they?

Yes _____ No _____ Don't Know _____

Make suggestions _____

_____

For Managers and Supervisors

1. Does your team carefully prepare preliminary demands before going to the negotiating table?

   Yes _____ No _____ Don't Know _____

2. Do you believe that the union demands really represent the wishes of its broad membership?

   Yes _____ No _____ Don't Know _____

   Make suggestions _____

3. Did too many grievances go to arbitration this past year that could have been settled if management had taken a more realistic position?

   Yes _____ No _____ Don't Know _____

   Make suggestions _____

4. Should management be more willing to discuss concerns with the union before they reach the grievance stage?

   Yes _____ No _____ Don't Know _____

5. Are first-level supervisors allowed to settle most grievances at their level?

   Yes _____ No _____ Don't Know _____

   Make suggestions _____

6. Does management conduct training sessions for supervisors in the area of contract implementation?

   Yes _____ No _____ Don't Know _____

7. Do administrators who review union grievances give enough consideration to the concerns of subadministrators whose decisions are being grieved?

   Yes _____ No _____ Don't Know _____

   Make suggestions _____

After the inhouse evaluation team has reviewed and summarized the questionnaire response and examined all pertinent documents of the institution, they could make a joint report, together with minority opinions, addressed to the selected visitation team and widely circulated on campus. The report should clearly summarize the issues which are unresolved and which appear to reduce the effectiveness of the bargaining process and the institution as a whole. Areas of agreement and disagreement could be summarized for quick reading at the beginning of the report. Many of the lesser problems that are raised will tend to solve themselves as corrective measures are taken by each party in areas that need little attention from the visitors. This type of internal self-corrective action could well become one of the most valuable outcomes of the evaluation.

The major responsibilities of the visitation team, consisting usually of one neutral acting as chairperson, one national union representative, and one management consultant, could be to (1) review the report and pertinent documents, (2) visit the campus and conduct interviews for additional information and verification, and (3) write its own report with special emphasis on possible solutions to the areas of disagreement. This report would obviously be addressed to all parties, namely, management, union membership, trustees, and, perhaps, to student association officers.

The premises underlying the entire evaluation are that collective bargaining is a dynamic process constantly changing in response to new conditions and that it can be constructively studied and redirected if the parties are willing to make the effort.

Regional Commissions

If the self-evaluation idea gains acceptability, regional evaluation commissions could be formed and charged with the responsibility for developing criteria, self-study procedures, visitation standards, and methods of reporting, along with a handbook which describes the service and suggests guidelines for conducting self-evaluation studies and on-site visits. Commissions should be available to encourage, counsel, and assist in the improvement of bargaining processes to help achieve reasonable goals for the good of the institution and the community served.

Another important function of the commission would be to orient and train people for on-site visitation and consultation. This would be an unusual challenge as the commissions would be dealing with teams of men and women with diverse attitudes and concerns about the bargaining process. Finally, each commission will have to coordinate site-evaluation visits to institutions within their regions in order to provide continuous service with high standards.

A regional commission must be composed of outstanding individuals from management and labor along with expert neutrals in personnel and labor relations. Neutrals would bring credibility and moderating influences to the deliberations of regional commissions and perhaps could be selected with the aid of the National Academy of Arbitrators, the American Arbitration Association, or the Federal Mediation and Conciliation Service.

The work of commissions could be expedited and encouraged by the fact that boards of trustees are beginning to reflect both a management and a labor viewpoint. People from both sides of the table are being appointed to boards of trustees. This phenomenon could have a positive effect in encouraging both management and labor to share responsibility for self-evaluation and on-site visitations.

Conclusions and Recommendations

Boards of trustees and administrators have not completely accepted the idea that collective bargaining is here to stay and that it must be dealt with constructively. Nor have many unions come to fully realize that their existence depends on the quality and success of the institutions served by their members. Yet times are changing and so are trustees, management, and union leadership. All can benefit from self-analysis and cooperation. And so can the entire movement of collective bargaining throughout the United States.

It is recommended that each unionized institution consider the possible benefits of a self-evaluation program. Let the courageous ones develop the frontiers, sort out the problems, and enjoy the benefits. Each successful evaluation should be reported to appropriate state and federal agencies, foundations, and accrediting agencies. Let regional programs develop from grass-roots experience. Sooner or later funds will be requested and made available from foundations to establish the first regional commission, and sooner or later the evaluation of contract negotiations and administration may become a function of revitalized and redirected regional "accreditation" agencies.

Leland Miles

30

⚬⚬⚬⚬⚬⚬⚬⚬

Collective bargaining adds one more pressure and complication to the already complicated life of a modern university president. On some campuses it has been possible for the president to marshal the forces of collective bargaining in such a way as to help achieve institutional goals. On other campuses, it is questionable whether the unions involved really want presidential leadership, which would seem precluded by such unions' extreme view of "shared authority."

Collective bargaining, however benign, has a severe impact on students, trustees, the community (alumni, donors, corporations, and foundations), the administration as would-be educational planners, and, perhaps most of all, on faculty. The responsibility of the president for statesmanlike leadership among faculty during the periods of emotional decision making (elections, unit determinations, and so forth) that precede bargaining and arise during bargaining (negotiations, impasses, grievances, and so forth)

552

Coordinating Faculty Bargaining with Other University Processes

❦❦❦❦❦❦❦❦

critically affect the destiny of the institution. The impact of collective bargaining on faculty is such a large topic that it is handled separately in Chapter Twenty-Seven by Joseph J. Orze. This chapter will discuss the other four areas of collective bargaining influence. In each instance, I will analyze the impact and reactions, will note what the president can do to balance such reactions, and, finally, I will explore some of the problems that may be caused by an attempted presidential initiative. My frame of reference is based upon my collective bargaining experience in a private urban university; my comments should be read in that light.

Students

In my experience there is one overriding impact of collective bargaining for students, namely, they feel that they are the innocent victims. Cartoons in student newspapers frequently show the prostrate student being kicked by both sides (administration and faculty) in the collective bargaining process. Students feel confused and upset by the charges and countercharges of the rival parties. Note the comments from a vice-president of a student council at a university which was recently embroiled in collective bargaining: "Collective bargaining seemed to us [she says] to be a very suspicious scheme designed to keep students removed from discussions which would affect their welfare. We questioned the motives of both parties to the bargaining process. We suspected that all the negotiations were based on the selfish arrogance of both bargaining teams. One method for correcting the situation is to provide a workshop for students on the collective bargaining process. In this way, student leaders who will be confronted with the problems of collective bargaining will at least be given a basic familiarity with the concept. It is also important that students be regularly briefed by a single, officially designated spokesperson. No single reliable source existed for us."

The reaction of students to such feelings of frustration is that they want to be involved in the collective bargaining process in order to at least know what is going on, and if possible in order to control or at least influence those events that seriously affect their welfare. Some student leaders have lobbied for legislation in this area. Note for example that Maine guarantees students a faculty bargaining role. (Semus, 1976, p. 4) In extreme cases, students have even talked of organizing a third union which would confront both faculty and administration. At the University of Massachusetts in 1976, students were successful in gaining some legislative support for a bill that would provide them the right to organize and bargain as a union. National experience indicates that students rarely side consistently with administration or faculty during the negotiation period. Either they vacillate, depending on the personalities or events of the moment, or they remain neutral in an attempt to put pressure on both sides. Lucy Miller (1976) has prepared a comprehensive summary of student reaction to collective bargaining. (See also Research Project on Students and Collective Bargaining, 1976.)

In the interests of collegial integrity and good communication, what can the university president do under such situations? First, the president can request that the union allow students to be present as observers. If the union accepts this request, students will hopefully be a mediating force at the bargaining table and at least will be an information channel back to the student body, thus relieving frustration at being uninformed. There are, of course, disadvantages to having student observers, who are often susceptible to the "grandstanding" of drama-conscious negotiators. However, it is important to remember that most student observers will soon become accustomed to the dramatics of bargaining and learn to perceive posturing and selfishness wherever it exists, on whichever side.

Second, if the union disallows students as observers, the president can consider appointing a student to the employer negotiating team.

Third, in response to union mass meetings announced by union circulars, the president or his designate can hold counter mass meetings announced by countercirculars. Obviously, the most articulate and respected administrative spokesperson should be assigned to such responsibilities.

Fourth, the administration can set up a "rumor desk" with telephones to stop rumors and false allegations. Here again articulate, highly respected people should be assigned, perhaps on a temporary basis, since news reporters and union representatives can be callers looking for hot news items that may increase rather than decrease rumors.

Fifth, as the same student vice-president suggested, the administration can hold workshops and briefing sessions for student leaders. It is also important to plan frequent meetings with student observers and officers to discuss potential or imminent emergency issues. The approach at such meetings should be that the president is attempting to enlist the understanding and suggestions of students. Presidents should consider the importance of establishing a pattern of such meetings well in advance of the first negotiations, so that later meetings do not take on a crisis atmosphere.

Finally, the president or his designee can meet frequently with student editors and radio station managers to explain the university's position. As reinforcement to such meetings, the administration can issue bulletins, quietly and objectively reporting what is happening at the bargaining table, unless there has been a writ-

New Opportunities for Leadership

ten agreement with the union in advance of bargaining that neither side will issue information to anyone until either agreement or impasse has been reached.

In connection with the above, it is important to stress that the union through its faculty membership can reach students daily through the classrooms. Hence, the administration must establish its own way of communicating directly and frequently with the student body. (Chapter Fourteen offers a detailed description of how students participated directly and effectively in faculty union negotiations at three institutions in Montana.)

Trustees

Trustees normally react with irritation or anger to the advent of academic bargaining unless one or more of them are representatives of industrial unions. Many trustees are corporation officials who accept, sometimes reluctantly, unions in their own industries but never dreamed that collective bargaining would come to the campus. The despair of some trustees at this development is typified by this statement from a former board chairman of a private urban university: "What about the university and its concern for excellence, as collective bargaining makes tenure essentially a provision for super-seniority rather than a protection of free speech and free expression for the teacher? Under collective bargaining the university must downgrade its search for excellence because job security has become a primary purpose of tenure."

Trustees, most of whom are conservative, take a hard line towards unions which some blame for the present economic situation in the United States. Some trustees feel, moreover, that they know more about unions than the president or the administration does. In point of fact, they view university administrators as being generally naive in this area. Perhaps trustees are right in this regard: some professional mediators insist that academic unions behave no differently from industrial unions, except that the latter are more rational. Whether this be so or not, most observers agree that campuses are different from industry and the governance of universities is different from the governance of business corporations.

Because trustees react normally with anger or consternation at the development of faculty collective bargaining on campuses, they quickly want a hand in negotiations or at least an opportunity to confront the union face to face. Thus, the previously mentioned board chairman states, "With the advent of collective bargaining, trustees are beginning to act more like corporation executives than like trustees." The implication here is that trustees are beginning to invade the prerogatives of management in dealing with unions.

While the trustees are seeking to confront the union face to face, the union is seeking the same objective. Having corralled department chairmanships, having partially bypassed deans and vice-presidents through contractual terms, and having successfully minimized presidential authority on many campuses, the unions next seek to pull the trustees directly into the collective bargaining caldron. The union's approach here is that they have never met the trustees; if they could just communicate with board members, everything would be different (and better). Put another way, some unions seek to "horizontalize" governance by creating two coequal bodies; namely, faculty and administration, whose disputes are then mediated by the trustees. Under this system, the administration loses its traditional authority, and trustees, in fact, become quasi-administrative in character. In short, collective bargaining puts enormous pressure on the president from both trustees and unions. The trustees want to "get at the union" and the union officers want to "get at the trustees."

Under this situation, the president has a number of alternatives. First, he can provide a select group of trustees an opportunity to meet periodically with faculty representatives (both union and nonunion) to discuss long-range institutional needs and options. Should such an approach be taken, the president should stress in advance that such meetings cannot legally constitute or preempt future negotiating sessions. Obviously, there are both advantages and dangers to such an approach. The obvious advantage is that such meetings will defuse the union's contention that they cannot reach trustees and may engender faculty understanding and constructive suggestions, especially if the discussions carefully avoid immediate issues. One disadvantage is that the meetings might degenerate into informal negotiating despite prior disavowals, thus undercutting the stability and effectiveness of both the administration and its negotiating team. Another possible alternative is for the president to select a small trustee group to advise him on collective bargaining strategy and especially public relations tactics as they affect the outside press and community perceptions.

In any event, a president should keep the board periodically briefed on all collective bargaining developments. In advance of negotiations he can seek their help in setting bottom-line parameters for negotiations.

Above all else, the president should insist that the board ratify all collective bargaining agreements. This should be announced to both parties before the first negotiation session. Such ratification is a manifestation and protection of the board's ultimate authority. It is also a protection against inadvertent error made by the administrative negotiating team during the confusion caused by marathon sessions. The faculty negotiating team is similarly protected by the faculty ratification process.

Alumni and Fund Raising

From a public relations, alumni, and fund-raising standpoint, an urban university is especially vulnerable to collective bargaining because it lives in a goldfish bowl. Most of its students come from nearby areas, its activities are of great interest to the city's news media, and the slightest conflict is immediately known to large numbers of people, including alumni, parents, corporations, foundations, and donors.

Collective bargaining disputes, if publicized, often create the impression of internal discord. The public gains the impression that the school is so racked by controversy that it cannot find direction. Such an image is hardly one to attract donors, parents, or students.

In this connection, hear the exasperated comments of an outstanding development director at an urban university:

> *In many cases, collective bargaining has hurt our development effort with foundations we are trying to cultivate for a first grant. The task of local fund raising has become much more difficult under collective bargaining. We must now constantly defend the university against highly publicized adversary union attacks on administration. A tremendous and disproportionate effort has to go into retaining public confidence built up over the years. . . . The fact*

*that we have a union does not create the problem; most corpo-
rations are used to dealing with unions. It is the adverse and
totally negative publicity issued by the faculty union that
has hurt.* Most unions in industry do not attack management in the way that our faculty attacks the administration *[Emphasis added]*. *Nor do industrial unions get
as much print space and public mention. Consequently, fund
raisers have the very difficult task of assuring a potential
large donor that his gift will not help finance the recent collective bargaining agreement. The success of an institution's
fund raising in a collective bargaining atmosphere is as
much the result of a reasonable union as it is the result of
the professional competency of its development staff.*

What is the reaction of the community to collective bargaining disputes on the campus, especially in an urban situation? First,
newspapers will frequently seize on collective bargaining conflicts
as a source for spectacular news. This situation is aggravated by
professorial contact with local papers and by the fact that reporters
for student newspapers sometimes double as "stringers" for the
off-campus outside press in urban communities.

Second, corporations tend to react tolerantly to collective
bargaining given their own historical immersion in the collective
bargaining process. However, foundations and lending agencies
are different. Most of them shy away from supporting campuses
where leadership is not focused on the board and the president.
For example, a large foundation recently refused to consider a grant
to an urban university until such time as it put its collective bargaining house in order. Even more crucially, a major lending agency
dragged its feet in making a key loan to an urban university on the
grounds that the agency did not have confidence that the administration was in charge.

However, most negative reactions to collective bargaining
come from individuals; for example, from parents who do not want
their children's education interrupted, from alumni who gasp at
the thought of old Dr. Chips on the picket line, and from big donors
who decline or withdraw gifts if the union seems to be "taking over."

It is crucial under these circumstances that the president
attempt to gain understanding and help from union leadership in

relating to outside donors. If such help is not forthcoming, the following alternatives are possible. First, the president can try to get the union to agree to a gag rule under which neither side will release materials to or make statements to the outside press. Failing this, the administration can seek the understanding of news media, in the city's and university's best interests, to moderate collective bargaining stories, regardless of which side initiates them.

Third, the president can form a public relations council from local corporate executives for advice on the public relations handling of labor disputes. Fourth, the president must, under all circumstances, convey a good-humored air of confidence whenever he finds himself being interrogated in social situations or in press interviews. He should stress that his own particular university is not unique in having a union. Five hundred campuses are now organized; it is a fact of life which everyone must accept and live with. The aim must be not to fight the fact of collective bargaining, but to attempt to maximize its possible benefits.

Assuming that large numbers of alumni and donors work in the immediate campus area, it is important that the president emphasize in oral and written statements that the trustees and administration intend to fully exercise all management rights and authority especially in such vital areas as position allocation, appointments, and fiscal control. The advice of a prominent alumni director is noteworthy:

> [It is] important that the president involve alumni at the earliest possible time in the collective bargaining process. Through the president of the alumni association, the facts of the bargaining should be delineated. As negotiations proceed and as possible impasses arise, the president should alert the alumni and anticipate their reactions, favorable and unfavorable. Without going into minute detail, the points of difference between the administration and faculty should be clearly defined by the president. He should state the university position and why it adopts same. The president should also, as objectively as possible, present the arguments of the opposing faculty team. When necessary, the president can ask the alumni board for a vote of confidence; and if he has been open and fair-minded, he can anticipate support for

his position from the alumni. When the settlement is reached, the president should inform the alumni of this fact and should be prepared to spell out, in general terms, the impact of the negotiation agreement on the overall well-being of the university community.

Educational Planning

It is in the area of educational planning that collective bargaining on many campuses may have had its most negative impact. One danger of unionism is that it may drain and divert administrative and faculty energy away from the university's central purpose of teaching and planning for the future. Deans, vice-presidents, and even the president can become so enmeshed in the collective bargaining process that innovative planning and reorganization is diminished or laid aside altogether. Where the adversarial relationship is at its height, political struggle and power-block politics, rather than curricular planning, may become the order of the day.

Under such circumstances, the president has a variety of options. For example, he can attempt to minimize adversarial relations by creating significant nonpolitical projects on which the administration and faculty can work together, for instance, the planning of an instructional development center or the launching of a long-range planning project.

Long-range planning stands the best chance of minimizing conflict because the university's future is most likely to transcend current politics. Also, a planning committee representing all constituencies can be a healing and cohesive force, especially if the union is willing to be involved in planning. Indeed, if a long-range plan is evolving at the time a contract is being bargained, the president might consider the feasibility of negotiating for union support of trustee-approved long-range goals in the impending contract.

The university senate can be used as a locus of faculty and staff reaction to planning ideas and processes. Any multiconstituency senate is a less political body than a union—even some union members behave differently after putting on the senatorial hat.

Whether or not the foregoing procedures work, the president can at least minimize the drain on administrative energy by concentrating all collective bargaining negotiations and contract administration in a single office. At some large institutions, a vice-chancellor of labor affairs is appointed with a staff of attorneys and other technicians. For medium and small institutions, it is probably more feasible simply to expand the personnel director's office and to concentrate therein all personnel matters including collective bargaining, affirmative action, and Title IX. Under this arrangement the personnel director can also handle grievances.

There is considerable advantage in having the same administrator in charge of negotiations, grievance hearings, arbitrations, regular meetings with union representatives, supervision of appointment records, education of supervisors, and so forth. One top-flight person in this position can change the entire tenor of labor relations throughout the campus. For this reason, the president's attitude toward faculty relations is probably most clearly expressed by the type of person he selects to be in charge of labor relations. A second-rate appointee spells trouble. A first-rate person assures and reaffirms the goal of institutional excellence.

Summary and Conclusion

The university president must, of course, do everything possible to minimize any negative impact of collective bargaining. What is far more important, however, is to take vigorous leadership in directing the opportunities, challenges, and forces of bargaining toward institutional integrity and excellence. He, alone, is responsible for seeing that all constituencies work together toward common goals. Certainly, the president must take the position, whether accepted or not by the union, that he is the president of the total university and, therefore, a *member of both faculty and administration*. As their presiding officer, he must demand justice for each party within an atmosphere of freedom and open search for better alternatives that characterize the institution's devotion to reason and scholarship. This attitude might irritate the administrative negotiating team, but it is, on balance, the only position which, in my judgment, makes any moral or legal sense.

In a sense, then, the president becomes an unofficial mediator who insists that the proper interests of students, faculty, administration, and all other constituencies be defended vigorously and impartially. However, presidential leadership in a collective bargaining milieu cannot be restricted solely to a mediator's role. He now has fresh opportunity and responsibility to insist that "excellence" become a common goal of *both* parties and that the "terms and conditions of employment" under negotiation are to be designed for the purpose of strengthening the institution's commitment to excellence. While the faculty is negotiating increased "faculty participation," the president can insist, for example, that the contract require that "shared governance" set high standards for evaluating faculty performance and that the contract recognize and illuminate the goals and objectives of the total institution. Such a contract can be strong evidence of institutional vitality and integrity.

All this requires some agility as well as omniscience on the part of the president. Although some unions attempt to polarize the constituencies and to make him the chief adversary, the president himself must help them to lift their sights and redirect their efforts. His sole aim must be to unify constituencies in a common search for freedom, knowledge, and humanity.

References

ACADEMIC COLLECTIVE BARGAINING INFORMATION SERVICE (ACBIS). *Analysis of Legislation in 24 States Enabling Faculty Collective Bargaining in Postsecondary Education.* Special Report No. 17, Update, Washington, D.C.: ACBIS, May 1976a.

ACADEMIC COLLECTIVE BARGAINING INFORMATION SERVICE (ACBIS). *Scope of Public Sector Bargaining in 14 Selected States.* Special Report No. 25, Washington, D.C.: ACBIS, April 1976b.

AGREEMENT BETWEEN BLOOMFIELD COLLEGE and the Bloomfield College Chapter of the American Association of University Professors, July 1, 1975 to June 30, 1976.

AGREEMENT BETWEEN THE BOARD OF REGENTS, State University System of Florida and the United Faculty of Florida, 1976–1978.

AGREEMENT BETWEEN THE BOARD OF TRUSTEES for the Nebraska State Colleges and the Higher Education Association of Nebraska, June 1974 to June 1978.

AGREEMENT BETWEEN OAKLAND UNIVERSITY and the Oakland University Chapter of the American Association of University Professors, July 1, 1975 to June 30, 1976.

AGREEMENT BETWEEN RIDER COLLEGE and the Rider College Chapter of the American Association of University Professors, 1974–1976.

AGREEMENT BETWEEN STATE UNIVERSITY OF NEW YORK and the United University Profession, Inc., 1974–1976.

AGREEMENT BETWEEN TEMPLE UNIVERSITY of the Commonwealth System of Higher Education and the Temple Chapter of the American Association of University Professors, July 1, 1973 to June 30, 1976.

AGREEMENT BETWEEN THE UNIVERSITY OF SAN FRANCISCO and the University of San Francisco Faculty Association, July 1, 1976 to June 30, 1981.

ALBANO, C. *Transactional Analysis on the Job and Communicating with Subordinates.* New York: American Management Association Bookstore, 1975.

ALLSHOUSE, M. "The New Academic Slalom: Mission—Personnel Planning—Financial Exigency—Due Process." *Liberal Education,* October 3, 1975, *61,* 349.

AMERICAN ASSOCIATION FOR HIGHER EDUCATION (AAHE). *Faculty Participation in Academic Governance.* Task Force on Faculty Representation and Academic Negotiations. Washington, D.C.: AAHE, 1967.

AMERICAN ASSOCIATION OF UNIVERSITY PROFESSORS (AAUP). "The Standards for Notice of Nonreappointment." *American Association of University Professors Bulletin,* 1967, *53,* 407.

AMERICAN ASSOCIATION OF UNIVERSITY PROFESSORS (AAUP). "1969 Recommended Institutional Regulations on Academic Freedom and Tenure." *American Association of University Professors Bulletin,* 1968, *54,* 448–452.

AMERICAN ASSOCIATION OF UNIVERSITY PROFESSORS (AAUP). *Operating Guidelines on Institutional Problems Resulting from Financial Exigency.* Washington, D.C.: AAUP, 1972.

AMERICAN ASSOCIATION OF UNIVERSITY PROFESSORS (AAUP). "Termination of Faculty Appointments Because of Financial Exigency, Discontinuance of a Program or Department, or Medical Reasons." *American Association of University Professors Bulletin,* 1975, *61,* 329–331.

AMERICAN MANAGEMENT ASSOCIATION (AMA). *Constructive Discipline on the Job.* Prime Audio I. Workbook, programmed notebook, tests, guide, and two cassettes, 1200-9. New York: AMA, 1975a.

AMERICAN MANAGEMENT ASSOCIATION (AMA). *Labor Relations and the Supervisor.* Prime Audio II. Workbook, programmed notebook, guide, and two cassettes, 1202-5. New York: AMA, 1975b.

AMERICAN MANAGEMENT ASSOCIATION (AMA). *Union or Not: The Supervisor's Role.* Prime Audio II, 1303-x. New York: AMA, 1975c.

AMERICAN MANAGEMENT ASSOCIATION (AMA). *How to Be a Successful Negotiator.* Workbook and twelve cassettes. New York: AMA, 1976a.

AMERICAN MANAGEMENT ASSOCIATION (AMA). *Know Your Employees—Individual Differences.* Film. New York: AMA, 1976b.

AMERICAN MANAGEMENT ASSOCIATION (AMA). *Transcendental Meditation.* Film, 2189-x. New York: AMA, 1976c.

BAER, W. *Grievance Handling.* New York: American Management Association Bookstore, 1970.

BAIRD, J., AND MCARTHUR, M. "Constitutional Due Process and the Negotiation of Grievance Procedures in Public Employment." *Journal of Law and Education,* 1976, *5,* 209–232.

BAKKE, E.W. *Mutual Survival.* New York: Harper, 1946.

BEGIN, J., SETTLE, T., AND ALEXANDER, P. *Academics on Strike.* Washington, D.C.: Academic Collective Bargaining Information Service, 1975.

BEGIN, J. "Bargaining History—Contract Summaries of New Jersey Community Colleges 1968–1975." Unpublished paper. Department of Research, Institute of Management and Labor Relations. New Brunswick, N.J.: Rutgers University, 1976.

BLAKE, R.R., SHEPARD, H.A., AND MOUTON, J.S. *Managing Intergroup Conflict in Industry.* Houston, Texas: Gulf Publishing, 1964.

BOWEN, F.M., AND GLENNY, L.A. "State Budgeting for Higher Education: The Response of Public Higher Education to Fiscal Stringency." Berkeley, Calif.: Center for Research and Development in Higher Education, 1976.

BROWN, R.S., JR. "Financial Exigency." *American Association of University Professors Bulletin,* 1976, *62,* 5–16.

BROWN, W.W., AND STONE, C.C. *An Emperical Analysis of the Impact of Collective Bargaining on Faculty Salary, Compensation, and Promotions in Higher Education.* Northridge, Calif.: Association of California State University Professors, 1976.

BIRNBAUM, R. "The Effects of Collective Bargaining on Faculty Compensation in Higher Education." Published proceedings of the Second Annual Conference. *Collective Bargaining in Higher Education.* New York: Baruch College, CUNY, National Center for the Study of Collective Bargaining in Higher Education, 1974.

BUCKLEW, N. S. "Collective Bargaining and Policymaking." In D. W. Vermilye (Ed.), *Lifelong Learners—A New Clientele for Higher Education.* San Francisco: Jossey-Bass, 1974.

BUCKLEW, N. S. "Students and Concerted Action." *Collective Bargaining In Higher Education: The Developing Law.* New York: Practicing Law Institute, 1975.

CARNEGIE COMMISSION ON HIGHER EDUCATION. *Governance of Higher Education: Six Priority Problems. A Report and Recommendations.* New York: McGraw-Hill, 1973.

CARR, R. K., AND VAN EYCK, D. K. *Collective Bargaining Comes to the Campus.* Washington, D.C.: American Council on Education, 1973.

CHESEBROUGH, R. S., AND ENCINIO, P. A. (Eds.) *Sample Master Contract for College and University.* Washington, D.C.: National Society of Professors, National Education Association, 1970.

COHEN, M. D., AND MARCH, J. G. *Leadership and Ambiguity: The American College President.* New York: McGraw-Hill, 1974.

COHEN, N. "What the Mediator Expects of the Parties." *Public Employment Relations Board News, New York State,* February 2, 1974, 7, 2.

COHEN, S. "A Comment On Arbitration in Higher Education." *The Arbitration Journal,* 1975, 30, 280–282.

COLLECTIVE BARGAINING AGREEMENT Between the Association of Pennsylvania State College and University Faculties (APSCUF) and the Commonwealth of Pennsylvania. September 1, 1974 to August 31, 1977.

COLLECTIVE BARGAINING AGREEMENT Between the Faculty Bargaining Coalition of Eastern Montana College and the Commissioner of Higher Education as Agent for the Board of Regents of Higher Education on behalf of Eastern Montana College. July 1, 1975 to June 30, 1977.

COLLECTIVE BARGAINING AGREEMENT Between the Western Montana College Unit of the Montana Education Association and the Commissioner of Higher Education, July 1, 1975 to June 30, 1977.

COLLECTIVE BARGAINING NEGOTIATIONS AND CONTRACTS: BASIC PATTERNS IN UNION CONTRACTS. Washington, D.C.: Bureau of National Affairs, 1976.

COMMITTEE FOR ECONOMIC DEVELOPMENT. *The Management and Financing of Colleges.* [477 Madison Avenue] New York: Research Policy Committee, 1973.

CONTRACT BETWEEN FAIRLEIGH DICKINSON UNIVERSITY and Fairleigh Dickinson University Council of American Association of University Professors Chapters. September 1, 1974 to August 31, 1976.

CONTRACT BETWEEN WAGNER COLLEGE and The Wagner College Chapter of the American Association of University Professors. September 1, 1974 to August 31, 1977.

CORWIN, R. G., AND EDELFELT, R. A. *Perspectives on Organizations.* Washington, D.C.: American Association of Colleges for Teacher Education and Association of Teacher Educators, 1976.

COSER, L. *The Functions of Social Conflict.* Glencoe, Ill.: The Free Press, 1956.

COX, A. "Rights Under a Labor Agreement." *Harvard Law Review,* 1956, *69,* 601–657.

DRESCH, S. P. "A Curmudgeon's View of the Future of Academe." Keynote address delivered to North East Association for Institutional Research, New Haven, Connecticut, November 6, 1975a.

DRESCH, S. P. "Educational Saturation: A Demographic-Economic Model." *American Association of University Professors Bulletin,* 1975b, *61,* 239–246.

DRUCKER, P. F. "Drucker on Management." Sound recording, eight cassettes with guide, 9060-3. New York: AMACOM, 1974.

DRUCKER, P. F. *Effective Executive.* Film series, five films. Washington, D.C.: Bureau of National Affairs, 1968.

DRUCKER, P. F. *Management.* New York: Harper & Row, 1973.

DURYEA, E. D., FISK, R. S., AND ASSOCIATES. *Faculty Unions and Collective Bargaining.* San Francisco: Jossey-Bass, 1973.

EMMETT, T. A., AND HOWE, R. "Collective Bargaining." Sound recording, three cassettes. Chicago: Teach 'Em Inc., 1975.

EWING, D. *Writing for Results*. New York: Wiley, 1974.

FAST, J. *Body Language*. New York: M. Evans, 1970.

FINKIN, M. W., GOLDSTEIN, R. A., AND OSBORNE, W. B. *A Primer on Collective Bargaining for College and University Faculty*. Washington, D.C.: American Association of University Professors, 1975.

FISCHER, T. C. *Due Process in the Student Institutional Relationship*. Washington, D.C.: American Association of State Colleges and Universities, 1973.

FISK, W. "A System of Law for the Campus: Some Reflections." *George Washington Law Review*, 1970, *38*, 1006–1025.

"$4,400 (in) Raises Negotiated Over Two Years by Affiliate in Youngstown." *NEA Advocate*, September 1975, *3*, 3.

FRATKIN, S. "Collective Bargaining and Affirmative Action." *The Journal of College and University Personnel Association*, 1975, *26*, 53–62.

FRIEDMAN, J. "Individual Rights in Grievance Arbitration." *The Arbitration Journal*, 1972, *27*, 252–273.

FULKERSON, W. M., JR. *Planning for Financial Exigency in State Colleges and Universities*. Washington, D.C.: American Association of State Colleges and Universities, 1974.

FURNISS, W. T. "Retrenchment, Layoff, and Termination." *Educational Record*, 1974, *55*, 159–170.

GARBARINO, J. W. *Faculty Bargaining: Change and Conflict*. New York: McGraw-Hill, 1975.

GARBARINO, J. W. "Professors at Sixty Campuses Elected Bargaining Representatives During the 1975–1976 Academic Year." *Government Employee Relations Report*, no. 661, June 14, 1976.

GARDNER, J. "Faced With A Union Organizing Drive?" *American School and University*, June 1976, *48*, 8–18.

GARDNER, J. *Excellence, Can We Be Equal and Excellent, Too?* New York: Harper & Row, 1961.

GEMMELL, J. *Collective Bargaining: A View From the Presidency*. Orientation Paper #6. Washington, D.C.: Academic Collective Bargaining Information Service (ACBIS), 1975.

GERSHENFELD, W. F., AND MORTIMER, K. P. *Faculty Collective Bargaining Activity in Pennsylvania: The First Five Years (1970–1975)*. University Park, Pa.: Center for the Study of Higher Education, Pennsylvania State University, April 1976.

GOLEMAN, D. "Meditation Helps Break the Stress Spiral." *Psychology Today,* February 1976, *9,* 82–93.

Grievance. Film. New York: McGraw-Hill, 1954.

Grievance, The. Film. New York: National Film Board of Canada, 1953.

Grievance Hearing. Film. New York: McGraw-Hill, 1953.

GUNNING, R. *How to Take the Fog Out of Writing.* Chicago: Dartnell, 1964.

HALL, E. T. *The Silent Language,* paperback ed. New York: Doubleday, 1973.

HALL, J. "What Makes a Manager Good, Bad or Average?" *Psychology Today,* August 1976, *10.*

HARRIS, A. H. "Conflicts in the Resource Allocation Process." Comments made in a panel discussion at the 16th Annual Forum of the Association for Institutional Research. Los Angeles, May 1976.

HIGHER EDUCATION DAILY, July 16, 1976.

HOLWAY, L. W., AND O'DONNELL, T. L. P. "Unfair Labor Practices in the Academic Setting." *Journal of College and University Law,* Summer 1974, *1,* 325–349.

HUGHES, C. R., UNDERBRINK, R. L., AND GORDON, C. O. *Collective Negotiations in Higher Education.* Carlinville, Ill.: Blackburn College Press, 1973.

IKLE, F. C. *How Nations Negotiate.* Millwood, N.Y.: Kraus, 1976.

INDUSTRIAL RELATIONS RESEARCH ASSOCIATION. *Collective Bargaining and Productivity.* Madison: University of Wisconsin Press, 1975.

"Iowa Board Rules for Statewide Bargaining Units; Teachers Appeal for Determination of Bargaining Representative." *Government Employee Relations Report,* no. 647, March 8, 1976.

JAKOWBAUSKI-SPECTOR. "Facilitating the Growth of Women Through Assertive Training." *Counseling Psychologist,* 1973, *4,* 75–86.

JENSEN, M. C. "Management Using Meditation to Unwind." *New York Sunday Times,* June 11, 1976.

KATZ, E. "Faculty Stakes in Collective Bargaining: Expectations and Realities." In J. H. Schuster (Ed.), *New Directions for Higher Education: Encountering the Unionized University,* no. 5. San Francisco: Jossey-Bass, 1974.

KELLEY, E. P., JR. *289 Institutions, With 482 Campuses, That Have Col-*

lective Bargaining Agents, Special Report #12 Update. Washington, D.C.: Academic Collective Bargaining Information Service (ACBIS), February, 1976.

KEMERER, F. R., AND BALDRIDGE, J. V. *Unions on Campus: A National Study of the Consequences of Faculty Bargaining.* San Francisco: Jossey-Bass, 1975.

KRESSEL, K. *Labor Mediation: An Exploratory Survey.* Albany, N.Y.: Association of Labor Mediation Agencies, 1972.

LADD, E., JR., AND LIPSET, S. *Professors, Unions, and American Higher Education.* Berkeley, Ca.: Carnegie Commission on Higher Education, 1973.

LANIER, L. H., AND ANDERSEN, C. J. *A Study of the Financial Conditions of Colleges and Universities 1972–1975.* Washington, D.C.: American Council on Education, 1975.

LESLIE, D. "Conflict Management in the Academy: An Exploration of the Issues." *Journal of Higher Education,* 1972, *43,* 702–719.

LESLIE, D. *Conflict and Collective Bargaining.* Washington, D.C.: ERIC Clearinghouse on Higher Education, 1975.

LEVINSON, H. *Psychological Man.* Cambridge, Mass.: Levinson Institute, 1976.

LONG, D. "Notes Toward a Theoretical Perspective." In Martin Kaplan (Ed.), *The Monday Morning Imagination: Report from the Boyer Workshop on State University Systems.* New York: Aspen Institute for Humanistic Studies, 1976.

LOZIER, G. G., AND MORTIMER, K. P. *Anatomy of a Collective Bargaining Election in Pennsylvania's State-Owned Colleges.* University Park, Pa.: Center for the Study of Higher Education, 1974.

LUSSIER, V. L. "Collective Bargaining and Affirmative Action." Paper presented at the First Annual Meeting of the American Association of Affirmative Action. Austin, Texas, April 1975.

MCGILL, M. E., AND WOOTEN, L. M. "Symposium: Management in the Third Sector." *Public Administrative Review,* September-October, 1975, *35,* 443–455.

MCGUINNES, K. C. *How To Take a Case Before the National Labor Relations Board.* Washington, D.C.: Bureau of National Affairs, 1976.

MAEROFF, G. I. "City University's Plan to Discharge the Tenured Is Assessed." *New York Times,* July 16, 1976.

MALI, P. *How To Manage by Objectives*. New York: Wiley, 1975.

Management by Objectives, EFM Series. Sound recording, six cassettes with workbook, 80019. New York: AMACOM, 1975.

MANGELSON, W. L., NORRIS, D. M., POULTON, N. L., AND SEELEY, J. A. *Projecting College and University Enrollments: Analyzing the Past and Focusing on the Future*. Ann Arbor, Mich.: Center for the Study of Higher Education, October 1973.

MANNIX, T. "Community College Grievance Procedures: A Review of Contract Content in Ninety-Four Colleges." *Journal of College and University Personnel Association,* 1974, *25,* 23–40.

MARCEAN, L. (Ed.). *Dealing With a Union*. New York: American Management Association, 1969.

MILLER, L. *Summary of Student Response to Academic Collective Bargaining*. Washington, D.C.: Research Project on Students and Collective Bargaining, 1976.

MORRIS, W. (Ed.). *The American Heritage Dictionary of the English Language*. New York: Houghton-Mifflin, 1969.

MORTIMER, K. P. (Ed.). *Faculty Bargaining, State Government and Campus Autonomy: The Experience in Eight States*. A joint publication by the Pennsylvania State University and the Education Commission of the States. Denver, Colo.: April 1976.

MORTIMER, K. P., AND LOZIER, G. G. *Collective Bargaining: Implications for Governance*. University Park, Pa.: Center for the Study of Higher Education, June 1972.

NAPLES, C. J. "Collective Bargaining: Opportunities for 'Management.'" In J. H. Schuster (Ed.), *New Directions for Higher Education: Encountering the Unionized University,* no. 5. San Francisco: Jossey-Bass, 1974.

NATIONAL ASSOCIATION OF COLLEGE AND UNIVERSITY ATTORNEYS. *The Journal of College and University Law*. Washington, D.C.

NATIONAL CENTER OF THE STUDY OF COLLECTIVE BARGAINING IN HIGHER EDUCATION. "Non-Discrimination Clauses in Contracts." *Newsletter,* 1974, *4,* 8–11.

NATIONAL SOCIETY OF PROFESSORS, NATIONAL EDUCATION ASSOCIATION. "Due Process and Tenure in Institutions of Higher Education." *Today's Education,* 1973, *62,* 60–62.

NOLTE, M. C. *Faculty and the Law*. Sound recording. Chicago: Teach 'Em Inc., 1975.

Nondiscrimination on the Basis of Sex in Education Programs and Activi-

ties Receiving or Benefitting from Federal Financial Assistance. 45 C.F.R. 86.

NORTHERN MONTANA COLLEGE FACULTY CONTRACT: 1975–1977, Ratified April 25, 1976. 8–11, Section 5.000.

ODIORNE, G. S. *Executive Skills.* Sound recording, twelve cassettes. Westfield, Mass.: Management by Objectives, 1972.

ORZE, J. J. "After It's Ratified That Contract Has To Work." *College Management,* February 1974, 15–17.

PARKER, G. C. *College Enrollments in the United States, 1975–1976.* American College Testing Special Report 17, 1976.

PEACH, D., AND LIVERNASH, E. R. *Grievance Initiation and Resolution: A Study in Basic Steel.* Cambridge, Mass.: Division of Research, Graduate School of Business Administration, Harvard University, 1974.

PERB NEWS. Annual Report Edition, 1976, *3.*

POLOWY, C. *Collective Bargaining and Discrimination Issues in Higher Education Institutions.* Washington, D.C.: Academic Collective Bargaining Information Service (ACBIS), 1975.

RESEARCH PROJECT ON STUDENTS AND COLLECTIVE BARGAINING. Washington, D.C. Monthly Report No. 8, May–June 1976.

ROBERTS, H. S. *Roberts' Dictionary of Industrial Relations.* Washington, D.C.: Bureau of National Affairs, 1966.

ROTTER, J. "Generalized Expectancies for Internal versus External Control of Reinforcement." *Psychology Monographs,* 1966, vol. 80, no. 609.

SANDLER, B. "Equal Employment Opportunity on the Campus." *Labor Relations for Higher Education. Criminal Law Course Handbook Series.* New York: The Practicing Law Institute, June–July 1974, *67,* 231–247.

SATRYB, R. P. *The Art of Settling Grievances: A Study in Campus Conflict Resolution,* Special Report #27. Washington, D.C.: Academic Collective Bargaining Information Service (ACBIS), August 1976.

SATRYB, R. P. "The Grievance Appeals Process within the State University of New York: A Descriptive Analysis." Ed.D. Dissertation, University of Virginia, 1974.

SCHWARTZ, G. E. "Part II. TM Relaxes Some People and Makes Them Feel Better!" *Psychology Today,* April 1974, *7,* 39–44.

SCHWARTZMAN, H. D. "The Administration's Approach to Collective

Bargaining." *Journal of College and University Law,* 1974, 351–369.

SELEKMAN, F.M. *Labor Relations and Human Relations.* New York: McGraw-Hill, 1947.

SEMUS, P.W. "Maine Guarantees Students a Faculty Bargaining Role." *Chronicle of Higher Education,* July 19, 1976, p. 4.

SEMUS, P.W. "Campus Salary Freezes Voted by 3 Legislatures." *Chronicle of Higher Education,* August 18, 1975, p. 6.

SHARK, A. *Current Status of College Students in Academic Collective Bargaining.* Special Report 22. Washington, D.C.: Academic Collective Bargaining Information Service (ACBIS), July 1975.

SIMKIN, W.E. *Mediation and the Dynamics of Collective Bargaining.* Washington, D.C.: Bureau of National Affairs, 1971.

SMITH, B.L., AND ASSOCIATES. *The Tenure Debate.* San Francisco: Jossey-Bass, 1973.

SMITH, G. "Faculty Women at the Bargaining Table." *American Association of University Professors Bulletin,* 1973, *59,* 402–405.

STAMPEN, J. *Patterns in Undergraduate Enrollment Growth Among State Colleges and Universities, 1966–1974.* Washington, D.C.: American Association of State Colleges and Universities, 1976.

STANLEY, J.D. *Handling Complaints and Grievances.* Sound recording, one cassette and manual, 9042-5. New York: AMACOM, 1966.

STATE OF NEW JERSEY, Public Employment Relations Commission. PERC No. 76-13, Rutgers, The State University and Rutgers Council of American Association of University Professors, Chapter 3, Trenton, January, 1976.

"State Trust Helps Retrain Pennsylvania Teachers." *Chronicle of Higher Education,* July 19, 1976, p. 4.

STRUNK, W., JR., AND WHITE, E.B. *The Elements of Style.* New York: Macmillan, 1959.

"Termination of Faculty Appointments Because of Financial Exigency, Discontinuance of Program or Department, or Medical Reasons" (1975 Proposed Revision). *American Association of University Professors Bulletin,* 1976, *62,* 17–19.

THOMAS, J.M, AND BENNIS, W.G. (Eds.) *Management of Change and Conflict.* Baltimore: Penguin Books, 1972.

TOMLINSON, K. Y. "A Tale of Two Teachers." *Reader's Digest.* November 1975, *107*, 29–35.

TROTTA, M. S. *Arbitration of Labor-Management Disputes.* New York: AMACOM, Division of American Management Association, 1974.

VAN ALSTYNE, W. "Tenure: A Summary Explanation and 'Defense.' " *American Association of University Professors Bulletin*, 1971, *58*, 328–333.

VAN DYNE, L. "The New York Tragedy." *Chronicle of Higher Education*, September 13, 1976a, p. 1.

VAN DYNE, L. "The Free-Tuition Fight Is Lost. The New York Tragedy-2." *Chronicle of Higher Education*, September 20, 1976b, 4–5.

VAN DYNE, L. "To Fit the Budget: Painful Layoffs, Sweeping Cutbacks. The New York Tragedy-3." *Chronicle of Higher Education*, September 27, 1976c, 6–7.

WEATHERSBY, G. B. "A Broad View of Individual Demand for Postsecondary Education: Major Policy Issues." Paper presented at the National Center for Higher Education Management Systems National Invitational Seminar. Reston, Virginia, May 16, 1974.

WEISBERGER, J. *Faculty Grievance Arbitration in Higher Education: Living with Collective Bargaining.* Ithaca, N.Y.: Institute of Public Employment, New York State School of Industrial and Labor Relations, Cornell University, 1976.

WESTERN INTERSTATE COMMISSION ON HIGHER EDUCATION. *Reports on Higher Education.* Boulder, Colorado, 1976.

WOLLETT, D.H. "Historical Development of Faculty Collective Bargaining and Current Extent." Paper presented to the First Annual National Conference of the National Center for the Study of Collective Bargaining in Higher Education, Baruch College, New York City, April 12, 1973.

YARMOLINSKY, A. "The Analogy with Other Systems." In Martin Kaplan (Ed.), *The Monday Morning Imagination: Report From the Boyer Workshop on State University Systems.* New York: Aspen Institute for Humanistic Studies, 1976.

Index

Funding: government, and strikes,
365; for graduate schools, 72; management decision, 15; sources of,
influence of union on, 558–561

G

Gardner, John, 175
Gateway Technical Institute, 241
Good faith bargaining, 298
Governance: as affected by bargaining,
328–329, 513; affected by statewide contract, 479, 480; in contract
terms, 219, 227–228, 374–389;
and retrenchment, 253; studied by
back-up team, 108
Government control: as backlash effect
of student revolt, 8; at bargaining
table, 145; over expenditures, 8,
9; testing traditional recruitment
strategies, 20; of universities through
collective bargaining, 47
Governors, 9, 49
Graduate school: questionnaire to determine includability in unit, 70–73;
unions prefer exclusion of, 70
Grants: for bargaining costs, from industry, 525–526; faculty-adminis-
tered, 43; responsibility for, 45
Grievance officer, 114, 206–207
Grievance procedure: academic vs.
industrial, 197; access to, 193–194,
208, 209, 229; appeals under, 190,
223; applicable only to contractual
items, 169; arbitration limited to,
55; on basis of principle, 188–217;
clause covering, 395; compared with
court system, 206; for complaints
not in contract, 199; contract terms
covering, 35, 220; costs of, 535–536;
described, 228–230; development
of, under flexible contract, 177;
and discrimination, 300; due process
in, as creating trust, 181, 186; dynamics of, 384–386; as heart of
contract, 393; as mandatory issue,
189, 197, 198; reciprocal, 162; samples of, 211–217; scope, 192; at
Southeastern Massachusetts University, 180; for students, 267, 270;
training for, by simulation, 113;
as way to recoup bargaining losses,
314; weeding out frivolous complaints as part of, 382–385; and

Grievance procedure (continued)
what is grievable, 192; zipper clause
to keep past practices out of, 319
Grievances: class vs. individual, 194,
203; defined, 376, 382; denied on
procedural grounds, 36, 436; and
faculty senate, 12, 131; formalizing
procedures for, 190–192; by management against union, 194, 229,
386; resolved at lowest level, 482;
review of, for second contract,
432–433; teaching administrators
what causes, 102; timely and sympathetic handling of, 385; used by
union to retain membership, 102

H

Handbooks, 114, 226, 271, 319, 543
Harvard, not unionized, ergo . . . ,
176, 187
Hawaii, 138, 354; University of, 236–
237
Health: mental and physical, of teams,
102–107, 115, 354, 366; subject
of self-evaluation, 543
HEW. See Title IX
"Hidden agenda" destructive of trust,
183
Hidden costs: of benefits, 289; of turn-
over, 287–288; of unpaid leave, 291
HUAC, undesirable on campus, 19

I

Idealism in union work, 26
Illinois, 48, 54
Impartial. See Neutral
Individual contracts, 182
Individual interests: best protected
by protecting group, 209; in conflict with academic excellence, 176;
in grievances, 193–194; presumed
protected, 209
Industrial model: and academic realities, 45–46, 159; as constraint on
change, 469; and public sector,
40–41, 53–54; use of in training
administrators to bargain, 97, 98
Informal meetings; 183. See also "Meet
and discuss"
Informal resolution of grievances,
190, 203, 206
Information: concealing not advisable,
34; controlled during negotiations,